21ST CENTURY
SCIENCE & HEALTH
WITH KEY TO THE SCRIPTURES

A modern version of Mary Baker
Eddy's *Science & Health*

CHERYL PETERSEN

Trafford rev. 05/19/2014

 www.trafford.com

North America & international
toll-free: 1 888 232 4444 (USA & Canada)
fax: 812 355 4082

Official Website:
www.HealingScienceToday.com

ACKNOWLEDGEMENTS

Appreciation goes to all those who support sharing the spirit of Mary Baker Eddy's writings. I'd especially like to acknowledge:

Marie Cummings, who provided the artwork for the book cover of this modern edition of *Science and Health*.

And, Etta Jamison, who financed the 5th edition of *21st Century Science and Health*.

CONTENTS

PREFACE
TO 21ST CENTURY SCIENCE AND HEALTH WITH KEY TO THE SCRIPTURES

Burned into my foster mothering psyche are two pictures: I see a 2-year old foster child, unable to communicate his confusion. And, I see a 9-year old, who thinks being unwanted is normal. In both cases (though different children), I felt them asking me the age-old questions, Why am I here? Why be good? What future?

Sometimes in life, we don't know how to communicate the gut feeling that there must be something more to life than what meets the eye.

In my search for cohesive answers, I've found the knowledge of truth and love to be vital.

Truth and love help us communicate.

Identifying with Truth and Love also helps to ease the conflict between the fortunate and the unfortunate, the good and the bad, the yin and the yang.

We can learn from unfortunate situations, but we don't have to allow their pushing and pulling to control our experience.

Stretching our mental barriers further, we learn that Truth and Love have control and that Truth and Love is God. This definition of God wipes out the common collective notion that God is a humanlike superman, or a contradictory force to reckon with, or a façade.

In reality, God is willing and able to give us a reason to live. The ideas in this book help us learn that we are wanted by God, not to do God's job, but to express life, soul, and a holy purpose.

The methodology read in *Science and Health* is timeless, first penned in the 19th century by Mary Baker Eddy and termed divine Science.

This modern version is not a revisionist divine Science, because the Principle of the rules in Science is constant. But the words and references in *Science and Health* have been updated to show how divine Science, as presented by Mary Baker Eddy, is applicable to today's situations.

The driving factor in *21ˢᵗ Century Science and Health* encourages progress in religion, science, family, society, and medicine. The book discusses a Mind-healing system.

The theme in *Science and Health* administers the potency of Spirit as the only substance and power, completely good. You can read the scientific statement of spiritual being, "There is no life, truth, intelligence, nor substance in matter. All is infinite Mind and its infinite manifestation, for God is All-in-all. Spirit is divine Truth; matter is human error. Spirit is the real and eternal; matter is the unreal and temporal. Spirit is God, and we are Spirit's image and likeness. Therefore person is not mortal, but is immortal."

The rhythmic prose in *21ˢᵗ Century Science and Health* appeals to our tradition of inhaling the new, while exhaling the old on a regular basis. You can begin reading wherever you want in the book. Each fresh breathe is infused with the spiritual reality that, "God is Mind, and God is infinite; and so all is Mind."

The vocabulary in *21ˢᵗ Century Science and Health* has been tagged with accessible terms. God is dignified as infinite Mind. "Person" is idea, image. The term "error" is used to denote anything unlike truth and love.

We read, "Remove error from thought, and it will not appear in effect."

For clarification, error is defined in *Science and Health,* as, "the theory that pleasure, pain, intelligence, substance, and life, are existent in human mind/body . . . Error is the contradiction of Truth. Error is a belief without understanding. Error is unreal because untrue. Error is that which seems to be and is not. If error were true, its truth would be error, and we should have a self-evident absurdity—namely, erroneous truth. If an erroneous truth were real, there would be no such thing as Truth."

The explanations of the unreality of error, or matter, must not be abused by the deluded optimism that asserts sickness is not real. Mary Baker Eddy wrote, "Sickness is neither imaginary nor unreal,—that is, to the frightened, false sense of the patient. Sickness is more than fancy, it is solid conviction. It is therefore to be dealt with through right apprehension of the truth of being."

Likewise, we read in this book, "Sickness is real, is true that is, to the patient's frightened perception. Problems are more than imagination, but are solid convictions of fear or ignorance, and therefore need to be dealt with through an accurate comprehension of the truth of being." Scientists must still deal with error correctly and this is done from the premise that anything unlike God is unreal in the spiritual cosmos. We read that through, "Spiritual reasoning and free thought . . ." do we discover trustworthy truth and love.

We also read that, "Spirituality is the basis of true healing. Whatever holds human thought in line with selfless love, receives directly the divine power.

"Systematic teaching and the student's spiritual growth and experience in practice are requisite for a thorough comprehension of the Science of Mind-healing. Some individuals realize truth more readily than others, but any student, who remains true to the divine rules of spiritual Science and becomes one with the spirit of Christ, can demonstrate Science, overcome error, heal the sick, and add continually to their supply of spiritual understanding, power, enlightenment, and success."

Please bear in mind, the above mentioned "divine rules" are not the same thing as the rules of a church organization. History shows that anytime the divine rules are placed secondary to church rules, spiritual success becomes dim and diminished. But we can wipe off the tarnish of human rules and respond to the gleam and shine of spiritual rules.

I've experienced profound spiritual healing in my life, including the healing of 2nd degree burns on half of my face. I attribute the healings to divine Science.

As a freelance writer, when writing, I often choose my subjects. But, I've found that the subject of divine Science choses me; and it's ever unfolding spiritual ideas continue to be communicated. Now in its 5th edition, the vital components of *21st Century Science and Health with Key to the Scriptures* are:

- Use of the latest research made in technical, Biblical, religious, and medical study
- New vocabulary from the expanding English language and today's idiom
- Footnotes
- The use of modern English versions of the Bible
- Treatment of today's social issues
- Gender-inclusive language

All first person references are Mrs. Eddy speaking.

Cheryl Petersen

INTRODUCTION

My introduction to *Science and Health* happened while I was working in New Zealand as a research scientist. I met an amazing person, a woman in her 80's, a well-known artist; a national treasure. She was loving and strong, exuding health and well-being. I wanted to learn how she approached life, because it was obviously working. I wanted to learn from her how to grow in spiritual beauty, instead of growing old and miserable.

She gave me a copy of *Science and Health* by Mary Baker Eddy. I found a paragraph and re-read it for a whole day before I could make any sense out of it. This clearly was not going to be an easy read. But I went to her church, and kept studying and spending time with my wonderful friend. She knew something, and she kept pointing to this book.

My friend told me to throw out negative thoughts. I had never before considered that I had a choice on what to think about. My thoughts were just my thoughts, right? Even though I had spent many years studying engineering, physics, and chemistry, and working as a scientist, it never occurred to me that thinking about whatever is true, noble, right, pure, lovely, and admirable, could elevate my mind and experience. I decided to try experimenting with thoughts, and discovered this "divine Science" works for me.

The word "science" has evolved since Mary Baker Eddy's time. In the 19th century, the word science was replacing "natural philosophy" in common usage. Science meant a study of the underlying truth or reality. Questioning and thinking were being applied in place of blind belief.

Mary Baker Eddy's proclivity to God as Truth, and her understanding that truth replaces blind belief, caused her to term her method divine Science, or Christian Science.

In the 20th century, however, the rigor of the questioning and thinking became more concrete, in all fields of learning. I was trained to think experimentation came from something physical in the world. We've come to think that having a measurement method is necessary for science.

Mary Baker Eddy used the word "science" in the sense that Truth was demonstrated by the healings that result from understanding all powerful Love.

There were many things in *Science and Health* that I found confusing. The concept was hard for me to get, and there were also words and references that were so dated that they had lost meaning or changed meaning.

If it was hard for me, a bookish nerd, to understand, how do other new comers to these profound important ideas read *Science and Health*?

I then moved back to the United States, and about 10 years ago, it was one of those Sundays, when I rushed to church. I wanted to stay home, and I was going to be a few minutes late, but oh well, it felt more right to go. An unknown woman marched right into church, late with me. I was feeling ashamed, but looking at her, I knew she had better things to think about than guilt.

I approached the woman after church and met Cheryl Petersen. Within minutes of speaking, I guessed, "You are revising *Science and Health* aren't you?" And I offered my help with editing.

The study of Christian Science works as I walk a fine line between the philosophical and practical. I feel the blessings of God. I use divine Science to remember not to try to control or manipulate those blessings. I want to rely on God, Love, to keep out the fear that creeps in if I lose clarity.

There are seventeen chapters in *Science and Health*. The first chapter on *Prayer* describes how to prepare and receive infinite blessings that are naturally given to us by an all-powerful and loving God. We are warned that it is important to work hard and be willing to grow, even when it is uncomfortable. The chapter ends with a beautiful prayer, known as the Lord's Prayer, along with a useful spiritual interpretation.

Reconciliation and Communion discusses atonement, describing it as being at one with God, Spirit, Love. This requires making choices on a daily basis to align with our spiritual truth, and not get sidetracked by the materialistic world. Jesus was a great teacher showing us the way and demonstrating Spirit, or Christ. An interpretation of Jesus' struggles is given to help us understand his message. Love prevails over hate, sin, disease, and death.

The *Marriage* chapter can be read by anyone in a relationship. It points out that in divine Spirit, we don't need conventions and institutions, but that marriage and other forms of commitment, can help us on our spiritual path here on earth. Advice on relationships is given, stressing the importance of honesty, respect, and compromise (with somewhat of a 19th century Victorian slant). Ultimately, creation unfolds and brings to light our true selfhood is perfect and eternal, with no pain or separation from God.

In the chapter, *Investigating Psychics and Spiritualism*, the reader finds an assertion that Spirit doesn't mix with matter. Spirit/God is infinite, whereas matter, including human minds and bodies, is short lived. Readers find an argument against popular beliefs in the 19th century: that communing with spirits of the dead can bring healing. Readers also find encouragement to "empower ourselves with the thought that all substance is purely spiritual." This leads a shift from the sick and limited egocentric view to an awareness of ourselves as one with divine Spirit, Love.

Chapter five, *Power of Suggestion; Crowd Thinking,* examines how the human mind can protect itself from being deceived by materialist suggestions or peer pressure. Chapter six is *Science, Theology, and Medicine,* fields of study all benefited by the metaphysical system of divine Science.

Physiology and Genetics tackles what we learn through the schools and media. While we keep learning, and because theories are constantly modified, we can unlearn that which deprives us of seeing our innate spiritual power. We read, "The supposed laws which result in weariness and disease are not God's laws. The legitimate and only possible action of Truth is the production of harmony. Laws of nature are laws of Spirit; but human beings commonly recognize as law that which hides the power of Spirit. Divine Mind rightly demands our entire obedience, affection, and strength."

Footsteps of Truth show the pro-active approach to divine Science. Truth is lived a step at a time. Our everyday life is infused with operative, functioning, working spiritual principles. The chapter *Creation* pushes the mind out of the restrictive notion that creation has a beginning and an end. We learn to advance toward the unchanging Truth of ongoing Being, while we stop clinging to changing truths.

Science of Being distinguishes between the metaphysical and physical. We read, "Metaphysics resolves things into thoughts and exchanges the objects of sense for the ideas of Soul." A sequenced dialogue closes the chapter, giving the reader a point-by-point paradigm of a thought process appropriate to today's mass consciousness.

Some Misconceptions Debunked addresses rumors surrounding Christian Science. The chapters, *Christian Science Practice* and *Teaching Christian Science* specifically address proper instruction in divine Science and its mental treatment. The *Review* chapter involves the question/answer approach to understanding divine Mind and its power to guide, bless, and heal humanity, holistically.

A spiritual interpretation of the first and last books in the Bible is then given in the chapters *Genesis* and *Revelation*. Reality is a revelation or unfoldment of Love, rather than something quantifiable.

The last chapter in *Science and Health* is the *Glossary*, where we read the definition of God as: "The great I AM; the all-knowing, all-seeing, all-acting, all-wise all-loving, and eternal; Principle; Mind; Soul; Spirit; Life; Truth; Love; all substance; intelligence."

Dr. Holly Shulman, Ph. D.

PREFACE
TO SCIENCE AND HEALTH WITH
KEY TO THE SCRIPTURES,
BY MARY BAKER EDDY

To those leaning on the sustaining infinite, today is big with blessings. The wakeful shepherd beholds the first faint morning beams, ere cometh the full radiance of a risen day. So shone the pale star to the prophet-shepherds; yet it traversed the night, and came where, in cradled obscurity, lay the Bethlehem babe, the human herald of Christ, Truth, who would make plain to benighted understanding the way of salvation through Christ Jesus, till across a night of error should dawn the morning beams and shine the guiding star of being. The Wisemen were led to behold and to follow this daystar of divine Science, lighting the way to eternal harmony.

The time for thinkers has come. Truth, independent of doctrines and time-honored systems, knocks at the portal of humanity. Contentment with the past and the cold conventionality of materialism are crumbling away. Ignorance of God is no longer the steppingstone to faith. The only guarantee of obedience is a right apprehension of Him whom to know aright is Life eternal. Though empires fall, "the Lord shall reign forever."

A book introduces new thoughts, but it cannot make them speedily understood. It is the task of the sturdy pioneer to hew the tall oak and to cut the rough granite. Future ages must declare what the pioneer has accomplished.

Since the author's discovery of the might of Truth in the treatment of disease as well as of sin, her system has been fully tested and has not been found wanting; but to reach the heights of Christian Science, man must live in obedience to its divine Principle. To develop the full might of this Science, the discords of corporeal sense must yield to the harmony of spiritual sense, even as the science of music corrects false tones and gives sweet concord to sound.

Theology and physics teach that both Spirit and matter are real and good, whereas the fact is that Spirit is good and real, and matter is Spirit's opposite. The question, What is Truth, is answered by demonstration,—by healing both disease and sin; and this demonstration shows that Christian healing confers the most health and makes the best men. On this basis Christian Science will have a fair fight. Sickness has been combated for centuries by doctors using material remedies; but the question arises, Is there less sickness because of these practitioners? A vigorous "No" is the response deducible from two connate facts,—the reputed longevity of the Antediluvians, and the rapid multiplication and increased violence of diseases since the flood.

In the author's work, *Retrospection and Introspection,* may be found a biographical sketch, narrating experiences which led her, in the year 1866, to the discovery of the system that she denominated Christian Science. As early as 1862 she began to write down and give to friends the results of her Scriptural study, for the Bible was her sole teacher; but these compositions were crude,—the first steps of a child in the newly discovered world of Spirit.

She also began to jot down her thoughts on the main subject, but these jottings were only infantile lispings of Truth. A child drinks in the outward world through the eyes and rejoices in the draught. He is as sure of the world's existence as he is of his own; yet he cannot describe the world. He finds a few words, and with these he stammeringly attempts to convey his feeling. Later, the tongue voices the more definite thought, though still imperfectly.

So was it with the author. As a certain poet says of himself, she "lisped in numbers, for the numbers came." Certain essays written at that early date are still in circulation among her first pupils; but they are feeble attempts to state the Principle and practice of Christian healing, and are not complete nor satisfactory expositions of Truth.

To-day, though rejoicing in some progress, she still finds herself a willing disciple at the heavenly gate, waiting for the mind of Christ.

Her first pamphlet on Christian Science was copyrighted in 1870; but it did not appear in print until 1876, as she had learned that this Science must be demonstrated by healing, before a work on the subject could be profitably studied. From 1867 until 1875, copies were, however, in friendly circulation.

Before writing this work, *Science and Health,* she made copious notes of Scriptural exposition, which have never been published. This was during the years 1867 and 1868. These efforts show her comparative ignorance of the stupendous Life-problem up to that time, and the degrees by which she came at length to its solution; but she values them as parent may treasure the memorials of a child's growth, and she would not have them changed.

The first edition of *Science and Health* was published in 1875. Various books on mental healing have since been issued, most of them incorrect in theory and filled with plagiarisms from *Science and Health.* They regard the human mind as a healing agent, whereas this mind is not a factor in the Principle of Christian Science. A few books, however, which are based on this book, are useful.

The author has not compromised conscience to suit the general drift of thought, but has bluntly and honestly given the text of Truth. She has made no effort to embellish, elaborate, or treat in full detail so infinite a theme. By thousands of well-authenticated cases of healing, she and her students have proved the worth of her teachings. These cases for the most part have been abandoned as hopeless by regular medical attendants. Few invalids will turn to God till all physical supports have failed, because there is so little faith in His disposition and power to heal disease.

The divine Principle of healing is proved in the personal experience of any sincere seeker of Truth. Its purpose is good, and its practice is safer and more potent than that of any other sanitary method. The unbiased Christian thought is soonest touched by Truth, and convinced of it. Only those quarrel with her method who do not understand her meaning, or discerning the truth, come not to the light lest their works be reproved. No intellectual proficiency is requisite in the learner, but sound morals are most desirable.

Many imagine that the phenomena of physical healing in Christian Science present only a phase of the action of the human mind, which action in some unexplained way results in the cure of disease. On the contrary, Christian Science rationally explains that all other pathological methods are the fruits of human faith in matter,— faith in the workings, not of Spirit, but of the fleshly mind which must yield to Science.

The physical healing of Christian Science results now, as in Jesus' time, from the operation of divine Principle, before which sin and disease lose their reality in human consciousness and disappear as naturally and as necessarily as darkness gives place to light and sin to reformation. Now, as then, these mighty works are not supernatural, but supremely natural. They are the sign of Immanuel, or "God with us,"—a divine influence ever present in human consciousness and repeating itself, coming now as was promised aforetime,

> To preach deliverance to the captives [of sense],
> And recovering of sight to the blind,
> To set at liberty them that are bruised.

When God called the author to proclaim His Gospel to this age, there came also the charge to plant and water His vineyard.

The first school of Christian Science Mind-healing was started by the author with only one student in Lynn, Massachusetts, about the year 1867. In 1881, she opened the Massachusetts Metaphysical College in Boston, under the seal of the Commonwealth, a law relative to colleges having been passed, which enabled her to get this institution chartered for medical purposes. No charters were granted to Christian Scientists for such institutions after 1883, and up to that date, hers was the only College of this character which had been established in the United States, where Christian Science was first introduced.

During seven years over four thousand students were taught by the author in this College. Meanwhile she was pastor of the first established Church of Christ, Scientist; President of the first Christian Scientists Association, convening monthly; publisher of her own works; and (for a portion of this time) sole editor and publisher of the Christian Science Journal, the first periodical issued by Christian Scientists. She closed her College, October 29, 1889, in the height of its prosperity with a deep-lying conviction that the next two years of her life should be given to the preparation of the revision of *Science and Health*, which was published in 1891. She retained her charter, and as its President, reopened the College in 1899 as auxiliary to her church. Until June 10, 1907, she had never read this book throughout consecutively in order to elucidate her idealism.

In the spirit of Christ's charity,—as one who "hopeth all things, endureth all things," and is joyful to bear consolation to the sorrowing and healing to the sick,—she commits these pages to honest seekers for Truth.

Mary Baker Eddy

PRAYER

I tell you the truth, if anyone says to this mountain, 'Go, throw yourself into the sea,' and does not doubt in his heart but believes that what he says will happen, it will be done for him. Therefore I tell you, whatever you ask for in prayer, believe that you have received it, and it will be yours.[1]

Your Father knows what you need before you ask him.[2]

The prayer that reforms and heals is an absolute faith in a God of infinite and good possibilities. Powerful prayer combines a spiritual understanding of God and an unselfish love. Regardless of what another person may say or think on this subject, I speak from experience. Humility, prayer, awareness, and action are God's gracious means for the spiritualization and health of humankind.

Unspoken thoughts are not unknown to God, also known as divine Mind. Prayer is desire. No loss can occur from trusting God to clarify and exalt our desires before they are put into words and action.

Right motives

What are the motives behind prayer? Do we pray to improve ourselves, or to benefit those who hear us? Do we meditate to enlighten the infinite? Do we pray so other people will see us? Is prayer beneficial? Yes, the aspiration that hungers after righteousness[3] is blessed by our heavenly Parent. The desire for spirituality does not return to us void.

---

1   Matt. 21:21-22; Mark 11:23-24

2   Matt. 6:8

3   Matt. 5:6; Luke 6:21

God's work is done. Prayer doesn't motivate God to do what has already been done. The Infinite can do nothing less than give all goodness since God is absolute good, wisdom, and Love—the all-knowing. God's manifestation doesn't appear simply on the ground of lip-service, but modest fervent affirmations of God's presence can kick-start prayer.

Spiritual being exists. Meditation is not meant to activate immortal existence, but it can bring us into sync with it. Prayer is not the mere habit of trying to persuade the divine Mind, as we persuade a human being. Methods of prayer that perpetually try to humanize God are sad mistakes—errors that impede spiritual growth. As a first step, we can ask God to deliver us, but by taking more steps, demonstrating spiritual goodness, we reach the living Truth.

God's standard

God is Love. Can we ask God, Mind, to be more? Love is intelligence. So, what could we possibly tell the all-knowing infinite Mind? Do we expect to change perfection? Will we plead for more at the open fountain, which is pouring forth more than we accept? Unspoken heartfelt desires bring us closer to the source of all existence and blessedness.

Asking God to *be* God is superfluous. God is "the same yesterday and today and forever."[1] God, who is immutably right, will do right without needing to be reminded. Human wisdom is not sufficient to authorize us to advise God.

Who would hold a calculator in their hand and pray for the science of mathematics to solve a math problem? The rule is already established, and it is our responsibility to work out the solution. Will we ask the divine Principle to solve what has already been solved? It is better to make our minds and bodies available to follow God's rule, because we then can receive Love's blessing and work out our own salvation.

Unless we reflect the divine Being, we are not the image and likeness of the patient, tender, and true, the One "altogether lovely."[2]

[1] Heb. 13:8

[2] Song of Songs 5:16

To understand God is the work of eternity, and it demands absolute commitment of thought, energy, and desire.

Are our thoughts of Deity empty? We admit theoretically that God is good, omnipotent, omnipresent, omniscient, and then we try to give information to this infinite Mind. We may even ask for undeserved forgiveness or benefits. We can rather ask, "Do I really appreciate the good already received?" If so, then we will put to good use the blessings we have and be prepared to receive more.

Appreciation is much more than a verbal expression of thanks. Action expresses more gratitude than speech. In some cases, there is a tendency to thank God for all our blessings, yet not really be grateful for Life, Truth, and Love. Don't be a hypocrite! You can't hide the ingratitude of a barren, superficial life. Jesus criticized hypocrites. If you find yourself ungrateful, quietly ponder your blessings.

The effective prayer is a fervent desire for growth in grace, expressed in patience, humility, love, and good deeds. Constant prayer is the habitual struggle to improve always. The motive of meditation is made evident in the rewards it brings, rewards that, even if not acknowledged in audible words, confirm our worthiness to experience divine Love.

Superficial worship is not sufficient to express persevering and unadulterated gratitude. Feeling indebted to the healing Wayshower, Christ Jesus, we must follow his example. Jesus said: "If you love me, you will obey what I command."[1]

Simply asking that we may love God will never make us love Spirit. Every day, our thoughts and actions need alignment with the divine character. An honest, intense effort to assimilate the divine character will format and design us anew until we awake in Love's likeness. The Science of spirituality is reached while we mirror the divine nature, but in a wicked world goodness will "be spoken of as evil."[2] Patience must bring experience.

---

[1] John 14:15

[2] Rom. 14:16

3

True devotion

Reformation and regeneration come with spiritual understanding. Voluminous regurgitations lack the ability to improve. Wordy prayers, superstition, and dogma interrupt the communications of Love, and disguise religion in human forms. Whatever defaces worship is an obstacle to spiritual progress and keeps us from demonstrating our power over error. Silent prayer, awareness, and sincere obedience to divine Love, clear the road for us to follow Jesus' example.

Sorrow and reformation

Being sorry for wrongdoing is only one step toward reform, and the easiest step. The next and great step required by wisdom is the test of our sincerity—namely reformation. During the reformation process we are placed under the stress of circumstances. Temptation will pressure us to repeat the offense. Heartache for backsliding may be felt until we are no longer tempted. This is the way it goes until we learn that there is no discount in the law of justice. We must pay "the last penny."[1] "The measure you use, it will be measured to you,"[2] and it will run over and "be poured into your lap."[3]

The followers of Christ drink from a full cup.[4] Ingratitude and persecution fill the cup to the brim. While drinking from this cup, however, the riches of God's love permeate our understanding and feelings, giving us the strength and spiritual reward we need. People who do right, and those who do wrong, get their full reward, but not always in this world. Offenders are seen, "flourishing like a green tree in its native soil;"[5] but looking further the Psalmist could see an end— the destruction of wrongdoing through suffering.

Prayer is not to be used as a confession, leaving the chance to repeat our offenses. Such an error holds back true religion. If prayer feeds the thinking that human beings are made better merely by praying, prayer is an evil. Repentance is needed. New thoughts are

---

[1]   Matt. 5:26

[2]   Matt. 7:2; Luke 6:38

[3]   Luke 6:38

[4]   Matt. 20:23; Mark 14:23; Luke 22:17; I Cor. 11:26

[5]   Ps. 37:35

needed. Those who imagine wrongdoing can be excused, and so repeat the wrongdoing, will worsen. Shady, sinister activities are forgiven only as they are replaced by the Christ idea—Truth and Life. Wrongdoing isn't cancelled, but is destroyed by truthful prayer.

We can't escape the consequence for wrongdoing. An apostle said, "The reason the Son of God [Christ] appeared was to destroy the devil's work."[1] The Scriptures say that if we disown the Christ spirit, "he will also disown us."[2] We can follow Jesus' divine example, and permit spirituality to replace all ill-doing—blunders and disease included.

Calling on Mind to forgive our unfinished or sloppy work is useless. To repeatedly ask for forgiveness, yet repeat lousy behavior, is ridiculous. Human beings may forgive, however, divine Principle reforms. Sometimes, human beings don't forgive, but if you have reformed, you can legitimately feel God's forgiveness. Divine Love corrects and governs. To reach heaven, the harmony of being, the divine Principle of being needs to be understood and the talents[3] given to us by God must be improved. God is not separate from the wisdom bestowed.

Suffering is a result of sin, and the means of sins self-destruction. Every supposed pleasure in sin will provide more than its equivalent of pain until belief in temporal life and sin is destroyed.

"God is love."[4] We cannot ask for more than infinite Love, we cannot go farther, and we cannot look deeper. To think that God forgives or punishes sin, according to whether or not we pray, is to misunderstand Love. Prayer is not a loophole for wrongdoing.

Before healing, Jesus uncovered and rebuked that which opposed God, Life. In regard to the crippled woman he said that Satan kept her bound.[5] Jesus even told his disciple, Peter, "You are a stumbling block

---

1   I John 3:8 (Brackets added by Mary Baker Eddy)

2   II Tim. 2:12

3   Matt. 25:15; Luke 19:13

4   I John 4:8

5   Luke 13:16

to me."[1] Jesus taught and showed us Life's potency to dissolve anything that opposes Truth. He said, "Every tree that does not produce good fruit will be cut down."[2]

It is believed by many that Jesus' rebukes were serious; he used strong language. The only polite comment Jesus had for error was, "Get behind me, Satan!"[3] His words support the necessity for a sharp, penetrating, mental stand when driving out devils and healing the sick. Does the evidence show us that downward spiraling thinking is reversed due to a forceful and direct mindset, backed by Spirit? Error must be compelled to quit itself. The false human perceptions must be replaced by true perceptions.

Showy, or emotional, prayers

Audible prayers can be impressive, even giving instant gratification and awe. But do they produce any lasting advantage? As we think about this more, we see that zeal "not based on knowledge,"[4] is precarious. Public prayers can tempt a reaction unfavorable to spiritual growth or resolve. Lip service can distort a healthy perception of our Godlike responsibilities. Pay attention! Make sure that the motive for prayer doesn't embrace the desire to be admired, because this will discourage spiritual growth.

It is physical sensation, and not Soul, that triggers an overexcited passion for God. Let spiritual perception be our guide, which in turn results in an improved experience. Selflessness and purity are connected to a better life. Fanaticism and self-satisfied devotion do not reveal spirituality. God is not influenced by human beings, no matter how radical you are. The divine ear is not an auditory nerve. The Divine is the all-hearing and all-knowing Mind, recognizing and supplying our every need.

Prayer can be dangerous if it tempts us to voice desires that aren't real. We become involuntary hypocrites when we use prayer to console ourselves, while yet make negligible effort to break out of illusory

---

1   Matt. 16:23

2   Matt. 3:10, 7:19; Luke 3:9

3   Matt. 16:23; Mark 8:33; Luke 4:8

4   Rom 10:2

mindsets. We can't stay in deceptive mindsets, thinking we can pray for forgiveness later. Hypocrisy is fatal to religion.

You do not need to lose heart if you are honest, however, if you only spasmodically face your materialist perceptions and then try to hide them, hopelessness will be felt. Words and prayers that offer a mild sense of self-justification make us phony. Contrived prayers hint at a deceitful character. Jesus spoke of superficiality as "like whitewashed tombs, which look beautiful on the outside but on the inside are full of dead men's bones and everything unclean."[1]

Ardent audible prayers are like charity in one respect—a charity that "covers a multitude of sins."[2] If someone appears to be passionate and prayerful, but also impure and insincere, what can we say? There is nothing to say if that person actually puts into practice his or her prayer. Praying for humility, even with a fervent expression, does not always mean a desire for it, but if we feel the aspiration, humility, gratitude, and love, which our words express, God accepts this. It is wise not to try to deceive ourselves or others, for "there is nothing concealed that will not be disclosed, or hidden that will not be made known."[3] If you turn away from people who have fewer advantages than you, you are not ready to be blessed by our divine Father-Mother who blesses everyone. You confess to having a materialist heart and ask that all negativity be revealed, but don't you already know more of this heart than you are willing to have your neighbor see?

Searching the heart

It is important to examine our inclinations and intentions. Mental examination is the way we learn what we honestly are. If a friend informs us of a fault, do we listen patiently to the criticism and reconsider our attitude? Or, do we react by giving thanks that we are "not like other people: thieves, rogues, adulterers, or even like this tax collector"?[4] During many years, I have been most grateful for

<hr>

[1] Matt. 23:27
[2] I Peter 4:8
[3] Matt. 10:26; Luke 12:2
[4] Luke 18:11 (NRSV)

constructive criticism. The misdeed is destructive careless criticism, which does no one any good.

The test of prayer is found in the answer to these questions: Do we love our neighbor better because of our prayer? Or, are we satisfied with our prayerful words and yet give no evidence of living consistently with our prayer? If selfishness has given place to kindness, we will regard our neighbor unselfishly and pray for our enemies;[1] but this great responsibility is never accomplished simply by asking that it may be done. Improvement of mind/body/spirit needs to be tangible before we can experience the achievement of our hope and faith.

Practical religion

Do you "love the Lord your God with all your heart and with all your soul and with all your mind"?[2] This counsel includes much, even the surrender of all mortal perceptions, restricted intentions, and materialistic worship. Loving God with all your heart is the Utopia of Christianity; it involves the Science of Life. The counsel of Love recognizes and respects only the divine control of Spirit, of which Soul is our master and mortal human mindsets have no place.

Are you willing to leave all for Truth, and be treated like a criminal? Do you really desire to follow Christ in all ways? Probably not! So why make long prayers about Christ's way if you do not care to walk in the footsteps of Jesus? If unwilling to follow his example, why bother saying, "In His name"? Consistent prayer is the will to do right. Prayer means that we become doers and not just talkers. We need to live the received enlightenment, even if it is uncomfortable. Patiently attentive to the Lord, we will leave our real intentions to be rewarded by Spirit.

The world must evolve into the spiritual understanding of prayer. If we are good enough to profit by Jesus' cup,[3] God will sustain us while we overcome the anguish that comes with his cup. Until we are divinely qualified and willing to drink his cup, millions of rerun prayers are useless to reveal the spiritual power "with indisputable

---

[1] Matt. 5:44

[2] Matt. 22:37; Mark 12:30; Luke 10:27

[3] Matt. 26:39, 42; Mark 14:36; Luke 22:42; John 18:11

evidence."[1] Divine Science reveals a necessity for overcoming not only worldliness, but also the flesh, thereby destroying all error.

Seeking is insufficient. Just saying you accept Christ Jesus is moot. An all-out effort to "do" enables us to change for the better and know eternalness. Spiritual achievements open the door to a higher understanding of divine Life.

Mechanical prayers or knee-jerk rituals are not progressive. Seeking Truth doesn't include paying someone else to give us a prayer. The advance guard of progress has paid for the privilege of prayer the price of persecution.

Asking with wrong motives

Experience teaches us that we do not always receive the answers we ask for in prayer. Some misunderstanding as to the source and means of all goodness and blessedness keeps us from receiving plausible answers. The Scriptures say: "When you ask, you do not receive, because you ask with wrong motives, that you may spend what you get on your pleasures."[2] What we desire and what we ask for is not always the best to receive, however, infinite Love knows what to grant. Do you ask wisdom to be merciful, or do you ask Soul to remove sin's self-punishment? Then "you ask in quite the wrong spirit."[3] Without punishment, sin would multiply. Jesus' prayer, "Forgive us our debts," specified the condition of forgiveness. When forgiving the adulterous woman he said, "Go now and leave your life of sin."[4]

A human judge sometimes remits the penalty but this may not be a moral benefit to the criminal. At best, it only saves the criminal from one form of punishment. The moral law, which has the right to acquit or condemn, always demands restitution before human beings can "move up to a better place."[5] Broken law brings penalty in order to compel progress.

---

[1] Mark 16:20 (The Message)
[2] James 4:3
[3] James 4:3 (Phillips NT)
[4] John 8:11
[5] Luke 14:10

Mere legal pardon leaves the offender free to repeat the offense. Sometimes the offender has suffered, and made others suffer so much, that they don't want to repeat the mistake. Jesus suffered, not to annul the divine sentence for other people's sin, but because sin inevitably hurts others. Truth doesn't excuse error, but wipes it out in the most effectual manner. Divine Principle causes us to correct our mistakes.

Repetitious prayers bring to mortals what they believe will be repeated. A desire for spirituality is requisite in order to gain it, and if we desire spirituality above all else, we will surrender all mortal thoughts. We must be willing to surrender mortal thoughts in order to walk securely in the only practical road to immortality. Prayer can't change the unalterable Truth, nor can prayer alone give us an understanding of Truth. Prayer, attached to an eager consistent intent to know and do God's will, brings us into all Truth. Prayer is best expressed in thought and in life.

Prayer for the sick

"The prayer offered in faith will make the sick person well,"[1] says Scripture. What is this healing prayer? It isn't begging. Summoning God to heal the sick has no power, since the divine presence is already at hand. Shallow prayers only produce shallow effects, even if sometimes they are beneficial. Shallow prayers remind us of blind faith, which only triggers the human mind to temporarily affect the body. Blind prayers only exchange one belief for another. For example, a belief in a supernatural humanlike but kind God who occasionally grants health, can temporarily replace a belief in sickness. Or, the belief in a trendy miraculous drug can replace the belief in a stubborn chemical imbalance.

Divine Science doesn't act through blind belief. Science doesn't act through human understanding. A prayer grounded in Truth advocates spiritual understanding. Jesus' humble prayers were deep and conscientious affirmations of Spirit—of man and woman's likeness to God and unity with Truth and Love.

Praying from the standpoint that God is part and parcel of the exotic, flimsy, undeveloped, pleasant, cruel human existence, affects

---

[1]   James 5:15

10

the sick like a drug. The prayer and drug have no efficacy of their own, but borrow their power from human faith and belief. Drugs don't ultimately or permanently do anything, because they have no intelligence. It is human belief, not the divine Principle, Love, that causes a drug to be poisonous or give temporary relief.

The common habit of praying that the sick recover finds help in blind belief, whereas help should come from enlightened understanding. Human thinking can change indefinitely, but if the changes are without spiritual understanding, they are only the merchandise of human thought. The result of divine Science is nonphysical, nonlocal, yet sacred and immeasurable.

Does Deity help one worshipper, but not another, even if they offer the same measure of prayer? In divine Science, where prayers are mental, *all* may profit from God, as "ready to help when we need him."[1] Love is impartial and universal in its spiritualization and generosity. The sick can recover when they pray, or are prayed for. The infinite Source calls out, "Come, all you who are thirsty, come to the waters."[2]

Can public prayers make our intentions honest? Do we gain the omnipotent ear sooner by words or thoughts? Will God more so hear our prayer if we tell other human beings about it? Public expressions tempt us to go beyond our true convictions. Prayer is more effective when we quietly desire, and actively strive, for the accomplishment of all we ask. Don't be "full of formulas and programs and advice."[3] If we cherish our hope honestly, silently, and humbly, we lessen the risk of overwhelming our real desires with a deluge of words. Stillness allows us to work willingly for what we ask, and we thereby feel God's reward.

If we pray to God as though God is a measurable unit, human doubts and fears rear their ugly heads and become obstacles. Because of the human minds unawareness of God as divine Spirit, there is an unawareness of divine Principle, Love. As a result, the Father of all

---

[1]   Ps. 46:1 (NASB)

[2]   Isa. 55:1

[3]   Matt. 6:7 (The Message)

is represented as a corporeal creator. Human beings then recognize themselves as merely physical and are ignorant of God's image as eternal incorporeal beings. Corporeality is not able to grasp the wonders brought about by incorporeal spiritual Love, to whom all things are possible. The brains electrochemical functioning is ignorant of the world of Truth—not wired to the reality of our immortal existence—for the world of materiality is not cognizant of life in Soul.

If we are sensitive to the body, and regard omnipotent Being as fleshly with an attention we need to get, we are not "away from the body and at home with the Lord."[1] In the life of Spirit, we can't "serve two masters."[2] To be "at home with the Lord,"[3] is to have not only faith, but the actual demonstration and understanding of Life as revealed in spiritual Science. To be "at home with the Lord"[4] is to be in obedience to the law of God. To be with God is to be influenced by infinite Mind, not by finite minds.

For a single moment, become aware that Life and intelligence are purely spiritual—neither in nor of that which is measurable—and the body will stop complaining. Depression is turned into joy and sickness is turned into wellness when the body is controlled by spiritual Life, Truth, and Love. Hence the hope of Jesus' promise: "Anyone who has faith in me will do what I have been doing . . . because I am going to the Father"[5]—because the spiritual self is absent from the body and present with Truth and Love.

The belief and dream of mortal being is entirely separate from the Life divine. Immortal Life reveals not only spiritual understanding, but also the consciousness of our dominion over that which is earthbound. This understanding overcomes error and heals the sick, and with it you can speak "as one who had authority."[6]

---

[1] II Cor. 5:8

[2] Matt. 6:24; Luke 16:13

[3] II Cor. 5:8

[4] II Cor. 5:8

[5] John 14:12

[6] Matt. 7:29

Jesus said, "When you pray, go into your room, close the door and pray to your Father, who is unseen. Then your Father, who sees what is done in secret, will reward you."[1]

The room symbolizes the sanctuary of Spirit with a door that shuts out the errors of physical senses and mortal perceptions. Closed to error, you are open to Truth and can respond to spiritual sense. God knows all things, and rewards according to motives, not according to speech. When we mute the mouth and silence the materialism, we can take audience with the divine Principle, Love.

Put an end to the chatter in your head and calmly enter spiritual consciousness. In the refuge of sincere intentions you must deny sin and affirm God's allness. Become committed, "pray continually,"[2] and go forward with a pure heart to work and watch for wisdom, Truth, and Love. Such meditation is answered insofar as you put your spiritual desires into practice. Christ Jesus' guidance is that we pray in secret and let our lives confirm our sincerity.

You can rejoice in secret beauty and abundance, hidden from worldliness, but known to God. Constant prayer spiritualizes thoughts and causes the mortal selfhood to be less demanding. A discerning practice gains the ear and right hand of omnipotence and assuredly calls down infinite blessings. Trustworthiness is the foundation of enlightened faith. We need to prepare for spirituality in order to receive spirituality.

A genuine sacrifice of temporal things comes before we recognize the advanced spiritual understanding. The highest prayer is not just faith, but faith and demonstration. Such prayer heals sickness and overcomes sin and death. Proof of spirituality distinguishes between the Truth that is sinless and the falsity of sinful sense.

Christ Jesus taught his disciples one brief prayer which we name the Lord's Prayer. The Lord's Prayer is the prayer of Spirit, not of mortal perceptions. Jesus said, "Pray, therefore, like this:"[3] and he gave that prayer which covers all human needs.

---

[1]   Matt. 6:6

[2]   I Thes. 5:17

[3]   Matt. 6:9 (Amplified)

In the phrase, "Deliver us from the evil one,"[1] the one evil is but another name for the first lie and all liars. Only as we ascend above all habituated feelings and sin can we reach heaven-born aspiration. The Lord's Prayer indicates the spiritual consciousness that instantaneously heals the sick.

Some Bible versions include an extra line at the end of the Lord's Prayer. Bible scholars think that a later copyist may have added it however it does not affect the meaning of the prayer itself and has been included here in what I understand to be the spiritual sense of the Lord's Prayer:

Our Father in heaven,

Our Father-Mother God, all-harmonious,

Hallowed be Your name,

One sacred nature,

Your kingdom come,

Your government is come; You are ever-present,

Your will be done on earth as it is in heaven.

Enable us to know—as in heaven, so on earth—God is omnipotent, supreme.

Give us this day our daily bread.

Give us grace for today; feed the starved intent.

And forgive us our debts, as we forgive our debtors.

And Love is reflected in love.

And lead us not into temptation, but deliver us from the evil one.

And God does not lead us into temptation, but delivers us from sin, disease, and death.

For Yours is the kingdom and the power and the glory forever.[2]

For God is infinite, all-power, all Life, Truth, Love, over all, and All.

---

[1]   Matt. 6:13

[2]   Matt. 6:13 (NKJV)

RECONCILIATION AND COMMUNION

Those who belong to Christ Jesus have crucified the sinful nature with its passions and desires.[1]

For Christ did not send me to baptize, but to preach the gospel.[2]

For I tell you I will not drink again of the fruit of the vine until the kingdom of God comes.[3]

Reconciliation illustrates oneness with the divine. It shows the unity between God and spiritual person, whereby man and woman reflect divine Truth, Life, and Love. Jesus of Nazareth taught and demonstrated oneness with Spirit. His life accomplishments are worthy of respect. On an individual and collective mission, Jesus' lifework was done in justice to himself and in mercy to humanity. Jesus gave an excellent example of reconciliation, however, he did not do our work for us. Jesus showed us how to be responsible for our own thoughts and actions. He acted boldly, not only against the self-authorized evidence of human perceptions, but also Pharisaical dogma and practices. With healing power, Jesus proved the powerlessness of all that opposed goodness.

Christ's conciliation unites person to God, not God to human beings. The divine Principle of Christ is God and God doesn't atone to Himself. It is therefore Christ's purpose to bring us to God. Christ can't reconcile Truth to error, for Truth and error are irreconcilable.

---

[1] Gal 5:24

[2] I Cor. 1:17 (NASB)

[3] Matt. 26:29; Mark 14:25; Luke 22:18

Jesus aided in uniting humanity to God by giving us a truer sense of Love, the divine Principle of Jesus' teachings. This truer, spiritual sense of Love redeems people from the law of matter, sin, and death by the law of Spirit—the law of divine Love.

The Teacher refrained from speaking the whole truth by declaring precisely what would destroy sickness, sin, and death. This did not make him popular. His teachings agitated the human mind, and brought to incomplete beliefs not peace, but a sword.

Every twinge of conscience and agony, every effort to reform, every improved attitude and undertaking, will help us not only understand Jesus' atonement, but also promote its usefulness. Mortals, asleep at the wheel of spiritual progress, cannot habitually pray and repent and still feel included in the atonement—in the at-one-ment with God. Repentance is more than contrition or feeling really bad. It must be lived out with sincerity. Effective repentance reforms thinking and enables human beings to do the will of wisdom. We feel secure in God's goodness when we try to demonstrate, even a little bit at a time, the divine Principle of the teachings and practice of the Teacher.

Jesus urged the commandment, "You shall have no other gods before me,"[1] which may be interpreted as, you will have no belief of Life as finite. You shall not know an evil life, for there is one Life which is God, good. Jesus gave "to Caesar what is Caesar's, and to God what is God's."[2] He did not praise, or obey, human-made doctrines or theories. He acted and spoke as he was moved not by spirits, but by divine Spirit.

To the ritualistic church authorities and hypocritical Pharisees, Jesus said, "The tax collectors and the prostitutes are entering the kingdom of God ahead of you."[3] Jesus' history made a new calendar, which we call the Christian era, but he established no ceremonial worship. He knew that people can be baptized, take sacrament, support the ministry, study Bible lessons, make long prayers, and yet be corrupt and unspiritual.

---

[1]   Exodus 20:3

[2]   Matt. 22:21; Mark 12:17; Luke 20:25

[3]   Matt. 21:31

Knowing the limitations of human thinking, Jesus tolerated humanity's weaknesses, and "by his wounds [the rejection of error] we are healed."[1] "Despised and rejected by men,"[2] yet returning good-will for cursing, Jesus taught spirituality, even the nature of God. When mistaken human minds felt the power of Truth, betrayal and terror were ready to attack the great Teacher. Yet Jesus did not change direction, knowing very well that obeying the divine order and trusting God saves from backtracking and re-healing the same problems again.

Human belief is slow to acknowledge what the spiritual fact implies. Paul wrote, "Let us also lay aside every weight and the sin that clings so closely, and let us run with perseverance the race that is set before us."[3] In other words, let us put aside the materialist self and its imperfect perceptions. Let us pursue the divine Principle and Science of all healing. Truth compels sure entrance into the realm of Love.

If Truth is overcoming error in your daily walk and talk, you are a better person and can finally say, "I have fought the good fight, I have finished the race, I have kept the faith."[4] This is having our part in the reconciliation with Truth and Love. Don't continue working and praying, with the expectation that because of another person's goodness, suffering, and triumph, that you will reach that person's harmony and reward. There is no surrogate savior.

Save yourself as Jesus saved. Strive. Advance spiritually. Constantly turn away from the objects of the human mind, and look toward the imperishable things of Spirit. If honest, you will be in earnest from the start, and joyfully gain a little each day in the right direction. If persistent, you will make the transition from limited substance to the substantial unlimited.

Inharmonious travelers

Who are we traveling with? If, from Boston, my friends are going to New Zealand while I am headed to California, we obviously are not

---

[1] Isa. 53:5 (Brackets added by Mary Baker Eddy)

[2] Isa. 53:3

[3] Heb. 12:1 (NRSV)

[4] II Tim. 4:7

traveling together. We have separate time-zones to consider, different routes to pursue, and opposite seasons to consider. Our journeys have diverged from the start and we don't have much opportunity to help each other. On the other hand, if my friends pursue my direction, we have the same itinerary and interests. If I take up their line of travel, they help me on, and our companionship may continue.

On our spiritual journey, if we sympathize with mortality, we will be at the beck and call of error and follow a zig-zag course getting nowhere. If we travel with the worldly minded, we get sucked into a nasty cycle. A good example of this is randomly walking around the shopping mall, making feel-good purchases, and eating junk food with friends. We return home, thinking we had a good time and feeling satisfied. However, when re-thinking the situation we realize that too much time and money was wasted. So, we repeat the trip to the mall but buy books on time and financial management, or dieting.

Our moral and spiritual progress will be monotonously slow if we constantly bounce back and forth between futile habits and the hope of forgiveness. Selfishness and stupidity cause constant retrogression. We must wake up to Christ's demand, however, the waking generally causes suffering. We feel like we are drowning. We struggle to stay above the water. And, through Christ's precious love our efforts are rewarded with success.

"Work out your salvation,"[1] is the demand of Life and Love, for to this end God works with you, "Until I come back."[2] Be patient, and "Let us not lose heart *and* grow weary *and* faint in acting nobly *and* doing right."[3] Don't go back to error, and don't become apathetic or offended even though you are trying hard and there are no immediate rewards. The reward will come.

When the difficult time has passed, you will experience a fullness of the good you have practiced. You will receive according to your efforts. Love is not in a hurry to rescue us from temptation, for Love means that we shall be tested and purified.

---

[1]   Phil. 2:12

[2]   Luke 19:13

[3]   Gal. 6:9 (Amplified)

Deliverance by doing our own work

Final deliverance from error is not reached by taking the easy way. There are no shortcuts. Deliverance is also not experienced by attaching our faith, without works, to someone else's effort. Whoever believes that violent anger is justified, or that divinity is appeased by human suffering, does not understand God. In our deliverance, we rejoice in peaceful honor, immortality, and spiritual freedom.

Justice requires reformation. Mercy cancels the debt only when justice approves. Revenge is unacceptable. Revenge only placates anger, whereas anger needs to be destroyed. Wisdom and Love may require many sacrifices of self to save us from sin. One sacrifice, however great, is insufficient to pay the debt of sin. The atonement requires the sinner constantly to swear off the mortal selfhood.

The atonement is a difficult problem in theology. That God's wrath against humankind should be vented on His beloved Son, is divinely unnatural—a human-made theory. Truth destroys the mistaken teaching with the scientific explanation that eventually both sin and suffering fall at the feet of everlasting Love.

Doctrines and faith

The custom of telling people, that if they take one doctrine and have total faith in it, they will be filled with the Holy Spirit, receives a strong rebuttal in the Scripture, "Faith by itself, if it is not accompanied by action, is dead."[1] Faith, if only belief, is like a motor piston shifting between nothing and something, having no fixity. Faith, advanced to spiritual understanding, however, gains evidence of Spirit. The evidence rebukes mistaken mindsets of every kind and establishes the claims of God.

In Hebrew, Greek, Latin, and English, the word faith, and its corresponding words have these two definitions, trustfulness and trustworthiness. One kind of faith trusts one's well-being to others. Another kind of faith understands divine Love and how to "work all the more strenuously at your salvation with reverence and trembling."[2]

---

[1]   James 2:17

[2]   Phil. 2:12 (Moffatt)

"I do believe; help me overcome my unbelief!"[1] This expresses the helplessness of a blind faith; whereas the directive, "Believe . . . and you will be saved,"[2] demands self-reliant trustworthiness, which includes spiritual understanding and confides all to God.

The Hebrew verb *to believe* means also to be firm or to be constant. This certainly applies to Truth and Love understood and practiced. Rigidity in mistaken mindsets will never save us.

We need to become familiar with original Bible texts and be willing to give up human beliefs and interpretations established by hierarchies or instigated by the worst passions of mortal beings. Familiarity with texts opens the way for divine Science to be understood and makes the Bible the map of life, where the healing steps of Truth are clearly pointed out.

As "the arm of the Lord"[3] is revealed, people will believe our report and rise to newness of life with regeneration. We can experience the reconciliation that Jesus endured. We can triumph. The ordinary theological views of reconciliation will continue to change and improve, just as opinions regarding predestination and future punishment have improved.

Purpose of crucifixion

If a theology stresses the view that Jesus' crucifixion served as an immediate pardon for all sinners who ask for it, then divine Science differs from that theology. Divine Science also differs from the theology that Jesus' death proved spirits can return to earth in the flesh. God is the one and only Spirit, never trapped in the flesh. We are images of Spirit.

The crucifixion was effective because of the practical tendencies and goodness it demonstrated for humanity. The truth had been lived among humankind, but until the disciples saw that it enabled their Teacher to triumph over the grave, they could not admit such an event to be possible. After the resurrection, even the unbelieving Thomas

---

[1]   Mark 9:24

[2]   Acts 16:31

[3]   Isa. 53:1

was forced to acknowledge how complete the great proof of Truth and Love was.

The spiritual significance of blood is sacrifice. The essence of Jesus' sacrifice is infinitely greater than can be expressed by our sense of human blood. The physical blood of Jesus was no more effective to cleanse from sin either before or after being shed on the cross. His sacrifice was being about his Father's business. God was his life. To eat Jesus' flesh and drink his blood is to participate in divine Life.

Jesus taught the way of Life by demonstration, that we may understand how this Principle heals the sick, drives out mistaken mindsets, and triumphs over death. Jesus presented the ideal of God better than any person whose origin was less spiritual. By his obedience to God, he demonstrated the Principle of being. Notice the force of his counsel, "If you love me you will keep my commandments."[1]

Although the great Teacher proved his control over sin and disease, he didn't relieve others from proving their own spiritual power. He worked as a guide, that people might demonstrate the power of divine Principle. Smothering Jesus with emotional affection, or claiming to be a devoted follower, will never alone make you like him. You must "go and do likewise,"[2] or you are not improving the great blessings that he worked and suffered to offer you. The spirituality of the Christ was made manifest in the humanity of Jesus.

We may revere Jesus and our heart may overflow with gratitude for what he did, however, our demonstration of love must be comparable to Jesus' until all are redeemed through divine Love. Jesus reached his glory alone, in speechless agony. He explored the way and we all have the same cup of poignant effort to drink. We are not spared a single experience if we follow faithfully.

The Christ was the Spirit that Jesus referred to in his own statements: "I am the way and the truth and the life;"[3] "I and the

---

[1] John 14:15 (JB)

[2] Luke 10:37

[3] John 14:6

21

Father are one."[1] This Christ, or divinity of the man Jesus, was his divine nature, the godliness that animated him. Divine Truth, Life, and Love gave Jesus authority over sin, sickness, and death. His mission was to reveal the Science of celestial being, to prove what God is and what spiritual intelligence does.

A musician teaches and demonstrates the beauty of the music in order to show the learner by way of practice as well as precept. Jesus' teaching and practice of Truth involved such a sacrifice as makes us admit its Principle to be Love. Sacrifice was the precious significance of the Teacher's sinless career and of his demonstration of power over death. He proved by his deeds that divine Science destroys sickness, sin, and death.

Jesus taught no mere theory, doctrine, or belief. It was the divine Principle of real being that he taught and practiced. His proof of spiritual enlightenment was not a form or system of religion and worship, but the Science of Christ-spirit, working out the harmony of Life and Love. When John the Baptist sent a messenger to ask Jesus if Christ had come, Jesus answered: "Go back and report to John what you hear and see: The blind receive sight, the lame walk, those who have leprosy are cured, the deaf hear, the dead are raised, and the good news is preached to the poor."[2] In other words, Tell John what the demonstration of divine power is and he will at once perceive God is with us.

Living temple

By his reappearance after the crucifixion, Jesus proved that Life is God. Jesus confirmed his scientific statement: "Destroy this temple, and I [Spirit] will raise it again in three days."[3] It is as if he said, the *I*—the Life, substance, and intelligence of the universe—is not in physical elements to be destroyed.

Jesus' parables explain that Life never associates with sin and death. God, Life, is not in or of matter. Through divine Science, material knowledge can be dematerialized.

---

[1]   John 10:30

[2]   Matt. 11:4; Luke 7:22

[3]   John 2:19 (Brackets added by Mary Baker Eddy)

Cowardly disciples and stubborn people

Understanding the Teacher's instruction keeps us in grace. At one time, Jesus sent out seventy-two students, but only eleven left an affirmative record. Tradition also credits Jesus the Christ with a few hundred other disciples who left no name. "Many are invited, but few are chosen."[1]

Why do those who profess to follow Christ, reject the essential religion he came to establish? The people who persecuted Jesus made their strongest attack on his basic religion; they even endeavored to hold him at the mercy of matter and stop him according to the physical law of death.

The Pharisees claimed to know and to teach the divine will, but they only hindered the success of Jesus' mission. Even many of his students were obstacles. If the Teacher hadn't taken a student and taught the unseen truths of God, he would not have been crucified. The determination to hold Spirit in the grasp of matter is the persecutor of Truth and Love.

While respecting all that is good in the Church or out of it, one's dedication to Christ is more on the ground of demonstration than of profession. In conscience, we can't stay in a mindset we have outgrown. We are enabled to heal the sick and overcome sin by understanding more of the divine Principle of the deathless Christ.

Misleading perceptions and false accusations

The origin, the character, and the work of Jesus were not generally understood. Even his righteousness and purity didn't stop the crowds from saying: He is a glutton and a friend of the impure, and Beelzebub is his supporter.[2] The materialist is unable to evaluate properly the nature of spirituality.

Remember, when you are persecuted because of your spirituality, it is enough if you are found worthy to untie the Teacher's sandals.[3] To suppose that oppression for righteousness' sake belongs to the past, and that Christianity today is at peace with the world because it is

---

[1]   Matt. 22:14; Luke 14:24

[2]   Matt. 11:19; Luke 7:34

[3]   Mark 1:7; Luke 3:16; John 1:27

honored by sects and societies, is to mistake the very nature of religion. Misguided mindsets repeat themselves. The trials encountered by prophet, disciple, and apostle, of "whom the world was not worthy,"[1] stalks every pioneer of truth.

Christ-like warfare

There is too much animal courage in society and not enough moral courage. Students of Truth and Love must take up arms against flawed mindsets at home and abroad. They must wrestle with sin in themselves and in others, and continue this warfare until they have finished the course. If they keep the faith, they will receive the honor of rejoicing.

Christ-like experience teaches faith in the right and doubt in the wrong. We learn the value of working more diligently in times of persecution, because that is when the work is really needed. The reward of self-sacrifice is great, although we may never receive it in this world.

Parenthood of God reveals spiritual conception

Dr. William Barclay wrote, "Jesus insists that the Christian should remember that he has one teacher only—and that teacher is Christ; and only one Father in the faith—and that Father is God."[2] Those instructed in Science have reached the glorious perception that God is the only Maker. The Virgin-mother conceived this idea of God, and gave to her ideal the name of Jesus, that is, Joshua, or Savior.

Mary's spiritual sense was illuminated, putting to silence physical law and its order of reproduction. Her child was conceived by the revelation of Truth, demonstrating God as the Parent. The Holy Spirit protected the innocent mother's illuminated sense with the full recognition that being is Spirit. Christ lives forever an idea in the bosom of God. The divine Principle of the man Jesus was faintly perceived by woman, before developing into its fullness in the life of Jesus.

---

[1] Heb. 11:38 (Amplified*)*

[2] Barclay, William. *The Gospel of Matthew.* Volume 2, Revised Edition. (Pennsylvania, Westminster Press) ISBN: 0-664-24101-8 (. 2). First published by The Saint Andrew Press, Edinburgh, Scotland.

As the offspring of God, individuals can be viewed as immortal evidence that Spirit is harmonious and eternal. Through spiritual conception, Mary's conscious communication with God resulted in Jesus. He went on not only to give us a higher idea of life, but also to demonstrate the Science of Love—his Father, or divine Principle.

Born of woman, Jesus appeared in the flesh. Although equipped with the divine Spirit, Jesus still felt a part of Mary's earthly condition, which accounts for his struggles in Gethsemane and on Calvary. If his origin hadn't been a typical human birth, Jesus wouldn't have been significant to human minds as "the way."[1] But as it was, the circumstance enabled him to be the mediator, or way-shower, between God and human beings.

People are taught the law Moses gave, which said: "Eye for eye,"[2] and "Whoever sheds the blood of a human, by a human shall that person's blood be shed."[3] Jesus, however, did not teach such retaliation. The new executor for God presented the divine law of Love which blesses even those who curse it.

As the individual ideal of Truth, Christ Jesus came to help us unlearn false teachings, sickness, and death. The purpose of Jesus' earthly career was to point out and demonstrate the way of Truth and Life. Jesus showed the difference between the offspring of Soul and of fleshly sense, of Truth and of error.

As we triumph over erroneous views and allow Soul to hold the control, we shall detest and correct sin under all its disguises. Only in this way can we bless our enemies, though they won't take it as a blessing. We can't choose for ourselves, but must work out our salvation in the way Jesus taught. With humility and spiritual courage he was found preaching the good news to the spiritually responsive. Arrogance and fear are unprepared to hold up the standard of Truth, and God will never place it in such hands.

Jesus pushed the boundaries when it came to fleshly or family ties. He said: "Do not call anyone on earth 'father,' for you have one Father,

---

[1]   John 14:6

[2]   Exodus 21:24; Lev. 24:20; Deut. 19:21

[3]   Gen. 9:6 (NRSV)

and he is in heaven."[1] Again he asked: "Who is my mother, and who are my brothers?"[2] Answering his own question, he pointed out that it is they who do the will of the Maker. Jesus recognized Spirit, God, as the only source, and therefore as the principle of all.

First in the list of spiritual responsibilities, Jesus taught his followers the healing power of Truth and Love. He attached no importance to dead ceremonies. It is the living Christ, the practical Truth, which makes Jesus "the resurrection and the life"[3] to all who follow his actions. Obeying his priceless precepts—following his demonstration so far as we understand it—we drink of his cup, share his bread, and are baptized with his purity. At last we can rest and sit down with Christ in a full understanding of divine Principle, which triumphs over death. For what did Paul say? "Whenever you eat this bread and drink this cup, you proclaim the Lord's death until he comes."[4]

Jesus said: "A time is coming and has now come when the true worshipers will worship the Father in spirit and truth."[5] Referring to the materiality of the age, and foreseeing the persecution that comes with the Science of Spirit, Jesus said: "They will put you out of the synagogue; in fact, a time is coming when anyone who kills you will think he is offering a service to God. They will do such things because they have not known the Father or me."[6]

In ancient Rome a soldier was required to swear loyalty to his general. The Latin word for this vow was *sacramentum*, and our English word "sacrament" is derived from it. Among the Jews it was an ancient custom for the master of a feast to pass each guest a cup of wine. But sacrament, or Communion, does not commemorate a Roman soldier's oath, nor was the wine (used on festive occasions), the cup of our Lord.

---

[1] Matt. 23:9

[2] Matt. 12:48; Mark 3:33

[3] John 11:25

[4] I Cor. 11:26

[5] John 4:23

[6] John 16:2-3

Jesus' cup shows forth his bitter experience—the cup that he prayed might pass from him, though he bowed in holy submission to the divine decree.

"While they were eating, Jesus took bread, gave thanks and broke it, and gave it to his disciples, saying, 'Take and eat; this is my body.' Then he took the cup, gave thanks and offered it to them, saying, 'Drink from it, all of you.'"[1]

The true sense is spiritually lost if the sacrament is confined to the use of bread and wine. The disciples had eaten, yet Jesus prayed and gave them bread. This would have been ridiculous in a literal sense; but in its spiritual meaning, it was natural and beautiful. Jesus prayed; he retreated from the mortal human perspectives and refreshed his heart with brighter, spiritual views.

The Passover, which Jesus ate with his disciples, in the month Nisan, on the night before his crucifixion, was a troubling occasion. As the day closed, there was sadness. The last supper ended Jesus' rituals, or compromises to human minds. Darkness quickly engulfed Jesus' glorious career.

Heavenly supplies

His followers, sorrowful and silent, anticipating the hour of their Master's betrayal, partook of the heavenly manna. Their bread came down from heaven, similar to the bread that fed Moses and the Israelites, when following Truth.[2] They were fed with the great truth of spiritual being—a truth that heals the sick and drives out error. Their Master had explained the truth. The disciples had carried this bread from house to house, breaking (explaining) it to others, and now it fed, sustained, and comforted them.

For the truth of spiritual being, their Teacher was about to suffer violence and drain to the dregs his cup of sorrow. He must leave them. With the great glory of an everlasting victory guarding him, he gave thanks and said, "Drink from it, all of you."[3]

---

[1]   Matt. 26:26-27; Mark 14:22-23

[2]   Ex. 16:31

[3]   Matt. 26:27; Mark 14:23; Luke 22:17 (NEB)

The holy struggle

When the human element in him resisted the divine, Jesus surrendered: "Not my will, but yours be done"[1]—that is, let not the flesh, but the Spirit, be represented in me. This is the new understanding of spiritual Love. It gives all for Christ, or Truth. It blesses its enemies, heals the sick, drives out error, raises the dead from trespasses and sins, and preaches the good news to humble hearts.

Are you drinking his cup? Have you shared the persecutions that attend a new and higher understanding of God? Are you willing to take up the cross and leave all for the Christ-principle? Are you eating bread and drinking wine to honor Jesus, or just to remember him for a few minutes? Why assign the inspiration of Eucharist to an anesthetic ritual? Instead, we want to show that Truth has come to the understanding, by driving out error and making our bodies "holy and pleasing to God"?[2] If Christ, Truth, has come to us in demonstration, no other sign of remembrance is requisite. Demonstration is Immanuel, or "God with us."[3] If a friend is with us, why do we need memorials of that friend?

If everyone who ate bread and drank of Jesus' cup really commemorated his sufferings, they would have revolutionized the world. If all who seek Jesus' remembrance through material symbols will instead take up the cross, heal the sick, cast out evils, and preach Christ, Truth, to the receptive thought, they will bring in the millennium.

Fellowship with Christ, Truth

Through experience, the disciples became more spiritual and better understood what the Teacher had taught. Jesus' resurrection was also their resurrection. The resurrection was a critical revival, for soon their dear Master would rise again in what has since been called the ascension, when Jesus was no longer heard or seen physically. Jesus' ascension was the reward for his faithfulness. The resurrection advances individual and collective consciousness. It moves the people's

---

[1]   Matt. 26:39; Mark 14:36; Luke 22:42

[2]   Rom. 12:1

[3]   Isa. 7:14; Matt. 1:23

thoughts out of spiritual dullness and blind belief into the perception of infinite possibilities.

What a contrast between our Lord's last supper before the crucifixion, and the spiritual breakfast with his disciples after the resurrection. In the bright morning hours on the shore of the Galilean Sea, his misery was seen to have passed away. Majesty prevailed. The disciples' grief transformed into repentance. Their arrogance was rebuked and their hearts were renewed. Convinced of their unprofitable toil in the dark, and wakened by their Teacher's voice, they changed their methods, turned away from temporal things, and threw their net on the right side. Their new understanding of Christ, Truth, gave them a new perspective on life in divine Mind, rather than in human mind.

We commemorate, in the dawn of a new light, this spiritual meeting with Christ. We bow before Christ, Truth, to receive more of Spirit's reappearing. We commune silently with the divine Principle, Love. We celebrate Christ's victory over death, his probation in the flesh, and his final ascension above matter (flesh).

Spiritual sacrament and final purpose

Our baptism is purification from all error. Our church is built on the divine Principle, Love. We can unite with this church only as we are newborn of Spirit. The Eucharist is spiritual communion with the one God. Our bread, "that comes down from heaven,"[1] is Truth. We reach the Life that is Truth and the Truth that is Life by bringing forth the fruits of Love—driving out error and healing the sick. The cup is the cross. The wine is the inspiration of Love, which the Teacher drank and commended to his followers.

The design of Love is to reform the sinner. So long as a person's thought continues in a confused sinful state, they will perceive suffering. Punishment can't be avoided, since justice is the instrument of mercy. If the suffering is insufficient to remove the sin, then heaven is hell to the sinner. People who do not experience purity and love will not find happiness and peace through death. In divine Science you must spare no effort to purify thought before and after death.

---

[1] John 6:33, 50

29

At the cross, Jesus was rejected by everyone except John and a few women. Jesus endured the shame. He never strayed from sharing goodness. His reward was worth it, although the earthly price for spirituality in a materialist age was terribly high. The great moral distance between spiritual Christianity and material sensualism, precludes divine Science from finding favor with the worldly minded.

Righteous retribution

It is just as impossible for sinners to receive their full punishment on this side of the grave as it is for the righteous to receive their full reward. A selfish and narrow mind may be unjust, but divine Mind is the immortal law of justice *and* mercy. It is inapt to think the wicked can gloat over their offences, die, and go to heaven. It is incorrect to think that Love is satisfied by giving us only stressful work, losses, cross-bearing, trials, and tribulations. God doesn't mock us in return for our efforts at well doing. Religious history repeats itself and shows that just people suffer due to the unjust.

Does God overlook the law of righteousness that destroys sinful thinking? No. They who sin must suffer. "With the measure you use, it will be measured to you—even more."[1]

History is full of records of suffering. "The blood of the martyrs is the seed of the Church."[2] In vain, mortals try to kill Truth with neglect, slander, and bullet. However, the sword of Spirit topples error. Martyrs are the human links that connect one stage with another in the history of religion. They are earth's luminaries, serving to enlighten and refine the materialist atmosphere. They permeate humanity with godly ideals. Consciousness of right-doing brings its own reward; but merit is not seen and appreciated by onlookers.

Doing as Jesus did

When will Jesus' professed followers learn to emulate him in *all* his ways and to imitate his mighty works? The people who procured the martyrdom of that righteous man would gladly have turned his sacred career into a mutilated doctrinal agenda. May the Christians of

---

[1]   Matt. 7:2; Mark 4:24; Luke 6:38

[2]   Tertullian (160-225) Christian author. Quote from *Apologeticus* or *Apologeticum*

today take up the more practical import of that career! It is possible—yes, it is the duty and privilege of every child, woman, and man—to follow in some degree the demonstration of Truth and Life, health and holiness. Hear these imperative commands: "Be perfect, therefore, as your heavenly Father is perfect!"[1] "Go and preach the good news to everyone in the world."[2] "Heal the sick"![3]

Why don't Jesus' demands motivate humankind to heal and be perfect? Because people think the precepts were intended for another time period, or for an exclusive group of followers. This belief, however, is more destructive than the doctrine of predestination—a few to be saved while the others are damned. Human-made doctrines produce lethargic mortals. The demands of Christian Science detach humanity from false doctrines.

Jesus said: "These signs will accompany those who believe: . . . they will place their hands on sick people, and they will get well."[4] Who believes him? He was addressing his disciples, yet he did not say, these signs will follow you, but those—"those who believe" in all time to come.

The word "hands" is used metaphorically, as in the text, "The Lord's right hand is lifted high."[5] The hand of God expresses spiritual power; otherwise the healing could not have been done spiritually. At another time Jesus prayed, not for the twelve only, but for as many as should believe "through their message."[6]

Jesus experienced few physical pleasures, and his sufferings were the by-products of other people's sins. The eternal Christ, his spiritual selfhood, never sinned or suffered. Jesus charted out the path for others. He uncovered Christ, the spiritual idea of divine Love. To those buried in the belief of sin and self, living only for fleshly pleasure or gratification, he said: "You have eyes: can you not see? You have

---

[1] Matt. 5:48
[2] Mark 16:15 (CEV)
[3] Matt. 10:8; Luke 9:2
[4] Mark 16:17-18
[5] Ps. 118:16
[6] John 17:20

ears: can you not hear?"[1] Jesus taught that the mortal senses shut out Truth and its healing power. By employing our spiritual senses, we change for the better and feel regenerated.

Mockery of truth cannot affect our present salvation

Humbly, Jesus confronted the ridicule thrown at him. His magnificence was unrecognized. Such indignities as he received, his followers will endure until spirituality's last triumph. Jesus earned perpetual respect. He overcame the world, the flesh, and all error, thereby proving their nothingness. He affected a full salvation from sin, sickness, and death. We need "Christ and him crucified."[2] Human beings must have trials and self-denials, as well as joys and victories, until all error is destroyed.

The educated belief that Soul is in the body causes human beings to regard death as a friend. The Bible calls death an enemy. Jesus defeated death *and* the grave, because death is not a steppingstone out of mortality, into immortality and bliss. Life and living is "the way."[3]

"Now," urged the apostle, "is the time of God's favor, now is the day of salvation."[4] This doesn't mean that now we must prepare for a future-world salvation or safety, but that right now we can experience salvation in spirit and in life. Now is the time for temporary pains and pleasures to pass away, for both are unreal. To break this earthly spell, human beings must get the true idea and divine Principle of all that really exists. The understanding of what governs the universe harmoniously is comprehended slowly, and comes with doubts and disappointments, as well as successes.

Sin, penalties, and suffering

Who will stop the learned behavior of resisting eternal Spirit while believing they are benefiting from temporal systems? When human beings admit that the temporal provides no lasting answer, they turn toward the eternal. Remove error from thought, and it will not appear in effect. The advanced thinker will perceive and advocate

---

[1]   Mark 8:18 (REB)

[2]   I Cor. 2:2

[3]   John 14:6

[4]   II Cor. 6:2

Mind-healing and its Science. Other people will say: "That's enough for now! You may leave. When I find it convenient, I will send for you."[1]

Divine Science adjusts the circumstances as Jesus adjusted them. While there is sin, there is penalty. Science removes the penalty only by first removing the sin that incurs the penalty. My interpretation of divine pardon is that God destroys sin. It is foolish to think our own sins will be less sinful if we attack someone else who we believe is sinful. Did the excommunication of Martin Luther[2] make the ritualistic hypocrisy of his enemies less criminal?

Was it fair for Jesus to suffer? No, but it was inevitable; otherwise he could not have shown us the way and the power of Truth. Remember though, another person's suffering can't lessen our own liability. If a career as great and good as that of Jesus could not avoid a felon's fate, then students of Truth must endure without complaining. Rejoice, and enter into companionship with Christ through the triumphal arch of Truth and Love.

Service and worship

Our heavenly Parent, divine Love, did not demand us to worship the personality of Jesus. The phrase "serving the Lord" doesn't mean public worship. Serving the Lord means work. It is essential to follow the example of the Teacher and his apostles.

The nature of spirituality is peaceful and blessed. In order to enter into the realm of Spirit, the anchor of hope must be thrown past the veil of matter into the Shekinah that Jesus showed us. This advance beyond superficial thinking comes through the joys and triumphs of the righteous, as well as through their sorrows and afflictions. We must leave mortal impressions of fleshly being, and advance into immortal expressions of spiritual being.

The God-inspired walk calmly on though with aching feet. Pampered hypocrites may ride on easy street here, but they can't

---

[1]   Acts 24:25

[2]   Martin Luther, (1483-1546) Christian theologian and Augustinian monk whose teachings inspired the Reformation and influenced the culture of the Lutheran and Protestant traditions.

forever break the Golden Rule[1] and escape the penalty due. We reap what we sow.

Spiritual healing was not pursued

Jesus' earthly mission was fulfilled with proofs of Truth, Life, and Love, by driving out error and healing the sick. Unfortunately, in the Christian Church, the demonstration of healing was lost about three centuries after the crucifixion. Ancient schools of philosophy, medicine, and theology more or less stopped teaching or demonstrating the divine healing of absolute Science.

Moving from city to city, his apostles still went about doing good deeds for which they were envied, hated, and stoned. Jesus was well aware that the Science of Truth would be disregarded before it was understood. His foreknowing wasn't an obstacle. The "man of sorrows"[2] was in no danger because he lacked salary or popularity. Jesus completed his God-mission and then sat down at the right hand of God.

The religious officials scoffed at the truth taught by Jesus. Why? Because truth demanded more than they were willing to work at. Human beings are content to believe in a political or theological deity, but those beliefs never made a disciple who can drive out evils and heal the sick.

Jesus' life proved, divinely and scientifically, that God is Love. Leaders and followers must be careful not to assert a mighty ruler who both loves and hates. The theology of a dualistic God gives no hint of the unchanging love of God.

The belief in death is cruel

The prevalent belief in death has no advantage. Death will eventually be found to be a human dream, which comes in darkness and disappears with the light. Death can't make Life or Truth apparent.

Jesus' brief triumphal entry into Jerusalem was followed by the desertion of everyone except a handful of friends. Though Jesus had

---

[1]   Matt. 7:12 "Do to others what you would have them do to you."

[2]   Isa. 53:3

God's approval and was entitled to respect, very few people followed him to the cross.

Death outdone

Jesus' body was the same before and after death, proving the mortal body is not the pith of being. The resurrection points to immortal being and a metaphysical science. The resurrection indicates that mortal mindsets die, while spiritual mindsets live. This testimony is important to mortals, because it shows that the true person is governed by God, by good, not evil. Jesus showed that temptation, sin, sickness, and death have no terror in the presence of the wondrous glory that God lavishes on us. Let people think they had killed the body! Afterward, he would show the people that Life-principle is not in, or of, the body.

Jesus taught his disciples metaphysical or divine Science. He enabled them to test his mysterious saying, "Anyone who has faith in me will do what I have been doing."[1] Divine Science was evident in the resurrection and the final triumph over body and matter. The belief that we have an existence or mind separate from God is a dying error. We understand more fully the Life-principle by driving out error, healing the sick, and raising the dead.

The dimension of Jesus' scientific work—his disappearance and reappearance before the physical eye—enabled the disciples to understand what Jesus had said. Previously, they had only believed his words, now they understood. Their spiritual enlightenment was parallel to the coming of the Holy Spirit on Pentecostal Day. The reappearance of divine Science repeats itself now.

Convincing evidence

Jesus' passion was the ultimate, the most convincing and profitable lesson. The spiteful attitude of his cruel persecutors and the treason and suicide of his betrayer were overruled by divine Love. The spiritual identity, which Jesus' persecutors had mocked and tried to obliterate, was glorified. The influence of Christ was perpetuated and extended rather than killed. The final manifest truth that Jesus taught, and for which he was crucified, opened a new era for the world.

---

[1]   John 14:12

35

Divine victory

After drinking the cup of bitterness, Jesus rose higher in his demonstration. Human law had condemned him, but he was living out divine law. While in the tomb—safe from the brutality of his enemies—Jesus defied matter and mortality. He acted according to, and was defended by, spiritual law. The Science Jesus taught and lived must triumph over all material beliefs related to life, substance, and intelligence, along with the many errors that grow from such beliefs. The divine must overcome the human at every point.

Love must prevail over animosity, Truth over misunderstanding, and Life over death, before the thorns can be laid aside for the crown. Then will follow the benediction "well done, good and faithful servant."[1]

The lonely space in the tomb gave Jesus a refuge from his enemies, a place in which to solve the great problem of being. His three days of mental work marked time with eternity. He proved Life to be deathless and Love to be the master of hate. On the basis of spiritual Science, Jesus met and conquered all the claims of medicine, surgery, and nutrition, by proving the power of Mind over matter.

After the crucifixion, Jesus took no drugs to relieve inflammation. He did not depend on oxygen, food, or physical therapy for recovery. He did not require the skill of a surgeon to stitch the torn hands and feet, yet they were employed as before.

Could it be called supernatural for the God of nature to sustain Jesus, while he proved spiritual dominion? It was a method of surgery beyond physical skill, but it was not a supernatural act. On the contrary, it was a divinely natural act whereby divinity brought to humanity the understanding of Truth-healing. Scientific Mind-healing was revealed as a method infinitely above that of human invention.

His disciples believed Jesus was dead. Hidden in the narrow tomb however, Jesus was alive, demonstrating the power of Spirit to overrule materialist perceptions. Rock-solid walls surrounded him, and a dense immense stone had to be rolled from the cave's mouth. Jesus reduced

---

[1]   Matt. 25: 21, 23

every concrete belief to nothing. He resisted every law of physics and stepped out of his gloomy resting-place crowned with the glory of an awe-inspiring success—an everlasting victory.

Success over the grave and after the resurrection

This Teacher fully and finally demonstrated divine Science in his victory over death and the grave. Jesus' deed was for the enlightenment of humanity and for the salvation of the whole world from death, sin, and sickness. Paul writes: "For if, when we were God's enemies, we were reconciled to him through the death of his Son, how much more, having been reconciled, shall we be saved through his life!"[1] Three days after the burial of his body, Jesus talked with his disciples. The persecutors had failed to hide immortal Truth and Love in a grave.

Praise to God and peace to the struggling hearts! Christ has removed the obstacle from the door of human hope and faith, and through the revelation and demonstration of life in God, we are elevated to possible at-one-ment with the spiritual idea of God and our divine Principle, Love.

The people, who first saw Jesus after the resurrection, observed the final proof of his teachings, but misinterpreted the event. Even his disciples called him a ghost, for they believed his body was dead. Jesus replied: "A ghost does not have flesh and bones, as you see I have."[2] The reappearing of Jesus was not the return of a spirit. He presented the same human body that he had before his crucifixion, and so sanctified the supremacy of Mind over human mind.

The resurrection was necessary for Jesus' students to be fully convinced of the truthfulness of all he taught. Before the crucifixion, the students were not sufficiently advanced to understand how to perform many wonderful works. When they finally admitted the idea of resurrection, they then were convinced of Jesus' teachings and went on to prove their own spiritual power.

---

[1]   Rom. 5:10

[2]   Luke 24:39

Spiritual interpretation and ascension

On the road to Emmaus,[1] Jesus was known to his friends by the words that made their hearts burn within, and by the breaking of bread. The divine Spirit, which identified Jesus centuries ago, has spoken through the inspired Word and will speak through it in every generation and milieu. Spirit is revealed to the receptive heart and is again seen driving out evil and healing the sick.

Physique is not Spirit, and Jesus proved this point. After his resurrection he proved to the physical senses that his body was not changed until he ascended in thought; in other words, until his understanding of Spirit, God, expanded. To convince Thomas that mortality has nothing to do with Spirit, Jesus caused him to examine the nail marks and the spear-wound.[2]

Jesus' unchanged physical state after the resurrection posits a progressive state beyond the grave. The spiritual growth that allowed Jesus to rise from the dead was increased even more to allow him to ascend. Jesus was "the way;"[3] that is, he marked the way for humankind. The final display, called the ascension, closed the earthly record of Jesus, and this world's human minds and physical senses could no longer detect Jesus.

After Jesus' ascension, his students received the Holy Spirit. Meaning, that by all they had witnessed and suffered they were wakened to a clearer understanding of divine Science. The scientific spiritual interpretation and understanding of Jesus' teachings and demonstrations gave them a faint conception of the Life that is God. This allowed them to stop interpreting people through human knowledge and turn their thoughts instead to divine knowledge. Through the Holy Spirit they gained the true interpretation of their glorified Master and became better healers, leaning no longer on matter or human mind, but on divine Principle. The appearance of light was sudden, likened to the overwhelming power on the Day of Pentecost.

---

[1] Luke 24:13

[2] John 20:27

[3] John 14:6

38

The traitor's conspiracy

The world's ingratitude and hatred toward Jesus affected his persecution. Judas Iscariot conspired against Jesus, choosing to betray him when the people were in doubt concerning his teachings. The traitor's reward was thirty coins and the smiles of the Pharisees.

Judas Iscariot's awareness of Jesus' goodness was a wedge between the two men. The spiritual distance compounded Judas Iscariot's envy and the wedge cracked open. Because the world generally loves a lie better than Truth, Judas had only to kiss Jesus and let those bent on revenge take the opening from there. The greed for money strengthened Judas' ingratitude, and for a time quieted his guilt. His scheme to betray Jesus was intended to gain popularity and promote himself, but Judas Iscariot's dark strategy fell to the ground, and the traitor fell with it.

The disciples' desertion of their Teacher in his last earthly struggle on the Mount of Olives was punished. When we desert someone who is affirming and living Truth, punishment will be felt.

Gethsemane glorified

During his night of gloom, and yet success, in the garden of Gethsemane,[1] Jesus realized the absolute error of a belief in any possible human intelligence. Neglect, bigotry, and indifference pained and devastated him. His students slept. Couldn't they care? Jesus was waiting and struggling in silent torment. He uncomplainingly was protecting a world. He asked them: "Could none of you stay awake with me for one hour?"[2] There was no response to that human request, and so Jesus turned forever away from earth to heaven, from sense to Soul.

Remembering the sweat of agony that fell in holy benediction on the grass of Gethsemane, shall the humblest or mightiest student complain when drinking from the same cup? Should we think, or even wish to escape the exalting ordeal of sin's revenge on its destroyer? Truth and Love offer little applause until our life-work is accomplished.

---

[1]   Matt. 26:36; Mark 14:32; Luke 22:39

[2]   Matt. 26:40; Mark 14:37 (REB)

Defensive thinking and its weapons

Judas Iscariot had the world's weapons. Jesus did not choose either the fight or flight method, but instead, "I was silent; I would not open my mouth."[1] When Jesus was arrested, Peter reacted and drew his sword, but Jesus rebuked resentment and animal courage and told Peter, "Put your sword away!"[2] The great demonstrator of Truth and Love was calm before envy and hate.

The governor, Pilate, was numb in the presence of his own momentous question, "What is truth?"[3] His cowardice was easily influenced by Jesus' enemies. Pilate stupidly went along with the demands of the crowd. His horrible choice against human rights and divine Love showed his ignorance—an ignorance that had no consequence to God, Life. Jesus took the advantage, and demonstrated what life is, and what the true knowledge of God can do for us.

The women who stood near Jesus' cross were able to answer Pilate's question, "What is truth?"[4] They knew what had inspired their devotion, motivated their faith, and opened the eyes of their understanding. They identified with the Principle that healed the sick, cast out evil, and caused the disciples to say to their Teacher: "Even the demons submit to us in your name."[5]

Student's ingratitude

Did only eleven disciples not conspire against Jesus? Where were the seventy-two whom Jesus sent forth? Did they forget this representative of God? Had they already lost interest in his great work? How did they so easily become oblivious to Jesus' struggles, deprivations, divine patience, courage, and unrequited affection? Why didn't they gratify his last human desire with one indication of commitment?

Jesus was mocked at the cross by the religious authorities, the same authorities before whom he humbly and courageously walked.

---

1   Ps. 39:9

2   Matt. 26:52; Luke 22:51; John 18:11

3   John 18:38

4   John 18:38

5   Luke 10:17

Contempt was thrown in Jesus' face by the people to whom he had given clear-cut proof of divine power. They said, "He saved others; let him save himself."[1] Arrogance and complacency denied Jesus "his rights before the Most High,"[2] and the people "thought his suffering was punishment from God."[3] "He was led like a lamb to the slaughter, and as a sheep before her shearers is silent, so he did not open his mouth."[4] "Who can speak of his descendants?"[5] Who will decide what truth and love are?

The last supreme moment of mockery, desertion, and torture—added to the overwhelming sense of the magnitude of his work—wrenched from Jesus' lips the cry, "My God, my God, why have you forsaken me?"[6] If a human parent was asked this heart-broken question, it would deny the justice and love of whom Jesus knew to be his Maker. Jesus appealed to his divine Principle, the God who is Love, and to himself, Love's pure idea. Had Life, Truth, and Love forsaken him in his highest demonstration? This was a startling question. No! God and Christ Jesus must remain united or that hour would be deprived of its mighty blessing for human beings.

If Jesus' recognition of eternal Life had for a moment given way before the evidence of the bodily senses, what would his accusers have said? Exactly what they did say—that Jesus' teachings were wrong, and that the teachings would be destroyed by his death. But the accusations were wrong.

The burden of that hour was terrible, beyond human conception. Jesus' mission was not trusted or believed by the minds of mortals. The people's refusal to believe the purpose of his mission was a million times sharper than the thorns that pierced his flesh. The real cross which Jesus endured on the hill of misery was the world's hatred of Truth and Love. It wasn't the spear and material cross that

---

1   Matt. 27:42; Mark 15:31; Luke 23:35
2   Lam. 3:35
3   Isa. 53:4 (CEV)
4   Isa. 53:7
5   Isa. 53:8; Acts 8:33
6   Matt. 27:46; Mark 15:34

extorted from his faithful lips the grief stricken cry, *"Eloi, Eloi, lama sabachthani?"*[1] He was moved by the possible loss of something more important than human life—the possible misunderstanding of the transcendent influence of his career. This dread added the drop of gall to his cup.

Life-power indestructible

Jesus could have withdrawn himself from his enemies. He had power to put aside a human sense of life for his spiritual identity in the likeness of the divine, but he allowed people to attempt to destroy the human body, in order that he might furnish the proof of spirituality. Jesus could give his temporal life into his enemies' hands because he knew that matter had no life and that real Life is God. He could no more be separated from his spiritual Life than God could be extinguished. When his earth-mission was accomplished, his spiritual life, indestructible and eternal, was found forever the same. Nothing can kill our Life.

Example for our salvation

Jesus' example was all-inclusive, not only was his life's work carried out to the end for himself, but the work was also done to show us deliverance. We must do what he did and what he taught us to do. His purpose in healing was not just to restore health, but to demonstrate his divine Principle. He was inspired by God, by Truth and Love, in all that he said and did. His persecutors were motivated by arrogance, envy, cruelty, and vengeance, inflicted on the physical Jesus, but aimed at the divine Principle, Love—the same Love that rebuked their unspiritual mindsets.

Jesus didn't assume a mortal selfhood. It was his spirituality that made it possible for Jesus to heal the sick, drive out evil, and raise the dead. His spiritual identity was distinct from the unspiritual minded and this caused the selfish materialist to hate him.

Even at a young age Jesus knew he was in his "Father's house."[2] His pursuits were different from the conventional pursuits of human beings. His master was Spirit; their master was material energy. He

---

1   Matt. 27:46; Mark 15:34

2   Luke 2:49

served God; they served money. His inclinations were pure; theirs were to indulge the flesh and ego. Jesus' senses drank in the spiritual evidence of health, holiness, and life. The world's senses absorb the material evidence of sickness, sin, and death. Divine perception and worldly perception witness polar-opposite to one another.

The imperfect and impure feel reprimanded by the ever present perfect and pure. That is why the world hated the just and perfect Jesus. Even the prophet Isaiah foresaw the welcome that error would give perfection. Isaiah explained graphically that the "Prince of Peace,"[1] would be "looked down on and passed over."[2] At Jesus' trial, Herod and Pilate stopped feuding long enough to team up and put to shame and death a great person. Today, as before, error and evil collaborate and work against those who are a model of, and advocate for, truth.

The "man of sorrows"[3] best understood two main points: the insubstantiality of temporal life and intelligence, and the substantial actuality of all-inclusive God, good. These points of Mind-healing, or divine Science, armed him with Love. The highest earthly representative of God, speaking of the human ability to reflect divine power, prophetically said to his disciples, "Anyone who has faith in me will do what I have been doing."[4] He also said, "These signs will accompany those who believe."[5]

Slander and reputation

The Pharisees accusations against Jesus were as self-contradictory as their religion. The bigot, the morally corrupt, and the hypocrite accused Jesus of being a glutton and drunk. They said: "By Beelzebub, the prince of demons, he is driving out demons,"[6] and he is "a friend of tax collectors and sinners."[7] The last accusation was true, but not in

---

[1]   Isa. 9:6
[2]   Isa. 53:3 (The Message)
[3]   Isa. 53:3 (NASB)
[4]   John 14:12
[5]   Mark 16:17
[6]   Matt. 12:24; Luke 11:15
[7]   Matt. 11:19; Luke 7:34

their meaning. Jesus was no ascetic. He did not fast as did John the Baptist's disciples; yet there never lived a man so far removed from appetites and fixations as Jesus. Without flinching, he admonished sinners straightforwardly because he was their friend; hence the cup he drank.

Jesus' reputation differed from his character. Why? Because his divine Principle and practice were misunderstood; Jesus' words and works were alien to the world's expectations and contrary to the world's religious views. Mortals believed in God as humanly mighty, rather than as divine infinite Love.

Out of the comfort zone

The world could not correctly interpret the discomfort that Jesus inspired. Therefore, the world could not correctly interpret the spiritual blessings that might flow from such discomfort. When an uncomfortable shock is produced by truth, Science shows the cause of shock to come from the great distance between the individual and Truth. Like Peter, it is better to weep over the warning, instead of deny the truth, or deride the lifelong sacrifice that goodness makes for the destruction of evil.

It was mortal sins that marked Jesus' body. He knew the palpable errors that constitute the material body and was able to destroy those errors. However, because he hadn't yet conquered all the beliefs of the flesh, or his own sense of temporal life, he tangibly felt our weaknesses. He carried our sins until he performed his final act of spiritual power in what is known as the ascension.

Jesus would not have been so sensitive to the beliefs of mortals if he had shared them. Through the magnitude of his human life, he demonstrated the divine Life. Out of the amplitude of his pure inclinations, he defined Love. With the affluence of Truth, he defeated error. Though the world may not have acknowledged his righteousness—not seen it—earth received the harmony his glorified example introduced.

Inspiration of sacrifice

Who is ready to follow his teaching and example? Sooner or later, we need to position ourselves in the true idea of God. Jesus paid a high price for his spiritual treasure. His intense human sacrifice was motivated by the desire to give generously to the empty or sin-filled storehouses of human beings. In witness of Jesus' divine commission, he presented the proof that Life, Truth, and Love heal the sinning and triumph over death through Mind, not matter. This was the highest proof he could have offered of divine Love. His hearers didn't understand his words or his works. Hearers still don't accept his humble interpretation of life, nor do they follow his example.

Jesus' earthly cup of bitterness was drained to the dregs. He had only a few unpretentious friends stay by his side. The religion of these spiritual friends was something more than a name. It was so vital that it allowed them to understand and share the glory of eternal life. Jesus said that those who follow him shall drink of his cup, and history has confirmed the prediction.

Injustice to the Savior

As mass consciousness advances to a perception of the invisible God, Mind-healing as instructed by Jesus, will be liable to misinterpretations; however, misinterpretations don't affect the invincible facts of Truth.

Perhaps the early Christian era did Jesus no more injustice than the later centuries have. Questions are posed today to people who profess to love Jesus: If that Godlike and glorified man were physically on earth today, would you reject him? Would you deny him the rights of humanity, if he entertained any other sense of being and religion than yours?

The healing Truth and spiritual idea of being are often disregarded at the pulpit, over the air, or through the internet. The curative mission (presenting the Savior in a clearer light than mere words), can't be omitted from our spiritual education, even if it is ruled out of the church or temple.

Truth's immortal idea is hovering over the centuries, gathering beneath its wings the sick and sinning. My weary hope tries to realize that happy day when human beings will recognize the Science of Christ, Truth, and love their neighbor as themselves. I hope you realize God's omnipotence and the healing power of divine Love, and what it does for humankind. The promises will be fulfilled. The time for the reappearing of the divine healing is throughout all time. Leaving all our earthly things at the altar of divine Science, we will drink from Truth's cup now and be provided with the spirit and power of scientific Mind-healing.

In the words of St. John: "He will give you another Counselor to be with you forever."[1] This Counselor I understand to be divine Science.

---

[1]   John 14:16

MARRIAGE

No one should separate a couple that God has joined together.[1]

At the resurrection people will neither marry nor be given in marriage; but they will be like the angels in heaven."[2]

When Jesus came to John the Baptist for baptism, John was astounded, yet reluctant. Jesus read John's confused thoughts and reassured him with the remark, "Permit it at this time; for in this way it is fitting for us to fulfill all righteousness."[3] Jesus acknowledged several human ceremonies as suitable means to advance spiritual good, including baptism and marriage.

Marriage is temporary but fidelity is required

Marriage is the legal and moral provision for reproduction among humankind. Until spiritual reality is discerned intact and understood—as when John the Revelator[4] envisioned God's universe on earth—marriage will continue subject to policies that secure increasing virtue.

Fidelity to the marriage vow is required to preserve collective well-being in society. Infidelity is "the pestilence that stalks in the darkness . . . the plague that destroys at midday."[5] The instruction,

---

1   Matt. 19:6, Mark 10:9 (CEV)
2   Matt. 22:30; Luke 20:34-36
3   Matt. 3:15 (NASB)
4   Rev. 21:1
5   Ps. 91:6

"You shall not commit adultery,"[1] is no less imperative than, "You shall not murder."[2]

Abstinence from immoral sexual activity leads to an advanced state of intellectual and cultural development in human society, marked by progress in the arts, science, and religion. Without integrity there is no social stability and the Science of Life can't be achieved.

Mental elements and demands

Union of the masculine and feminine qualities *represents*, not *is*, completeness. The qualities, regarded as feminine or masculine, reach a higher tone through a blending of certain elements such as courage, strength, and empathy. The harmony of spiritual oneness is felt as the differing elements join naturally with each other. All persons, regardless of gender, should be forgiving, chaste, bold, tender, and strong. The attraction between these spiritual qualities will be perpetual only as they are pure and true, being constantly renewed like the returning springtime.

The demands of the affections will never be satisfied if you pursue a sexy, rich, or sanctimonious partner, so make sure to engage with wisdom, sincerity, and open-mindedness. Spiritual happiness lasts because it is constantly poured forth from Truth and Love. Genuine happiness can't exist alone, because it has to be shared.

It may seem vain to share our love with someone who doesn't give it back, but it isn't a waste as long as we allow spiritual Love to enlarge, purify, and elevate the circumstance. If spite, revenge, and arrogance do uproot and scatter our affections, this separation of fleshly ties serves to unite thought more closely to God, for Love supports the struggling heart until it ceases to sigh over the world. Love recognizes the spiritual cosmos.

Promising relationships correlate with the motive to participate in activities adapted to improve society. Marriage is fortunate or unfortunate according to the expectations it involves and fulfills. Unity of spirit gives new energy to a sense of joy, whereas lame or unreasonable expectations drag joy through the mud.

---

[1]   Ex. 20:14; Deut. 5:18; Matt. 5:27

[2]   Ex. 20:13; Deut. 5:17

Musical notes can be arranged to make harmony. Tones of the human mind are just as diverse as musical notes, and harmony is apparent as tones of unselfish ambition, noble life-motives, and honesty blend properly. Spiritual harmony constitutes individual and collective happiness, strength, and permanence.

Mutual freedom

Spiritual and moral freedom is found in Soul. Guard against narrowness and jealousy, or they will confine a wife or husband to restricted behavior. Home is not a boundary of the affections, but is a framework from which to grow spiritually. Do not desire all your partner's attention and time. Circulate happiness and compassion in the community to promote the sweet interchange of confidence and love, but be sure not to generate a wandering desire for incessant amusement outside the home circle.

In his book, *Survival in the Killing Fields*,[1] Haing Ngor, survivor of the Khmer Rouge regime, acknowledges the special trust between he and his wife, which did not include quibbling. Hard feelings are avoided when spouses use common sense, have respect for one another, and do not become extravagant or lazy. Having money and possessions may remove some barriers to a happy marriage, but nothing can replace the loving care in a union.

Fully recognize your ongoing responsibilities before entering matrimony. "A married woman is concerned . . . how she can please her husband,"[2] says the Bible. Success is guaranteed when both spouses are pleasant. Have a mindful interest in one another's progress, and reciprocate appreciation in a relationship.

Mutual compromises, or a prenuptial agreement, will often preserve an arrangement which might otherwise become unbearable. Agree on a realistic intent of the marriage and share the responsibilities to meet that intent. As you both fulfill the different demands of your united spheres, you will feel supported, confident,

---

[1]   Haing Ngor, with Roger Warner, *Survival in the Killing Fields*. (New York, NY: Carroll & Graf Publishers, 2003)

[2]   I Cor. 7:34

and thus sanctify the union of wellbeing in which the heart finds peace and home.

Renewal

Gentle words, and an unselfish attention to detail in what promotes the success of your spouse, will prove valuable in prolonging one another's health and smiles. Don't practice stolid indifference or resentment. Remember, a simple heartfelt word or deed is powerful enough to renew the romance.

It is regressive to complain about incompatibility. Do not deceive yourself, or one another, as to why you are getting married or staying married. Deception is fatal to happiness. Honesty allows you to understand a sensible motive for marriage, if not before, then after the legal union.

Permanent obligation

The frequency of divorce shows that the sacredness of this relationship is losing its influence. Serious mistakes are undermining the foundation of marriage. Separation need not take place if both husband and wife genuinely put into practice spiritual rules of Truth and Love. Spiritual knowledge inevitably lifts one's being higher in the scale of harmony and happiness. When the moral obligations are kept intact, why annul the nuptial vow?

Permanent affection

Similar tastes, intents, and aspirations are necessary to form a loving and permanent companionship. The beautiful in character is also the good, securing indissolubly the links of affection. From the logic of events we learn that selfishness and impurity are short-lived and that wisdom ultimately will separate what she did not join together.

The parent's affection cannot be weaned from their children, because parent-love includes purity and constancy, both of which are immortal. Parental care lives on under all situations.

Marriage should improve the human species, becoming a barrier against stupidity, a protection and encouragement to the spouses, and a nucleus for the expressed feelings. When marriage is used to blame, control, or prove one another wrong, spiritual growth is neglected.

Effort spent living in the past, pursuing superficial goals, or showing off, is effort wasted.

Spiritual harmony

A badly trained ear, not appreciating harmony, thinks noisy melodrama is normal. So human perception, untrained to discern true happiness, thinks unhappiness is normal. Divine Science will correct the misperceptions and teach us life's sweeter harmonies.

Happiness can't be defined by personal perceptions. The perceptions of human beings confer no lasting enjoyment. Higher enjoyments alone can satisfy the cravings of immortal person. Soul has infinite resources with which to bless humankind, and happiness is more readily responded to and more secure in our keeping, if found in Soul.

Ascendency of good

Happiness is won as good has ascendency over evil and the spiritual over the animal. The attainment of this spiritual condition improves our progeny, diminishes crime, and gives higher aims to ambition. Every valley of materialism must be exalted and every mountain of selfishness must be brought low, that the highway of our God may be prepared in Science. The offspring of heavenly-minded parents inherit more intellect, better balanced minds, and more reliable health.

Propensities inherited

If some unfortunate circumstance places promising children in the arms of gross parents, often these beautiful children wither like tropical flowers born in the snowy Alps. If by chance those children live to become parents themselves, they may pass along to their children the grosser traits of what they were taught when growing up. Society can ask: What noble ambition can inspire the child to overcome the bad traits? What hope of happiness can be gained so as to head off reducing the child to a hopeless wreck?

Raising children is a great responsibility, a more solemn trust than climbing the corporate ladder or accumulating material possessions. Take immense care not to transmit to children what is unworthy of perpetuity.

In order to advance humankind, the development of mortals must improve. The scientific mental spirit of marriage is unity. Having sex is acceptable for the purpose of reproducing a higher human species. Every stage of child-bearing must be kept mentally pure and have the sanctity of virginity.

Educate the children to form habits agreeable to moral and spiritual laws. Children are better prepared to meet and master the limitations imposed by physical laws—especially the laws that breed disease and disorder—when they are obedient to moral and spiritual laws.

Inheritance observed

Parents, if you allow your children incessantly to play computer games, want stuff, or be picky, don't complain later in life if your children are complicated or frivolous. Be accountable. Worry less "about your life, what you will eat or drink; or about your body, what you will wear,"[1] and pro-actively grow together in the understanding of man and woman's higher nature. Children can still retain their innocence while maturing. You will do more than imaginable when you also continue to mature along with the children.

The Mind creative

By attributing more and more intelligence to spirituality, and giving less and less power to physical laws and human beings, we promote wisdom and health. The divine Mind, which forms the bud and blossom, will care for the human body, even as it clothes the lily.[2] Do not let mortals interfere with God's natural order of existence by thrusting in laws of mistaken human perceptions.

Bear in mind, the higher nature of a person is not controlled by the lower more baneful nature; if it were the order of wisdom would be reversed. Our immature views of life hide eternal harmony and produce the problems of which we complain. Even though human beings believe in mortal laws—which by default causes people to disbelieve the Science of Mind—that believing does not make the mortal laws superior to the laws of Soul. You would not believe food

---

1   Matt. 6:25, 31; Luke 12:29

2   Matt. 6:28; Luke 12:27

supplements were better for warding off disease than the influential Mind if you understood the Science of being.

Spiritual origin

In spiritual knowledge, we are the offspring of Spirit, Mind. The beautiful, whole, and pure constitute our ancestry. Our origin is not like that of mortals, programmed to pass through human stages prior to reaching intelligence. Spirit is our primordial and ultimate source of being. God is our Father-Mother, and Life is the law of our being.

Civil laws are created to implement fairness and equity between the rights of the sexes but more progress is needed, to say the least. Civilization and Science stand strong on the side of justice, and encourage the elimination of discrimination, however, every time an effort is made to remedy unfairness, we must be alert that the effort doesn't encourage difficulties of greater magnitude. Higher aims and motives, as well as improved mental character, must be considered as the feasible and rational means of progress.

Dealing with discrimination

If a spouse deserts the partnership, certainly the lone mate can single-handedly be self-reliant and independent. Women and men are equally capable to succeed in the business world, earn an education, own real estate, and care for the children and home, without interference.

Global injustice between the sexes is a crying evil caused by the arrogance and inhumanity of mortals. We must exercise our faith in the direction taught by the Apostle James, when he said: "Religion that God and Father accepts as pure and faultless is this: to look after orphans and widows in their distress and to keep oneself from being polluted by the world."[1]

Husbands and wives, who keep empathy and generosity to themselves, will become tyrants. Do not let selfishness, suspicion, or bitterness control one another's activities. Christianity includes humanitarian efforts to help people who are less fortunate, and we can assist others without becoming unfaithful to our partner.

---

[1]   James 1:27

Progressive development

A solid marriage is one that signifies a union of hearts. The time comes when Jesus declared that in the resurrection "people will neither marry nor be given in marriage; but they will be like the angels in heaven."[1]

Until it is learned that God is Father-Mother, marriage will be useful as long as mortals do not permit an unlawfulness that leads to a worse state of society than now exists. Sincerity and virtue ensure the stability of the marriage promise. Marriage won't lose its luster as the love/hate emotions give way to the rejoicing of Soul. Recognize your ability to unite masculine and feminine insight, love, spiritual understanding, and perpetual peace.

Mortals ultimately claim nothing in the end, and Spirit receives its own. Learn from experience. Learn respect, self-control, patience, and a reliable happiness that comes from spiritual growth. May Christ, Truth, be present at every bridal altar, to turn the water into wine[2] and inspire your life with the vision of a serene and immortal existence.

If the starting point of your relationship is consistent with progress, the relationship will be strong and enduring. However, unions suffer confusing dysfunction. Divorces warn us that some fundamental error lingers in marriage. To achieve divine Science and its harmony, it pays to regard life more metaphysically.

Powerless promises

Evil is conspicuously broadcast today, showing off itself in consumerism, materialism, and sensualism. Evil is struggling against the advancing spiritual era. The world may lack spirituality, and people may not be able to keep a promise or make a home happy, but human minds are demanding spiritual understanding and a reformed attitude.

Transition and reform

As with any reform, a transition period will be felt. Transition periods are often unsettling and undesirable, however, why buck the trend when the reform compels us to find permanence and peace in a more spiritual devotion?

---

[1] Matt. 22:30

[2] John 2:9

The mental development that has brought infidelity to the surface will need to keep improving so as to bring about faithfulness. Infidelity weakens marriage whereas faithfulness strengthens marriage.

Rick Warren wrote in *The Purpose Drive Life*, "Your most profound and intimate experiences of worship will likely be in your darkest days—when your heart is broken, when you feel abandoned, when you're out of options, when the pain is great—and you turn to God alone."[1]

Adversity teaches human beings not to lean on a collapsible crutch. Spiritual development doesn't come from planting seeds in the dirt of materialist views. Those seeds rot whereas Love nurtures the higher joys of Spirit, which have no taint of earth. We forget this when life is fine. But when mortals belch, or the economy goes sour, or people think their partner is boring, the heart is pierced with sadness until we remember that sorrow can be therapeutic, forcing us to enter the domain of spiritual happiness and reliance. God will take care of us as we travel a trajectory unfolding new views of divine goodness and love.

When a relationship is going well, pay attention, otherwise an increasing dependence on one another may yank the rug out from under your feet. If, on the other hand, your relationship is rocky, don't react, but hope, pray, and wait patiently on divine wisdom to point the way.

Patience is wisdom

Husbands and wives should never separate if there is no Christian demand for it. The logic of events will reveal itself. In those cases when one spouse is better, then the better spouse is good company for the worse. Dr. Oral Roberts discussed his philosophy for a successful marriage. He and his wife, Evelyn, who was better company for a time, patiently told her very busy husband that he was "making a terrible

---

[1] Warren, Rick. *The Purpose Driven Life*. Michigan: Zondervan, 2002. www.zondervan.com

mistake,"[1] by neglecting the family. Her words struck Mr. Robert's conscience and he disciplined himself to put God and family first before work.

If our outlook is expanded and purified, the unhappiness will lift. It is life-giving to learn the lessons God teaches. The furnace separates the gold from the dross that the precious metal may be graven with the image of God.

Weathering the storm

When navigating aircraft through a storm, the pressure is shifting, the wind is shrieking, and air pockets are hiding in the air currents. We ask the pilot: "Do you know your course? Can you aviate safely among this turbulence?" Though brave, the dauntless aviator is not sure of safety because even aeronautical science is not equal to the Science of Mind. Yet, acting on his or her highest understanding, the pilot doesn't avoid responsibility, but keeps working, ready to act on divine guidance. This example of behavior can be useful in any stressful relationship, including a seething marriage. Be accountable, hope and work, willingly act on divine guidance, not private interest. Divine guidance will either force a graceful change, or calm the enraged atmosphere.

Spiritual power

To assume an alpha male or female attitude adds to one's character is absurd. Through spiritual ascendency our Lord and Master healed the sick, raised the dead, and commanded even the winds and waves to obey him. Grace and Truth are potent beyond all other means and methods.

The lack of spiritual power in today's demonstrations of popular Christianity does not put to silence the labor of the centuries. Spiritual, not material consciousness is needed. Men and women, delivered from conflict, disease, and death will epitomize the true likeness of God's image.

---

[1] Roberts, Oral. *When You See the Invisible You Can Do the Impossible.* Copyright 2002, used by permission of Destiny Image Publishers, 167 Walnut Bottom Road. Shippensburg, PA 17257 www.destinyimage.com

Basis of true religion

Religious and medical systems treat physical pains and pleasures as if they are normal, but Jesus rebuked the suffering from any such cause or effect. The epoch approaches when true religion will be built on the understanding of the truth of being. However, people are slow to understand truth because they are obsessed with fashion, pride, bodies, and opinion. The fixation of materiality makes us weary and old because it goes against our higher nature. At some point, we will break through the fleeting and false and learn how Spirit, the great architect, has created men and women in Science.

Envy buries trust and love. Mistrust is a rotten apple in a relationship. Build a confidence in the commitment and responsibility that comes with a union. Don't rush into a relationship teetering on infatuation or fear. Be aware of how your promises to another will influence your own growth and other people's lives.

I discredit the belief that asexual propagation applies to the human species.

God's creation intact

Spiritual Science presents unfoldment, not accumulation. Mind-science presents revelation, not big bang. There is no growth from material molecule to mind. Creation is a manifest impartation of divine Mind to man and woman and the universe. As human generation ceases, the unbroken links of eternal harmonious being will be discerned; and person, not of the mortal flesh, but coexistent with God, will appear. The scientific fact that man and woman and the universe are evolved from Spirit, and so are spiritual, is as fixed in divine Science as is the proof that mortals gain the experience of health only as they lose the sense of destruction and disease. Mortals can never understand God's creation while believing that human beings are creators. Whether marriage or reproduction happen or not, God's children, spiritual beings, already created, will be recognized as we awake to the truth of being. Spiritually to understand that there is but one creator, God, reveals all creation, confirms Scripture and brings the sweet assurance of no parting and no pain, which in turn exposes the deathless, perfect, and eternal ideal.

When practicing Christian Science and educating your own offspring spiritually, know that you can educate others spiritually and not conflict with the scientific sense of God's creation. One day, a child will ask, "Do you keep the First Commandment? Do you have one God and creator, or are human beings creators?" If you answer, "God creates human beings through human beings," the child may retort, "Do you teach that Spirit creates materially, or do you teach that Spirit is infinite and creates spiritually?" Jesus said, "The people of this age marry and are given in marriage. But those who are considered worthy of taking part in that age and in the resurrection from the dead will neither marry nor be given in marriage."[1]

---

[1]   Matt. 22:30; Mark 12:25; Luke 20:34-35

INVESTIGATING PSYCHICS
AND SPIRITUALISM

When people tell you, "Try out the fortunetellers. Consult the spiritualist. Why not tap into the spirit-world, get in touch with the dead?" Tell them, "No, we're going to study the Scriptures."[1]

I tell you the truth, if anyone keeps my word, he will never see death.' At this the Jews exclaimed, 'now we know that you are demon-possessed![2]

Physical existence and human minds are enigmas. Every day is a mystery. The physical senses can't tell us of what is real or what is delusive, whereas the revelations of divine Science unlock the treasures of Truth. There is but one Spirit. We are never God. Our spirituality is made in the likeness of Spirit. We reflect God. In this scientific reflection, the Ego and the divine Parent are inseparable. The assumptions that human egos are spirits, or that there are good and bad spirits, are mistakes.

The divine Mind maintains all identities as distinct and eternal, from a blade of grass to a star. The questions are: What are the identities of God? What is Soul? Does life or soul exist trapped inside a thing or person?

Nothing is real and eternal—nothing is Spirit—except God and God's idea. Evil has no reality. Evil is not a person, place, or thing, but

---

1   Isaiah 8:19 (The Message)
2   John 8:51-52

is in the end a misinterpretation of reality, an illusion of human mortal perceptions.

The identity or idea of reality continues forever. Soul is synonymous with Spirit, God; the creative, governing, infinite Principle, which is reflected by creation. Spirit is never inside a finite form.

Lessons from dreams

You may dream that you see a flower—that you touch and smell it. You learn that the flower is a product of the human mind, a formation of thought rather than of matter. With a greater imagination, you may see landscapes, auras, chakras, men, and women. The images even simulate mind, life, and intelligence. We learn that these are images which human mind embraces, evolves, and manipulates. These lessons of the imagination teach us that the human mind and material particles are not the image or likeness of God and that immortal Mind is not directly or indirectly in anything changeable.

When the Science of Mind is understood, psychics, spiritualism, and channeling will be found lacking, having no scientific basis, no origin, no proof, and no power outside of human testimony. It is the human mind and physical sensation that gives temporal life to psychics and spiritualism. There is no physical sensation in divine Spirit

The basis and structure of psychics and spiritualism are material and physical. The spirits of psychics are many bodies; quantifiable and restricted in character and quality. Channeling therefore is presuming Spirit, which is ever infinite, to be divisible. The theory of a quantifiable being is contrary to Christian Science.

There is only one spiritual existence, the Life of which physical senses can't grasp. Divine Principle speaks through spiritual sense. If a material body—in other words, a mental embodiment of mortality and materialism—were permeated by Spirit, that body would disappear to fleshly sense, would be deathless. A condition precedent to communion with Spirit is the gain of spiritual life.

Spirits outmoded

High-level guides, spirits, personality entities, and so on, are but limited communicators. God is the only truth-giver. As light destroys darkness and in the place of darkness all is light, so in absolute Science,

Soul, or God, destroys mortality and in the place of mortality all is immortality. Fire and frost mingle as readily as Spirit and spirits. In either case, one does not support the other. Human belief (the limited sense of life) and immortal Truth (the spiritual sense) are the weeds and the wheat,[1] separated by progress. The joys of interaction and socializing become the farce of sin when bad influences and suffering become contagious.

Perfection is not expressed through imperfection. Spirit is not made manifest through its antipode, human energy. Biofields and bioenergy do not transmit truth.

God, good, being ever-present, it follows in divine logic that evil, the suppositional opposite of good, is never present. Sin, sickness, and death are not transferable or scientific. In Science, individual good derived from God, the infinite All-in-all, may flow to human beings from other people or from those who are no longer on this earth, but evil is neither communicable nor scientific. A sinning earthly mortal is neither the reality of Life nor the channel through which truth passes to earth. Not clairvoyant reading or interpersonal communication, but divine law is the communicator of truth, health, and harmony to earth and humanity.

Why say spirit is stuck inside a human being? Why call one person living in this world, physical, but then call the person a spirit after they die? The fact is that neither are infinite Spirit, for Spirit is God. Man and woman is the likeness of Spirit.

One government

The belief that one person, as spirit, can control another person, as matter, upsets the individuality and Science of God's child, image. Mind controls all images, and God is the only Spirit. Any other control or attraction of so-called spirit is a mortal belief, which ought to be known by its fruit—the repetition of evil.

If Spirit, or God, communed with human beings or controlled them through channelers—or any other form of matter/energy—the divine order and the Science of omnipotent, omnipresent Spirit would be destroyed.

---

[1] Matt. 13:29

The belief that material bodies return to dust hereafter to rise up as spiritual bodies with fleshly sensations and desires is incorrect. Equally incorrect is the belief that spiritual beings are squeezed into a human body and then freed by death. If freed from a fleshly body, how are the flesh sensations retained?

Science corrects the grave mistakes that suppose matter to be any part of the reality of intelligent existence, or that Spirit and matter, intelligence and non-intelligence, can commune together. The sensual can't be made the mouthpiece of the spiritual, nor can the finite become the channel of the infinite. There is no communication between the physical and spiritual existence because spiritual life is not subject to death.

It's impossible to return to a particular physical or mental condition after having left it. An acorn, after having dropped to the ground and sprouted, will never return to its pervious condition. The germinated seed has a new form and a different state of existence. When here or hereafter the belief of an imperfect life is extinct, the error which has held the belief dissolves with the belief, and never returns to the old condition. The dream of having died is dramatically different from the dream of still being alive in a biological body; therefore information can't pass between the two mindsets.

The caterpillar transformed into a beautiful butterfly is no longer a worm. The butterfly doesn't return to fraternize with or control the worm. Such a retrograde transformation is impossible in Science. Darkness and light, infancy and adulthood, sickness and health, are opposites—different beliefs, which never blend. Who will say that infancy can articulate the ideas of adulthood or that darkness can represent light? Who will insist they are on the moon when they are on earth? There is no bridge across the gap which divides such opposite conditions as the spiritual and the physical.

In divine Science there is never a backward step, never a return to positions outgrown. Those who are termed dead and those who are termed living can't commune together, for they are in separate states of being or consciousness.

The truth of peerless Spirit lays bare the training that people die as matter and return to life as spirit. The dead would need to be physically tangible on this earth plane in order to be recognized as more than imagination.

Psychics and spiritualism is an attempt to keep people restricted to a limited sense. This gross materialism is scientifically impossible, since to infinite Spirit there can be no restriction, no matter/energy, no space/time.

Raising the dead

Jesus said: "Our friend Lazarus has fallen asleep; but I am going there to wake him up."[1] Jesus restored Lazarus by the understanding that Lazarus never died—not by believing his body died and lived again. Had Jesus believed that Lazarus died or lived in his body, the Master would have stood on the same plane of belief as those who buried the body, and he could not have resuscitated it.

When you can waken yourself or others out of the belief that everyone must die, only then can you exercise Jesus' spiritual power to reproduce the presence of those who have thought they died.

The moment previous to the death transition, is the only moment when those living on earth and those called dead can communicate. This is the moment when the opposite beliefs blend. During the interlude when a person passes from one dream to another dream, he or she may hear the glad welcome of people who have gone before. The dying person may even describe to people living on this earth plane what they see and hear. This is similar to someone standing before the Northern Lights, with eyes open only to the wonder, forgetting all else, hearing a beckoning call, and voicing aloud his or her awe.

Real Life is God and sinless joy

When being is understood, Life will be recognized as not material or finite, but as infinite—as God, universal good, and the belief that life or mind was ever in a finite form, or that good is in evil, will vanish. Then it will be understood that Spirit never entered matter and therefore never came from matter. When advanced to spiritual being and the understanding of God, we can no longer commune with matter. We can't return to an outgrown point of view, any more than a frog can return to a tadpole (pollywog). Spiritual advancement

---

[1]   John 11:11

63

matures into the view that individual consciousness is characterized by the divine Spirit as idea, not matter.

Suffering, self-destructive, dying beliefs are unreal. When divine Science is universally understood, a negative consciousness will have no power over us, for we are spiritual and live by divine authority.

The sinless joy is the perfect harmony and immortality of Life, possessing unlimited divine beauty and goodness without a single bodily pleasure or pain. Our real indestructible being embodies sinless joy. This state of being is scientific and intact. It is a state of perfection discernible only by those who have the final understanding of God's idea in divine Science. Death can never produce immortality or spirituality, for death must be overcome, not submitted to, before immortality appears.

The recognition of Spirit and of infinity does not come all at once, but throughout eternity. *Haba na haba*, a Swahili phrase for little by little, or step by step, has relevance. Human beings do not change from error to truth in an instant.

Second death and a vanishing dream

Existence continues to be a perception of divided body energies until the Science of being is reached. Erroneous belief systems bring their own self-destruction both here and hereafter because mortal mind creates its own mortal conditions. Death will occur on the next plane of existence as on this until the spiritual understanding of Life is achieved. Then, and not until then, will it be demonstrated that "the second death has no power over them."[1]

The time required for this dream of material life to disappear from consciousness, "No one knows, not even the angels in heaven, nor the Son, but only the Father."[2] The time it takes for us to stop embracing delusive pleasures and pains will be drawn out, or shortened, depending on the tenacity of error. Of what advantage is it to prolong the illusion either of a catatonic soul or of a dying sufferer trapped in a body? What is better, to add years to mortal life, or, to add life to years?

---

[1]   Rev. 20:6

[2]   Matt. 24:36 (ESV)

Is it progress or purgatory?

Even if communications from spirits to human consciousness were possible, such communications would grow beautifully less with every advanced stage of existence. The departed would gradually rise above ignorance and materiality, and mediums would outgrow the belief that they need other spirits. Psychics consign the dead to a state resembling that of limbo or abject purgatory. What are the chances for continued spiritual improvement if the spirit entities are lowering their vibration levels, or constantly returning to their old standpoints of material knowledge, in order to communicate?

The decaying flower, the damaged bud, the gnarled oak, the ferocious beast, are unnatural, just as the chaotic lifestyle of disease, sin, and death are unnatural. Abnormalities and dysfunctions are not the eternal realities of Mind but are false perceptions, the changing deviations of human mind.

It is unreasonable to believe that we are wearing out life, accelerating toward death, and at the same time communing with immortality. If those who have gone before us are in rapport with mortality, they are not spiritual, but must still be fleshly, sinning, suffering, and dying. Then why look to them, even if communication were possible, for proofs of immortality? Why accept human spirits as infallible guides? Communications based on, or gathered from, a lack of good reason, is pernicious in tendency.

Any communication requiring bioenergy would destroy the supremacy of Spirit. If Spirit pervades all space, it needs no physical method for the transmission of messages. Spirit does not need biofields, quantum physics, or physical energy in order to be omnipresent.

Spirit tangible to spiritual sense

There is no confluence of God's power and fluctuating powers. Hypnotism and channeling are not the agents of God's government. Many spirits is the same as many gods. Because Spirit is not physically tangible, it doesn't communicate through tangible electromagnetism or physical energy fields. If God was physically tangible, we would have to conclude that the majesty and omnipotence of Spirit was vulnerable to radioactive decay, or could be lost to death.

Spirit blesses, but we cannot "tell where it comes from or where it is going."[1] By Spirit the sick are healed, the stressed are comforted, and the sinning are reformed. These are the effects of one universal God, the invisible good dwelling in eternal Science.

Mistaken methods and hypothesis

The act of describing disease—its symptoms, history and fatality—is not scientific. Warning people against death has a tendency to frighten into death those who are unfamiliar with Life as God. Thousands of instances could be cited of health restored by changing the patient's thoughts regarding death.

A scientific mental method promotes more well-being than the use of drugs. Science must examine the entire mind and remove every harmful influence. Christian Science relies on the higher understanding of God which removes beliefs and hypotheses; whereas the metaphysics of psychics tends to rely upon human beliefs and hypotheses. Science, in its revelation of spirituality, introduces the harmony of being by resting on divine Principle, rather than resting on material personalities.

The Apostle Paul encouraged people to have the Mind that was in Christ.[2] Jesus cast out evil spirits, or false beliefs. He did his own work by the one Spirit. Jesus said: "My Father has worked [even] until now, [He has never ceased working; He is still working] and I, too, must be at [divine] work."[3] The Master never described disease, as far as can be learned from the Gospels, but he healed disease.

The unscientific practitioner reads and says: "You are sick. You are stressed out, you must rest. Your body is weak, it must be strengthened. You have a neurological problem and must be treated for it." Science pierces through negative information and strives for the rights of intelligence, asserting that Mind controls body and brain. Caffeine and other related stimulants aren't equal to truth when you need energy or inspiration.

---

[1] John 3:8

[2] I Cor. 2:16; Phil. 2:5

[3] John 5:17 (Amplified)

Divine strength

Mind-science teaches mortals "Don't get tired of helping others."[1] It dissipates fatigue to do good deeds. In service to our Maker, generosity will not deprive us, likewise, holding back our wealth does not make us richer. Our strength is increased with our increased understanding of truth. Strength is not minimized by voicing truth.

Debra Lynne Katz, a professional clairvoyant reader, healer, and spiritual counselor, says in her book, *You are Psychic: The Art of Clairvoyant Reading & Healing,* "We are all energetically connected." Katz also shares with readers the importance of not continuously expecting to be strengthened by other people's energy, "The best energy, or fuel, for your body is your own."[2] This is valuable advice, preparing human thought to take the next step of recognizing divine Spirit as the infinite source of divine strength and immortality. Human energy is mortal and claims separate spirits. Divine energy unites everyone's consciousness to God, the one immortal Spirit.

I entertain no doubt of the altruism and philanthropy of many readers, psychics, and spiritualists, but I can't coincide with the views of a mystical, supernatural being or force. Science never removes phenomena from the realm of reason into mystique. Science puts an end to mystery and explains extraordinary phenomena as ordinary. If psychics understood the Science of being, their belief in channeling would vanish.

It should not seem supernatural that mind, without the aid of hands, can move or alter an object, when we already know that it is mind-power which moves both the object and hand. Studies in parapsychology and psychokinetic ability basically confirm the human mind's control over its substratum, called matter.

Human belief makes the choice to move, but the movements are not scientific or rational. Humans, either by means of thought or the body, cause objects to move, but it is mortal mind which causes its

---

[1] Gal. 6:9 (CEV)

[2] Katz, Debra Lynne. *You Are Psychic: The Art of Clairvoyant Reading & Healing.* First Edition, Third printing. Minnesota: Llewellyn Publications, 2005.

substratum, matter, to move, to have an ulcer or seizure. TheMoving matter stems from the common convictions that mind and matter cooperate both visibly and invisibly, or that matter is intelligent.

There is more evidence of suffering and sensation than there is of communications between the dead and the living. Mind-science is shaking up beliefs in regard to matter and life.

At the very best and on its own theories, spiritualism can only prove that certain individuals have a continued existence after death and maintain their attachment with mortal sensations. But this fact offers no certainty of everlasting life. A person who asserts that they are immortal doesn't prove immortality any more than the assertion that they are mortal would disprove immortality. Just because alleged spirits teach immortality, doesn't mean it is true. Life, Love, Truth, is the only proof of immortality. Person in the likeness of Truth is inevitably immortal.

Mind's manifestations are immortal

Though the grass seems to wither and the flower to fade, they reappear. Erase the figures which express numbers, silence the tones of music, give the human being called person to the bacteria, and yet the producing, governing divine Principle lives on, in the case of people as truly as in the case of numbers and music. All this is true despite the laws of human mind which define people as mortal. Though the problems resulting from limited perspectives hide the harmony of Science, these problems can't destroy the divine Principle of Science. In Science, our indestructibility depends on that of God, good, and follows as a necessary consequence of the immortality of good.

We think of an absent friend as easily as we do a present friend. It is just as easy to read distant thoughts as near. We read the thoughts of the deceased through their writings. Chaucer[1] wrote centuries ago, yet we still read his thought in his verse. What is study of the classics, but

---

[1]   Chaucer, (1343-1400) English author, poet, philosopher.

the discernment of the minds, even the minds of Homer,[1] and Virgil,[2] of whose personal existence we may be in doubt? But, there is no real communication.

Impossible communication

If spiritual life has been won, they can't return to a material existence because different states of consciousness are involved. Consider two people sleeping. They are wandering in different mazes of consciousness and unable to communicate. An awake person can't communicate with a sleeping person.

The conscious state of a departed friend is different from those still alive. Different mental realms prevent communication. The mental states are so unlike, that intercommunication is as impossible as it would be between a flea and a human being. Different dreams and different awakenings signify different frames of mind. When wandering in the jungles of South America, do we look for help to the Eskimo in snowy North America?

In a world where sin and sensuality scramble to rise in the ranks of power, it is wise earnestly to consider whether we are being influenced by the human mind or the divine Mind. Beware of ingenious human-made devices that merely claim to equal the work of wisdom. What the prophets of the Lord did, the worshippers of Baal failed to do (e.g. I Kings 18:16-40).

Only Science can explain the incredible good and evil elements that keep surfacing. Human beings must find protection in Truth in order to escape the errors of today. Nothing is more antagonistic to divine Science than a blind belief without understanding, for such a belief hides Truth and builds on error.

Miracles seem impossible due to the strong belief that the universe, including people, is governed by physical laws. Occasionally, religion and medicine think that Spirit sets aside these physical laws and a miracle occurs, however this belief belittles omnipotent wisdom, and

---

[1]   Homer, a legendary Greek poet, assumed to have lived in the 8th century BC.

[2]   Publius Vergillus Maro, later called Virgil. (70 BC-19 BC) Ancient Roman poet and author.

gives to matter the precedence over Spirit. Science interprets miracles as explainable, natural. The scientific manifestation of power is from the divine nature and is not supernatural.

Scientific reason and foresight and foreknowing

It is contrary to divine Science to suppose that life is either physically or organically spiritual. Between divine Science and all forms of bio-spirituality or superstition, a great chasm is fixed, as impassable as the abyss between The Rich Man and Lazarus.[1] Immortal Mind-reading is a revelation of divine purpose through spiritual understanding by which we gain the divine Principle and explanation of all things. Immortal Science doesn't coordinate with the premises or conclusions of mortal beliefs.

Mortal mind-reading and immortal Mind-reading, interpret cause and effect differently. The act of reading mortal human mind investigates and touches only human beliefs.

The ancient prophets received their foresight from a spiritual, metaphysical position, not by predicting evil and mistaking fiction as fact. Reading the future from the premise of fleshly and human belief is not scientific foresight. When sufficiently advanced in Science to be in agreement with the truth of being, people become seers and prophets involuntarily. Prophecy is not controlled by spirits, demons, or quantum entities, but by the one Spirit. It is the prerogative of the ever-present divine Mind, and of thought which is in alignment with this Mind, to know the past, the present, and the future.

As we become better acquainted with the Science of being, we are better able to communicate with the divine Mind. Spiritual knowledge not only allows people to foresee and foretell events which concern the universal welfare, but it also inspires people divinely to reach the dimension of unfettered Mind, Spirit.

Mind is not bound by physicality. Mind is not dependent on the fleshly ear and eye for sound or sight. Mind is not contingent on corporeal muscles and bones for movement. To understand incorporeal Mind is to perceive that Mind is infinite. This perception of boundless Mind extends toward Mind-science and toward a perception of

---

[1]   Luke 16:26

our true nature and existence, which does not include material personalities. Therefore the truth of our existence does not allow the belief of psychics or spiritualism, because without personalities called spirits, there is no basis for the spiritualist's belief.

All we correctly know of Spirit comes from God, divine Principle, and is learned through Truth and divine Science. If this Science has been thoroughly taken in and properly digested, we can know the truth more accurately than the astronomer can detect a nebula or calculate an eclipse. Scientific Mind-reading greatly differs from clairvoyance, psychics, or extrasensory perception (ESP). The reading of divine Mind is the illumination of spiritual understanding. Enlightened understanding demonstrates the capacity of Soul, not the capacity of human imprints. This Soul-reading comes to the human mind as the human mind yields to divine Mind.

Value of intuition

Spiritual intuition reveals whatever constitutes and perpetuates harmony, enabling one to do good, but not evil. You will reach the perfect Science of healing when you are able to read the human mind spiritually and discern the error you would destroy. The Samaritan woman said: "Come out and see the man who told me everything I've ever done! Can this be Christ?"[1]

It has been recorded that the Hebrew prophets intuitively foretold important events. It has also been recorded that when Jesus was with his students he "knew their thoughts"[2]—read them scientifically. In like manner he discerned disease and healed the sick. Jesus admonished the lack of Mind-reading power when he said: "You hypocrites, you know how to decipher the look of earth and sky; how is it you cannot decipher the meaning of this era?"[3]

Hypocrisy not good

Some people may have keen "supernatural" or "natural" physical senses, but humans need spiritual sense. Jesus knew the people to be wicked and adulterous, seeking the material more than the spiritual.

---

[1]   John 4:29 (Phillips NT)

[2]   Matt. 9:4, 12:25; Mark 2:8; Luke 5:22, 6:8, 11:17

[3]   Matt. 16:3; Luke 12:56 (Moffatt)

He said: "You should have practiced the latter, without neglecting the former."[1] His jabs at materialist thoughts were sharp, but needed. Jesus never spared hypocrisy from its stern self-condemnation. There is one cause and effect. Truth communicates itself but never imparts error.

Mental contact

Jesus once asked, "Who touched me?"[2] Peter, assuming he meant a physical touch answered, "Master, the people are crowding and pressing against you."[3] Jesus knew, as others did not, that it was not matter, but human mind, whose touch called for aid. So, he asked the question again and was answered by the faith of a sick woman.[4] His quick response to the mental call illustrated his spirituality. The disciples' misreading of the situation showed their unawareness of spirituality. Jesus possessed more spiritual receptivity than the disciples and was able to heal the woman.

Images of thought explained

Mortals evolve images of thought. They may appear to the learner to be apparitions, but they are mysterious only because it is unusual to see thoughts—although we can feel their influence. Ghosts and strange noises brought out in dark séances either involve pranks or they are images and sounds evolved involuntarily by human mind. Seeing is no less a quality of physical sense than is feeling. Here it can be asked, why is it more difficult to see a thought than to feel one? Education alone determines the difference. In reality there is no difference between seeing and feeling a thought.

Phenomena explained

Portraits, songs, writings, and conversations can all be detected and read from thought and memory. Pictures are mentally formed before the artist conveys them to canvas, and it is this way with all human concepts. Mind-readers perceive these pictures of thought, even seeing thoughts that have been lost to the memory of the mind in which they were discovered. Human mind sees what it believes as

---

1   Matt. 23:23; Luke 11:42

2   Mark 5:30; Luke 8:45

3   Mark 5:31; Luke 8:45

4   Matt. 9:22; Mark 5:33; Luke 8:47

certainly as it believes what it sees. It feels, hears, and sees its own thoughts.

Mental environment

It is needless for the thought or for the person holding the thought to be individually and consciously present. Although individuals have passed away, their mental environment remains to be discerned and described. Even when someone has moved far away and has been forgotten, their vibrations or whisperings are still in the general atmosphere of human mind.

The term "sixth sense" has been used to describe intuitive vision, or knowingness, when more accurately it could be called "first sense." Our intuitive perception discerns essential facts. Science enables a person to read the human mind, but not as a clairvoyant. Science enables one to heal through Mind, but not as a hypnotist.

The computer doesn't know what software programs are installed on its hardware. Outer-space isn't aware of the comets propelling through its atmosphere. The sea is unaware of the oil buried under its waters. Yet this stuff is all there. Do not assume that any mental concept is gone because you do not think of it. The strong impressions produced on human mind by friendship or by any intense feeling are lasting, and mind-readers can perceive and reproduce these impressions. The true concept is never lost.

Test this. While wide-awake, close your eyes and recall objects which are thousands of miles away or altogether gone from physical sight and sense. Memory can reproduce voices that have for a long time been silent. In a day-dream we can even evoke the heart's desire, as expressed by the poet Tennyson—

The touch of a vanished hand,

And the sound of a voice that is still.[1]

The mind can also be aware of a flavor or odor, when no foodstuff touches the taste buds and no scent signals the olfactory receptors.

Illusions are not ideas

How do we distinguish real thoughts from illusive thoughts? By learning what is the starting point of the thoughts. Real ideas

---

[1]   Tennyson, Alfred, (1809-1892) English Poet. *Break, Break, Break.*

flow from the divine Mind. Unreal thoughts, coming from the brain or from auras, are extensions of the human mind; they are an accumulation of imprinted mortal beliefs and experiences. Ideas are spiritual, harmonious, and eternal. Illusive thoughts, or objects, proceed from the physical senses and are vulnerable to death.

To love our neighbor's spiritual nature as we love our own spirituality, is a divine idea; but this idea can never be seen, felt, or understood through the physical senses. Excite the organ of admiration or religious faith and a person manifests profound adoration. Excite the feelings of anger or pessimism and the person curses God. These effects, however, do not proceed from spirituality. Idolization and irreverence are both a spin-off of mortal belief.

Eloquence re-echoes the tones of Truth and Love. It is due to inspiration rather than book learning or channeling and shows the possibilities derived from divine Mind. Sometimes, the eloquence is determined to be a gift from departed spirits, but what is the medium capable of knowing or saying when the spirit is absent? This question leads to the answer that beliefs can be undone. The medium first believes they are ignorant and can't speak. That belief is let loose and the medium then believes another mind possesses and is speaking through them.

Destroy the belief in an outside influence, and fluency disappears. The former limits of the belief return. The speaker says, "I am uneducated and incapable of eloquent words." Instances such as these reaffirm the Scriptural word concerning a person, "For as he thinks in his heart, so is he."[1] If a person believes that they cannot be a public speaker without study or without an outside influence, the body responds to this attitude and the tongue is tied.

Scientific improvisation

Mind is not necessarily dependent on the education process. Mind possesses of itself all beauty and poetry. Mind has the power to express prose. Spirit, God, is heard when the human mind's noise is silent. We are all capable of more than we do. The influence or action of

---

[1]   Prov. 23:7 (Amplified*)*

74

Soul confers a freedom which explains the phenomena of excellent impromptu speeches, admirable video scripts, or meaningful texts.

Material energy is neither intelligent nor creative. The tree is not the inventor of itself. Sound is not the originator of music, and man and woman is not the parent of person. Cain[1] naturally concluded that if life was in the body and human beings gave that life, then human beings had the right to take it away. Cain killed his brother, showing that the belief of life in matter was "a murderer from the beginning."[2]

If seed is necessary to produce wheat, and wheat to produce flour, or an animal is necessary to produce meat, how then can we account for their initial origin? How were the loaves[3] and fishes multiplied[4] without flour or egg from which bread or fish could come?

Mind is substance

The earth's orbit and the imaginary line called the equator are not substance. The earth's motion and position are sustained by Mind alone. Empower yourself with the thought that substance is purely spiritual and the movements and transitions possible for the human mind will be found equally possible for the body. Being is alive. Death is obsolete, although some insist that death is the necessary prelude to immortality.

A dreamer can find their self in distant places meeting friends. The dreamer's body is carried through the air and over the ocean. But, the onlooker sees the dreamer's body lying in bed. This shows the possibilities of thought. Hallucinogenic drugs also may temporarily cause the user to mentally travel far and work wonders, yet their bodies stay in one place. Mortal delusions and temporal states of consciousness show that mortal mentality and knowledge are illusory.

Admitting to our self that person is God's own likeness sets us free to master the infinite idea. This conviction shuts the door on death, and opens it wide toward spirituality. The understanding and recognition of Spirit must finally come, and we may as well improve

[1] Gen. 4:8

[2] John 8:44

[3] II Kings 4:42-44

[4] Matt. 14:15-21, 15:32-38; Mark 6:37-44, 8:2-9; Luke 9:12-17; John 6:5-13

our time in solving the mysteries of being through an understanding of divine Principle. At this moment, we do not know what man and woman is, but we certainly will know this when we reflect God.

The Revelator tells us of "a new heaven and new earth."[1] Have you ever pictured this heaven and earth, inhabited by beings under the control of supreme wisdom?

Let us rid our self of the belief that we are separate from God, and obey only the divine Principle, Life and Love. Here is the launching pad to all true spiritual growth.

It is difficult for the narcissistic attitude to accept divine Science, because Science exposes the nonbeing of a separate self. The sooner error is reduced to its native nothingness, the sooner realness appears and our genuine being is understood. The destruction of error is by no means the destruction of Truth or Love, but is the acknowledgment of them.

Absorbed in mortal human selfhood, we discern and reflect faintly the substance of Life or Mind. So, disengage thought from a mortal selfhood and permit the discernment of man and woman's spiritual and eternal individuality. Any erroneous knowledge gained from other spirits, or from the physical senses, can be destroyed as our spiritual image is affirmed.

Erroneous postulates considered

Certain erroneous postulates are now considered in order to better comprehend spiritual facts:

1. That substance, life, and intelligence can be something separate from God.
2. That person is both mental and physical.
3. That Mind is both evil and good.
4. That matter is intelligent, and people have physical bodies which are a part of self
5. That matter/energy holds in itself the issues of life and death and is not only capable of experiencing pleasure and pain, but also capable of imparting these sensations.

---

[1]   Rev. 21:1

From these mistaken postulates comes the decomposition of mortal bodies in what is termed death.

Mind is not an entity inside the brain with the power to go against Life, Truth, and Love, now or anytime. The real Mind cannot be evil or the channeler of evil, for Mind is God.

Knowledge of good and evil

In old Scriptural pictures we see a serpent coiled around the tree of knowledge speaking to Adam and Eve. This represents an alleged talking serpent in the act of commending to fictional first parents the knowledge of good and evil. The fatal knowledge is gained from limited perspectives, instead of from knowing Spirit. The portrayal is still graphically accurate. The common conception of a mortal human—a parody of God's child—is an outgrowth of human knowledge.

Uncover error, and it turns the lie on you. Until the nonbeing of error appears, the moral demand will not be met and the ability to make nothing of error will fall short. We should wince when insisting the unreal is real. The foundation of evil is laid on a belief in something besides God. Believing there is another being other than God tends to urge two opposite powers, instead of inspiring the claims of Truth alone. The mistake of thinking that error can be real, when it is merely the absence of truth, leads to belief in the superiority of error.

Do you say that the time is not yet here in which to recognize Soul as substantial and able to control the body? Remember Jesus, who over twenty centuries ago demonstrated the power of Spirit, was accounted to say, "Whoever believes in me will perform the same works as I do myself,"[1] and, "The time is coming, yes, and has *already come*, when true worshippers will worship the Father in spirit and in reality."[2] It is a privilege to read Paul's words, "I tell you, *now* is the time of God's favor, *now* is the day of salvation."[3]

---

[1]   John 14:12 (JB)

[2]   John 4:23 (Phillips NT) (Italics added by Mary Baker Eddy)

[3]   II Cor. 6:2 (Italics added by Mary Baker Eddy)

Logic and revelation

Divine reason and revelation coincide. If we believe otherwise, we may be sure that either our logic is a fault or that we have misinterpreted revelation. Good never causes evil and good doesn't create anything that can cause evil.

Good does not design a mind susceptible of causing evil or of being confused, for evil and confusion contend with creation. Destructive energy is not the outcome of infinite good. Whatever contradicts the real nature of the divine *esse*, though human faith may cover the contradiction in an angelic costume, is without foundation.

The self-contradictory belief that Spirit is finite as well as infinite has darkened all history. In divine Science, Spirit, as a proper noun, is the name of the Supreme Being. It means quantity and quality, and applies exclusively to God. The modifying derivatives of the word *spirit* refer only to quality, not to God. Man and woman is not God, Spirit, but is spiritual. If spiritual being was Spirit, then people would be spirits, gods. The belief that the infinite can be contained in the finite embodies a mortal spirit, and tends to darken our perception of the kingdom of heaven, and disturb the reign of harmony in the Science of being.

Scientific spiritual being

Jesus taught but one God, one Spirit, who makes spiritual being in the image and likeness of Love, of Mind—not in the likeness of human mind. Person reflects infinite Truth, Life, and Love. The understanding of our essence includes all that is implied by the terms "image" and "likeness"[1] as used in Scripture. The truly Christian and scientific statement of the relationship between spiritual being and God, with the demonstration which accompanied it, incensed the religious leaders, and they said: "Crucify him!"[2] "We have a law, and according to that law he must die, because he claimed to be the Son of God."[3]

---

[1]   Gen. 1:26-27

[2]   Mark 15:13, 14; Luke 23:20; John 19:6

[3]   John 19:7

Torture, dictatorship, repression, intolerance, and bloodshed, wherever found, arise from the belief that the infinite is formed after the paradigm of human personality, passions, and urges. Nations owe their untrustworthy governments to their prevalent misconceptions of God.

Ingratitude and denial do not stop spiritual insight

The progress of truth confirms its claims and Jesus confirmed his words by his works. His healing power evoked denial, ingratitude, and betrayal, arising from an ignorance of spiritual being. Of the ten lepers whom Jesus healed, only one person returned to give God thanks,[1] to acknowledge the divine Principle which had healed him.

The Teacher easily read the thoughts of humankind, and this insight better enabled him to direct those thoughts usefully. What would be said today of an irreverent blasphemer who hints that Jesus used his power to hurt others? Jesus read human minds on a scientific basis, that of the omnipresence of Mind. Readings that resemble Jesus' readings indicate spiritual improvement and a unity with the infinite capacities of the one Mind. Jesus could injure no one by his Mind-reading. The effect of his Mind-reading was always to heal and to save, and this is the only genuine Science of reading human mind. Jesus' holy motives and aims were blamed and condemned by the sinners of that period, as they would be today if Jesus were personally present. We approach God, Life, as our fidelity to Truth and Love expands; and in that ratio we can know all human need and be able to discern the thought of the sick and the sinning for the purpose of healing them. Error of any kind can't hide from the law of God. Paul said, "The mind controlled by the Spirit is life and peace."[2]

Whoever reaches the spiritual point of moral culture and goodness can't harm others, and must do them good. The greater or lesser ability of a Mind-reader to discern thought scientifically depends upon his or her genuine spirituality. The special characteristic of spiritually intuitive mind-reading is not clairvoyance, but is important to success in healing.

[1] Luke 17:18

[2] Rom. 8:6

We welcome the increase of knowledge and the end of error, because even human invention must have its day. We want that day to be prospered by divine Science and Christ-like reality. Midnight foretells the dawn. In the midst of darkness, the Magi[1] detected the solitary star leading to the Messiahship of Truth. Is it true that Christ is always reappearing? Is the wise person of today believed when he or she reads the light which heralds Truth's eternal dawn and describes it radiance?

The darkest hour is sometimes before spiritual awakening

Conditioned by mind-stultifying illusions, people let the hours slip away. Conventional views do not reveal the facts of existence, but immortal perceptions lift human consciousness into eternal Truth. Humanity advances slowly out of old thought patterns. The unwillingness to learn all things correctly, binds spiritual understanding in chains.

Love will finally mark the hour of harmony and spiritualization will follow, for Love is Spirit. Before error is wholly destroyed there will be interruptions of the general human routine. Earth will become dreary and desolate, but summer and winter, seedtime and harvest (though in changed forms) will continue to the end—until the final spiritualization of all things. C. S. Lewis illustrates the idea of Spirit's force in his novel, *The Lion, the Witch and the Wardrobe.*[2] Main character, Aslan, was killed in lieu of Edmonds. Susan and Lucy (Edmond's sisters) saw Aslan's death and were miserable, feeling as if life had stopped, until Lucy noticed light was appearing in the horizon and lively modest activity was going on around Aslan, eventually to prove that Life and Love never end.

This material world is becoming the arena for conflicting forces. On one side there will be disorder and disappointment; on the other side there will be Science and peace. The breaking up of material beliefs may seem to be famine and pestilence, deficit and depression, sin, sickness, and death, which assume new phases until their

---

[1]   Matt. 2:1-2

[2]   C. S. Lewis. *The Lion, the Witch and the Wardrobe.* New York: HarperCollins

nothingness appears. These disturbances will continue until the end of error when all disorder will be swallowed up in spiritual Truth.

Mortal error will vanish in a moral reaction. The mental turmoil of transition has begun and will continue until all errors of belief yield to understanding. Belief is changeable, but spiritual understanding is changeless.

As changeable knowledge diminishes and spiritual understanding increases, real objects will be comprehended mentally instead of materially. As this consummation draws closer, those who have shaped their course in accordance with divine Science will endure to the end.

During a final conflict, nefarious minds will endeavor to find means by which to accomplish more evil. People who discern divine reality will hold crime in check; they will help in the ejection of error. They will maintain law and order, and cheerfully serve the certainty of ultimate perfection.

Dangerous resemblances

Humanity believes that nuclear fission is fierce and the electric current swift, yet in spiritual Science the discharge of one and the flash of the other will become harmless. The more destructive matter becomes, the more its nonbeing will appear, until matter reaches its mortal extreme in illusion and completely self-destructs. The more closely error simulates truth—and the more matter resembles its essence, human mind—the more impotent error becomes as a belief. When a false belief becomes a first-rate copy of truth, it is ready for defeat, even if it hasn't yet passed the boundary of complete self-destruction. The more material the belief, the more obvious its error until divine Spirit, Love, supreme in its domain, dominates all matter and original person is found in the likeness of Spirit.

Universal facts naturally trigger anything that is false to work against its self, bringing error out from under cover. It requires courage to voice truth. The higher Truth's voice is lifted, the louder error will scream until its inarticulate noise is forever silenced in oblivion.

"He lifts his voice, the earth melts."[1] This Scripture indicates that all mortality will disappear before the supremacy of Spirit.

---

[1]   Ps. 46:6

Spirituality still rejected

Spirituality is again demonstrating the Life that is Truth, and the Truth that is Life by the apostolic work of defeating error and healing the sick. Earth has no repayment for the persecutions which attend a new step in Christianity. The spiritual recompense of the persecuted is assured in the elevation of existence above the disorder, and in the gift of divine Love.

The prophet of today sees in the mental horizon the signs of these times, the reappearance of Christianity's essence which heals the sick and destroys error. No other sign will be given. Body can't be saved except through Mind. The Science of Christianity is misinterpreted by a material age, because brain imprints and physical sense can't comprehend Spirit. The healing influence of Spirit is discerned by spiritual sense. Creeds, doctrines, and human hypotheses do not express Christian Science; much less can they demonstrate it.

Beyond the frail premises of human beliefs, above the loosening clutches of human policies, the demonstration of spiritual Mind-healing stands a revealed and practical Science. Throughout all time/space, scientific demonstration is imperative as Christ's revelation of Truth, of Life, and of Love, remaining inviolate for humanity to understand and to practice.

Science and religion not so foreign to one another

For centuries—yes, always—natural science has not really been considered a part of religion. Even now many people consider science to have no proper connection with faith and spirituality. However, mystery does not obscure Christ's teachings. Truth's instructions are not theoretical and fragmentary, but are practical, and complete; and being practical and complete, they are not deprived of their essential vitality.

Key to the kingdom

The way through which immortality and life are learned is not ecclesiastical but divine, not human but holy, not physical but metaphysical, not material but scientifically spiritual. Human philosophy, ethics, and superstition afford no demonstrable divine Principle by which human beings can escape from sin and mortality; yet to find safety in Love is what the Bible demands. "Work out your salvation with fear and trembling," says the apostle, and he straightway adds, "for it is God who works in you to will and to act according to his good purpose."[1] Truth has furnished the key to the kingdom, and with this key Christian Science has opened the door of the human understanding. None may pick the lock nor enter by some other door. The secular teachings are material and not spiritual. Christian Science teaches only that which is spiritual and divine. Spiritual Science is unmistaken and ongoing; whereas, the human perceptions are fallible.

Bear in mind, people who adopt New Age techniques, mysticism, or hypnotism, may be more spiritual than individuals who shun or avoid their practices. Therefore my contest is not with the individual person, but with the false systems. I love humanity, and will continue to labor and to endure.

The calm, strong forces of true spirituality are manifest as health, purity, and a magnanimous self. Spiritual mindedness must expand the human experience until the beliefs of temporal being are clearly exposed as impositions. Confusion, danger, and disorder will then give everlasting place to the scientific demonstration of divine Spirit and to God's radiant offspring.

---

[1]   Phil. 2:12-13

POWER OF SUGGESTION;
CROWD THINKING

> For out of the heart come evil intentions, murder, adultery,
> fornication, theft, false witness, slander. These are what
> defile a person.[1]

The power of suggestion has a long and capricious history.
Research of the human mind and its functions became rather
primitively active in the 18th century with Franz Anton Mesmer.[2]
He recognized that human beings can be manipulated, but didn't
understand the process. Mesmer theorized this manipulation occurred
by means of a physical magnetic fluid. Mesmer even concluded that
this magnetic fluid could be transmitted from one breathing creature
to another as a therapeutic influential agent. He termed his theory
animal magnetism. Today, it is realized that he had actually hit
upon the power of suggestion or collective mentality. Concerning
Mesmer's theory, the *Encyclopedia Americana* states, "Although it was
later deemed a pseudoscience, the theory helped pioneer the study
of the unconscious mind, hypnosis, and the development of medical
psychiatry."[3] Mesmer and his therapeutic animal magnetic fluid were
eventually discredited. The *Encyclopedia Americana* continues, "Two
separate commissions composed mainly of leading French scientists
concluded that no such physical substance as animal magnetism

---

[1]   Matt. 15:19-20 (NRSV)

[2]   Mesmer, Franz Anton (1734-1815) German physician

[3]   The Encyclopedia Americana International Edition, Volume 18.
      Connecticut: Grolier Incorporated, 2003.

exists."[1] Ironically however, Mesmer's name is preserved in the term, "mesmerize". When people are being influenced by mortal's persuasion or peer pressure, or when they are getting caught up in groupthink, or obsessed by some event, they are "mesmerized."

In the 19th century, the term "hypnotism" came into vogue, describing the process that characteristically induces the mental state of suggestibility. Today, hypnotism is studied, used as a form of entertainment, and sometimes utilized in the treatment of mental and physical disorders, but the scattered experimentation and observations are still not completely understood. Human beings can feel hypnotized for no apparent reason doing things they wouldn't normally do, while on the other hand there are some persons who just can't be hypnotized. Why?

Humankind is advancing toward an understanding of mental phenomena, of crowd thinking or hypnosis. In the 20th century, Carl Jung[2] distinguished three psychic levels: (1) consciousness, (2) the personal unconscious, and (3) the collective unconscious.

Observations of the workings of hypnosis, the collective unconscious, or crowd thinking, offer convincing evidence that they are not remedial agents. I am convinced that the effects of outside mortal mental influences on those who practice it, and on the people who do not resist it, lead to moral and physical death.

If hypnotism seems to heal disease—or mental collective noise seems to alleviate loneliness—this appearance is deceptive, since error cannot remove the effects of error. Discomfort under error is preferable to comfort. In every instance, the effect of suggestion is just the effect of illusion. Any seeming benefit derived from mental manipulation is proportional to one's faith in magic.

Openness to outside influence is denial of inner influence

The process, either unconsciously or consciously, of thought manipulation has no scientific foundation, for God is uninfluenced and always conscious—always consciously governing all that is real,

---

[1]   Ibid

[2]   Carl Gustav Jung (1875-1961) Swiss psychiatrist and founder of the school of analytical psychology.

harmonious, and eternal. God expresses divine consciousness in us. God did not give us an animal or human consciousness to lose control of or control. In Science, a hypnotic state is a belief, a denial of the one spiritual influence. Crowd thinking, mass human consciousness, or mental noise, possesses no intelligence, power, or reality. Human physical senses can't distinguish crowd thinking or mental noise because they are unreal concepts of the so-called human, mortal mind.

There is only one real attraction, that of Spirit. The pointing of the needle to the North Pole symbolizes this all-embracing power or attraction of God, divine Mind.

Gravitational pulls, the stars, and electromagnetic forces do not have power over us, just as they have no power over our Maker. God governs the universe. We reflect God's power have the dominion not to be influenced by the planets, by earth and its mortal people.

The mild forms of suggestion are disappearing and its aggressive features are coming to the front. The mechanism of crime, hidden in the dark recesses of mortal thought, is every hour producing more complicated and subtle confusion. So inconceivable are the present methods of the human mind's influences that they trick people into indolence and produce the very apathy on the subjects which the criminal desires. The power of suggestion, with its many different disguises such as herd mentality and the adoption of unoriginal thinking, causes people to make errors throughout the thought process.

In a psychology textbook, readers are asked, "Hypnosis: Altered consciousness or Role Playing?"[1] Answering that question is not as important as realizing that we need to spiritually think for our self; otherwise, indifferent, self-destructive, and depressed behavior is believed to be our own thinking, and it will be exhibited. We also need to encourage in others the right and responsibility to think for themselves as God created them able to do.

Mental terrorism defeated

Humanity must learn that the influences of propaganda or crowd thinking are powerless. Crowd thinking is oppressive, but only a

---

[1]   Weiten, Wayne. P*sychology Themes and Variations, Briefer version 6th Edition.* Thomson Wadsworth, 2005.

phase of nothingness. Christian Science devastates the vacuum of evil thinking and preeminently promotes good-will and virtue in families and therefore in the community. The Apostle Paul refers to the personification of evil as "the god of this age,"[1] and further defines it as dishonesty and false teachings. Sin was the Assyrian moon-god.

Humanity is fortunate when the noise of human mortal mind is defeated through Science. We can escape from sin and mortality as we overcome the mythological and primitive suggestions of human mind. In the first-steps of mental liberation, however, the knowledge of good and evil isn't scientifically seen because evil isn't real.

Mind-science has nothing to do with sitting-on-the-fence of impertinent knowledge, because Mind-science is of God and demonstrates the divine Principle, working out the purposes of good only. The maximum of good is the infinite God and God's idea, the All-in-all. Anything unlike the conscious infinite is a suggested lie.

As named in Christian Science, mesmerism or crowd thinking is the specific term for error, or human mortal mind. They are the false belief that mind is inside it's thought (matter), and is both evil and good, or that evil is as real as good and more powerful. This penchant to live out a mortal life has not one quality of Truth and is either ignorant or malicious. The malicious form of hypnotic suggestion ends in moral idiocy. The truths of immortal Mind annihilates the human mind's weak and stupid predilections, which are like blind bugs, flying in circles to the artificial light and getting burned.

Thought transfer

In reality there is no human mortal mind and consequently no transfer of temporal thought and will-power. Life and being are of God. In Christian Science, human beings can do no harm because scientific thoughts are eternal thoughts, passing from God to humanity.

When Christian Science and impulsive crowd thinking are both comprehended, as they will be at no distant date, it will be seen why

---

[1]   II Cor. 4:4

honest, hardworking people are unfairly persecuted and undermined by wolves in sheep's clothing.[1]

Arthur Schopenhauer[2] has been credited to say, "All truth passes through three stages. First, it is ridiculed. Second, it is violently opposed. Third, it is accepted as being self-evident." Or, in words attributed to George Bernard Shaw, [3] "All great truths begin as blasphemies."

Divine Science goes to the bottom of mental action. Spiritual knowledge reveals the theodicy which indicates the rightness of all divine action as the emanation of divine Mind. Spiritual knowledge also reveals the consequent wrongness of opposite actions deemed supernatural, paranormal, magic, voodoo, evil, hypnotism.

The medicine of Science is divine Mind, not human mind. The human attitudes of dishonesty, sensuality, greed, revenge, and malice, cannot heal the sick. Thoughts that try to control another person are crude tendencies and by no means the mental qualities which heal. The hypnotizer employs one error to destroy another. The mental mal-practitioner heals sickness through a belief, when it was a belief which originally caused the sickness. This is a case of a greater error overcoming a lesser. The greater error thereafter occupies the ground, leaving the case worse than before.

Motives and mental crimes considered

Our courts recognize evidence to prove the motive as well as the act of a crime. Clearly, the human mind must move the body to a wicked act. Isn't mortal mind the murderer? The hands, without human minds to direct them, could not commit a murder.

Can wave/particles commit a crime? Can material atoms be punished? Can you separate the mentality from the body over which courts hold jurisdiction? Human mortal mind, not matter, is the criminal in every case; and human law rightly estimates crime, and courts reasonably pass sentence, according to the motive. Courts and juries judge and sentence human beings in order to restrain crime,

---

[1]   Matt. 7:15

[2]   Schopenhauer, Arthur, (1788-1860) German philosopher.

[3]   Shaw, George Bernard, (1856-1950) Irish Playright.

to prevent violence, or to punish the wrongdoer. To say that these courts have no jurisdiction over the human or mortal mind would be to contradict precedent. It doesn't make sense to admit that law is restricted to matter or physical bodies, while the real outlaw, the human mortal mind, defies justice and is recommended to mercy.

Our laws will eventually take cognizance of mental crime and no longer apply legal rulings entirely too physical offences. It will go down in history that how we think, or what we think, directly or indirectly affects action, including the action of what we call physical bodies. The medical field is even somewhat recognizing the power of metaphysics. Dr. Dharma Singh Khalsa, M.D., a pioneer in integrative medicine, testifies that, "Meditation is a wondrously powerful medical modality . . . the meditation that I teach employs not just patients' mental energies, but also their physical energies"[1]

Mental manipulators let loose

Whoever uses their developed mental energies or powers to commit opportune atrocities is never safe. God will arrest those people. Divine justice will confine them. Their sins will be millstones about their necks, weighing them down to the depths of disgrace and death. The aggravation of error foretells its doom and confirms the ancient axiom: Whom the gods would destroy, they first make mad.

Proper self-government

Conventional medicine advocates drugs, even harmful drugs, and is far from divine Science. Learning the dangers or the uselessness of intrusive medicine, humanity looks in new directions for healing. Humanity begins to understand the power of mind over matter and the importance of better thinking. Be aware: some thought influences can pretend to be good or in our best interest, but are just as dangerous as harmful drugs. This is mental *mal*practice and is criminal, working against common humanity, honesty, and justice. Divine Mind-practice requires human mind to yield to the

---

[1]   From *Pain Cure, The* by Dharma Khalsa. Copyright ©. By permission of Warner Books, Inc. All rights reserved. To purchase copies of this book, please call 1-800-759-0190.

divine consciousness and to unite with the spiritual thought moving heavenward.

Like our nation, Christian Science has its Declaration of Independence. God has endowed us with inalienable rights, among which are self-government, reason, and conscience. We are properly self-governed only when we are guided rightly and governed by our Maker, divine Truth and Love. Our rights are invaded when the divine order is interfered with and the mental mal-practitioner incurs the divine penalty for this crime.

Right methods

When judging Christian Science, sanction only such methods as are demonstrable in Truth and known by their fruits. Classify other methods that suggest futile or backward behavior as did Paul in his great epistle to the Galatians, when he wrote as follows:

"The acts of the sinful nature are obvious: sexual immorality, impurity and debauchery; idolatry and witchcraft; hatred, discord, jealousy, fits of rage, selfish ambition, dissensions, factions and envy; drunkenness, orgies, and the like. I warn you, as I did before, that those who live like this will not inherit the kingdom of God. But the fruit of the Spirit is love, joy, peace, patience, kindness, goodness, faithfulness, gentleness and self-control. Against such things there is no law."[1]

---

[1]   Gal. 5:19-23

SCIENCE, THEOLOGY, MEDICINE

I want you to know, brothers, that the gospel I preached is not something that man made up. I did not receive it from any man, nor was I taught it; rather, I received it by revelation from Jesus Christ.[1]

The kingdom of heaven is like yeast that a woman took and mixed into a large amount of flour until it worked all through the dough.[2]

In the year 1866, I discovered spiritual Science or the divine laws of Life, Truth, and Love, and branded the discovery Christian Science. For many years, God graciously prepared me to receive the conclusive revelation of the absolute divine Principle of scientific mental healing.

Work of divine Science

This indisputable Principle points to the revelation of Immanuel, "God with us,"[3] the sovereign ever-presence, delivering the children of human beings from every ill "that flesh is heir to."[4] Through divine Science, religion and medicine are inspired with a more God-like nature and essence. Science gives new strength to faith and understanding, and thoughts intelligently acquaint themselves with God.

Dissatisfaction with human life

We are inundated with the feeling and consciousness that life exists in the material body, yet we remember that in reality God is our

---

[1]   Gal. 1:11

[2]   Matt. 13:33; Luke 13:21

[3]   Isa. 7:14; Matt. 1:23

[4]   Shakespeare, William, (1564-1616) *Hamlet,* Act III. Scene I.

Life. We look at human events and timidly realize the day will come when we say, "I find no pleasure in them."[1]

How does the heavenly conviction of spiritual existence come? How does a conviction so antagonistic to the testimony of the physical senses appear? According to Paul, it is "the gift of God's grace given me through the working of his power."[2] Neale Donald Walsch, author of *The New Revelations: A Conversation with God* wrote, "Divine inspiration is the birthright of every human being."[3] The divine law of Life and Love unfolds the demonstrable facts that matter (human mind) possesses neither sensation nor life; that human experiences show the falsity of all temporal things; and that spiritual desires establish the truth that the only sufferer is human mind. The divine Mind can't suffer.

Demonstrable evidence

My conclusions were reached by allowing the evidence of this revelation to multiply with mathematical certainty. The lesser demonstration proved the greater. Just as the product of three multiplied by three, equaling nine, proves conclusively that three times three trillion must be nine trillion—not a fraction more, not a unit less.

Light shining in darkness

When I felt as though I was near the edge of mortal existence, standing within the "valley of the shadow of death,"[4] I learned the following truths in divine Science. 1) All real being is in God, the divine Mind, and that Life, Truth, and Love are all-powerful and ever-present. 2) The opposite of Truth—called error, sin, sickness, disease, death, fleshly mind—is the false testimony of temporal perception, of mind in matter. 3) The temporal perception evolves, in belief, a subjective state of human mind which this same so-called mind names *matter*, thereby shutting out the true perception of Spirit.

---

1   Ecc. 12:1

2   Eph. 3:7

3   Walsch, Neale Donald. *The New Revelations: A Conversation with God.* New York: Atria Books, 2002.

4   Ps. 23:4

New lines of thought

My discovery—that human misnamed *mind* produces all biological functions and actions of the human body—set my thoughts to work in new directions. The new direction inspired my demonstration of the proposal that infinite Mind is All and human mortal mind is nothing in Mind-science.

Scientific evidence

Divine Science reveals unquestionably that Mind is All-in-all and that the only realities are the divine Mind and idea. This great fact is not seen to be supported by sensible evidence until its divine Principle is demonstrated by healing the sick and thus proved absolute and divine. After experiencing and seeing this proof, no other conclusion can be reached.

For three years after my discovery, I pursued the answer to the problem of Mind-healing, focusing on the Scriptures. Time and energy were devoted to discovering a positive rule. The search was sweet, calm, and buoyant with hope—not selfish or depressing. I knew the Principle of all harmonious Mind-action to be God, and that cures were produced in primitive Christian healing by holy, inspiring faith. Wanting to know the Science of this healing, I won my way to absolute conclusions through divine revelation, reason, and demonstration. The revelation of Truth in the understanding comes gradually and apparently through divine power. When a new spiritual idea is born to earth, the prophetic Scripture of Isaiah is again fulfilled: "For to us a child is born . . . and he will be called Wonderful Counselor."[1]

"Jesus answered, My teaching is not my own. It comes from him who sent me. If anyone chooses to do God's will, he will find out whether my teaching comes from God or whether I speak on my own."[2]

God's allness learned

There are three great certainties of Spirit: omnipotence, omnipresence, omniscience—Spirit possessing all power, filling all

---

[1] Isa. 9:6

[2] John 7:16-17

space, constituting all Science. These great truths contradict the belief that human mind can be actual. Spirit's truth reveals primitive existence as the radiant reality of God's creation, in which everything Mind's wisdom made is pronounced good.

Learning the allness of God is how I perceived as never before, the awful unreality called evil. Consequently, with equal force, another glorious proposal was brought to light—man and woman's perfectibility and the establishment of the kingdom of heaven on earth.

In following these leadings of scientific revelation, the Bible was my only textbook. The Scriptures were illumined; reason and revelation were reconciled, and afterward the truth of divine Science was demonstrated. No human pen or tongue taught me the Science contained in this book, *Science and Health*. Tongue or pen can't overthrow Science. This book may be distorted by shallow criticism or by negligent or malicious students, and its ideas may be temporarily abused and misrepresented; but the Science and truth therein will forever remain to be discerned and demonstrated.

The demonstration lost and found

Jesus illustrated the power of divine Science to heal human minds and bodies. But this power was lost sight of and must again be spiritually discerned, taught, and demonstrated as commanded by Truth, with "accompanying signs."[1] Its Science must be understood by as many as believe on Christ and spiritually comprehend Truth.

No analogy exists between the demonstrable truths of Christian Science, and the vague hypotheses of agnosticism, pantheism, spiritualism, Wicca, psychics, and New Age concepts. Willfulness, or the sensuous reason of the human mind, opposes the divine Mind as expressed through divine Science.

Spiritual Science is natural, but not physical. The Science of God and person is not supernatural, but understandable to everyone. Mystery or miracle is not included in Science, just as it is not included in the science of numbers. The Science of God, Spirit, cannot be denied its right to the name of Science. The Principle of

---

[1] Mark 16:20 (ESV)

divine metaphysics is God; the practice of divine metaphysics is the utilization of the power of Truth over error; its rules demonstrate its Science. The explanations of divine metaphysics reverses perverted and physical hypotheses concerning God, just as optical illusions are explained by physical science.

Pertinent proposals

The John Templeton Foundation seeks to promote a deeper understanding of the influence spirituality, beliefs and values can have on human health. By promoting collaboration and clinical research into the relationship between spirituality and health, and by documenting the positive medical aspects of spiritual practice, the Foundation hopes to contribute to the reintegration of faith into modern life. This is an example of how the advancement of spiritual discoveries is not only being encouraged, but also is helping to offset the world's tendency to attribute physical effects to physical causes rather than to a spiritual cause. Divine Science is meeting humanities desire for spirituality.

Tests confirming truth

Mind controls the body, not partially but completely. This fact became evident to me after I fully examined my discovery and its demonstration in healing the sick. I submitted this metaphysical system of treating disease to a broad range of practical tests. This system gained ground and has proved itself to be a very effective curative agent, when scientifically employed.

Is there more than one instruction of Christian Science? Divine Science is demonstrable. There can be but one suitable arrangement of ideas in its teaching. Those who depart from this approach forfeit their claims to belong to its Science. A student of Christian Science does not adhere to a doctrinal system taught by particular teachers; and does not adhere to a teaching peculiar to a human organization or a philosopher. In other words, there is no adherence to, or adoption of, the *opinions* of Socrates, Plato, Jean-Paul Sartre, Michel Foucault, or some other thinker. Although the opinions of great thinkers have gleams of divinity, borrowed from that truly divine Science which eschews human-made teaching practices, these opinions remain human in their origin and tendency and are not scientifically Christ-like.

Unchanging Principle

From the infinite One in divine Science comes one Principle and its infinite idea. From this infinite one Source come spiritual rules, laws, and their demonstration, and is "the same yesterday and today and forever."[1] The divine Principle of healing and the Christ-idea characterized in the epistle to the Hebrews is infinite, unchanging.

Any theory or teaching which departs from what has already been stated and proved to be true, affords no foundation on which to establish a genuine school of this Science. A new school of Christian Science who appropriately credits me is valid, because it is obeying the commandment, "You shall not steal."[2]

Principle and practice

God is the Principle of divine metaphysics. As there is but one God, there can be but one divine Principle of all Science. There must be fixed rules for the demonstration of this divine Principle. The letter of Science plentifully reaches humanity today, but its spirit comes only in small degrees. The vital part, the heart and soul of divine Science, is Love. Without Love, the letter is but the dead body of Science—obsolete, isolated, and barren.

Here is a summary of four fundamental propositions of divine metaphysics. To me, they are *self-evident*. The propositions agree in statement and proof even if reversed.

1. God is All-in-all.
2. God is good. Good is Mind.
3. God, Spirit, being all, nothing is matter.
4. Life, God, omnipotent good, deny death, evil, sin, disease.—Disease, sin, evil, death, deny good, omnipotent God, Life.

---

[1]   Heb. 13:8

[2]   Ex. 20:15; Deut. 5:19

Which of the denials in proposition four is true? Both are not, cannot be, true. According to the Scripture, I find that God is true, "though every human being is false and a liar."[1]

Mental reasoning

The divine metaphysics of spiritual Science, like the method in mathematics, proves the rule by inversion. Eleven plus three is fourteen, and fourteen minus three is eleven. There is no pain in Truth, and no truth in pain; no temporal sensations in Mind, and no mind in temporal sensations; no illusion in Mind, and no mind in illusion; no mortality in Life, and no life in mortality; no matter in good, and no good in matter.

Definition of human mind

Conventional thinking classes both evil and good together as *mind*. To be understood, I call sick and sinful humanity *human mind*— meaning by this term the flesh, or physical anatomy, opposing Spirit. The human mind and evil resist the divine Mind, or Truth and good. The spiritually unscientific definition of mind is based on the evidence of the physical senses, which makes minds many and calls *mind* both human and divine.

In Science, Mind is *one,* including noumenon and phenomena, God and Mind's thoughts.

Imperfect terminology

Human mind is a grammatical error in language, and involves an improper use of the word *mind.* As Mind is spiritual, the phrase *human mind* implies something untrue and therefore unreal. In teaching divine Science, the phrases human mind, human energy, chemically based mind, mortal or materialistic mind is meant to designate that which has no real existence. Certainly, if better words or phrases could be suggested, they would be used. In expressing the new tongue we must sometimes resort to the old and imperfect, and the new wine of the Spirit has to be poured into the old wineskins[2] of the letter.

---

1   Rom. 3:4 (Amplified)

2   Matt. 9:17; Mark 2:22; Luke 5:37

Mental cause

Divine Science explains all cause and effect as mental, not physical. It lifts the veil of mystery from Soul and body. Science shows the scientific relation of person to God and unravels the interwoven ambiguities of being, setting free the imprisoned thought. In divine Science, the universe, including man and woman, is spiritual, harmonious, and eternal. Science shows that what is termed *matter* is but the subjective state of what I term *human mind.*

Philological inadequacy

Apart from the usual opposition to everything new, the one great obstacle to receiving spirituality through which the understanding of Mind-science comes, is the inadequacy of terminology for metaphysical statements. It is difficult to make metaphysical ideas comprehensible to the reader who has not personally demonstrated divine Science as brought forth in my discovery. Job says: "The ear tests words as the tongue tastes food."[1] When translating material terms back into the original spiritual tongue, it is difficult to give the correct impression.

SCIENTIFIC TRANSLATION OF SPIRITUAL DIVINE MIND

GOD: Divine Principle, Mind, Soul, Life, Love, Truth, Spirit.

PERSON (man and woman): God's spiritual idea, individual, perfect, eternal.

IDEA: An image in Mind; "**Synonyms** idea, concept, conception, thought, notion, impression, means what exists in the mind as a representation (as of something comprehended) or as a formulation (as of a plan)."[2]

SCIENTIFIC TRANSLATION OF HUMAN MIND

First Degree: **Spiritual unawareness.**

PHYSICAL. Evil thinking, obsessions and negative appetites, fear, corrupt will, self-justification, arrogance, envy, deceit, hatred, revenge, sin, sickness, disease, death.

Second Degree: **Disappearance of self-destructive thinking**.

---

[1]   Job 34:3

[2]   By permission. From the *Merriam-Webster OnLine,*©2007 by Merriam-Webster, Incorporated (www.Merriam-Webster.com).

MORAL. Humanity, honesty, constructive inclinations, compassion, hope, faith, humility, moderation.

Third Degree: **Understanding**.

SPIRITUAL. Wisdom, purity, spiritual understanding, spiritual power, love, health, holiness.

Spiritual universe

In the third degree, human mind disappears and man and woman as God's image appear. Science reverses the evidence before the physical human senses. Science makes this Scriptural testimony true in our hearts, "Many who are first will be last, and many who are last will be first,"[1] so that God and Her idea may be to us what divinity really is and must of necessity be—all-embracing.

Aim of Science

A correct view of Christian Science and of its application to healing includes vastly more than can be seen at first. Many works on metaphysics do not recognize the power of Mind as the Messiah, leaving the grand point untouched. We want to carry the day against physical enemies—even to the extinction of all belief in materialism, evil, disease, and death. Pure metaphysics insists on the fact that God is all, therefore, temporal substance is nothing but an image in human mind.

Divine personality

Human personalities have material bodies, but God is Spirit, Love. Divine Science strongly emphasizes the thought that God is not *bodily,* but *bodiless,* yet personal.

The words *person* and *personal* need to be employed correctly when applied to God. We can refer to God as infinite Person, in the sense of infinite individuality, but our conception of divinity is confused and erroneous when Deity is thought to have human personalities. An infinite Person in a finite personality is impossible.

The term *individuality* is also open to debate. An individual may be one of a series, or one of many, as an individual person or an individual car; whereas God is *One*—not one of a series, but one alone and without an equal.

---

[1]   Matt. 19:30; Mark 9:35, 10:31; Luke 13:30

Spiritual language

God is Spirit; therefore the language of Spirit must be, and is, spiritual. Divine Science attaches no physical characters and significance to the Supreme Being and manifestation. Only human beings attach physicality to Spirit. God's essential language is spoken of in the last chapter of Mark's Gospel as the new tongue, the spiritual meaning of which is attained through the "signs that accompanied it."[1]

The miracles of Jesus

The pure language of Spirit "is more than eyes have seen or ears have heard."[2] Jesus taught spirituality by parables and stories. As a student of the divine, Jesus unfolded God to us, illustrating and demonstrating Life and Truth by his power over the sick and sinning. Human theories are inadequate to interpret the divine Principle involved in the miracles performed by Jesus, and are especially inadequate to explain his unparalleled and triumphant exit from the flesh.

Mindless sensory system

Evidence drawn from the five physical senses only relate to human reason. Human reason is unresponsive to the true light and therefore dimly reflects and feebly transmits Jesus' works and words. Truth is a revelation.

Leaven of Truth

Jesus warned his disciples to "be on your guard against the yeast of the Pharisees, which is hypocrisy."[3] He defined this yeast as human doctrines or teachings. Jesus' parable of the "yeast which a woman took and mixed with three measures of flour till it was all leavened,"[4] implies that spiritual yeast signifies the Science of Christ and its spiritual interpretation—an inference far above the merely ecclesiastical and formal applications of the illustration.

---

[1] Mark 16:20

[2] I Cor. 2:9 (CEV)

[3] Mark 8:15; Luke 12:1

[4] Matt. 13:33; Luke 13:21 (REB)

Did this parable have a moral that brings attention to a prophecy? Did it foretell the second appearing in the flesh of the Christ, Truth, hidden in sacred secrecy from the visible world?

Ages pass, but this yeast of Truth is always at work. It must destroy the entire mass of error, and so be eternally glorified in man and woman's spiritual freedom.

Contrasting the divine and human

Thinking further about the parable of the yeast, Could the three measures of flour be three modes of mortal thought, science, theology, and medicine? In their spiritual significance, science, theology, and medicine are means of divine thought, which include spiritual laws emanating from the invisible and infinite power and grace. However, a materialist view perverts these spiritual laws. In all mortal forms of thought, dust is dignified as the natural status of person and things. What's more, the modes of physical movement are honored with the name of *laws*. This perversion of the divine continues until the yeast of Spirit changes the whole of human thought, as yeast changes the chemical properties of flour.

Certain contradictions

When law is portrayed as physical instead of spiritual, natural science represents a kingdom divided against its self.[1] In absolute Love, nature and God are one, law is spiritual and the natural order of heaven comes down to earth.

Inescapable dilemma

We disown the Almighty when we try to attribute spiritual power to matter. Every time human theories give material elements power, we run into the quandaries of believing: The self-evolution and self-government of matter; or, that matter is the product of Spirit. The first assumption, matter as a power in and of itself, leaves the creator out of His own universe. The second presumption, regarding God as the creator of matter, automatically makes God responsible for all disasters; physical and moral. The unavoidable dilemma of empowering matter also makes infinite Life not only the source of

---

[1]   Matt. 12:26; Mark 3:24; Luke 11:17

destruction, but also makes Spirit guilty of maintaining perpetual disorder, all under the name of natural law.

God and nature

In one sense God is identical with nature, but this nature is spiritual and is not expressed in quanta or atomic structure. The lawgiver is the divine ideal of omnipresent Love, and never strikes the child at prayer. God is natural good and is represented only by the idea of goodness, whereas evil and destruction should be regarded as unnatural, because it is opposed to the nature of Spirit, God.

The science of astronomy has reversed the deceptive evidence of a geocentric system that says the sun is moving around the earth. When we watch the sunrise, human beings rarely deny heliocentrism. We knowledgably admit the fact that the earth is spinning and circling the sun. So also, the Science of Mind reverses the delusive evidence that soul is in a body. We can admit the facts that Soul is not in a body and that the body is accountable to Mind. People are the humble expressions of calm Mind, though it seems otherwise to our immature perceptions. We will never understand spiritual facts if we don't metaphysically reverse the outward appearance. Man and woman are not a dichotomy of non-intelligence and intelligence. We coexist with and reflect God, Soul, substance, unchangeable and intelligent.

Science reverses the false testimony of the physical senses. Mortals arrive at the fundamental facts of being by this reversal. The question inevitably arises: Is a person sick if the physical senses indicate that they are in good health? No! Matter can make no conditions for man and woman. And is a person well if the senses say they are sick? Yes, they are well in Science in which health is normal and disease is abnormal.

Health and the physical senses

Health is not a condition of matter, but of Mind. The flesh cannot bear reliable testimony on the subject of health. The Science of Mind-healing shows it to be impossible for anything other than Mind to honestly point to, or set forth, the real status of man and woman. The divine Principle of Science, reversing the testimony of the physical senses, reveals person as harmoniously existent in Truth. The only basis for health is through the Science that denies disease, overrules false evidence, and heals the sick.

Any conclusion *pro* or *con,* deduced from matter's assumed consciousness leads to disease. Science, however, reverses the consciousness of disease and presents that which is legitimate.

History illustrates truth

Sputnik and NASA changed the world view when launching into outer space. Setbacks happened, but courage set the precedence. Consequently, outgrown philosophies, based on what physical senses say, have become extinct. The physical law of gravity can't define us. Space exploration, thought expansion, bravery, and open-mindedness, continues.

Albert Einstein[1] recognized, and made public, the General Theory of Relativity. Time, space, and mass are relative, or in other words not absolute. Now that time, space, and mass are better identified, they are more correctly studied and scientific corrections and modifications continue.

Chaldean Wisemen read in the stars the future. Although no better revelation than the horoscope was seen in the stellar system, earth and heaven were bright. Birds and blossoms are thankful in God's perennial and happy sunshine, golden with Truth. So we have goodness and beauty to cheer the heart. But left to the hypotheses of mortal perceptions, unexplained by divine Science, we seem to be wandering comets—are as Maya Angelou wrote:

> Manless and friendless
> No cave my home
> This is my torture
> My long nights, lone.[2]

Science shows that appearances are often mistaken, leading to false judgments and conclusions. To correct the mistakes, we follow

---

[1]   Albert Einstein, (1879-1955) German-American physicist.

[2]   *The Traveler.* from "And Still I Rise" by Maya Angelou, copyright © 1978 by Maya Angelou. Used by permission of Random House, Inc.

the simple rule that the greater controls the lesser. For example; the clearer view that the infinite controls the finite has brought to light new discoveries. The idea of infinity discounted the mistake of a "static universe." Although indistinguishable to the temporal senses, the universe is not fixed, but expanding and contracting. Furthermore, the rate of expansion is greater than the contracting and the cosmos is moving away *with* space, not even *through* space. The universe exemplifies the infinite. There is no edge to the universe. From anywhere in the universe, it appears as though it is the center of an ever-expanding heaven. Even our solar system, orbiting in the outer edge of a spiral galaxy, the Milky Way, is indefinitely expanding and rotating in its own unique path.

The pattern of astronomy imitates the action of divine Principle. Therefore, the idea of God is brought nearer the spiritual fact, and is allied to divine Science as displayed in the everlasting control of the universe.

What the physical senses tell us often reverses or rearranges the real Science of being. This rearrangement assigns seeming authority to sin, sickness, and death. But the great facts of Life, rightly understood, defeat this triad of errors, contradict their false witnesses, and reveal the power of heaven—the actual authority of harmony on earth. The material senses' rearrangement of the Science of Soul was exposed in a practical way twenty centuries ago by the demonstrations of Jesus. Yet we are trained to believe that the human mind is secondary to mortal body, and that certain sections of matter, such as brain and nerves, are put in charge of pain and pleasure. Sadly, this derangement looks to matter to report to the mind the status of happiness or misery.

There are many proofs of the illusion of physical sense. For example, when driving on the highway, the paved road ahead sometimes appears to have water on it. The barometer points to fair weather in the midst of murky clouds and drenching rain. What about the body? Physical senses tell us the body is solid, but the body isn't solid. Cosmic rays, neutrinos, radio and TV waves are zinging through the body as if it is transparent. The examples of illusive, unreliable appearances could go on. Life teaches us to correct what the physical senses and human imprints claim as fact.

Spiritual sense of life

To physical sense, a cut jugular vein takes away life; but to spiritual sense and in Science, Life goes on unchanged. Existence is eternal. Temporal life is a false sense of being.

Change in worldview changes thought

Human-made theories make the same mistake regarding Soul and body that René Descartes[1] made regarding the brain as a complex fixed machine. Adherents of Descartes theories culminates in localizationism, the belief in a hard-wired brain in which each mental function has a strict location. However modern brain science is showing, "[Brain] plasticity is a normal phenomenon, and brain maps are constantly changing."[2] Moreover, Christian Science is showing that mind is not subject to the brain or matter, and soul is not in the body. The order of Science can't be reversed by human theories that assign to matter the power and prerogative of Spirit, a paradigm in which people become the most absolutely weak and pitiful creatures in the universe. Scientific blunders can't affect the harmony of being.

Seeming and being

The truth of Mind shows conclusively how it is that matter seems to be, but is not. Divine Science, rising above physical theories, excludes matter, resolves *things* into *thoughts,* and replaces the objects of physical sense with spiritual ideas.

I introduced the term CHRISTIAN SCIENCE to designate the scientific system of divine healing.

The revelation consists of two parts:

1. The discovery of this divine Science of Mind-healing, through a spiritual sense of Scriptures and through the teachings of the Counselor,[3] as promised by Jesus.

---

[1] René Descartes, (1596-1650) French mathematician, scientist and philosopher.

[2] *The Brain that Changes Itself: Stories of Personal Triumph from the Frontiers of Brain Science* Norman Doidge, M.D. (Viking Penguin Books, New York, 2007)

[3] John 16:7

2. The proof, by present-day demonstration, that the miracles of Jesus did not specially belong to a privileged few or at a time now ended. Miracles illustrate an ever-operative divine Principle which indicates the eternality of the scientific order and continuity of being.

Scientific starting point

Divine Science differs from the hard and soft sciences, because it has a complete theory. The Science of Christ is preeminently scientific because it is based on Truth, the Principle of all science.

Physical science not a starting point

Hard sciences are human knowledge; beliefs; human inventions; a shaved Samson[1] without strength. When human beliefs lack organizations to support them, their foundations are gone. Not having moral might, spiritual basis, or a holy Principle of its own, a belief mistakes effect for cause and seeks to find life and intelligence in matter, thus limiting Life and adhering to disorder and death. Basically, human beliefs are blind conclusions made from unreliable reasoning. A mortal sense of things is forever silenced by immortal Spirit.

Correct interpretation

The universe and person is to be interpreted by Science from its divine Principle, God, and then it can be understood. When explained on the basis of physical sense and represented as exposed to change, accumulation and decay, the universe, like man and woman, is an enigma.

Mental force, energy

Gravitational, electromagnetic, and nuclear forces are properties of Mind. They belong to divine Principle and support the equilibrium of that same thought-force which launched the earth in its orbit and said to the proud wave, "this far you may come and no farther."[2]

Spirit is the life, substance, and continuity of all things. We move on forces. Withdraw them and creation must collapse. Human

---

[1] Judges 16:19
[2] Job 38:11

knowledge calls them forces of matter. Divine Science restores the forces by classifying them spiritually and by declaring them inherently and wholly to belong to divine Mind.

Bodily and environmental changes

The elements of the physical world and the functions of the physical body will change as human mind changes its beliefs. What is now considered the best condition for biological and functional health may no longer be found indispensable to health in the future. Moral conditions will always be found harmonious and health-giving. Biological inaction and over-action are not beyond God's control. People will be found normal and natural as mortal thought grows out of the states which human belief creates and sanctions.

As human thought changes from one stage to another, from conscious pain to painlessness, from sorrow to joy, from fear to hope, and from faith to understanding, the visible manifestation will at last be self-governed by Soul. Reflecting God's control, you are no longer controlled by physical sense or mind. When subordinate to the divine Spirit, we cannot be controlled by sin or death, thus proving our material theories about laws of health to be valueless.

The astronomer no longer looks up to the stars—but looks out from them upon the universe. The florist finds the flower before its seed. Every cell can be seen before its multiplication. The seasons will come and go with changes of time and tide, cold and heat, latitude and longitude. Farmers will find that these changes can't affect the crops. "Like clothing You will change them and they will be changed."[1] The navigator can have dominion over the weather, over the great deep, over the fish of the sea and the fowls of the air. Time will not affect life.

Mortal is void of originality

Matter will finally be proved nothing more than an erroneous virtual reality, wholly inadequate to affect a person through its supposed action or existence. Error, belief, will no longer be used in stating truth. The problem of the dust-to-dust reality will be solved, and human mind will be without form and void. Mortality will cease

---

[1]   Ps. 102:26 (NASB)

when we behold God's reflection—just as we see our reflection in a mirror.

All Science is divine. Human thought never devised a tiny bit of true being. Human belief looks for and interprets in its own way the echo of Spirit, and seems to have reversed it and repeated it materially. The human mind never produces a real tone or sends forth a positive sound.

Natural versus supernatural

The point at issue between Christian Science on one hand and popular theology on the other is this: Shall Science explain cause and effect as both natural and spiritual? Or, shall all that is beyond the recognition of the physical senses be called supernatural, and be left to the mercy of speculative hypotheses?

I have set forth divine Science and its application to the treatment of disease just as I have discovered it. I have demonstrated through Mind, the effects of Truth on the health, longevity, and morals of human beings. I have found nothing in ancient or in modern systems on which to found my discovery except the teachings and demonstrations of Christ Jesus and the lives of prophets and apostles. The Bible has been my only authority. "Small is the gate and narrow the road,"[1] that leads to Truth.

If Christendom resists my application of the word Science to Christianity, or questions my use of the word Science, I will not therefore lose faith in Christianity, nor will Christianity lose its hold on me. If God, the All-in-all, be the creator of the spiritual universe, including man and woman, then everything entitled to a classification as truth, or Science, must be comprised in a knowledge or understanding of God. There can be nothing beyond illimitable divinity.

Scientific terms

The terms divine Science, spiritual Science, metaphysical Science, the Science of Truth and Love, Christian Science, or Science alone, are employed interchangeably according to the requirements of the context. These synonymous terms stand for everything relating to

---

[1]   Matt. 7:14

God, the infinite, supreme, eternal Mind. It may be said, however, that the term Christian Science relates especially to Science as applied to humanity. Divine Science reveals God, not as the author of sin, sickness, and death, but as absolute Principle, Supreme Being, Mind, exempt from all evil. It teaches that materialism or limitation is the falsity, not the fact, of existence. Nerves, brain, stomach, lungs, and so forth, have—as matter—no intelligence, life, or sensation.

No physical science

There is no physical science, as all truth proceeds from the divine Mind. Truth is not a law of matter and is not mortal. Matter is not a lawgiver. Spiritual Science comes from divine Mind, and is the only means of rightly interpreting God, Spirit, substance. Science has a Godlike, not humanlike, origin. It is a divine affirmation, the Counselor guiding "into all truth."[1]

Divine Science isn't what we call the hard or soft sciences (e.g. chemistry, biology, physics, and psychology). The conditions of the hard and soft sciences are built on the false hypotheses that matter or the human mind is its own lawgiver, whereas Spirit is the only lawgiver. The might of divine Mind can't be overruled by those sciences. Spirituality is natural and primary.

Practical Science

The term Science, properly understood, refers only to the laws of God and to Spirit's government of the universe, including all people. From this it follows that business professionals, scholars, and the common people have found that divine Science increases their perseverance and mental powers. The knowledge of spiritual Science expands people's perception of character, gives them alertness and the ability to be thorough and multitask usefully. The human mind, inspired with spiritual understanding, becomes more resilient and is capable of increased stamina. The human mind can escape somewhat from itself and won't require so much sleep. Knowledge of the Science of being develops our dormant abilities and potential. Spiritual discernment opens the mind and we attain access to far-reaching and

---

[1]   John 16:13

grand realms. As spiritual thinkers, we are elevated into our natural state of being insightful and quick to understand.

A fragrance becomes favorable only as it escapes into the surrounding atmosphere. The same is true in regard to our knowledge of Truth. Spiritual understanding, shared, can help waken others who are overrun with negativity. This is similar to waking someone up from a paralyzing nightmare. If the awakened person does not argue, they will not resist Truth, but be helped. The substance of Truth not only banishes temporal evidence with spiritual evidence, but also removes the stench of vile traits.

Logic

Science relates to Mind, not matter. It rests on fixed Principle and not upon the judgment of false sensation. The logic involved in divine Science is based on the premise that Truth is ever truthful. All conclusions made in Science must compute harmonious truth. The logic of Science cannot tolerate error, disorder, or contradictions in premise or conclusion.

If you wish to discover the spiritual fact then mentally perceive the limited situation you are in. It makes no difference whether the situation agrees or disagrees with your preconceptions.

Pantheism and nature worship may be defined as a belief in the intelligence of matter—a mindset which Science overthrows. In those days there will be "great distress, unequaled from the beginning of the world."[1] Earth will echo the cry, "Have you [Truth] come here to torture us before the appointed time?"[2] Mysticism, agnosticism, atheism, theosophy, neopaganism, and other systems of disbelief are antagonistic to true being and are fatal to the demonstration of Being.

Study of spiritual being needed

We must abandon pharmaceutics and take up the study of *Being*. Look deep into realism instead of only accepting the superficial, illusive sense of things. Be elevated in thought in every situation. Can we gather peaches from a pine tree or learn from disorder the order of being? Continue to recognize the nothingness of illusions—stay on the

---

[1]   Matt. 24:21; Mark 13:19

[2]   Matt. 8:29; Mark 5:7 Luke 8:28 (Brackets added by Mary Baker Eddy)

path Science is walking—and the ingrained illusions of human beings will be replaced with reality.

Reluctant guests and excuses

The body may object to the attitude that pays little attention to food. The sinner squirms when seeing that the system taught in this book requires obedience to the demands of God. The narrow-minded intellect rankles by the constant need to be responsible to infinite Mind. The licentious disposition is discouraged over its meager spiritual prospects. When the people are invited to the wedding banquet, the excuses come. One person has a machine to fix, others have an errand to run or a business to attend to,[1] and therefore they can't approve and accept.

It is vain to speak of divine Science dishonestly when you can demonstrate the realness of Science by destroying disorder. It is unwise to doubt if reality is in perfect harmony with God, divine Principle.

Children and adults

Science, when understood and demonstrated, will destroy all disorder. From the premise that God is omnipotent, comes the conclusion that good has all-power. Divine Science, properly understood, disengages material beliefs from the human mind. In order to make room for truth, beliefs warring against spiritual facts must be rejected and removed. You can't add to a glass already full. Some adults are full of faith in mortality, making it difficult to inculcate a grain of faith in God, or an inkling of Spirit's ability to make the body harmonious. We can remember Jesus' love of receptive little children and know how truly they belong to the heavenly kingdom.

All evil unnatural

Human thought is startled at the strong claims of Science and doubts the supremacy of good, Truth. Why aren't we startled at the vigorous claims of evil? Why don't we doubt negativism or depression? Why do we think it natural, almost necessary, to love that which works against life, truth, and love? Why do we imagine lack to be pervasive and good absent? Truth should not seem as surprising and

---

[1]   Matt. 22:5; Luke 14:18-19

111

unnatural as error, and error should not seem as real as truth. Sickness should not seem as real as health. There is no error in Science, and our lives must be influenced by reality in order to be in agreement with God, the divine Principle of all being.

When error is destroyed by divine Science, the false evidence before the physical senses disappears. Fleshly sensory experiences oppose the Science of Soul, as expounded in the Scriptural verse, "The sinful mind is hostile to God."[1] The central fact of the Bible is the superiority of spiritual over physical power.

THEOLOGY

Church neglects Science

Must Christian Science come through the Christian churches as some people insist? Divine Science has already come after the manner of God's appointing, but the churches don't seem ready to receive it. Scriptures say, "He came to that which was his own, but his own did not receive him."[2] Jesus once said: "I praise you, Father, Lord of heaven and earth, because you have hidden these things from the wise and learned, and revealed them to little children. Yes, Father, for this was your good pleasure."[3] The spirit of Christ, which takes away the rituals and doctrines of human beings, is not accepted until their hearts are made ready for it.

Jesus' mission confirmed prophecy and explained the miracles of olden time as natural demonstrations of divine power, demonstrations which were not understood at the time. Jesus' works established his claim to the Messiah. In reply to John's inquiry, "Are you the one who was to come?"[4] Jesus answered, not with a reference to his doctrine, but with a summary of his works. Confident that examples of divine healing power would fully answer John's question, Jesus said, "Go back and report to John what you hear and see. The blind receive sight,

---

[1]   Rom. 8:7

[2]   John 1:11

[3]   Matt. 11:25-26; Luke 10:21

[4]   Matt. 11:3; Luke 7:19

the lame walk, those who have leprosy are cured, the deaf hear, the dead are raised, and the good news is preached to the poor. Blessed is anyone who takes no offense at me."[1] Jesus' benediction is given to anyone who doesn't deny that such effects coming from divine Mind prove the unity of God—the divine Principle which brings out all harmony.

Christ rejected

The Pharisees of old shoved the spiritual idea and the man who lived it out of their synagogues, and returned like leeches to fasten themselves tighter to their materialist beliefs about God. Jesus' approach didn't receive support or approval from health-care or religious systems, and it is still generally not accepted. Today, as before, blind belief is unconscious of the reappearing of the spiritual idea, thereby shutting the door on it and condemning the cure of the sick and sinning if it is accomplished on any but a temporal or doctrinal theory. Jesus anticipated the rejection of the true idea of God—the salvation from physical and mental error, and asked, "When the Son of Man comes, will he find faith on the earth?"[2]

John's misgivings

Did the doctrines of John the Baptist give him healing power or provide him with the best idea of Christ? This righteous preacher once pointed his disciples to Jesus as "the Lamb of God;"[3] yet afterward he seriously questioned the signs of the Messianic appearing, and sent the inquiry to Jesus, "Are You the Expected One, or shall we look for someone else?"[4]

Faith and works

Was John's faith greater than that of the Samaritan woman, who said, "Could this be the Christ?"[5] A faithful centurion caused Jesus to say, "I have not found anyone in Israel with such great faith."[6]

---

[1]   Matt. 11:4-6; Luke 7:22-23 (NRSV)

[2]   Luke 18:8

[3]   John 1:29, 36

[4]   Matt. 11:3; Luke 7:19 (NASB)

[5]   John 4:29

[6]   Matt. 8:10; Luke 7:9

In Egypt it was Mind which saved the Israelites from belief in the plagues. In the wilderness, streams flowed from the rock,[1] and manna fell from the sky.[2] The Israelites looked at the bronze serpent that Moses had made and then believed they were healed of venomous snake bites.[3] Miracles attended the successes of the Hebrews. Even when in captivity among foreign nations, the divine Principle worked wonders for the people of God in the blazing furnace[4] and in kings' palaces. But when they departed from the true idea their demoralization began.

Beliefs that engender a national theology or political religion are the antithesis of true Christianity. Narrow systems and theories concerning God, human beings, health, and a religious society, are restrictive. Jesus, who set Christianity on the foundation of Spirit, was accused of "making himself equal with God."[5] Jesus taught as he was inspired by the Maker and would recognize no life, intelligence, or substance outside of God.

As the true knowledge of God becomes evident, the outdated concept of God as a mighty hero, lord, or king, will continue to vanish. Creeds and rituals still need to wash their hands of religious lore. Years ago, spiritual advancement was opposed by sword and spear. Today, idolatry anger, envy, arrogance, and egotism, whisper "Crucify! Crucify!"[6]

The word *martyr* from the Greek means *witness*; but those who testified for Truth were so often persecuted to death, that the word *martyr* was narrowed in its definition to mean someone who suffers for their convictions. The new faith in Truth so roused hatred that the followers of Spirit were burned, crucified, persecuted, and so it came about that human rights were canonized by the gallows and cross.

---

[1]   Ex. 17:6; Num. 20:11

[2]   Ex. 16:14; John 6:31

[3]   Num. 21:9

[4]   Dan. 3:26

[5]   John 5:18

[6]   Mark 15:13-14; Luke 23:20; John 19:6

Absence of Christ-power

Human-made doctrines are failing. They have not grown strong in times of trouble. Void of Truth-power, how can human-made theology illustrate the doctrines of Christ or the miracles of grace? Denial of the possibility of spiritual healing robs Christianity of the very element which gave it divine force and its astonishing and unequalled success in the first century.

Basis of miracles

The true Logos is demonstrably divine Science, the natural law of harmony which overcomes the pseudo-law of disorder. Science is not supernatural or superhuman, nor is it an infraction of divine law, but it is the unchangeable law of God, good, overcoming disorder. Jesus, speaking to Mind, said: "I knew indeed that you always hear me;"[1] and he raised Lazarus from the dead, calmed the storm, healed the sick, walked on the water. There is divine authority for believing in the superiority of spiritual power over material resistance.

A miracle doesn't violate but fulfills God's law. This fact can seem more mysterious than the miracle itself. The Psalmist sang: "Why was it, O sea, that you fled, O Jordan, that you turned back, you mountains, that you skipped like rams, you hills, like lambs? Tremble, O earth, at the presence of the Lord, at the presence of the God of Jacob."[2] The miracle introduces no disorder, but unfolds the permanency of spiritual order. It establishes the Science of God's unchangeable law. Only spiritual evolution is worthy of the exercise of divine power.

Fear and sickness are identical

The same power which heals sin also heals sickness. The "beauty of holiness"[3] is when Truth heals the sick, and drives out evils and disease. When Christ was casting out the devil of dumbness, "the man who had been mute spoke."[4] There is today danger of repeating the

---

1   John 11:42 (JB)

2   Ps. 114:5-6

3   Ps. 29:2, 96:9 (NKJV)

4   Luke 11:14

offence recorded in the Bible by limiting the Holy One of Israel and asking: "Can God spread a table in the desert?"[1] What can't God do?

The unity of Science and Theology

Theology must be Science, and Science must be theology, else one or the other is false and useless. Science and Christian theology are important, true, and alike in demonstration. This proves one to be identical with the other. Christian theology as Jesus taught it was not a creed, nor a system of scared ceremonies, nor a special gift from a ritualistic Yahweh; but it was the demonstration of divine Love overcoming error and healing the sick. Jesus taught action, not merely in the *name* of Truth, but in the nature—the demonstration of Truth, as must be the case in the cycles of divine light.

Christ mission

Jesus established his church and maintained his mission on a spiritual foundation of Truth-healing. His followers were taught that religion has a divine Principle which would overcome error and heal both the sick and the sinning. Jesus claimed no intelligence, action, or life separate from God. Despite the persecution brought on him, Jesus used his divine power to save men and women, mind/body/spirit.

How did Jesus heal the sick? The same question is asked today. Jesus answered the question but his answer was rejected. He appealed to his students: "Who do people say the Son of Man is?"[2] That is: Who or what is identified with driving out evils and healing the sick? They replied, "Some say John the Baptist; others say Elijah; and still others, Jeremiah or one of the prophets."[3] These prophets were considered dead, and this reply may indicate that some of the people believed that Jesus was a medium, controlled by the spirit of John or Elijah.

King Herod repeated the superstitious thinking and blathered whether, "John, the man I beheaded, has been raised from the dead!"[4] That a wicked king and corrupt husband should have no appreciation

---

[1] Ps. 78:19

[2] Matt. 16:13; Mark 8:27; Luke 9:18

[3] Matt. 16:14; Mark 8:28; Luke 9:19

[4] Matt. 14:2; Mark 6:16; Luke 9:9

of divine Science and the great work of the Master was not a shocker. How could a sinner comprehend what the disciples did not fully understand? It's no wonder that Herod desired to see the new Teacher.

Doubting disciples

The disciples understood their Teacher better than other people, yet still questioned Jesus because they didn't fully comprehend what he said. Jesus patiently persisted in teaching and demonstrating the truth of being. Although Jesus' students saw this power of Truth heal the sick, drive out evil, and raise the dead, they did not spiritually discern the ultimate of this wonderful work until after the crucifixion, when their remarkable Master stood before them, the victor over sickness, sin, disease, death, and the grave.

Rejecting their first answer and longing to be understood, Jesus repeated, "Who do you say I am?"[1] He discarded the narrow-minded opinions or rumors about himself. The renewed inquiry meant: Who or what is it that is able to do the work so mysterious to the popular human mind?

A divine response

With his usual impetuosity, Simon replied for the disciples. His reply set forward a great fact: "You are the Christ, the Son of the living God."[2] That is: The Messiah is what you have declared—Christ, the spirit of God, of Truth, Life, and Love, which heals mentally. This answer elicited from Jesus the benediction, "Blessed are you, Simon son of Jonah, for this was not revealed to you by man, but by my Father in heaven;"[3] that is, Love has shown you the way of Life!

Before this, the impulsive disciple had been called only by his common name, Simon son of Jonah; but now Jesus gave him a spiritual name in these words: "And I tell you, you are Peter [Greek, *Petros*—a large piece of rock], and on this rock [Greek, *petra*—a huge rock like Gibraltar] I will build My church, and the gates of Hades (the powers of the infernal region) shall not overpower it [or be strong to

---

[1]   Matt. 16:15; Mark 8:29; Luke 9:20

[2]   Matt. 16:16; Mark 8:29; Luke 9:20

[3]   Matt. 16:17

its detriment or hold out against it.]"[1] Jesus intended to establish his society on the God-power which impelled Peter's confession of the true Messiah. Jesus did not establish church on the personal Peter as a human being.

It was now evident to Peter that divine Life, Truth, and Love, and not a human personality, was the healer of the sick and a rock, a firm foundation in the realm of harmony. On this spiritually scientific basis Jesus explained his cures, which appeared miraculous to outsiders. He showed that diseases were not removed by surgery, medicine, or health care regimes, but by the divine Spirit, casting out the errors of human mind. The supremacy of Spirit was the foundation on which Jesus built, and his exceptional standard of living points to the religion of Love.

Jesus established the precedent for all Christianity, theology, and healing. People are accountable now, as they have been forever, to be Christ-like, to possess the Christ-spirit, to follow the Christ-example, and to heal the sick as well as the sinning. It is easier to drive out sickness than it is to drive out sin because we are more willing to part with suffering than to give up the sinful pleasures. People can prove this today as readily as it was proved centuries ago.

Theology that stimulates health

Jesus said, "Go out to the whole world; proclaim the Good News to all creation,"[2] "Heal the sick,"[3] "Love your neighbor as yourself."[4] Jesus' theology heals. *Science and Health* reiterates Jesus' theology and its spiritual meaning, causing the materialist to "forsake their way, and the unrighteous their thoughts."[5] It was Jesus' theology that the ungodly endeavored to destroy.

From beginning to end, the Scriptures are full of accounts of the triumph of Spirit, Mind, over mortality. Moses proved the power of Mind by what people called miracles; so did Joshua, Elijah, and

---

[1]   Matt. 16:18 (Amplified)

[2]   Mark 16:15 (JB)

[3]   Matt. 10:1, 8; Luke 9:2, 10:9

[4]   Matt. 5:43, 19:19, 22:39; Mark 12:31; Luke 10:27

[5]   Isa. 55:7 (NRSV)

Elisha. What was eventually tagged the Christian era was ushered in with signs and wonders, yet the reformations were accompanied by bloodshed and persecution, even when the end has been brightness and peace. The present new, yet old, reform in religious faith will patiently and wisely teach us not to give in to sectarian bitterness when it flows inward.

Science obscured

The divine Science of the Scriptures, seen from Genesis to Revelation, can't be totally obscured even with all the odds against it. We've had Church committees vote to decide what should or shouldn't be considered Holy Writ. Mistakes were made in the ancient translations and today, with the many thousand different versions of the Testaments, misinterpretations occur. However, the prophets' healing work can't be annulled or lost, and Jesus' demonstration is intact, confirming that "the stone the builders rejected has become the capstone."[1]

Helping even those who oppose

Atheism, pantheism, theosophy, and agnosticism are opposed to divine Science, as they are to ordinary religion, however, a person who identifies with those belief systems can still be healed by Science. The moral condition of such a person demands the remedy of Truth more than is needed in most cases; and Science is more than usually effectual in the treatment of moral weaknesses.

God is invisible to the physical senses

Nobody can affirm that God is a bodily being. The Bible represents Spirit as saying: "you cannot see my face, for no one may see me and live."[2] Not materially, but spiritually we know God as divine Mind, as Life, Truth, and Love. We become more respectful and caring as we get to know the divine nature better and love Soul understandingly. The struggle over physicality will be replaced by a rejoicing in the affluence of our God. Religion will then be of the

---

[1] Ps. 118:22; Matt. 21:42; Mark 12:10; Luke 20:17

[2] Ex. 33:20

heart and not of the head. Humankind will no longer be tyrannical from lack of love—straining out gnats and swallowing camels.[1]

True worship

We worship spiritually, only as we cease to worship materially. The devotion to Spirit is the soul of spirituality. Worshipping through the medium of matter is not productive. Human-made rituals are but types and shadows of true worship. "The true worshippers will worship the Father in spirit and truth."[2]

Anthropomorphism

The tribal Yahweh was a human-projected God, liable to wrath, repentance, and human moodiness. The Christian Science God is unchanging, universal, eternal, divine Love. This God does not cause evil, disease or death. In the beginning God created children in God's image; but human beings would procreate man and woman, and make God in their own mortal image. What is the god of a human, but a human magnified? It is depressing when the meaning of Scripture is reversed.

Do more than profess

A reversal of Scripture shows the distinction between theological and ritualistic religion. The truth preached by Jesus was more than just talk and robotic behavior. A life of spirituality is requisite. Few understand or adhere to Jesus' divine precepts for living and healing. Why? We don't emulate Jesus, because we don't want to set aside personal agendas, human beliefs, habits, and learned information. In Bible terms, we don't want to cut off the right hand[3] and gouge out the right eye.[4] It is requisite to leave all for Christ.

No religious, scholarly, or hierarchal monopoly

Default thinking assumes that all revelation must come from a scholarly or ecclesiastical lineage, like kings crowned from a royal dynasty. Those assumptions disallow inspired understanding and the demonstration of God's healing power. For this Principle there is no

[1] Matt. 23:24
[2] John 4:23
[3] Matt. 5:30
[4] Matt. 5:29

ecclesiastical monopoly, no human lineage of teachers, no successor. The priest is the spiritualized person. Immortal rulings are crowned. In healing the sick and sinning, Jesus actively brought attention to the fact that the healing effect followed the understanding of the divine Principle and of the Christ-spirit which controlled his physical self. As divine Principle is scientifically understood, you can comprehend and experience for yourself the works of Christ, Truth. The Bible declares that all believers "will be called priests of the Lord."[1]

A change demanded

It requires a mental unlearning, restructuring and reorganization before we can adopt scientific religion and the divine healing which overcomes sickness, sin and death. Let our pulpits do justice to divine Science. Let Science have fair representation by the media. If Science is given the opportunity in our schools and workplace, we will then discover it takes less time to eradicate sickness and sin. The systems of fundamentalist theology and uninspired psychotherapy, devised for subduing mortality, always falls short.

In times past, the followers of Truth measured Christianity by its power over sickness, sin, and death. Modern religions generally omit all but one of these powers—the power over sin. We must work for the seamless garment.[2] Truth provides us with absolute evidence as we seek and prove the whole Christ.

Selfishness and loss

If religious people accept church salaries and build churches, yet turn away the poor and stranger, they are shutting the door on progress. Let the story of Jesus' birth in a manger, and death on a cross, deflate that arrogance and human egotism. Gratification of the physical senses will numb the right hand and cause the left to let go of its grasp on the divine.

Cleaning out the church

Jesus showed us a whip[3] is needed to drive tyranny and arrogance out of church. The strong cords of scientific demonstration, as twisted

---

[1]   Ex. 19:6; Isa. 61:6; Rev. 1:6

[2]   John 19:23

[3]   John 2:15

and wielded by Jesus, are still needed to purge churches of their vain traffic in worldly worship. Church should be made "a house of prayer for all nations,"[1] where humility and divine Science are welcome.

MEDICINE

Question of precedence

Which was first, Mind or medicine? If Mind was first and self-existent, then Mind, not matter, must have been the first medicine. God being All-in-all, made medicine; but that medicine was Mind. Medicine can't be physical particles because that would depart from the nature and character of intelligence, God. Truth is God's remedy for error of every kind, and Truth destroys only what is untrue. Hence the fact that today, as yesterday, Christ drives out evils and heals the sick.

Methods rejected

Has anyone seen God take medicinal drugs? God doesn't provide drugs or a particular health care program. Jesus didn't recommend and employ drugs in his healing work. The sick are more regrettably lost than the sinning, if the sick can't rely on God for help and sinners can. The divine Mind never called matter medicine, and matter required a mortal and human belief before it could be considered as medicine.

Error doesn't cure

Sometimes the human mind uses one error to medicine another error. Forced to choose between two difficulties, the human mind takes the lesser problem to relieve the greater. For example, in order to relieve an uncomfortable eye condition, the human mind may choose eye-drops. On this basis it saves from suffering by temporarily quieting the problem with drops made in a factory. Do we admit that mind influences the body somewhat, but conclude that the organs, hormones, nerves, bones, etc., outweigh the power of Spirit? Controlled by this kind of thinking, people unthinkingly repeat learned reactions. They lean on the artificial or the unintelligent, never

---

[1]   Isa. 56:7; Mark 11:17; Luke 19:46

discerning how this deprives them of the available superiority of divine Mind. The body is not controlled scientifically by a negative mind.

Divine Mind and human mind will never go together

Mind is the grand revelator, and there can be no power except that which is derived from Mind. If Mind was first chronologically, is first potentially, and must be first eternally, then give to Mind the glory, honor, dominion, and power everlastingly due its holy name. Inferior and unspiritual methods of healing may try to make Mind and drugs coalesce, but the two will not mingle scientifically. Why would we force divine Mind and human mind to work together, since no good can come of it? The mortal gives way to the immortal.

If Mind, Life, is foremost and superior, you can rely on Mind, which doesn't need any cooperation from lower powers. The lower powers are real to the human mind, but divine Mind, Love, ultimately prevails.

> As the sun rises in the east
> So He shall split the eastern sky[1]

Soul consciousness versus human consciousness

The more concrete a belief, the more obstinately tenacious is its error and the less signs there are of Soul. The various human beliefs formulated in human philosophy, physiology, psychology, and health care, are mainly predicated of matter or human consciousness and they only give faint hints of God, Truth.

Watch out for will-power

Human will-power is not Science. Be aware; do not approve of the detrimental human will. Willing the sick to recover is not the metaphysical practice of divine Science, but is mesmerism through and through and intrudes on the rights of humanity. Human willfulness breeds evil continually, and is not a factor in the realism of being. Truth, not the willful flesh or animal instinct, is the divine power which says to disease, "Quiet! Be still!"[2]

---

[1]   Paris, Twila. *Every Knee Shall Bow* lyrics

[2]   Matt. 8:26; Mark 4:39; Luke 8:24

Conservative attitudes

The "old school" thinking still opposes Christian Science because spiritual Science wars with conservatism and physical science, even as Truth wars with error. Ignorance, arrogance, or prejudice closes the door to whatever is not stereotyped. When the Science of being is universally understood, every person will be their own physician and Truth will be the universal remedy, even as truth removes error.

Ancient healers

It is a question, whether the ancient inspired healers understood the Science of spiritual healing, or whether they caught its sweet tones as the natural musician catches the tones of harmony without being able to explain them. Past healers were so divinely animated with the spirit of Science, that the lack of the letter could not impede their work. The letter without the spirit voids the healing practice.

The struggle and victory

Recovery is a struggle, not between material methods, but between human minds and spiritual Mind. It makes no difference what temporal method a patient may adopt, whether it is a faith in drugs or counseling, or a trust in physical therapy, Reiki, or a reliance on time. The victory will be on the patient's side only as spiritual Mind through Christ, Truth, subdues the human belief in disease.

Mystery of godliness

Scientific healing has this advantage over other methods—that in it Truth controls error. From this fact arise its ethical as well as physical effects, which are indissolubly connected. If there is any mystery in healing by means of Truth, the mystery comes from an unawareness of the laws of perfect Mind. Godliness is always a mystery to the ungodly.

Matter diminishing itself

Temporal methods of healing generate antagonism. For example, we take one pill to relieve a problem, but the pill creates another problem for which we need surgery, and then complications come about after the surgery for which we need another pill. The warfare between Spirit and the flesh goes on. Antibodies kill good bacteria along with the bad. Viruses become immune to antibiotics. Drugs are addictive. These rivalries cause the human mind to weaken its own assumed power.

How healing was lost

The theology of divine Science includes healing the sick. The ancient Christians were healers. Jesus taught, lived, and proved a scientific healing faith. Why has this living faith been lost? Compassionate, unobtrusive, intelligent healing is lost because our systems of religion are governed more or less by our systems of material medicine. The first idolatry was faith in matter. Society, advertisements, pharmaceutical companies, and the schools have made faith in drugs the fashion, rather than faith in God. By trusting matter to destroy its own disorder, health and harmony have been sacrificed. Temporal systems are barren of the vitality of spiritual power by which physical sense is made the servant of Science, and religion becomes Christ-like.

Drugs and divinity

The materialist's medicine substitutes drugs for the power of God, and the might of Mind goes unnoticed. Intellectualism clings to the person of Jesus for salvation, instead of divine Principle, and the curing power of God is silenced. Truth deprives drugs of their imaginary power and clothes Spirit with supremacy. Science is the "alien within your gates,"[1] remembered not, even when its elevating effects pragmatically prove its divine origin and efficacy.

Christian Science originates with God

The healing power of Truth must have existed before Jesus' time. It is as ancient as "the Ancient of Days."[2] It lives through all Life, and extends throughout all space. The validity of divine Science is found in the Bible, yet the divine origin of Science is demonstrated through the holy influence of Truth in healing sickness and sin.

Divine metaphysics has been adapted to today's thought. The Mind-healing system taught in this book enables the learner to demonstrate the divine Principle upon which Jesus' healing was based, and to apply its sacred rules for the cure of disease.

---

[1] Ex. 20:10; Deut. 5:14

[2] Dan. 7:9, 13, 22

Late in the nineteenth century I demonstrated the divine rules of Science. The rules were submitted to broad practical testing, and when honestly applied under circumstances where demonstration is humanly possible, the results showed that Truth is still effective in healing. Even though centuries have passed away since Jesus practiced these rules on the hills of Judea and in the valleys of Galilee, the rules are still effective.

Study and practice to discover definite rule

Although this book contains the complete Science of Mind-healing, never believe that you can absorb its whole meaning by skimming it. *Science and Health* needs to be *studied*. As the rules of scientific healing are discovered and practiced, you will become secure on the groundwork of divine Science. Your healing experiences will lift you high above fossilized human theories already antiquated, and enable you to grasp the spiritual facts of being, even if at first the facts don't seem accessible or crystal clear.

Christ Jesus healed the sick, practiced healing, and taught the general idea of divine Principle to his students. However, he did not leave a definite rule for demonstrating this Principle of healing and preventing disease. This rule remained to be discovered in divine Science. A pure affection takes form in goodness, but Science alone reveals the divine Principle of goodness and illustrates its rules.

Jesus never spoke of disease as dangerous or as difficult to heal. When his students brought to him a case they had failed to heal, he said to them, "O [faithless ones] unbelieving *and* without trust in God, a perverse (wayward, crooked and warped) generation!"[1] His answer implies that the requisite power to heal was in Mind. Jesus didn't prescribe drugs or urge obedience to fleshly demands, but acted in direct disobedience to them.

Anatomy and theology

Anatomy can't describe God's child, created by Spirit. Anatomy explains the child of human beings, which are not the counterpart, but the counterfeit of God's child. Anatomy has no Spirit, no true tone, and accepts disorder. Moreover, theologies that start from the false

---

[1]   Matt. 17:17; Mark 9:19; Luke 9:41 (Amplified)

premise that God created human beings, try to convert a disordered person into a Christian. These teachings that define people as both physical and mental, with a mind at the mercy of matter for every function, formation, and manifestation, start from the lowest instead of the highest concept of being, and reject the divine Principle which created man and woman spiritually. We can't produce the harmony and unity of Spirit from an anatomical or bio-theological position.

Deficient-ology

Physiology and biotechnology promotes matter, debars Mind, and claims to rule by temporal laws instead of spiritual laws. This process ignores Spirit as able and willing to help. When human beings sin they are left to the guidance of a theology which admits God to be the healer of sin but not of sickness. Our Master demonstrated that Truth saves from sickness as well as from sin.

Blunders and blunderers

Is the medicine of humankind a science or a cluster of theoretical human speculations? The prescription which succeeds in one instance, but fails in another, is due to the different mental states of the patient. Only in divine Science can these mindsets be explained and comprehended. The power of Mind excels the power of drugs in the cure of disease. Mind's rule and its perfection of operation never vary in Science. If you fail to succeed in any case, it is because you have not demonstrated the life of Christ, Truth, more in your own life. The more excellent way in every case is following the rule and proving the Principle of divine Science.

Old school thinking

A fairly common remark heard in society today is: "We know that mind affects the body somewhat, and we try to be hopeful and optimistic and to take as little medicine as possible; but mind can never cure biological difficulties." The logic is lame, and facts contradict it. I have cured the diseases of organs as readily as I have cured purely functional disease, and with no power but the divine Mind.

Today's tests

God, divine Mind, administers to all, not partially but wholly. Predicting disease does not dignify therapeutics. Whatever guides thought spiritually, benefits mind/body/spirit. We need to understand the affirmations of divine Science, dismiss superstition, and live truth according to Christ. The world is home to many representatives, living the virtue and healing power of Truth.

Main purpose

The healing power of Truth is no longer random, but widely practiced as an inherent, ongoing Science. Spiritual healing is the good news constantly appearing; it is "on earth peace among those whom he favors!"[1] The appearance of good, as was promised by Jesus, establishes the divine system among humanity. Now, as in earlier times, signs and wonders are meant to elucidate the divine origin and substantiate the reality of Truth. The higher mission of Science is not physical healing, but is to take away the sins of the world.

Exploded doctrine

Physical sciences would make us believe that both matter and mind are liable to disease, even in spite of our protests. Our moral agency is infringed upon until we see it's all a big mistake, similar to the error of predestination. The doctrines that our harmony is governed by physical conditions all our earthly days are fading. Matter is not superior to the law of Mind.

Disease is mental

The god of temporal medicine is flooding the world with diseases. It treats the sick person as if the body is the only factor in the case. But, the spiritual thinker becomes aware that the human mind and body are myths. They realize that infinite Mind could not possibly create a remedy outside of itself, let alone a remedy that is unsustainable. It is only the human mind that has an absolute need of something beyond itself for redemption and healing, but we are spiritual.

Be sure to respect good intentions

Great respect is due to the motives and philanthropy of the higher class of physicians. As they understand the Science of Mind-healing and its power to benefit all peoples physically and spiritually, they will rejoice with us. Even this one reform in medicine would ultimately

---

[1] Luke 2:14 (NRSV)

deliver humankind from the awful and oppressive burdens now enforced by false theories, and from which multitudes would gladly escape.

Being governed by Mind

Mortal belief says that fear can cause death, but fear never stopped being and its action. The hormones, blood, heart, lungs, brain, etc., can't do anything to Life, God. Every function is controlled by the divine intelligence. The human mind has no power to kill or to cure, and it has no control over God's child. The divine Mind that made us, maintains us. The human mind is opposed to God and must be put off,[1] as Paul declares in Ephesians. All that really exists is the divine Mind and its idea, and in this Mind the entire existence is found harmonious and eternal. The straight and narrow way is to see and acknowledge this fact, unite with this power, and follow the guidance of truth.

Human mind is overthrown

We have overwhelming proof that the human mind pretends to control every organ of the mortal body. But, this mind is a myth and must by its own consent yield to Truth. Although the human mind throws its weight around, it is powerless. The immortal divine Mind takes away all the human minds assumed expertise and saves human mind from itself. I have endeavored to make the ideas in this book the medicine of mind/body/spirit, giving hope and healing to the needy, even if they don't know how the work is done. Truth has a healing effect even when not fully understood.

All activity is from thought

Anatomy says thoughts can move the muscles—sometimes. Such errors plague every material theory in which one statement contradicts another over and over again. It is related that Sir Humphry Davy[2] once apparently cured a case of paralysis simply by introducing a thermometer into the patient's mouth. The thermometer was intended to ascertain the patient's body temperature; but the sick man, supposed

---

[1] Eph. 4:22; Col. 2:11, 3:8

[2] Davy, Sir Humphry, (1778-1829) Cornish chemist and physicist.

this ceremony was intended to heal him, and he recovered accordingly. Such a fact illustrates that all bodily activity comes from thought.

I experimented in medicine

My medical researches and experiments prepared my thought for the metaphysics of divine Science. I was searching for truth and discovered that all dependence on temporal medicine failed to help. I now understand why and can see the means by which human beings are divinely driven to a spiritual source for health and happiness.

When I experimented with homeopathy, I became skeptical as to alternative methods. Books on homeopathy, natural cures, and so on, discuss general symptoms and signs of health problems, and then suggest different remedies. Homeopathic drugs are diluted to such a degree that not a trace of active ingredient remains. Obviously, it is not the drug which removes or changes the symptoms of disease.

To cure a patient dying of typhoid fever, I diluted common table-salt until the sodium chloride had "become tasteless."[1] One drop of the attenuation in a cup of water, and a teaspoonful of the water administered at intervals of three hours, proved the active ingredient went from matter to mind. The drug was not the curative power. This discovery leads to more light and we can learn whether human faith or divine Mind is the healer.

Origin of pain

You say shingles are painful; but that is impossible, because matter without mind is not painful. Shingles simply manifest, through eruptions and rashes, a belief in pain and this belief is called shingles. Now administer mentally to your patient a high attenuation of truth and it will soon cure shingles. The fact that pain can't exist where there is no human mind to feel it is a proof that this mind makes its own pain—that is, its own *belief* in pain.

Source of contagion

We cry because others cry, we yawn because they yawn, and we have the flu because others have it; but human mind, not matter, contains and carries the infection. When this mental contagion is understood we will be more careful with our mental conditions. We

---

[1]   Matt. 5:13; Luke 14:34 (NASB)

will avoid continually talking about disease just as we would avoid advocating crime. It is to our advantage never to let sympathy and society tempt us to cherish error in any form, and certainly we should not be error's advocate.

Diseases appear like other mental states, through association. Erroneous thoughts connect to one another and the condition is classified as a disease. Some diseases are regarded as contagious. Contagion is a human activity where sick thoughts get copied-and-pasted from one mind and body to another.

Imaginary contagion

Illustrations can be found to show how contagion is fickle. Dr. Albert Schweitzer[1] has been quoted to say, "Serious illness doesn't bother me for long because I am too inhospitable a host," whereas some people will catch a contagious disease without coming into contact with the disease.

Working with children

If a child is exposed to a contagious disease, the parent is frightened and says, "My child will get sick." The law of human mind and the parent's fears control the child more than the child's mind controls him or herself. The sickness might have been prevented with different thinking.

Our responses need improvement if we typically say things like, "You look sick," "You must be tired?" or "You need a pill."

Why do people run to a child who has fallen, and whine childishly "Oh, poor thing, I know you hurt"? The better and more successful response to adopt is: "You're Okay, let's think about what's good." Soon the child forgets all about the accident, and is directed to positive activity.

Drug-power mental

Why do drugs cause recovery? According to the faith will be the effect. General belief, culminating in individual faith, heals. Even if you take away the individual's confidence in the drug, you have not yet divorced the drug from the collective faith. Mass

---

[1]   Dr. Albert Schweitzer (1875-1965) Alsatian theologian, philosopher, organist, physical, and medical missionary.

consciousness—including the pharmacist, the chemist, the therapist, the doctor, and the nurse—equips the medicine with their faith in the drug, and gives it the upper hand. To buck the collective thinking, individual dissent or faith must rest on Science, otherwise the belief is governed by the majority, not the minority.

Conviction in physics

The universal belief in physics weighs against the high and mighty truths of spiritual metaphysics. The widespread belief in physics, which sustains medicine and produces all medical results, works against divine Science. The percentage of power on the side of this Science must mightily outweigh the power of popular belief in order to heal metaphysically a single case of disease. The human mind can offset the discords of matter and the ills of flesh by giving less power to physics and more to spirituality.

Nature of drugs

Homeopathy diminishes the drug, but the potency of the medicine increases as the drug disappears. Herbs, homeopathy, and alternative health treatments have diminished drugging; but if drugs are an antidote to disease, why lessen the antidote? If drugs are good things, why not take more? What makes drugs beneficial or harmful for human beings? We learn the strength and remedial qualities of drugs are mental.

Placebos

A case of edema, given up by the doctors, fell into my hands. It was a terrible case. Tapping had been employed. The patient was awfully swollen. I prescribed a homeopathic remedy. She improved a little bit. I then found out her former doctor had prescribed the same remedy and I became afraid that a prolonged use of this medicine may aggravate her symptoms; and I also was still learning to trust God. I told her it would be better not to take her medicine, but she was unwilling to give it up. It then occurred to me to give her placebos and watch the result. I did so, and she continued to improve. Finally she said that she would give up her medicine for one day, and risk the effects. After trying this, she informed me that she could get along two days without medicine; but on the third day she suffered and was relieved by taking the placebos. She continued taking the placebos, receiving occasional visits from me—using no other means—and she was cured.

Advancement

Metaphysics, as taught in Christian Science, is the next advanced step beyond holistic methods. In metaphysics, matter disappears from the remedy entirely, and Mind takes its rightful and supreme place. Holistic methods take mental symptoms into consideration in its diagnosis of disease, but divine Science deals wholly with the mental cause in judging and destroying disease. It succeeds where holistic methods fail, because the one recognized Principle of healing is Mind, and the whole force of the mental element is employed through the Science of Mind, which never shares its rights with inanimate matter.

Divine Science eliminates the drug and rests on Mind alone as the curative Principle, acknowledging that the divine Mind has all power.

The narrative of spiritual creation in the first chapter of Genesis, pronounces *good* all that was created. Then how can drugs be poisonous? Matter is unintelligent, therefore it is not self-creative. The *Homo sapiens* mind grants power to the drugs. If Spirit did create drugs and design them for medicinal use, why didn't Jesus employ or recommend them? If God created drugs inherently bad, they should not be used.

Narcotics quiet human mind and relieve the body; but they leave both mind and body worse for this submission. Science impresses the entire corporeality—namely, mind/body/spirit—and brings out the proof that Life is continuous and harmonious. Science neutralizes error, destroys it, and humanity is the better for it.

Mythology and medicine

The profession of medicine may have originated in idolatry with pagan priests who looked to the gods to heal the sick. Apollo has been designated as the god of medicine, but he is also the bringer of disease. Hippocrates turned from image-gods to vegetable and mineral based drugs for healing. The future history of material medicine may correspond with that of Apollo who was banished from heaven and endured great sufferings on earth. What we need is the truth which heals both mind and body.

Drugs, ointments, and narcotics are reckless substitutes for the dignity and potency of divine Mind and its effective healing power. It is pitiful to tempt human beings with addictive prescriptions. Why create victims who acquire an educated appetite for intoxicating treatments?

Advancing degrees

Evidence of progress and of spiritualization can definitely be seen in the world. People are realizing the power of mind. We are learning to question drug systems and surgical procedures. Less obtrusive drugs, alternative health care treatments, responsible eating, consistent exercise, and homeopathy are being pursued. The substance of medicine is being transferred from matter to mind.

Effects of fear on human mind

A woman in the city of Lynn, Massachusetts, was anesthetized and died in consequence. Her physicians insisted that it would be unsafe to perform a needed surgical operation without anesthetic. After the autopsy, the woman's sister testified that the deceased had protested against inhaling the anesthesia, saying it would kill her, but that she was compelled by her physician to take it. Her sister's hands were held and she was forced into submission. The case was brought to trial. The evidence was found to be conclusive and a verdict was returned that death was occasioned, not by the anesthetic, but by fear of inhaling it.

This sequel proved that the Lynn woman died from effects produced by human mind, and not from the anesthetic, disease, or operation.

Is it skillful or scientific surgery not to consider the patient's mental condition? The patient is more than mindless matter. The patient is more than a weak and manipulative mind. Divine Mind needs to be consulted.

False source of knowledge

The medical schools attempt to learn the state of human beings from matter or machines, instead of from Mind. They measure the blood pressure, electrolytes, body temperature, etc., in order to ascertain how much health matter is permitting to matter. MRIs,

X-rays, and other images are examined in order to diagnose how much normalcy one form of matter is allowing another form of matter.

Ignorant of the fact that human thinking produces disease and all its symptoms, ordinary physicians are liable to increase disease with their own mind. Instead, they can work to destroy disease through the power of the divine Mind.

The systems of physics act against metaphysics, and vice versa. When human beings abandon the material for the spiritual basis of action, drugs lose their healing force because they have no innate power. As human faith quits supporting a drug, the drug becomes powerless.

Obedient muscles

The human mind directs internal organs as well as the arm. Think about it, when human mind quits the body, the heart becomes as inactive as the arm.

Anatomy and mind

Anatomy and physiology require nerves to tell the mind to move the muscles. But what does anatomy say when the muscle cramp? Did human mind stop talking to the muscle? Did the mind tell it to go berserk? Can muscles, bones, blood, and nerves rebel against mind in one instance and not in another? Can the muscles have a spasm, despite a mental protest?

Unless muscles are self-acting at all times, they never are—never are capable of acting contrary to mental direction. Muscles are either self-directing all the time or never. So why do we consult anatomy or physiology to learn how muscles govern?

Mind over matter

Are we a material fungus without Mind to help us? Are contracted muscles, tendinitis, or arthritis laws? Or, is God the only creator, creating laws of health?

You say, "I have burned my finger." This is an exact statement, more exact than you suppose; for human mind and not matter, burns the finger. Spiritual inspiration has revealed mindsets able to nullify the action of flames, as in the Bible case of the three young

Hebrew captives,[1] whereas, an opposite mental state might produce spontaneous combustion.

Restrictive regulations

Health insurance companies are recognizing the power of thought. Not only are the costs of psychiatry or counseling covered, but some policies also cover alternative health care costs. These examples of unrestricting the practice of medicine are in harmony with our Constitution and Bill of Rights, with that immortal sentiment of the Declaration, "Man is endowed by his Maker with certain inalienable rights, among which are life, liberty, and the pursuit of happiness."

Oppressive policies or agendas that restrict right thinking can be removed from power. Nelson Mandela wrote, "There was no particular day on which I said, From henceforth I will devote myself to the liberation of my people; instead, I simply found myself doing so, and could not do otherwise."[2]

Metaphysics challenges physics

The ordinary doctor examines the body, tells the patient they are sick, and treats the case according to the physical diagnosis. This naturally induces the very disease imposed by human mind. Such unconscious mistakes would not occur if this old class of philanthropists looked as deeply for cause and effect into mind as into matter. The physician agrees with the "adversary quickly,"[3] but on different terms than the metaphysician. The matter-physician agrees with the disease, while the metaphysician agrees with health and challenges disease.

Truth stimulates health

Divine Science brings to the body the sunlight of Truth, which invigorates and purifies. Christian Science acts as a medicinal, neutralizing error with Truth. It balances the hormonal reactions, expels harmful fluids, dissolves tumors, rehabilitates degenerated or injured muscles, and restores bones to wellness. The effect of this

---

[1]   Dan. 3

[2]   Mandela, Nelson. *Long Walk to Freedom* (New York: Little, Brown and Company, 1994, 1995

[3]   Matt. 5:25 (NKJV)

Science is to adapt the human mind to an improved attitude from which it may yield to the peace and order of divine Mind.

Experiments support the fact that mind governs the body, not in one instance, but in every instance. The indestructible faculties of Spirit exist without the conditions of matter and also without the false beliefs of a mortal existence. Working out the rules of Science in practice, I have restored health in cases of both acute and chronic disease in their severest forms. Secretions have been changed, the structure has been renewed, shortened limbs have been elongated, stiff joints have been made supple, and carious bones have been restored to healthy conditions. I have restored diseased lungs and organs. Christian Science heals every kind of disease or malfunction, for it requires only a fuller understanding of the divine Principle of divine Science to demonstrate the higher rule.

Statements from leading practitioners and scientists

With due respect, here are some statements to think about.

"The materials we need to reach a new level of discourse are in our grasp; we have only to abandon outmoded approaches/disciplines to achieve an enlightening beginning for a new science." From *The Anthropology of Medicine: From Culture to Method,* Third Edition.[1]

"The Starting Point of Biblical Theology: We have already observed that every scholarly endeavor inevitably is based upon presuppositions."[2] HarperCollins Bible Dictionary.

"We physicians often pay lip service to the importance of the mind in health and illness, yet in practice we equate it with the brain. This is obvious in our reliance on drugs when mental problems arise . . . A refreshing contrast is alternative or complementary medicine, which has emerged as a major social force shaping medical care in the United

---

[1]   *The Anthropology of Medicine: From Culture to Method,* Third Edition. Edited by Lola Romanucci-Ross, Daniel E. Moerman, Laurence R. Tancredi. Copyright © 1997 by Lola Romanucci-Ross, Daniel E. Moerman, and Laurence R. Tancredi. Reproduced with permission of Greenwood Publishing Group, Inc., Westport, CT.

[2]   HarperCollins Bible Dictionary. Paul J. Achtemeier, General Editor, With the Society of Biblical Literature (HaperCollins Publishes, New York: 1996)

States." From *Reinventing Medicine: Beyond Mind/Body to a New Era of Healing.*[1]

"Both The Social Theory and The New Genetics have proved in their different ways to be blind alleys, quite unable to deliver on their promise. Their failure is 'The Fall' of modern medicine."[2] James Le Fanu, M.D., medical columnist, London.

"We know from history that much of what doctors do at any particular time is ineffective or even dangerous when viewed in retrospect. Years ago a famous professor warned his graduating medical students that half of what he'd taught them was wrong, but the trouble was he didn't know which half. Medical practice has evolved significantly since then, but the principle still applies: we don't know which of the well-intentioned therapies of the present will end up looking like the leeches and bloodletting of ancient time or like the thalidomide, Dalkon shields, and routine tonsillectomies of a more recent era gone by. Accordingly, the pronouncements of doctors should be viewed with healthy skepticism."[3] Timothy B. McCall, M.D. a practicing physician in Boston.

"We physicians do not fully understand the relationship between mind, body, and that intangible element known as spirit . . . Medical educators have often taught that religion is an irrelevant or even detrimental factor in physical and emotional well-being. But a growing body of research has established that religious people, both young and old, often enjoy the psychological and physical benefits of a positive emotional outlook."[4] Harold G. Koenig, M D., Director of Duke University's Center for the Study of Religion/Spirituality and Health.

---

[1]   *Reinventing Medicine: Beyond Mind/Body To a New Era of Healing,* by Larry Dossey, M.D. (HarperCollins, NY:1999)

[2]   Le Fanu, James. *The Rise and Fall of Modern Medicine.* New York: Carroll & Graf, 2000.

[3]   McCall, Timothy B., *Examining Your Doctor, A Patient's Guide to Avoiding Harmful Medical Care.* New York: Carol Publishing, 1995

[4]   Koenig, Harold G. *The Healing Power of Faith: Science Explores Medicine's Last Great Frontier.* New York: Simon and Shuster, 1999.

From an interview by Bill Moyers: **"MOYERS**: Is there a scientific basis for the idea that optimism makes a difference?

"ORNISH: It's not so much optimism in the sense of telling jokes and making light of things. But I think there is a scientific basis to the idea that beliefs are powerful. If you believe that you have some control over your life, and that you have the ability to make choices instead of being the passive recipient of medical care, or the victim of bad luck or bad genes, then you are more likely to make changes that are going to do you good in terms both of your behavior and of the direct effects of your mind on your body."[1] Bill Moyers interviewing Dean Ornish, M.D., Assistant Clinical Professor Medicine and President and Director of the Preventive Medicine Research Institute at the School of Medicine, University of California, San Francisco.

A sampling of other recommended reading: *Complications: A Surgeon's Notes on an Imperfect Science,"* by Atul Gawande; *A History of God: The 4000-Year Quest of Judaism, Christianity and Islam,* by Karen Armstrong; *Second Opinions, Stories of Intuition and Choice in the Changing World of Medicine,* by Jerome Groopman; *The Future of Faith,* by Harvey Cox.

It is right to say that the educated class of scientists and medical doctors are great people. They are more scientific than are false claimants to Christian Science. There is much that yet remains to be said and done before all humankind is saved and all the mental microbes of sin and disease thought-germs are exterminated. Also, bear in mind, all human systems based on temporal premises lack the anointing of divine Science.

If you or I should appear to die, we should not be dead. Death is caused by the collective human thinking that we must die, or by mental assassins, but this does not in the least disprove divine Science. Rather it evidences the truth of its basic proposition that human thoughts rule the mis-called life in the body or in matter. However,

---

[1] *Healing and the Mind: Bill Moyers.* Ed. Betty Sue Flowers and David Grubin. Copyright © 1993 by Public Affairs Television, Inc., and David Grubin (New York: First Main Street Books Edition by arrangement with Doubleday, 1995)

the fact remains paramount that Life, Truth, and Love save from sin, disease, and death. "When the perishable has been clothed with the imperishable, and the mortal with immortality, then the saying that is written will come true: 'Death has been swallowed up in victory.'"[1]

---

[1] I Cor. 15:54

PHYSIOLOGY AND GENETICS

Therefore I tell you, do not worry about your life, what you will eat or drink; or about your body, what you will wear. Is not life more important than food, and the body more important than clothing?[1]

He sent forth his word and healed them; he rescued them from the grave.[2]

Our real being is not structural

Physiology and genetics are fruit from "the tree of the knowledge of good and evil."[3] Evil declared that eating this fruit would open our eyes and make us as a god. Instead, it closed the eyes of human beings to our God-given dominion over mortality.

Strength and intelligence are not limited to muscles and brain. Measuring muscles or IQ's (Intelligence Quotient), or testing people's cognitive approach to problem solving and decision making, are inadequate appraisals. Strength and intelligence are not at the mercy of non-intelligent matter.

Obedience to the physical laws of health has not diminished sickness. Diseases multiply when theories based on material realities take the place of spiritual truth.

Causes of sickness

A person may say that indigestion, fatigue, and insomnia cause distressed stomachs and aching heads. They have to consult their ever-re-wiring brain in order to remember the troublesome cause when the

---

1   Matt. 6:25
2   Ps. 107:20
3   Gen. 2:9

remedy lies in forgetting the earthbound experiences. Matter has no sensation of its own, and the human mind is all that can produce or feel pain.

As people think, so are they. Mind is all that feels, acts, or interferes with action. Unaware of this, or shrinking from its implied responsibility, the healing effort is made on the wrong side, and thus the conscious control over the body is lost.

Delusions and false worship

Worshippers more interested in religious ceremonies than in the principles behind the religion, will believe that a ritual, person, place, or thing is necessary for the salvation of their soul. Doctors and pharmacists who believe drugs have power will think their prescription will save a life. The belief that ceremonies will save the soul is a delusion. The belief that drugs will save a life is a medical mistake.

Health from reliance on spirituality

The human mind is in conflict with itself. From its own mindset appears the disordered body. It is an ignorant judgment to think God is of little use when we are sick. Don't wait for a strong healthy body before acknowledging God. Learn that God can do all things for us in sickness as in health.

Failing to recover health through treatments based on physiology or gene therapy, the despairing invalid often drops them. Only now, as a last resort, does the patient take the extreme step of turning to God. The person would have resorted to Mind first if they had more faith in the divine Mind than in drugs, time, and genes. Medical systems grant more power to be with matter than Spirit, however, when Mind asserts its mastery over all problems, we are found to be harmonious and spiritual.

What would be better? To beg a human-like God to heal the sick out of His free will? Or, would it make more sense to understand the infinite divine Principle which heals? If our thinking is no better than blind faith, the Science of healing is not attained and Soul-existence, in the place of molecular existence, is not comprehended. We understand Life in divine Science only as we let go of limited views and attain spiritual views. The amount of good or of evil admitted determines the harmony of our existence—our health, our longevity, and our spirituality.

The two masters

We cannot serve two masters, nor perceive divine Science with the physical senses. Drugs and DNA technology cannot successfully take the place and power of the divine source of all health and perfection. If God made people both good and evil then they must remain so. What can improve God's work? Again, an error in the premise must appear in the conclusion. To have one God and to experience the power of Spirit, you must love God, spiritual good, supremely.

Half-way success

"For the sinful nature desires what is contrary to the Spirit."[1] Sinful desires can never unite in action with Spirit, just as good never meets at some point with evil. It is foolish to take a hesitant position or sit on the fence when it comes to our spirituality. Expecting to work equally with Spirit and matter, Truth and error, is not wise. There is but one way—namely, God and Truth's idea—which leads to spiritual being. The scientific government of the body must be accomplished through the divine Mind. It is impossible to gain control over the body in any other way. On this fundamental point, cowardly conservatism is absolutely unacceptable. Only by advancing from the root of Truth can scientific healing power be realized.

Substituting good words for a good life, pretending to have a straightforward character, is a feeble change for the weak and worldly, who think the standard of divine Science too high.

Belief on the wrong side

If the balance is evenly adjusted, the removal of a single weight from either scale offsets the other side. Whatever influence you put on the side of human mind, you take away from divine Mind, which would otherwise outweigh all else. Your thinking can work against your health, so it is better to employ your thinking on the side of health. You make yourself sick through the false belief of sickness even before you rush after drugs, get blood tests, and avoid society for fear of germs.

---

[1]   Gal. 5:17

The divine authority

Because human-made systems insist that we can become sick and useless, suffer and die, all in agreement with the laws of God, or nature, are we to believe it? Are we to believe an authority which denies God's spiritual command relating to perfection—an authority which Jesus proved to be false? Jesus did the will of the Father. He healed sickness in defiance of what is called physical law, but in accordance with Mind's law.

Disease foreseen

I have detected disease in the human mind and recognized the patient's fear of it, months before the disease made its appearance in the body. Disease being a belief, a latent illusion of human mind, the sensation would not appear if the erroneous thinking was met and destroyed by truth.

Changed mentality

Note: There are mental reactions similar to chemical reactions. A mental reaction is the process by which human mind (and consequently body) undergoes a change of thought from a material to a spiritual basis.

Scientific foresight

Mental reactions (chemicalization) can aggravate the symptoms, but when the mentality has improved, the body will follow. For example, because I am aware of chemicalization, I have had the scientific foresight to notice the mental improvement of a patient and know the danger was over and tell a patient, "You are healed." Sometimes, because of their unbelief, the patient was frustrated to hear such a statement until their body completely responded to the improved thinking.

Facts such as the one just mentioned show that disease has a mental, mortal origin. Faith in the rules of genetics or drugs procreates and fosters disease. A faith in mortality attracts the mind to the subject of sickness by exciting fear of disease and by dosing the body with chemicals in order to avoid a problem. Faith can, however, find a stronger support and a higher home in Spirit. If we understood the control of Mind over body, we should put no faith in material means.

Mind the only healer

Science not only reveals the source of all disease as mental, but it also declares that all disease is cured by divine Mind. There can be no healing except by this Mind however much we trust a drug or any other means toward which human faith or endeavor is directed. It is human mind, not matter, which brings to the sick whatever good they may seem to receive from conventional medicine or biotechnology. The sick are never really healed except by means of the divine power. Only the action of Truth, Life, and Love can give harmony.

Types of matter

The good that a poisonous drug seems to do is bad because it robs us of our reliance of God. It is twisted thinking to use poisons in treatments since according to belief the treatment is toxic to the human system. The disorder which calls for these twisted methods is the result of the exercise of faith in matter instead of in Spirit. Practices, in which good is perverted, cannot form either a moral or a spiritual system. Whatever teaches us to have convoluted ideals and to acknowledge powers other than the divine Mind, opposes spirituality.

Was Jesus as savvy to our nutritional needs, as the dieticians of today are? Spiritual ideas, such as shared by Jesus, certainly present what human theories exclude—the Principle of our well-being. The text, "Everyone who lives and believes in Me will never die,"[1] not only contradicts human systems, but also points to the self-sustaining and eternal Truth.

The demands of Truth are spiritual and reach the body through Mind. The best interpreter of our needs said: "Stop being perpetually uneasy (anxious and worried) about your life, what you shall eat *or what you shall drink.*"[2]

If there are physical laws which prevent disease, what then causes disease? Spiritual law did not cause disease. Jesus, obedient to Spirit, healed the sick and cast out error always in defiance to physics.

---

[1]   John 11:26 (NASB)

[2]   Matt. 6:25; Luke 12:22 (Amplified)

Cause considered

Spiritual cause is the one question to be considered, for more than all others spiritual causation relates to human progress. The collective mass consciousness is approaching this subject and pondering somewhat the supremacy of Spirit. Touching the fringe of Truth's "cloak"[1] is a worthy goal.

The description of people as purely molecular, or as a mixture of molecules and spirituality—but in either case dependent upon their physical organization—is a can of worms. Opening up this can, we find all ills, especially depression. Materiality takes divine power into its own hands and claims to be a creator, but it is only a fabricated fiction. In this fabrication, idolatry and lust are so encouraged by society that humankind has caught their moral contagion.

Paradise regained

We can discover the spiritual opposite of materiality. Even the way through Christ, Truth, allows us to reopen, with the key of divine Science, the gates of Paradise which human beliefs have closed. There will then be no need to consult reference books for the probabilities of life. It will be unnecessary to study DNA or neurons in order to learn the state of our substance and purpose. We can find our self not fallen, but upright, pure, and free.

A closed question

Mind's control over the universe and humankind is no longer an open question, but is demonstrable Science. Jesus illustrated the divine Principle and the power of spiritual Mind by healing sickness and sin and destroying the sources of death.

Matter versus Spirit

Mistaking our origin and nature, we believe we are a combination of atoms and Spirit. This leads to believing that Spirit is broken down through matter, transported by a nerve, and exposed to removal by an operation. The intellectual, the moral, the spiritual—subject to non-intelligence!

---

[1]   Matt. 9:20; Matt. 14:36; Mark 6:56

No more like-mindedness exists between the flesh and Spirit than between Belial and Christ.[1]

The laws of matter are nothing but the mindset that intelligence and life are present where Mind is not. Mindlessness is the procuring cause of all sin and disease. The opposite truth, that Mind is infinite and that intelligence and life are spiritual, can destroy sin, sickness, and death.

The fundamental error is to suppose we are the result of matter and that the knowledge of good and evil, caught through the physical senses, constitute our happiness or misery.

Godless evolution

Insisting that human beings went through a chain of development from a single-celled organism to a monkey to a person is unproductive.

The chain of a material evolution is a conundrum. If we came from a single-celled organism, why aren't all single-celled organisms human beings? Why do we still have monkeys? Did the chain of material evolution break at some point? Spirit can't form a link in a supposed chain of material being. Divine Science reveals the eternal chain of existence as uninterrupted and wholly spiritual. Spirituality can only be realized as the false sense of being disappears.

Degrees of development

If we ever were material beings, we must have passed through all the forms of matter in order to be where we are. If the material body is person, we are a part of dirt. On the contrary, our true self is the image and likeness of Spirit. The belief that Soul is in sense, or that Life is in organized atoms, obtains in human beings (human mind) to which the apostle refers when he says that we must "put off your old self, which is being corrupted by its deceitful desires."[2]

Identity not lost

How can the temporal brain, heart, blood, DNA, etc. be our identity? If our real nature is the bodily structure, a portion of our being would be gone if a limb was amputated; a surgeon could remove our manhood or womanhood; or bacteria would annihilate

---

[1]   II Cor. 6:15

[2]   Eph. 4:22

our existence. What happens to the identity of an organ recipient? How can DNA be the foundation of our identity when it mutates and replicates? After a person is gone their DNA is still here on earth, so where is the individual? On another note, people have repeatedly proven that the loss of a limb cannot take away their manliness or womanliness. Many people, classified as disabled, have presented more nobility, more manliness and womanliness, than the polished athlete or glamour model—teaching society that true identity and nature comes from spirituality, consciousness.

When people are God's child

When we admit that matter (hormones, DNA, neurons, etc.), acting through the five physical senses, constitutes a person, we fail to see how physiology can distinguish between humanity and animals. Animals also have hormones, DNA, and neurons. Do some pets act more humane than people? Physiology and anatomy have a difficult time determining when people are really people.

Supposing that the potter is subject to the clay is like saying the genetic engineer is subject to, or constrained by, the genetically altered organism. When God isn't understood as our source, attempts are made to reduce truth to the level of error where the sensible is required to be made manifest through the insensible.

What are called molecules or dark matter manifests nothing but a limited mentality. The substance or manifestation of Spirit is not obtainable through matter. Spirit is positive. Matter is negative; the absence of Spirit. For positive Spirit to pass through a negative condition would be Spirit's destruction.

Anatomy teaches that our being is structural. Physiology continues this explanation, measuring human strength by bones and muscles. Genetics chimes in and insists that genes can instruct our virtues or faults. Psychology makes a person aggressive or honest according to the body's chemical levels or according to how the person developed through human experiences. Material structure is mortal. Anatomy, physiology, genetics, or psychiatry does not define our spiritual individuality, whereas divine Science does.

Human reason and religion come slowly to the recognition of spiritual facts. Human belief systems continue to call upon matter to remove the error which the human mind alone has created.

The idols of domestication are far more fatal to health and longevity than are the idols of the undomesticated. The idols of domestication call into action less faith than the doctrines of a human deity. Village Guardians and the Shaman restore health by incantations as consciously as do modern practitioners by their more culturally esteemed methods.

Is civilization only a higher form of idolatry, where humankind makes gods out of massage, drugs, diet, exercise, or vitamins? Nothing except divine power is capable of doing more for human beings than we do for ourselves.

Advance of thought

The movement of thought, advancing past limiting standpoints is slow and warns the spiritual traveler of the long haul ahead. However, the angels of Love's presence—the spiritual intuitions that tell us when "the night is nearly over; the day is almost here"[1]—are our guardians in the gloom. Whoever opens the way in divine Science is a pioneer and stranger, marking out the path for generations yet unborn.

The thunder of Sinai and the Sermon on the Mount are pursuing and will overtake the evolving thoughts. In this course, all error is rebuked and the kingdom of heaven on earth is proclaimed. Truth is made known. It needs only to be practiced.

Medical errors

Human belief is all that enables a drug to cure mortal ailments. Anatomy admits that mind is somewhere in man or woman, though out of sight. Then, if an individual is sick, why treat the body alone and administer a dose of despair to the mind? Why declare that the body is diseased, and picture this disease to the mind? Why savor the image of disease as if it is sweet candy by holding it before the thought of both physician and patient? It is useful to understand that the cause of disease obtains in the mortal human mind, and its cure comes from the immortal divine Mind. Delete the outlines of disease

---

[1]   Rom. 13:12

already programmed in the minds of human beings and prevent other images of disease from taking form in thought.

Trendy diseases

When there are fewer prescriptions and more thought is given to moral and spiritual subjects, there will be improved metabolisms and less disease. A hundred years ago, who ever heard of AIDS, Autism, and Attention Deficient Disorder?

What about food allergies? Isn't it a form of abuse to say that food, the sustenance of God, can produce suffering! The presence of natural nourishment should encourage self-disciplined, grateful thought. It should discourage any sense of worry or inflammation. The thought that the taste of food can cause inflamed glands or hives, can be reversed.

Random problems crushed

If a random thought, calling itself indigestion, tries to tyrannize productive people, it is routed out by their independence and energy; because they who don't have time for selfishness, coddling, and sicko chit-chat. It has not been proven beneficial for humanity to dwell on advice concerning the exact amount of food the stomach can digest. The latest food fad is not a health law.

Damp atmospheres and freezing snow can give rosy complexions. For pulmonary health, you don't have to indulge in the refinement of inflamed bronchial tubes. You don't have to fear pneumonia, or depend on antibiotics, vapor therapy, or antihistamines. You can rely on something better than the fruit of the "knowledge of good and evil."[1]

The action of human mind on the body was not so injurious before curiosity took up medical study and then distracted thought away from spiritual healing. "Where ignorance is bliss, 'tis folly to be wise,"[2] and there is truth in this sentiment.

Permit the stomach and bowels to act in obedience to nature. Give the gospel a chance to be seen in its glorious effects upon the

---

[1] Gen. 2:9

[2] Thomas Gray, (1716-1771) English poet. *Ode On a Distant Prospect of Eton College.*

body. Dismiss the ghastly collection of diseases paraded before your imagination. Keep to "sermons in stones, and good in everything."[1] When the mechanism of the human mind gives place to the divine Mind, selfishness and sin, disease and death, will lose their grip.

Human fear of pollution would load the air of Eden with disease. Fear weighs down humanity with superimposed and conjectural evils. Human mind is the worst enemy of the body, while divine Mind is its best friend.

Diseases not to be classified

Should all cases of fleshly disease be treated by a doctor, and the Christian Scientist use truth only in cases of hysteria, hypochondria, and hallucination? One disease is no more real than another. All disease is the result of education, and disease can carry its ill-effects no farther than mortal mind plots out. It is the human mind, not matter that supposedly feels, suffers, and enjoys. Hence decided types of acute disease are quite as ready to yield to Truth as the less distinct type and chronic form of disease. Truth deals with the most malignant contagion with perfect assurance.

One basis for all sickness

Human mind produces diseases of the flesh or genetic disorders as certainly as it produces hysteria, and it must relinquish all its errors, sicknesses, and sins. I have demonstrated this beyond all doubt. The evidence of divine Mind's healing power and absolute control is to me as certain as the evidence of my own existence.

Mentally and physically one

Human mind and body are one. Neither exists without the other, and both must be replaced by spiritual Mind. A material body is an embodied concept of human mind. This mortal mind builds its own superstructure of which the fleshly body is the denser portion. From first to last, the body is a sensuous mythical human concept.

The effect of names

In the Scriptural allegory of human history, Adam (representing the lie of humanized dirt or atoms), had the job of naming all that was material. These names indicated the properties, qualities, and forms

---

1   Shakespeare, William, (1564-1616) *As You Like It*, Act 2, Scene 1.

151

of matter, but lacked the idea of real substance. A lie, the opposite of Truth, cannot name the qualities and effects of eternal substance. A lie cannot create the alleged laws of the flesh, nor can a lie hold the predominate power in any direction against God, Spirit.

Poison defined mentally

If a dose of poison is swallowed by mistake and the patient dies even though physician and patient are expecting favorable results, does human belief cause this death? Yes, and as directly as if the poison had been taken intentionally.

In this case, only a few people believe the poison swallowed by the patient to be harmless. Otherwise, the vast majority, the collective consciousness of humankind believes the sleeping pills, strychnine, antianxiety drugs, or whatever the poison, to be toxic. Bear in mind, although mass consciousness knows nothing about this particular case and patient, the drug is still marked down as a poison by human mind. Consequently, the result is controlled by the majority of collective opinions, not by the infinitesimal minority of opinions in the sick room.

Heredity isn't dangerous. Heredity isn't law. Just because people in the past believed in a disease doesn't mean it has priority and a connection to the present. The predisposing cause and the exciting cause are mental.

Perhaps the fright of a parent produced a birth defect and the deformity continued into the child's adulthood. Forced away from human belief and based on Science or divine Mind, to which all things are possible, that chronic case is not difficult to cure.

Destroying the power of suggestion

Human mind, acting from the basis of sensation in matter, is susceptible to suggestions. This so-called mind from which comes all evil, contradicts itself, and must finally yield to the eternal Truth, or the divine Mind, as expressed in Science. In proportion to our understanding of Christian Science, we are freed from the suggestions of physical inheritance or mind in matter. We disarm sin of its imaginary power as we scientifically understand the status of spiritual being.

Unaware of the methods and the basis of metaphysical healing, you may attempt to unite it with hypnotism, brain manipulation, or psychics. However, none of these methods benefit metaphysical healing.

Whoever reaches the understanding of divine Science in its proper significance will perform the sudden cures of which it is capable. Nevertheless, this can be done only by facing and overcoming fears and mistaken thoughts, and following divine Spirit in our everyday experiences.

Absent patients

Science can heal the sick who are absent from their healers, as well as those present, since space is not an obstacle to Mind. Immortal Mind heals what eye has not seen. The spiritual ability to comprehend thought and to heal by the Truth-power is won only as we are found reflecting the divine nature. Put in other words, self-glorification, arrogance, anger, and the like, are not found in Truth healing.

Bad teaching

Every medical method has its advocates. The preference of human mind for a certain methodology creates a demand for that method, and the body then seems to require such treatment. You can even educate a healthy horse to believe it will catch a cold without a blanket. Whereas, the wild animals left to their instincts, sniffs the wind with delight. The outbreak of a cold is a humanly evolved ailment.

Reports in psychiatry, physiology, and genetics, sustained by what is termed material law, promote sickness and disease. It should not be true, that so long as you read medical reports you will be sick.

This constant thinking of something other than Spirit can inadvertently sow seeds of reliance on matter. Take a persistent healer who utilizes complementary alternative methods. They intently study the latest homeopathic remedies and automatically recommend doses for every itch, twinge, or burp. Clients may reap the effect of this mistaken reliance if healers impulsively endorse counselors, homeopathic powders, acupuncture needles, or magnets as a cure-all.

Descriptions and advertisements of disease, given by physicians, pharmaceutical companies, genetic engineers, and Health Departments, are prolific sources of sickness. The human mind is the agriculturist of error, but we can teach the human mind not to harm the body. We can root out of human mind all the weeds of sickness.

The patient's outlook

Ignorant that the human mind governs its phenomenon, the body, the sufferer may unconsciously add more fear to the mental reservoir already overflowing with that emotion. Tolerant sufferers try to be satisfied when they see their would-be healer busy. Faith in the healer's efforts is somewhat helpful to everyone involved; however in Science, people must understand the resuscitating law of Life. Understanding the self-sustaining Life is in accord with the "plants bearing seed according to their kinds."[1]

It is constructive for physicians, therapists, and practitioners to know and act on the truth that Mind *is* existent. Healers should not take the position that matter is the only cause.

Better way

Doctors, it is best not to implant disease in the thoughts of your patients by declaring disease to be a fixed fact, even before you go to work to eradicate the disease through the material faith inspired. Instead of furnishing thought with fear, try to correct the turbulent emotion by the influence of divine Love, which removes fear.

When governed by God, the ever-present Mind who understands all things, we know that with God all things are possible. One example, of this way to living Truth which heals the sick, is found in the Science of divine Mind as taught and demonstrated by Christ Jesus.

The important decision

To reduce inflammation, dissolve a tumor, or cure disease, I have found divine Truth more potent than all temporal remedies. And why not, since Mind, God, is the source and condition of all existence? Before deciding that the body (molecular organization) is disordered, it would be better to ask, "Who indeed are you, a human being, to argue with God? Will what is molded say to the one who molds it, 'Why have you made me like this?'"[2] Matter, which can neither suffer nor

---

[1]   Gen. 1:12

[2]   Rom 9:20; Isa. 29:16; Isa. 45:9 (NRSV)

enjoy, has no partnership with pain and pleasure, but human belief has such a partnership.

Manipulation unscientific

When the body is being treated through wordy prayers, massage, chiropractic's, Jin Shin Do, acupuncture, or other remedial methods, it is detrimental to trust the treatment or manipulation instead of Truth. Do not weaken or destroy your healing power by employing matter instead of Mind.

Be honest. Don't say massage or manipulation is benign in the healing work, but then insist on doing it. If it isn't a point then why do it? Because you are ignorant of the baneful effects of mortal mind-control or you are not sufficiently spiritual to depend on Spirit. Whether you are utilizing temporal healing methods, or praying from a tenuous standpoint that relies on ceremonies and creeds, you must improve your mindset until you attain the understanding of spiritual Science which heals.

Not words but deeds

Words are unsatisfying when there are no good works included. The people who adhere to incongruous manifestations are being asked the question "Where are you?"[1] Love the Science of Spirit and trust Truth. It is unnecessary to employ anything other than Mind in order to satisfy the sick that you are doing something for them. If they are cured, they generally know it and are content.

"Where your treasure is, there your heart will be also."[2] If you have more faith in time or in chemicals than in Truth, this faith will incline you to the side of limitation and error. Any hypnotic power you may exercise will deteriorate your ability to become a Scientist, and vice versa. The act of healing the sick through divine Mind alone, of replacing error with Truth, shows your position as a scientist of Spirit, Soul.

Physiology or Spirit

The demands of God appeal to thought only; but the claims of mortality and what are termed laws of nature, appertain to matter.

---

[1] Gen. 3:9

[2] Matt. 6:21; Luke 12:34

Which, then, are we to accept as legitimate and capable of producing the highest human good? We cannot obey both biology and Spirit. We pay attention to one or the other. It is impossible to work from two standpoints. If we attempt it, we will, "be devoted to the one and despise the other."[1]

The theories of human beings are antagonistic to Science and cannot mix with it. This is clear to those who heal the sick on the basis of divine Science.

No laws of limitations or opposites

Mind's government of the body must supersede the laws of matter. Obedience to material laws prevents full obedience to spiritual law—the law which overcomes material conditions and puts matter under the feet of Mind. Mortals ask the divine Mind to heal the sick and then shut out the aid of Mind by using temporal means. Our God-given ability to demonstrate Mind's sacred power is denied when we work against ourselves and against our prayers by vacillating between Mind and matter. Pleas for drugs and the latest health fad come from some sad incident or else from ignorance of divine Science and its transcendent power.

To admit that sickness is a circumstance over which God has no control is to presuppose that omnipotence is powerless on some occasions. The law of Christ, or Truth, makes all things possible to Spirit. The laws of human mind attempt to render Spirit of no avail, and demand obedience to materialist codes, thus departing from the basis of one God, one lawmaker. To suppose that God constitutes laws of chaos is a mistake. Balance and peace are supported by nature and divine law, even when everything else says otherwise.

We ask, can we eat and live without natural laws and agriculture? The answer is no, and yet the Scriptures inform us that sin, or error, first caused the condemnation of humankind to till the ground.[2] Scriptures also indicate that obedience to God will remove the necessity to rely on material food, air, or technology. Truth never made error necessary nor devised a law to perpetuate error.

---

[1]   Matt. 6:24; Luke 16:13

[2]   Gen. 3:17

Laws of nature are spiritual

The supposed laws which result in weariness and disease are not God's laws. The legitimate and only possible action of Truth is the production of harmony. Laws of nature are laws of Spirit; but human beings commonly recognize as law that which hides the power of Spirit. Divine Mind rightly demands our entire obedience, affection, and strength. No reservation is made for any lesser commitment. Obedience to truth gives us power and strength. Obedience to error coincides with a loss of power.

Belief and understanding

Through spiritual law, Truth disposes of evil and materialist methods. Spiritual law gives sight to the bind, hearing to the deaf, voice to the dumb, feet to the lame.[1] If Christian Science dishonors human belief, it honors spiritual understanding and the one Mind.

The so-called laws of health are simply laws that the human mind was trained to believe. If the premise for physical and mental health is limited to the human mind, the conclusions will be limited and erroneous. Truth makes no laws to regulate sickness, sin, and death, for these are unknown to Truth and should not be recognized as reality.

Belief produces the results of belief, and penalties are inseparably attached so long as the belief continues. The remedy consists in investigating the trouble thoroughly. Find, and cast out by denial, the mistaken thinking which produces human problems. Make sure never to honor a flawed conviction by calling it a law. Do not cede obedience to materialism. Affirm that the spiritual lawgivers, Truth, Life, and Love, are the only legitimate and eternal demands on us. Spirit enforces obedience through divine statutes.

Laws of human belief

Controlled by divine intelligence, we are harmonious and eternal. Whatever is regulated by a negative attitude is shiftless and mortal. We say people suffer from the effects of noise, heat, and fatigue; but this is a human creed, not the truth of being, for matter cannot suffer. Human mind alone suffers—not because a law of matter has been

---

[1]   Matt. 11:5

157

violated, but because a law of this mind has been disobeyed. I have demonstrated this as a rule of divine Science by destroying the delusion of suffering from what was termed a fatally broken physical law.

A woman, whom I cured of tuberculosis, always breathed with great difficulty when the wind was from the east. I sat silently by her side for a few moments. Her breath came gently. The inspirations were deep and natural. I then requested her to look at the weather-vane. She looked and saw that it pointed due east. The wind had not changed, but her thought of it had and so her difficulty in breathing had gone. The wind had not produced the difficulty. My metaphysical treatment changed the action of her thinking on the lungs, and she never suffered again from east winds, but was restored to health.

A bogus mind cure

There are many self-help books on the market that assist us in yielding to a Higher Power, however "mind-cures," or "mental medicines" that operate through human mind or the earth's energy are as material as conventional medicine. The treatments don't break their own barriers and only try to mimic divine Science. This is similar to when Moses had Aaron throw his staff on the ground before Pharaoh, and the staff became a snake. Imitating Aaron, Pharaoh's cohorts threw their sticks down to become snakes, but Aaron's snake swallowed the copies.[1] The system of divine Science is purely mental. We must embrace spiritual Mind with its power to cure. God, Love, Mind, is the healing factor. Christian Science rests on the conception of God as the only Life, substance, intelligence, and the only factor in the healing work.

Jesus and the power of suggestion

Jesus cast out vice and healed the sick, not only without drugs, but also without hypnotism. The ethics and pathology of Christian Science do not include chemicals and external mind suggestions.

Mental practice on the human level may seem for a time to benefit the sick, but the recovery is not permanent. Methods that act on and through the human mind, and its counterpart the brain, are only manipulations of the accumulated human imprints and activities.

---

[1]   Ex. 7:8-12

False stimulus

If a patient is under the influence of human mind, that influence is removed by emptying the mind of its false stimulus and reaction of will-power, and filling it with the divine energies of Truth.

Divine Science replaces materialist thinking through the understanding of Spirit, and the thoroughness of this work determines health. Erring mind-forces are trickery and do their work under the name of good. Spirit and matter, good and evil, light and darkness, cannot mingle.

Evil is negative and self-destructive

Evil is nonbeing, because it lacks truth. It is nothing, because it is the absence of something. It is unreal, because it presupposes the absence of God, the omnipotent and omnipresent. Every human being must learn that there is neither power nor reality in evil.

Evil is self-assertive. It says: "I am a real entity, overmastering good." This falsehood should strip evil of all pretensions. Self-destruction is the only power of evil, and it can never destroy one iota of good. Every attempt of evil to destroy goodness is a failure, and only aids in decisively punishing the evil-doer. If we allow the same reality to discord as to harmony, discord has as lasting a claim on us as harmony. If evil is as real as good, evil is also immortal. If death is as real as Life, immortality is a myth. If pain is as real as the absence of pain, both must be immortal; and if so, harmony cannot be the law of being.

Uninformed idolatry

Human mind is unaware of its false ego or it could never be self-deceived. If this mortal mind knew how to be better, it would. When human mind tries to believe in something besides itself, it only promotes its own image as deity, thereby becoming an idolater. Out of the necessity to maintain its identity the human mind has other gods and believes in more than one Mind.

As human beings do not comprehend even mortal existence, they must be ignorant of the all-knowing Mind and of the creation of Spirit.

Physical sense creates its own forms of thought, and gives the forms imaginative titles, before worshiping and fearing them. Often, the forms are attributed with abilities beyond themselves. Basically, the beliefs of the human mind commit self-robbery and self-enslavement and then charge the result to another illusive personification named Satan.

Action of the human mind

The human mind always tells the body what to do. Quite often the body goes through a motion so often that after a while the movement appears to be involuntary. Human mind tells the heart valves to open and close as directly as it tells the hand to wave hello. Anatomy admits that human-will waves the hand, but it doesn't see human mind directing the heart.

We say, "My hand did it." What is this *my* but human mind, the cause of all mortal action. All voluntary and involuntary action of the mortal body is governed by mortal mind, not by chemicals or electricity. There is no involuntary action. The divine Mind includes all action and will, and in Science we are governed by this Mind. The human mind tries to classify action as voluntary and involuntary and suffers from the attempt.

Death and the body

If you take away the human mind, the temporal physical body loses all appearance of life or action and the human mind calls itself dead. However, the human mind still holds in belief a body, through which it acts and which appears to its self to live until the body is put off. Only as the mortal, false mind yields to God or spiritual Mind, is our identity found in the image of Love.

Undeveloped, unmotivated negative thoughts

What is termed disease does not exist in spiritual Mind. Disease is neither mind nor matter. The belief of sin, which has grown terrible in strength and influence, is an unconscious error in the beginning. Negativity is like an undeveloped thought with no motive, but afterward it controls human beings. Infatuation, self-destructive appetites, dishonesty, envy, hatred, and revenge ripen into action, only to pass from shame and despair to their final self-punishment.

Disease a dream

Mortal existence is a dream of temporal substance, a dream of pain, pleasure, sickness, and death. It is similar to the dream we have in sleep, in which everyone recognizes their condition to be wholly a state of mind. In both the waking and the sleeping dream, the dreamer thinks that the body is their own individual unit that can feel pain or pleasure.

The smile on the face of a sleeping baby implies that a dream produced a pleasant sensation. In the same mental nonsensical way, pain and pleasure, sickness and degeneration, are traced upon human beings by unmistakable signs.

Sickness is an extension of error, reaching out from fear or inaccurate knowledge. Error spreads error. What causes disease cannot cure it. The soil of disease is human mind, and you have an abundant or sparse crop of disease according to the seedlings of fear. Sin and the fear of disease must be uprooted and thrown out.

Sense yields to understanding

When darkness comes over the earth, the physical senses have no direct evidence of a sun. The human eye doesn't know where the light of day is, or if it exists. Astronomy gives the desired information. The physical senses accept the authority of astronomy. If our eyes see no sun for a week, we still believe that there is solar light and heat. Natural science advances human thought past the crude theories of the human mind and dissolves fear.

Human beings do not deny the existence of good weather when a hurricane is raging. They know good weather exists and will return. In like manner, it is profitable for human beings to accept the authority of divine Science and its power to explain the effect of human mind on the body and establish harmony, though the cause is unseen. The sins of others should not make good people suffer.

Ascending the scale

Whether we call the body material or spiritual, but it is only what the human mind and brain believe. The human mortal mind, by an inevitable perversion, makes all things start from the lowest instead of from the highest mortal thought. The reverse is the case with all the formations of the immortal divine Mind which proceed from the divine source and constantly ascends in infinite being.

Human reproduction

From human mind comes the reproduction of the species—first the belief of inanimate (DNA), and then of animate (conscious) matter. According to human thought, embryonic human mind begins in the central nervous system and develops into a brain, always keeping in line with matter, which is the subjective condition of human mind.

Next, we have the formation of an emerging human mind, defined as a human being. All this while flesh is ignorant of its self and of what it is producing. Why do we go along with the theory that an unconscious network of nerve cells evolve and produce both body and mind? The mortal's mind, and certainly the immortal Mind, is not found in brain or elsewhere in matter or in human beings.

Human stature

This genotypic and physiological mortal humanity in turn fills itself with thoughts of pain and pleasure, life and death. The belief of humanized molecules also arranges itself into five so-called senses, which presently measure mind and body by the number of synapses in the brain, and mass weight.

Human frailty

Human birth, growth, maturity, and decay are as the grass springing from the soil with beautiful green blades, afterward to wither and return to its native nothingness. These human impressions are temporal; they never merge into spiritual being, but finally disappear, and spiritual being, which is eternal, is found to be the real.

The Hebrew poet, swayed by human thoughts, is a bit melancholy:

> As for mortals, their days are as grass;
> they flourish like a flower of the field;
> for the wind passes over it, and it is gone,
> And its place knows it no more.[1]

When hope was inspired in the human heart, the poet sang:

> And I—in righteousness I will see your face;

---

[1]   Ps. 103:15 (NRSV)

when I awake, I will be satisfied with seeing your likeness.[1]
For with you is the fountain of life;
In your light we see light.[2]

The brain can give no idea of God's child. It can take no cognizance of Mind. Matter is not the organ of infinite Mind.

As human beings give up the delusion that there is more than one Mind, more than one God, spiritual individuality in God's likeness will appear. Our eternal identity includes no illusive element.

The immortal birth

As a physical, theoretical life-basis is found to be a misinterpretation of existence, the scientific and divine Principle of our spirituality dawns upon human thought. Consciousness is guided to "where the child was"[3]—even to the birth of a new-old idea, to the spiritual sense of being and of what Life includes. Thus the whole earth will be transformed by Truth as enlightened thought displaces the darkness of error.

Spiritual freedom

The human thought must free itself from self-imposed materiality and bondage. Don't take the effort to ask the genome, heart, or lungs: What are our prospects for life? Ask Mind about life. Mind is not helpless. Intelligence is not mute before non-intelligence.

Not by its own determination does a star proceed to shine, a leaf unfold its fair outlines, and a flower open.

The Science of being reveals individual spirituality as based on Soul. Physical sense defines humanity as based on matter and from this premise infers the mortality of the body.

No physical affinity

Self-delusion may imagine that opposites attract; but in Christ's Science, Truth never mingles with error. Mind has no affinity with material limitation and therefore Truth is able to cast out the ills of the flesh. Mind, God, sends forth the aroma of Spirit, the atmosphere

---

[1]   Ps. 17:15

[2]   Ps. 36:9

[3]   Matt. 2:9

of intelligence. Believing that gray matter and white matter, plus the chemicals inside the skull, is mind, is a mockery of intelligence—a mimicry of Mind.

We are Scientists of Spirit only as we quit our reliance upon that which is false and grasp the truth. We are not metaphysical Scientists until we leave human opinions for spiritual Truth. Human attitudes come from the hearing of the ear, from physicality, instead of from Principle. Limited perceptions come from the mortal, instead of from the immortal. Spirit is not separate from God. Spirit *is* God.

Human power is a blind force

Erring power is a material belief, a blind miscalled force, the offspring of false intent and not of wisdom, of the human mind and not of the spiritual. Human power is the reckless flood, the devouring flame, the exploding meteor. It is lightning and hurricane. Human power is all that is selfish, wicked, dishonest, and impure.

The one real power

Moral and spiritual power belongs to Spirit, who gathers the "wind in the hollow of the hands."[1] This metaphysical teaching agrees with Science and harmony. In Science, you can have no power opposed to God and the physical senses must give up their false testimony. Your influence for good depends on the weight you throw into the right scale. The good you do and embody gives you the only power obtainable. Evil is not power, but a mockery of strength, which ultimately betrays its weakness and falls, never to rise.

We walk in the footsteps of Truth and Love by following the example of Jesus in the understanding of divine metaphysics. Spirituality is the basis of true healing. Whatever holds human thought in line with selfless love, receives directly the divine power.

Mind cures hip problem

I was called to visit Mr. Clark in Lynn, who had been confined to his bed six months with hip-disease. On entering the house I met his physician who said that the patient was dying. The physician had just probed the ulcer on the hip and told me the bone was carious for several inches. He even showed me the probe, which had on it

---

[1]   Prov. 30:4

the evidence of this condition of the bone. The doctor went out. Mr. Clark lay with his eyes fixed and sightless. The dew of death was on his brow. I went to his bedside. In a few moments his face changed; its death-pallor gave place to a natural hue. The eyelids closed gently and the breathing became natural; he was asleep. In about ten minutes he opened his eyes and said: "I feel like a new man. My suffering is all gone." It was between three and four o'clock in the afternoon when this took place.

I told him to get up, dress himself, and eat supper with his family. He did so. The next day I saw him in the yard. Since then I have not seen him, but am informed that he went to work in two weeks. The discharge from the sore stopped and the sore was healed. The diseased condition had been there ever since he was a boy when he had injured himself after falling on a wooden spike.

Since his recovery I have been informed that his physician claims to have cured him, and that the patient's mother has been threatened with incarceration in a mental health facility for saying: "It was none other than God and that woman who healed him." I cannot attest the truth of that report, but what I saw and did for that man and what his physician said of the case, occurred just as I have narrated.

It has been demonstrated to me that Life is God and that the might of omnipotent Spirit doesn't share its strength with matter or with human will. Reviewing this brief experience, I cannot fail to discern the coincidence of the spiritual idea of man and woman with the divine Mind.

Change of belief

A change in human thought changes all the physical symptoms and determines a case for better or for worse. When one's false belief is corrected, Truth sends a report of health over the body.

Destruction of the auditory nerve and paralysis of the optic nerve are not necessary to ensure deafness and blindness. If human mind says, "I am deaf and blind," it will be so without an injured tissue. Every theory opposed to this fact would claim we are mortal in belief, rather than immortal in spiritual understanding.

Power of habit

Research points to the frailty and inadequacy of human minds and brains. Professor Susan Greenfield reports online at www.dailymail. co.uk, that, "Today's technology is already producing a marked shift in the way we think and behave, particularly among the young." Specifically talking about pleasure, Greenfield continues, "For some, pleasure means wine, women and song; for others, more recently, sex, drugs and rock-n-roll; and for millions today, endless hours at the computer console."[1]

These cases prove physical senses are beliefs formed by education or trained behavior. The hours and days spent in front of the computer video games would be appalling to the person who was enjoys a walk in the park. Sounds and sights from multichannel televisions and MP3 players that thrill some viewers, can convulse other people trained in an opposite direction.

Useful knowledge

The point to decide is whether human mind or spiritual Mind acts as the cause. It is much more productive to forsake the basis of matter for the metaphysical basis of Science and its divine Principle.

Whatever resembles an idea governed by Principle, furnishes food for thought. Through astronomy, art, natural history, chemistry, music, and mathematics, thought passes naturally from effect back to cause.

Academics of the right sort are requisite. Observation, invention, study, and original thought are expansive. They should promote the advancement of human mind out of itself to a consciousness that escapes mortality.

Sensationalized education is deplorable. The mere dogma, the frightening speculations, and the nauseous fiction can be filtered out. Novels and movies remarkable only for their exaggerated pictures, unrealistic ideals, and models of rudeness, fill the viewer and reader with wrong tastes and attitudes. Commercialism is lowering the

---

[1] Greenfield, Susan, "Modern technology changing way brains work says neuroscientist," http://www.dailymail.co.uk/sciencetech/article-565207/Modern-technology-changing-way-brains-work-says-neuroscientist.html#ixzz2xrjH2Ima Accessed 4/3/2014

intellectual standard to accommodate the bank account and to meet a foolish demand for entertainment instead of for improvement. Incorrect views lower the standard of truth.

The power of human mind over its own body is not understood very well. Human beings have "made a mess of things,"[1] not realizing yet that knowledge can save from the dire effects of knowledge. If materialistic knowledge is power, it is not wisdom. Temporal knowledge is but a vain force.

Sin destroyed through suffering

Suffering can awaken human mind from its fleshly dream, and is better than the false pleasures which tend to perpetuate this dream. Only sin brings death, for sin is the element of destruction.

"Be afraid of the One who can destroy both soul and body in hell,"[2] said Jesus. A careful study of this text shows that here the word *soul* means a false perception or temporal consciousness. The command was a warning to beware, not of human governments, Satan, nor of God, but of sin. Sin makes its own hell, and goodness makes its own heaven. Sickness, sin, and death are not companions of Life or Truth. No law supports them. They have no relation to God wherewith to establish their power.

Preventing dangerous crowd thinking

Instead of impressing on the mind forcible descriptions and medical details, delete them. Constructive and informative literature, images, and movies will help rule disease out of human mind and abate and destroy sickness.

Many a hopeless case of disease is induced by a single post mortem examination—by fear of disease and the images brought before the mind. Disease is a mental state, which is afterward outlined on the body.

Problems caused by the media

The press, internet, and media unwittingly send forth many sorrows among the human family. It does this by giving names to diseases and by printing long descriptions which mirror images

---

1   Eccl. 7:29 (The Message)

2   Matt. 10:28; Luke 12:5

of disorder and dysfunction distinctly in thought. A new name for an ailment affects people like the latest craze. Every one jumps on the band wagon to join the party of problems. A minutely described disease costs many human beings their earthly days of comfort. What a price for human knowledge! But the price does not exceed the original cost. God said of the tree of knowledge, which bears the fruit of sin, disease, and death, "When you eat of it you will surely die."[1]

Higher standard for humanity

The less that is said of physical structure and laws, the higher will be the standard of living. The more that is thought and said about moral and spiritual law, the further human beings will be removed from imbecility or disease.

Fear is to be overcome, instead of cultivated. Fear makes us wimpy, dishonest, touchy, and egotistical.

Diet and digestion

We are told that certain foods make us healthy, but that is a mistake. Yesterday's diet would not cure today's indigestion. With rules of health in the head and the most digestible food in the stomach, there are still digestive problems. Unwell bodies will become healthy as individual opinions improve and human belief loses some portion of its error.

Harm done by some physicians

The doctor's mind reaches that of the patient. Doctors should suppress their fear of disease, or else their belief in its reality and fatality will harm their patients even more than the chemotherapy, radiation, or morphine. This fact is explained in that the human mind has in belief more power to harm humankind than its substratum, matter. A patient hears the doctor's verdict as a criminal hears his death-sentence. After hearing bad news, the patient may seem calm, but this is not so. Fortitude may sustain the patient, but the fear, which has already developed the disease, is gaining the mastery and is increased by the physician's words.

---

[1] Gen. 2:17

Disease depicted

Doctors, therapists, and so on, though humane, are artists who outline their thoughts relative to disease. They then fill in their delineations with sketches from textbooks. It is better to prevent disease from forming in human mind afterward to appear on the body; but to do this requires attention. The thought of disease is formed before a doctor's visit, even before the doctor undertakes to dispel it with an antibiotic, a blood thinner, or a surgical operation.

A patient's belief is molded more or less by the doctor's belief in the case, even if the doctor says nothing. Given another direction to faith, the physician prescribes drugs until the flexibility of human thought, by chance, causes a vigorous reaction upon itself and reproduces a picture of health and harmony. The physician's thoughts and their patient's commingle, and the stronger thoughts rule the weaker. This is why it is important for doctors to study and practice the universal law of Truth and Love.

Mind over matter

Weight-lifters develop their muscles, but it doesn't mean that exercise has produced the result, or that a less used arm must be weak. If exercise was the cause of enlarged muscles, we can ask, Why didn't the weights increase in size? The muscles are as material as barbells. Furthermore, Can the muscles lift the weights without the impulse of human mind? This discrepancy between mind and matter is because nobody believes that mind is producing such a result on the weights.

Muscles are not self-acting. If mind does not move them, they are motionless. Hence the great fact that Mind alone enlarges and empowers through its mandate—by reason of its demand for and supply of power. Not because of exercise, but by reason of the weight-lifters faith in exercise do the muscles become stronger.

Dormant fear under control

Human beings develop their own bodies or make them sick according to how they influence them through mortal mind. To know whether this development is produced consciously or unconsciously is of less importance than knowledge of the fact. The skills of the gymnast prove that latent mental fears are subdued in thought. The commitment of thought to an honest achievement makes the achievement possible. Exceptions only confirm this rule, proving that failure is occasioned by a strong faith in failure.

If athletes believed it impossible to accomplish record-breaking feats, they could never do it. Their belief that they can achieve something spectacular gives their thought forces, called muscles, the flexibility and power which the unscientific might attribute to adrenaline or genes. Fear must disappear before the power of putting resolve into action can appear.

Spiritualized worship

For some cultures, worship began with muscularity, but the law of Sinai lifts thought into the song of David. Moses advanced a nation to the worship of God in Spirit instead of matter and illustrated the grand human capacities of being bestowed by immortal Mind.

A mortal is not person

Whoever is incompetent to explain Soul is wise not to undertake the explanation of body. Life is, always has been, and ever will be independent of matter/energy. Life is spiritual good, not formed physically, but metaphysically. Our real life is the idea of spiritual good and is not liable to decay and dust. The Psalmist said: "You have given them dominion over the works of your hands; you have put all things under their feet."[1]

The great truth in the Science of being, that our spirituality was, is, and ever shall be perfect, is indisputable. Our true self is the image, reflection, of God. God's children are not inverted or subverted, but upright and Godlike.

The self-styled human soul or spirit is not the divine infinite Spirit. In other words, the physiological and genetic view of spirit is diametrically opposed to Spirit—the flesh warring against Love. These mortal limited views must yield to the infinite Spirit, named God.

Paul said: "For I resolved to know nothing while I was with you except Jesus Christ and him crucified."[2] The Science of Christ, Truth, says: I am determined not to know anything among you, save Jesus Christ, and him revealed (glorified).

---

[1]   Ps. 8:6 (NRSV)

[2]   I Cor. 2:2

FOOTSTEPS OF TRUTH

Remember, Lord, how your servant has been mocked, how
I bear in my heart the taunts of all the nations, the taunts
with which your enemies have mocked, O Lord, with which
they have mocked every step of your anointed one.[1]

The best sermon ever preached is the practice and manifestation of
the Truth that replaces sickness, sin, and death. We can be committed
to only one ideal. Knowing this, Jesus was quoted to have said, "You
can't worship two gods at once."[2]

It is not safe to build on false foundations. Truth makes a new
creature, where "old things passed away; behold, new things have
come."[3] Obsessions, selfishness, misleading appetites, hatred, fear, and
lust give way to spirituality, and the superabundance of being is on the
side of God, good.

We cannot fill vessels already full. Vessels full of the impracticable
must first be emptied. Let us strip off error and stand in the showers of
God and come clean.

The way to extract error from human mind is to pour in truth
through flood-waters of Love. Spiritual perfection, including
Christian perfection, is won on no other basis.

Grafting spirituality onto something not spiritual is as foolish as
trying to "strain out a gnat" and "swallow a camel!"[4] Sin needs to be
abandoned before forgiven.

---

[1] Ps. 89:50-51
[2] Matt. 6:24; Luke 16:13 (The Message)
[3] II Cor. 5:17 (NASB)
[4] Matt. 23:24

The scientific relationship which exists between us and God must be worked out in life-practice. The will of God must universally be done.

Divine study and life-work

As we shift our faith and attention from the pains and pleasures of temporal sense to the study of the Science of divine Mind, we get better instead of worse. Suffering, imprisonment, and death are not natural disciplinarians. The whole human family can be redeemed through the excellence of Christ—through the perception and acceptance of Truth. For this magnificent result, Christian Science lights the torch of spiritual understanding.

Outside of divine Science all is relative. Earthly experience exposes the relativity of error, indirectly leading to the infinite capacities of Truth. Spiritual beings agree with the absolute and harmonious Principle of being. Immortality does not sin, suffer, or die and our spiritual experiences will multiply instead of diminish as God's kingdom comes on earth. The spiritual way leads to Life instead of to death and we realize our God-given dominion to overcome temporal limitations.

Belief and practice need to be the same

The thinking that God is all-power contradicts the practice of giving power to drugs or the human mind. Error abounds where Truth should "much more abound."[1] We admit that God has almighty power and is "an ever-present help in trouble,"[2] and yet we rely on drugs and the power of suggestion to heal disease and bad habits. Senseless matter or erring human mind has no power because omnipotent Spirit has all power.

Common opinion admits that a human being may catch a cold in the act of doing a good deed. Some people even fear and expect the cold to develop into a fatal pulmonary disease. Evil cannot overpower the law of Love and stop the reward for doing good deeds. In the Science of spirituality, Mind—omnipotence—has all-power. Divine

---

[1]   Rom. 5:20 (KJV)

[2]   Ps. 46:1

Mind, God assigns sure rewards to spiritual righteousness and shows that matter cannot heal or make sick, create or destroy.

If God were understood instead of only believed, this understanding would establish health. The church leaders of old accused Jesus, "because he claimed to be the Son of God."[1] The accusation was really the justification of Jesus, for to the Christ-like follower, the only true spirit is Godlike. The godly thought impels a more exalted worship and self-discipline. Spiritual perception brings out the possibilities of being and destroys reliance on anything accept God. Action and thought were made to image forth our Maker.

We are susceptible to believe in more than one supreme Ruler, or in some power less than God. We imagine that Mind can be imbedded in a sensuous body. What happens when the material body takes a turn for the worse and gives out? What happens when the belief of life in matter overloads and crashes? Do you believe the deathless Principle, or Soul, escapes from matter and lives on? But, this is unworkable. Death is not a springboard to eternal Life and happiness. The person who neglects their spirituality is a suicide. Sin kills the sinner and will continue to kill so long as sin is committed. The ranting and raving of illegitimate living and of fearful and pitiful dying should disappear on the shore of time where the waves of sin, sorrow, and death beat in vain.

God, divine good, does not kill humanity in order to give us eternal Life, for God alone is our life. It is evil that dies; good doesn't die. No matter where you are in the universe, God is the center and circumference of existence.

Spirit the only intelligence and substance

All forms of error support the false conclusion that there is more than one Life—a material life and a spiritual life. But, material history is not as real and living as spiritual history. Material or temporal evidence can't uphold itself as conclusively real. All erroneous evidence defends two separate antagonistic entities and beings, two powers— namely, Spirit and matter—resulting in a third power, called human beings, who carry out the delusions of sin, sickness, and death.

---

[1]   John 19:7

The power of Spirit is admitted to be good, an intelligence or Mind called God. The second power, called matter or evil, supposes there is something unlike good, but if the second power is unlike Mind then it is not intelligence. Consequently, the third power, believed to be human beings, is a supposed mixture of the first and second antagonistic powers, a mix of intelligence and non-intelligence, of Spirit and matter.

The theories that include many powers are erroneous and don't stand the test of divine Science. Judging them by their fruits, they are rotten. When will you understand your spiritual beingness and realize there is only one God, one Life or intelligence?

False and self-assertive theories have given sinners the notion that they can create what God cannot—namely, sinful mortals in God's image. This attitude takes God's name without the nature of the image of divine Mind. In Science, it is not true that people have a mind of their own, distinct from God. Everyone reflects, uniquely, the *all* Mind.

It is pantheistic to believe that the material universe is divine. God doesn't live in matter. We must look beyond the natural universe for divine Mind, otherwise the spiritual blindness causes us to stumble with lameness, drop with drunkenness, lean on matter, and consume with disease. Spiritual enlightenment confirms that God will not continue to be hidden from humanity.

Creation, divine image, perfect and perceptible

When will the error of believing that there is life in matter and that sin, sickness, and death are creations of God be exposed? When will it be understood that the inventions of human mind have no intelligence, life, or sensation? When will it be known that the prolific source of all suffering is the insistence that matter/energy has life and intelligence? God created all through Mind, and made all perfect and eternal. It is a belief to think we need to be created again.

We have a difficult time glimpsing God when we get distracted by material energy. By adjusting the out-of-tune thinking and getting in tune with Truth, we then can perceive the divine image in some word or deed, which indicates the true idea—the supremacy and reality of good, the nothingness and unreality of evil.

Redemption from selfishness

The divine law of loving our neighbor as ourselves unfolds as we realize that there is one Mind. On the flip side, a belief in many ruling minds hinders humanity's advancement toward the one Mind, one God. The assumption that there are numerous minds takes us down dead end roads where selfishness dominates.

Selfishness pulls the weight of human existence toward the side of error, not toward Truth. Denying the oneness of Mind also causes our energy to be put on the wrong side, not of Spirit, good, but of matter, mortality.

When we fully understand our relation to the Divine, we can have no other Mind—no other Love, wisdom, or Truth. In the divine relationship, there is no other sense of Life and no consciousness of the existence of matter or error.

Unrighteous will-power

It is only productive to exercise human will-power in subordination to Truth. Human-will has the tendency to misguide our decisions and bring out inferior tendencies. Mistaken human thoughts injure our self and others. It is the function of spiritual sense to direct man and woman aright.

Human will-power is liable to all evil. The willfulness of human mind can never heal the sick. Contrastingly, the exercise of spirituality—hope, faith, love—is the prayer of the righteous. The prayer governed by Science instead of human mortal selfhood, heals.

In our scientific relationship to God, we find that whatever blesses one blesses all. Jesus showed with the loaves and the fishes[1] that Spirit, not matter, is the source of supply.

Birth and death unreal

Does God give the parent a child, then take the child away by death? Can there be any birth or death for the spiritual image and likeness of God? Instead of God sending sickness and death, Spirit destroys them, and brings to light spirituality, of which there is no sickness and death. Omnipotent and infinite Mind made all and

---

[1]   Matt. 14:19; Matt. 15:36; Mark 6:44; Mark 8:6 Luke 9:16; John 6:11

includes all. This Mind does not make mistakes and subsequently correct them. God does not cause us to sin, to be sick, or to die.

Does God create anew what Life has already created? Nothing is new to God. The Scriptures are definite on this point, declaring that God's work was *finished*,[1] and that it was *good*.[2]

No evil in Spirit

There are evil beliefs, often called evil spirits; however, these evils are not Spirit, for there is no evil in Spirit. As we advance spiritually, evil becomes more apparent and obnoxious. Continuing to advance spiritually, material evil will disappear from our lives, because God is Spirit, reality. This fact proves our position, for every scientific affirmation in Christianity has its proof. Error of statement leads to error in action.

Subordination of evil

God is not the creator of an evil mind. Indeed, evil is not Mind. We must learn that evil is the awful deception and unreality of existence. Evil is not supreme; good is not helpless; nor are the so-called laws of matter primary and the law of Spirit secondary. Without this lesson, we lose sight of the perfect Source, or the divine Principle of spiritual selfhood.

Evident impossibilities

Body is not first and Soul last, nor is evil mightier than good. The Science of being rejects self-evident impossibilities, such as an alliance of Truth and error in cause or effect. Science separates the weeds and wheat in time of harvest.[3]

One primal cause

There is but one original cause. Therefore there can be no effect from any other cause, and there can be no reality in aught which does not proceed from this great and only cause. Sin, sickness, disease, and death belong not to the Science of being. Human beings ultimately cannot create their own reality; in other words, they cannot presume the absence of spiritual Truth, Life, or Love.

---

[1] Gen. 2:2

[2] Gen. 1:31

[3] Matt. 13:36-39

The spiritual reality is the scientific fact in all things. The spiritual fact, repeated in the action of person and the whole universe, is harmonious and is the ideal of Truth. Spirituality is not reverse. The contraposition, which bears no resemblance to spirituality, is not real. The only evidence of a reversal comes from the erroneous perceptions that offer no proof of God, Spirit, or of the spiritual creation. Mortal perceptions define all things temporally and have a finite sense of the infinite.

Seemingly independent authority

The Scriptures say, "For in him we live and move and have our being."[1] What then is this seeming power, independent of God, which causes disease and cures it? It is mortal thinking being projected outward—a law of human mind, a mistaken power, wrong in every sense, embracing sin, sickness, and death. The ostensible power of mortal thinking is the complete contrast to sacred Mind, to Truth, and to spiritual law. Temporal law has no agreement with the goodness of God's character. Soul cannot decide to make children sick and then leave the children to heal themselves. It is absurd to suppose that matter can both cause and cure disease or that Spirit, God, produces disease and leaves the remedy to matter.

Joyce Meyer wrote in her book *The Battlefield of the Mind*, "The mind is the leader or forerunner of all actions."[2] Statements such as are as a "voice of one calling in the desert,"[3] preparing humanity for the real and eternal. They lead thought to look past the superficial. Let us come to know the way of divine Science. Let us prepare for the supremacy of Spirit, the kingdom of heaven—the government and law of universal harmony, which cannot be lost or remain forever unseen.

Sickness as only thought

Mind, not matter, is causation. A material body only expresses a temporal and human mind. Human beings possess this body and make it harmonious or discordant according to the images of thought

---

[1]   Acts 17:28

[2]   Meyer, Joyce. *Battlefield of the Mind: Winning the Battle in Your Mind*. New York: Warner, 1995.

[3]   Isa. 40:3; Matt. 3:3; Mark 1:3; Luke 3:4

imprinted upon it. You embrace your body in your thought. Be sure to outline on the body thoughts of health, not of sickness. Make the effort to banish all thoughts of disease and sin and of other beliefs connected to mortality. Man and woman, being spiritual, have a perfect indestructible life. It is the mortal thinking which makes the body disordered and diseased in proportion as spiritual unawareness, *fear*, or human-will governs human beings.

Totality of Truth

Mind, supreme over all its formations and governing them all, is the central sun of its own systems of ideas. God is the life and light of all its own incalculable creation. We acknowledge divine Mind. The measurable human body or mind is not God's child.

The world would collapse without Mind, without the intelligence which holds the "winds"[1] in its grasp. Neither philosophy nor skepticism can hinder the movement of Science, which is ever revealing the supremacy of Mind. The intuitive sense of Mind-power reinforces the glory of Mind. Nearness, not distance, lends delight to this view.

Spiritual translation

Quantum mechanics; water on Mars; molecular structures and reactions; the patterns and relationships between masses and forces; wavelengths and so on, are of no real importance, when we remember that they all must give place to the spiritual fact by the translation of the universe and man and woman back into Spirit. As this transformation occurs, our true selfhood and the universe will be found harmonious and spiritual.

Genome sequences, radiometric dating, seismic surveys, data from satellites and space stations, and the paradigms of speculative theories, will all vanish in the presence of the infinite calculus of Spirit. Anything based on the hypothesis of physical law, or life and intelligence resident in matter, ultimately fades away.

Spiritual sense is a conscious, constant capacity to understand God. Spiritual sense shows the supremacy of faith "accompanied by

---

[1] Rev. 7:1

action,"[1] over faith in words. Spiritual ideas are expressed only in "new tongues."[2] These ideas are interpreted by the translation of the spiritual original into the language which human thought can comprehend.

Jesus' disregard of matter, human mind

Spiritual sense discerns the Principle and proof of the manifestation of God. Jesus was instrumental in setting forth Principle. His Christ-like proofs showed—by healing the sick, driving out evils, and destroying death ("the last enemy to be destroyed"[3]), his disregard of human mind and its fragmented laws.

Knowing that the attributes of Soul were forever manifested through man and woman, the Master gave sight to the blind, hearing to the deaf, feet to the lame, and healed the sick. Christ Jesus brought to light the scientific action of the divine Mind on human minds and bodies. He gave a better understanding of Soul and salvation. The Teacher healed sickness and sin by one and the same metaphysical process.

Divine Mind is not mortal

The expression *human mind* is really a grammatical error, because Mind is immortal. Truth pierces the ambiguous error of mortal humanity as a sunbeam penetrates the cloud. Error will always "sow the wind and reap the whirlwind."[4] The human mind is mortal, self-destructive, because it can't obey or disobey the spiritual law of Life, Truth.

Mindless matter/energy

What is termed matter, being unintelligent, cannot say, "I suffer, I die, I am sick, or I am well." It is the so-called human mind which voices this and appears to make good its claim. To human sense, sin and suffering are real, but spiritual sense includes no evil or epidemic. Because spiritual mind has no error of sense, it has no sense of error; therefore it is without a destructive element.

---

1   James 2:17
2   Mark 16:17
3   I Cor. 15:26
4   Hosea 8:7

Who will say whether Truth or error is greater? Are brain, nerves, and the stomach, intelligent? If they talk to us, tell us their condition and report how they feel—then Spirit and matter, Truth and error, commingle and produce sickness and health, good and evil, life and death.

The sensations of the body must either be the sensations of a human mind or of matter flesh. Nerves are not mind. It is provable that Mind, God, is not mortal. Is it not equally true that human mind and its matter flesh do not appear in the spiritual understanding of being?

Matter is without sensation

The sensation of sickness and the impulse to sin seem to come by the human mind. When a tear starts, doesn't this so-called mind produce the effect seen in the lacrimal gland? Without human mind, the tear could not appear; and this action shows the nature of all material cause and effect.

Do not fall back on the saying that "the fathers have eaten sour grapes, and the children's teeth are set on edge."[1] Sympathy with error should disappear. Science renders impossible the transfer of mistaken thoughts from one mind to another.

Nerves painless

Is it true that nerves have sensation? Does matter have intelligence? Do the material organs cause the eyes to see and the ears to hear? If so, when the body is dematerialized, these faculties must be lost, for their immortality is not in Spirit. The fact is, that only through a metaphysical dematerialization, can these faculties be conceived of as immortal.

Nerves are not the source of pain or pleasure. We suffer or enjoy in our dreams, but this pain or pleasure is not communicated through a nerve. Why, after pulling a bad tooth, can there sometimes be a continued belief of a toothache? What about phantom limb? A limb is felt, but there are no nerves. If the feeling can return, or be prolonged, why can't the limb reappear?

---

[1] Jer. 31:29; Ez. 18:2

Why does pain rather than pleasure, usually come to human perception? The memory of pain is more vivid than the memory of pleasure. I have seen an unconscious attempt to scratch the end of a finger which had been amputated. When the nerve is gone, which we say was the occasion of pain, and the pain still remains, it proves sensation to be in the human mind, not in matter. Reverse the process; take away this so-called mind instead of a piece of the flesh, and the nerves have no sensation.

Human fabrications

Human beings have a modus of their own, not directed and not sustained by God. They produce a rose through seed or grafts, and bring the rose into contact with the olfactory nerves that they may smell it. In the meantime, they automatically believe that organized matter produced the flower. God alone makes and clothes the lilies of the field,[1] and this is done by means of Mind, not matter.

No miracles in Mind-methods

Because all the methods of divine Mind are not understood, our conclusions are inconclusive. We think the lips or hands must move in order to convey thought. We think wave/particles are necessary to convey sound. And, what we don't understand we call a miracle. Whoever contradicts these conclusions is called a deceiver, or is said to be deceived, when in fact, Mind's normal action and the origin of all things, are unseen to human sense. It has been said of human beings, "As he thinks in his heart, so is he,"[2] but the realities of being can't be reversed conclusively. As we spiritually *understand*, so are we in truth.

Good is indefinable

Human mind conceives of something as gas, liquid, solid, or granular, and then classifies it quantitatively. Infinite and spiritual facts exist apart from limited conceptions. God, good, is self-existent and self-expressed, though indefinable as a whole. Every step toward spirituality is a step away from materiality and is a tendency toward God, Spirit. Material theories partially paralyze this attraction

---

[1]   Matt. 6:28; Luke 12:27

[2]   Prov. 23:7 (Amplified)

toward infinite and eternal good by a distraction to the measurable, flamboyant, and chaotic.

The physical ear does not really hear. Sound is a mental impression made on human belief. Divine Science reveals sound as communicated through the senses of Soul—through spiritual understanding.

Music, rhythm of head and heart

Mozart experienced more than he expressed. The exquisiteness of his grandest symphonies was never heard. He was a musician beyond what the world knew. This was even more strikingly true of Beethoven, who was for so long hopelessly deaf. Mental melodies and tones of sweet music supersede conscious sound. Music is the rhythm of head and heart. Human mind is the harp of many strings, conferring either discord or harmony, depending on whether the hand which sweeps over it is mortal or divine.

To believe in beginnings and endings is to abandon divine Mind as infinite Being. Before human-made learning plunged into the depths of a false perception of things, it is possible that the impressions from Truth were as distinct as sound, and that they came as sound to the early prophets. If the instrument of hearing is wholly spiritual, it is normal and indestructible.

Enoch's perception was not confined to the evidence before his physical senses. Therefore, he "walked with God"[1]—he ascended—Enoch was guided into the demonstration of life eternal.

Adam and the physical senses

Adam, represented in the Scriptures as formed from dust, is a case in point for the human mind. The physical senses, like Adam, originate in matter and return to dust. They are proved non-intelligent. Limited senses go out as they came in, for they are still the error, not the truth of being. When it is learned that the spiritual sense, and not the material, conveys the impressions of Mind, then Being will be understood and found to be harmonious.

Idolatrous illusions

We lend our self to matter and entertain limited thoughts of God the same way unbelievers do with their false gods. Human beings are

---

[1]   Gen. 5:24; Heb. 11:5

inclined to fear and to obey what they consider a material body more than they do a spiritual God. All knowledge based on matter, like the original "tree of knowledge,"[1] multiplies our pains, for mortal illusions would rob God and kill us. In the meantime, temporary knowledge spreads like cancer and gives thanks.

The senses of Soul

Human sight is unreliable when a wound on the retina may end the power of light and lens. But the real sight or sense is not lost. Accidents, or getting older, can't interfere with the senses of Soul, and there are no other real senses. Evidence confirms that the body, as a blob of matter, has no sensation of its own, and there is no oblivion for Soul and its faculties. Spirit's senses are without pain and they are forever at peace. Nothing can hide from spiritual sense the harmony of all things and the might and permanence of Truth.

Real being is never missing

If Spirit, Soul, could sin or be lost, then being and immortality would be lost, along with all the faculties of Mind; but being cannot be lost while God exists. Soul and matter stand apart from the very necessity of their opposite natures. Humanity is unacquainted with the reality of existence, because matter and mortality do not reflect the facts of Spirit.

Spiritual vision is not dependent on a physical location. Vision governed by God is never for an instant deprived of the light and might of intelligence and Life.

Light and darkness

We are sometimes led to believe that darkness is as real as light. Science affirms darkness to be only a human sense of the absence of light. Darkness loses the appearance of reality in the presence of light. So sin and sorrow, disease and death, are the supposed absence of Life, God, and vanish before truth and love.

With its divine proof, Science reverses the evidence of limited sense. Every quality and condition of mortality is swallowed up in spirituality. Mortals are the opposite of immortals in origin, in existence, and in their relation to God.

---

[1]   Gen. 2:9

Faith of Socrates

Socrates[1] did not fear his death sentence by hemlock poison, because he understood the superiority and immortality of good. The faith of his philosophy was audacious in the face of physical timidity. Having pursued spirituality, Socrates recognized the immortality of man and woman. Although Socrates was worthy of respect, the ignorance and malice of that time period killed him because of his faith in Soul and his indifference to the body.

The snake of error

Who will say that God's children are alive today, but may be dead tomorrow? What has touched Life, God, to such strange issues? Here theories cease, and Science unveils the mystery and solves the problem of man and woman. Error strikes the heel of truth, but cannot kill truth. Truth crushes the head[2] of error—destroys error. Spirituality lays open siege to materialism. On which side are we fighting?

Servants and masters

The understanding that the Ego, I AM, is Mind, and that there is but one Mind or intelligence, begins at once to destroy the errors of human sense and to supply the truth of spiritual sense. This understanding makes the body harmonious; it makes the nerves, bones, brain, etc., servants, instead of masters. If humanity is governed by the law of divine Mind, the body is obedient to everlasting Life and Truth and Love. The great mistake of human beings is to suppose that person, God's image and likeness, is both matter and Spirit, both good and evil.

If the decision were left to the physical senses, evil would appear to be the master of good and sickness the rule of existence. Health is not the exception, death is not the inevitable, and life is not pointless. Paul asked: "How can there be harmony between Christ and the devil?"[3]

---

[1] Socrates, (469-399BC) Greek philosopher. Charged, tried, and condemned to die in 399BC.

[2] Gen. 3:15

[3] II Cor. 6:15 (Phillips NT)

Personal identity

When we say things like, "My body is physical; my body is a shell, my body is spiritual," I say with Paul: Be "away from the body and at home with the Lord."[1] Give up your temporal belief that mind is in brain and have but one Mind, even God; for this Mind forms its own likeness. You will not lose your identity through the understanding which Science gives. The possibility of a lost identity is more absurd than to conclude that individual musical tones are lost in a grand symphony.

Paul's experience

Medical schools may inform us that the healing work of Christian Science—which proves Mind to be scientifically distinct from matter—implies an unnatural mental state. We could also be told that Paul's conversion indicates an abnormal mental and bodily condition, even hysteria or catalepsy. Notwithstanding, if we turn to the Scriptures, what do we read? "If anyone keeps my word, he will never see death."[2] And, "Regard no one from a worldly point of view."[3]

Fatigue is mental

That scientific methods are superior to others is seen by their effects. When you have conquered a diseased condition of the body through Mind, that condition never recurs and you advance in divine Science. For example, when a purified mentality gives rest to the body, the next toil will fatigue you less, for you are working out the problem of being in divine metaphysics. The scientific and permanent remedy for fatigue is to learn the power of Mind over the body or over any illusion of physical weariness. Material particles can't be weary and stressed. Remember, in proportion as you understand the control which Mind has over materialized human mind, you will be able to demonstrate this control.

You say, "This job tires me." But what is this *me*? Is it muscle or mind? What is fatigued and so speaks? Without mind, could the muscles be tired? Do the muscles talk, or do you talk for them? Matter

---

1   II Cor. 5:8

2   John 8:51

3   II Cor. 5:16

is non-intelligent. Human mind does the false talking and that which affirms weariness, made that weariness.

Mind never weary

You do not say a moving wheel is fatigued; and yet the body is as material as the wheel. Like the wheel, the body would never be weary, except for when the human mind says it is. The consciousness of Truth rejuvenates us more than hours of unconsciousness.

Coalition of sin and sickness

The body assumes to say, "I am ill." The reports of sickness may form a coalition with the reports of sin, and say, "I am revenge, lust, appetite, envy, hate." Sin and sickness are difficult to cure because the human mind is the sinner, refusing self-correction. Human mind insists the body can be sick independently of itself and that the divine Mind has no jurisdiction over the body.

Sickness related to sin (wrong-thinking)

Why pray for the recovery of the sick, if you are without faith in God's willingness and ability to heal? If you do believe in God, why do you substitute drugs for the Almighty's power? Why employ means which lead only into temporary, material ways of obtaining help, instead of turning in time of need to God, divine Love, who is an ever-present, permanent help?

Treat a thought of sickness as you would sin, with sudden refusal. Resist the temptation to believe in matter as intelligent, as having sensation or power.

The Scriptures say, "Those who look to the Lord will win new strength, they will soar as on eagles' wings; they will run and not feel faint, march on and not grow weary."[1] The meaning of that passage is not perverted by applying it literally to moments of fatigue, for the moral and physical are as one in their results. When we wake to the truth of being, all disease, pain, weakness, weariness, sorrow, sin, death, will be unknown, and the mortal dream will forever cease. My method of treating fatigue applies to all bodily ailments, since Mind should be, and is, supreme, absolute, and final.

---

[1]   Isa. 40:31 (REB)

Affirmation and result

In mathematics, we do not multiply when we need to subtract, and then say the answer is correct. No more can we say in Science that muscles give strength, or that nerves give pain or pleasure, or that genes and chemicals govern, and then expect that the result will be harmony. Material muscles, nerves, DNA, or bones are nothing without mind, but human mind keeps beating its head "against brick walls,"[1] whereas divine Mind heals.

When divine Mind's action is understood, we will never affirm concerning the body what we do not wish to experience. We will not call the body weak, if we would have it strong. The belief in feebleness must obtain in the human mind before it can be made manifest on the body. As the thinking that we are weak is removed, so are its effects. Science includes no rule of disorder, but governs harmoniously. "The wish," wrote Shakespeare "is ever father to the thought."[2]

Scientific beginning

We may hear a sweet melody and yet misunderstand the science that governs it. Those who are healed through metaphysical Science may not understand the Principle of the cure. They may even impute their recovery to change of air or diet, not rendering to God the honor due to Spirit alone. Entire immunity from the belief in sin, suffering, and death may not be reached at this level, but we may expect a decrease in these evils; and this scientific beginning is in the right direction.

Physical health regimes ineffectual

We hear it said: "I exercise every day and take vitamin C so I won't catch a cold. Yet, I always get a cold, have a runny nose, and cough non-stop." Admitting this is a first step to opening the mind to the futility of constantly paying attention to the material body. Futility often nudges us to look in other more effective directions for cause and cure.

Instinct is better than misguided reason, even as nature declares. The violet lifts her blue eye to greet the early spring. Tree leaves clap

---

[1]   Isa. 1:5 (The Message)

[2]   Shakespeare, William, (1564-1616) *Henry IV*, part 2, act IV, sc. 5, line 91.

187

their hands as lively worshippers as the wind gusts. The snowbird sings while securing a summer residence, never mind wet cold feet. Human beings on the other hand, overlook instinct and make things difficult. Earth's atmosphere is kinder than the atmosphere of human mind— kinder than the milieu crowded with thoughts of perfectionism, flu, colds, and allergies. Sicknesses and contagion are produced solely by human theories.

Self-deluded

Human mind procreates its own phenomena, and then credits them to something else—like a kitten glancing into the mirror at itself and thinking it sees another kitten.

A clergyman once adopted a diet of bread and water to increase his spirituality. Finding his health failing, he gave up his asceticism and advised others never to try dietetics for growth in grace.

The act of willing or determining something

The mistake of thinking that either fasting or feasting makes us better morally or physically is one of the fruits of "the tree of the knowledge of good and evil," concerning which God said, "you must not eat from."[1] Human mind forms all conditions of the human body and controls the organs, bones, genes, cells, blood, etc., as directly as the determination or will moves the hand.

Mind and stomach

I knew a person who when quite a child adopted a whole wheat and vegetarian diet to cure indigestion. For many years, he ate only bread and vegetables, and drank nothing but water. His dyspepsia increasing, he decided that his diet should be more rigid. So, he ate only one meal every twenty-four hours, a meal consisting of only a thin slice of bread. His physician recommended that he should not moisten his parched throat until three hours after eating. The person passed many weary years in hunger and weakness, almost in starvation. The skill of the doctors was exhausted and they kindly informed him that death was indeed his only alternative, so he finally made up his mind to die. Then divine Science saved him, and perfect health was restored without a reminder of the old complaint.

---

[1]   Gen. 2:17

188

This person learned that suffering and disease were the self-imposed beliefs of mortals, and not the facts of being. He recognized that God never decreed dis-ease—never ordained a law that fasting should be a means of health. Hence semi-starvation is not acceptable to wisdom, and it is equally far from Science, in which being is sustained by God, Mind. These truths opened the sufferer's eyes, relieved his stomach, and he ate without suffering, "giving God thanks." But, disciplined by self-denial and divine Science, he never enjoyed his food as he imagined he would back in the day when he was constantly hungry.

Starvation and eating issues

This new-born understanding that neither food nor the stomach, without the consent of human mind, can make us suffer, brings with it another lesson, that self-indulgence, gluttony, or bulimia, are sensual illusions and can't give you satisfaction. This phantasm disappears as we better understand our spiritual existence and walk the line of a balanced life.

Food affects the body only as fleshly mind has its material methods of working. One method is to believe that proper food supplies nutriment and strength to the human system. Another method is to believe we have no self-control. The human mind's recipe for health never gets it right, whereas Truth regenerates this fleshly mind and feeds thought with the bread of Life.

Food has less power to help or to hurt us after our thought has transformed to the spiritual. Without the consent of human mind, food and the stomach can't make you suffer. It is a human deception to believe you have to eat if you feel hungry. It is another deception to believe purging food will help you stay thin. As for the person mentioned above, taking less thought about what he ought to eat or drink, and consulting the stomach less and God more about the best way to live, he recovered strength and flesh rapidly. For many years he had been kept alive, as was believed, only by the strictest attention to fleshly health, and yet he continued ill all the while. After dropping drugs and his routine of severe dieting, he gave his attention to spiritual health, acted according to the improved mentality, and was well.

This person also learned that an afflicted person is nowhere close to being the image and likeness of God—nowhere close to being able to "rule over the fish of the sea and the birds of the air and over every living creature that moves on the ground,"[1] especially if eating a bit of animal flesh could overpower him. He finally concluded that God never made indigestion, while fear, diet, physiology, and physics did—contrary to God's order.

Life only in Spirit

In seeking a cure for digestive and food related problems, don't consult matter. You can understand how to eat what is put in front of you, "without raising questions of conscience."[2] We must destroy the false knowledge that life and intelligence are in matter. We must desire to establish ourselves in what is pure and perfect. Paul said, "Walk and live [habitually] in the [Holy] Spirit [responsive to *and* controlled *and* guided by the Spirit]; then you will certainly not gratify the cravings and desires of the flesh (of human nature without God)."[3] Sooner or later we will learn that restraints on our human abilities are pounded into us by the illusion that we live in body instead of in Soul.

Soul greater than body

Physical particle/waves do not express Spirit. God is infinite omnipresent Spirit. If Spirit is *all* and is everywhere, what and where is this limited so-called substance? Remember, truth is greater than error and we cannot put the greater into the lesser. Soul is Spirit, and Spirit is greater than body. If Spirit were once within the body, Spirit would be bound and therefore could not be infinite Spirit.

The question, "What is Truth," convulses the world. Many are ready to meet this inquiry with the assurance which comes of understanding. However, more people are blinded by their old misinterpretations and try to pass the question off. "If one blind person guides another, both will fall into a pit."[4]

---

[1]   Gen. 1:28

[2]   I Cor. 10:25, 27

[3]   Gal. 5:16 (Amplified)

[4]   Matt. 15:14 (NRSV)

The efforts to answer the question, "What is Truth," by some *ology* are vain. Spiritual reasoning and free thought accompany approaching Science, and cannot be put down. Divine logic and metaphysics will liberate humanity and strategically remove and displace unscientific means and laws.

Science getting our attention

Peals that should startle the trance-like thinker out of its erroneous dream are neglected. The last trump has yet to sound. Marvels, disasters, and sin will increase to urge human beings to stop resisting the claims of Truth. The awful daring of sin destroys sin and foreshadows the triumph of truth. God will overturn, until "He comes whose right it is."[1] Longevity is increasing and the power of sin diminishing, for the world feels the renewing effect of truth through every pore.

As the crude footprints of the past disappear from the dissolving paths of the present, we shall better understand the Science which governs these changes, and stand on firmer ground. Every sensuous pleasure or pain is self-destroyed through suffering. There can be painless progress, attended by life and peace instead of disorder and death.

Sectarianism and opposition

In the annals of Christianity, there are many sects but not enough spirituality. Centuries ago, religionists were ready to call on an anthropomorphic God and lavishly delegate human-like power with pomp and ceremony. However, this is not the manner of truth's appearing. The sign of suffering is more like it. The Roman era whip may have been more tangible than today's modern whip, but they both cut. Cold contempt, stubborn resistance, church opposition, state laws, and the press, still try to stop truth's full-orbed appearing.

A higher and more practical Christianity, demonstrating justice and meeting the needs of human beings in sickness and in health, stands at the door of this age, knocking for admission. Will you open or close the door upon this angel visitor? Will you welcome the angel who comes quietly, unpretentiously?

---

1   Ezk. 21:27 (NASB)

Gaining mental freedom

Truth encourages the elements of freedom. The Soul-inspired headline reads, "Terrorism Eliminated." The power of God brings deliverance. No power can withstand divine Love. What or who is it that makes the rules of exploitation and depression? What is it that draws us away from Spirit? How do we become saddled by wants and whims? What is it that holds human beings in the clutches of sin, sickness, and death? Truth makes us free.

Truth's ordeal

At first, Truth leads the few and faithful. As time marches on, the few and faithful thoughts of Truth move forward with the motto of freedom. The powers of this world will react and the old-guard will try to stop truth and make it submit to their human standards and systems. Science, not distracted by threats or assaults, continues to progress. There is always some chaos; however a mobilization to truth's standard is inevitable.

Immortal sentences

Improvement comes as mindsets improve. World history illustrates the might of Mind and shows human power to be proportionate to its embodiment of right thinking or spiritual clarity. Words and actions, breathing the omnipotence of divine justice and wisdom, are what powerfully break through discrimination, human agendas, and diminishing returns. Not by weapons and blood does the breath of freedom come. Love is the liberator.

Terrorism abolished

Legally to abolish terrorism in the world is difficult, but the elimination of mental terrors is a more difficult task. The domineering tendencies inherent in the human mind, and always germinating in new forms of tyranny, must be rooted out through the action of the divine Mind.

Men and women of all environments and cultures are still under the control of terrorists and bullies, ignorant how to obtain their freedom. However, the rights of humanity are being vindicated as people fight for equal rights and remove dictators from office. This pro-action is prophetic of furthering the banishment of world-wide oppression found on higher planes of existence and under more subtle and depraving forms.

Liberty's crusade

The voice of God in behalf of the people is reverberating around the world as the spokesperson of the new crusade sounds the keynote of universal mental freedom. A fuller acknowledgement of the rights of man and woman as useful spiritual beings demands that the terrors of sin, sickness, and death be exterminated from the human mind. Spiritual freedom is gained, not through human warfare, but through spiritual Science.

Cramping systems

God has built on divine claims, a higher platform of human rights. These claims are not made through human regulations or creeds, but in demonstration of "Peace upon earth among men of goodwill!"[1] Human policies, scholastic theology, and human health care systems lock our faith and spiritual understanding in hand cuffs. Divine Science rescues us, and our birthright of sole allegiance to our Maker asserts itself.

We can be saved from the bureaucracies and educational systems of today's Pharaohs. The disabled, the deaf, the dumb, the visually impaired, the sick, the sensualist, the sinner, can be saved from the terrors of their own beliefs. When I saw the sick, wearing out years of servitude to an unreal master in the belief that the body governed them, rather than Mind, I wanted to help. I saw before me the awful conflict, the Red Sea and the wilderness; however, I pressed on through faith in God, trusting Truth, the strong deliverer, to guide thought into the land of divine Science. In this land, or state of consciousness, limitations are overcome and the rights of man and woman are fully known and acknowledged.

Focus on higher law to end bondage

Oppressive laws are disputed and human beings are taught their right to freedom. From this same standpoint, the self-sabotaging physical senses must be denied and succeeded. The law of the divine Mind must end human repression, or human beings will continue to

---

[1]   Luke 2:14 (Phillips NT)

be unaware of their inalienable rights. People will be prone to hopeless obsessions because some public teachers permit an unawareness of divine power—an unawareness that is the foundation of anguish.

Native freedom

Discerning the rights of people, we can't fail to foresee the doom of all oppression. Trepidation and shock are not legitimate states of people. God made us free. Paul said, "I was born a citizen."[1] Humanity should be free to help themselves and society. "Where the Spirit of the Lord is, there is freedom."[2] Love and Truth make free, whereas evil and error lead into captivity.

Standard of liberty

Divine Science raises the standard of freedom and says: "Follow me! Escape from the control of sickness, sin, and death!" Jesus designated the way. Citizens of the world, accept the "glorious freedom of the children of God,"[3] and be free! This is your divine right. The self-deluded idolatrous views, not divine law, has captivated you, made you arthritic, made you a procrastinator, weakened your body, and ruined your reputation.

God did not institute physical laws to control us. We do not have to get sick because we went against a human-made health law. Jesus healed in direct opposition to, and in defiance of, all material laws and conditions. Jesus would not have disregarded any of God's governing laws.

No fleshly heredity

Genetics is a prolific subject for human belief to attach theories to; but if we learn that nothing is real but the right, we shall have no dangerous inheritances and fleshly ills will disappear. It would be impossible to transmit disease or certain human traits if this great fact of being was learned—namely, that nothing inharmonious can enter being, for Life *is* God.

---

[1]   Acts 22:28

[2]   II Cor. 3:17

[3]   Rom. 8:21

God-given dominion to be perfect

To be dependent on that which is constantly changing is not reasonable. False dependencies will cease as we recognize our God-given dominion over the temporal senses and enter into our heritage of freedom. Human beings will someday assert their freedom in the name of Almighty God. Dropping our present beliefs, we will recognize harmony as the spiritual reality, and disorder as the temporal unreality, and then control our own bodies through the understanding of divine Science.

Jesus said, "Do not worry about your life."[1] If we follow the direction of Jesus, we can depend less and less on bodily conditions, structure, or economy. We can be masters of the body, dictate its features, and form and control it with Truth.

The arrogance of church officials is humbled

There is no power apart from Mind. Omnipotence has all-power, and to acknowledge any other power is to dishonor God. The humble Nazarene overthrew the assumption that sin, sickness, and death have power. He proved them powerless. It should have humbled the arrogance of the priests when they saw the demonstration of spirituality excel the influence of their dead faith and ceremonies.

If Mind is not supreme over sin, sickness, and death, they are immortal. Particle/waves are the basis and support of sin and disease. Matter/energy has yet to prove it can destroy sin and disease.

Opposites don't unite

We should hesitate to say that Yahweh sins or suffers. If sin and suffering are realities of being, how did they first come about? God made all that was made, and Mind signifies God—infinity, not finity. The belief which unites opposites such as sickness and health is not far removed from infidelity. To believe that holiness comes into contact with that which is unholy—calling both the offspring of spirit, and at the same time admitting that Spirit is God—virtually declares God is good in one instance and evil in another.

By universal consent, the mortal mindset has constituted itself a law to obligate human beings to sickness, sin, and death. This

---

[1]   Matt. 6:25; Luke 12:22

programmed mindset and the individual who upholds it is mistaken in theory and in practice. The so-called law of human mind, conjectural and speculative, is made void by the law of spiritual Mind. Be sure to trample false law under foot.

Reasoning through typical conclusions

If God causes a person to be sick, sickness must be good, and therefore health must be evil, for all that He makes is good and will stand forever. Or, if violating God's law produces sickness, it is right to be sick; and we cannot if we would, and should not if we could, annul the decrees of wisdom. However, it is the transgression of a belief of human mind, not of a law of matter nor of divine Mind, which causes the belief of sickness. The remedy is Truth, not mortality—the truth that disease is illusion, *unreal.*

If sickness is real, it belongs to spirituality; if true, it is a part of Truth. Would you attempt with drugs, or without, to destroy a quality or condition of Truth? On the flipside, if sickness and sin are unfiltered and unprocessed images, divine Science can filter and process the images and show us health, holiness, and spirituality. This process or clarification of information is accomplished through Spirit, Christ, or the advanced appearing of Truth which is benefiting people and healing the sick. This is the salvation which comes through God, the divine Principle, Love, as demonstrated by Jesus.

God never inconsistent

It would be contrary to our highest ideas of God to suppose She makes unwise decisions, or is capable of arranging law and causation so as to bring about certain evil results. Would God punish helpless victims for doing what they could not avoid doing? Good is not, cannot be, the author of experimental sins. God, good, can no more produce evil or sickness, than health can produce disease.

Mental narcotics

Does wisdom make gross mistakes which afterward must be corrected by man or woman? Does a law of God produce sickness, and can we put that law under our feet by healing sickness? According to Holy Writ, the sick are never really healed by drugs, hygiene, or any material method. Temporal methods merely evade the question and are soothing syrups to put children to sleep, satisfy human belief, and avoid fear.

The true healing

We think that we are healed when a disease disappears, though it is liable to reappear. We are never thoroughly healed until the liability to be ill is removed. Mortal mind is the distant, near, and quickening cause of all suffering. The cause of disease must be obliterated through Truth, in divine Science, or the physical senses will get the victory.

Destruction of all evil

Unless an ill is rightly met and fairly overcome by Truth, the ill is never conquered. If God does not destroy sin, sickness, and death, they are not destroyed in the mind of human beings and seem to be immortal. We do not need to attempt to do what God can't do. If God doesn't heal the sick, they are not healed, for no lesser power equals the infinite All-power; however, God, Truth, Life, Love, does heal the sick through the prayer of the righteous.

If God makes sin, if good produces evil, if truth results in error, then Science and Christianity are helpless; but there are no antagonistic powers nor laws (spiritual or material), creating and governing us through perpetual warfare. God is not the author of fleshly disorders. Therefore, we accept the conclusion that disorders have only a fabulous existence and are human beliefs which divine Truth and Love destroy.

Superiority to sickness and sin

To hold yourself superior to sin, because God made you superior to it and governs us, is true wisdom. To fear sin is to misunderstand the power of Love and the divine Science of being in our relation to God—to doubt and distrust Soul's omnipotent care. To hold yourself superior to sickness and death is equally wise, and is in accordance with divine Science. To fear them is impossible, when you fully understand God and know that disease and dying are no part of Life's existence.

Under the umbrella of our Maker, we can have no other Mind. Secure on the Evangelist's statement that "all things were made;

without him nothing was made that has been made,"[1] we can triumph over sin, sickness, and death.

Denials of divine power

Many theories relative to God and creation do not make a lovable God or harmonious children. The beliefs we commonly entertain about happiness and life actually lack evidence of permanent joy and life. The unspoiled claims of harmonious and eternal being are discovered only in divine Science.

Scripture informs us that "with God all things are possible"[2]—all good is possible to Spirit. Prevalent theories practically deny this and make healing possible only through matter, however, these theories are not true, because spiritual good is possible to God. Christianity is not false, but religions which contradict its Principle are false.

Spirituality is again demonstrating the power of divine Principle, as it did over twenty centuries ago, by healing the sick and triumphing over death. Jesus never taught that drugs, food, air, and exercise could make people healthy. Jesus also didn't teach or practice that drugs, food, air, and exercise could destroy human life. He assigned harmony to Mind, not to matter/energy. He was very clear on God's ruling which condemned sin, bad health, and dying.

Signs following

Voices of solemn import are heard in the sacred sanctuary of Truth. Are we heeding these voices? If so, we are burying error and resurrecting to spiritual life. These signs are seen when the temporary pleasures and pains pass away from our lives.

Profession and proof

There is neither place nor opportunity in Science for error of any sort. Every day makes its demands upon us for better proofs rather than verbal claims of Christian power. These proofs consist solely in the destruction of sin, sickness, and death by the power of Spirit, as Jesus destroyed them. This is an element of progress and progress is the law of God whose law demands of us only what we can certainly fulfill.

---

[1]   John 1:3

[2]   Matt. 19:26

Perfection gained slowly

Surrounded by imperfection, perfection is seen and acknowledged only by degrees. People must slowly work toward perfection. How long it must be before we arrive at the demonstration of scientific being, no person knows—not even "the son, but only the Father."[1] The false claim of error continues its delusions until the goal of goodness is steadfastly earned and won.

Christ's mission

Already the shadow of God's right hand rests on the hour. For those of you who "know how to interpret the appearance of the sky,"[2] the physical sign—how much better is it to discern the mental sign? Mental interpretation destroys spiritual unawareness and ill-health by overcoming the thoughts which produce them and by understanding the spiritual idea which corrects and replaces them. Jesus' mission was to reveal the truth of spiritual reality to all humankind, even to the hearts which rejected him.

Effectiveness of truth

When numbers have been divided according to a fixed rule, the answer is unquestionable. The scientific tests I have made concerning the effects of truth upon the sick are just as unquestionable. The counter fact relative to any disease is required to cure it. Truth spoken and realized is designed to disprove and destroy error. Why shouldn't truth also destroy sickness, which is solely the result of disharmony?

Spiritual involvement heals, while material attachment interferes with truth, even as ritualism and creed stifle spirituality. If we trust matter, we distrust Spirit.

Crumbs of comfort

Song, sermon, and Science—crumbs of comfort—are capable to inspire us with wisdom, Truth, and Love. Spiritual comfort blesses the human family, feeds the unsatisfied, and gives living water to the thirsty.

---

[1] Mark 13:32

[2] Matt. 16:3; Luke 12:56

Welcome health and goodness

It is most beneficial to become more familiar with good than with evil. We can guard against false beliefs as diligently as we bolt our doors against the approach of thieves and murderers. We should love our enemies and help them on the basis of the Golden Rule, "Do to others what you would have them do to you."[1] Avoid throwing "your pearls to pigs,"[2] because then everyone loses out.

Cleaning the mind

If human beings would properly guard against human mind, the aggravating posterity of evils would be cleared out. We must begin with the human mind and empty out its negativity and self-delusion, or negativity and self-delusion will never cease. The conventional human systems disappoint the weary searcher who is looking for a divine theology, a theology adequate to teach rightly.

Sin and disease are thought before they are manifest. You must control evil thoughts in the first instance or they will control you in the second. Jesus declared that to look with desire on forbidden objects was to break a moral precept. He laid great stress on the action of the human mind, unseen to the senses.

Evil thoughts and aims reach no farther and do no more harm than one's thinking permits. Lusts and malicious purposes can't move around like wandering viruses from one human mind to another if virtue and truth build a strong defense. Not even the unsuspecting host can be contaminated. It is important to be aware of your mental environment so as not to be a naive receptor of evil thoughts. You would rather choose a doctor who has the flu to treat you, than be treated mentally by a metaphysician who isn't obeying the requirements of divine Science.

Educator's functions

Character development should be strongly fortified with virtue. It is not so much academic education, as an ethical and spiritual learning which improves the character. The pure and uplifting thoughts from teachers and instructors, constantly imparted to pupils, reach higher

---

[1] Matt. 7:12

[2] Matt. 7:6

than the heavens of astronomy. Corrupt and dubious minds, though gifted with scholarly attainment, will degrade the characters it should inform and elevate. Strive to see the whole picture when selecting teachers and speakers. It is imperative to consider the instructor's morality along with their credentials and skill level.

Physicians' privilege

Physicians, whom the sick employ in their helplessness, should be models of integrity. They should be wise spiritual guides to health and hope. To the frightened patient on the brink of death, physicians can be prepared to share an understanding of the Truth that is Life. When the soul is willing and the flesh is weak, the patient may be willing to learn of the ever-perpetuating Life, and plant their feet on the rock of Christ, the true idea of spiritual power.

The duty of spiritual leaders

Clergy, chaplains, and spiritual leaders, observing the world, should advance the standard of Truth. They can inspire their hearers spiritually so that listeners will love to grapple with a new right idea, and broaden their views. Love of spirituality, rather than love of popularity, should stimulate work and progress. Truth should emanate from the pulpit, but never be strangled there. A special privilege is commissioned in the ministry. How will it be used? The privilege of the ministry should be used sacredly in the interests of humanity, not of sect.

Aren't prestige and profit, rather than the dignity of God's laws, what many leaders pursue? Let's face it, these inferior motives indirectly lead to the furious attacks on the purely motivated people who are healing through divine Mind.

Responsibility of parent

A parent is the strongest educator either for or against crime. Parental thoughts form the embryo of another human mind and unconsciously shape it, either after a model that niggles the parent, or through divine influence "after the pattern for them, which was shown to you on the mountain."[1] Spiritual Science helps us learn of the one Mind and of the availability of good as the remedy for every problem.

---

[1]   Ex. 25:40 (NASB)

Children's adaptability

Teaching children, at the earliest stages possible, the realities of health and holiness is extremely beneficial. Children are more tractable than adults, and learn more readily to love the simple truths that will make them happy and good. Children can learn that obedience to parents and guardians promotes self-control. Disobedience blights.

Jesus loved little children because of their freedom from wrong and their receptiveness to right. While adults hesitate between two opinions or argue with false beliefs, youth makes easy and rapid strides toward Truth.

A little girl, who had occasionally listened to my explanations, badly wounded her finger. She seemed not to notice the wound. On being questioned about it she answered ingenuously, "There is no sensation in matter." Running off with happy eyes, she presently added, "Mamma, my finger is not a bit sore."

Soil and seed

It might have been months or years before the child's parents would have laid aside their drugs or reached the mental height their little daughter so naturally attained. The more stubborn beliefs and theories of parents often choke the good seed in the minds of themselves and their offspring. Superstition, like "the birds of the air,"[1] snatches away the good seed before it has sprouted.

Instructing children

Teaching children divine Science among their first lessons is useful. This includes monitoring and reducing discussions, theories, or thoughts about sickness. To prevent the experience of error and its sufferings, keep out of the minds of your children either sinful or diseased thoughts. Diseased thoughts are excluded on the same principle as the exclusion of sinful thoughts. This makes divine Science available early on in life.

Deluded invalids

Some invalids are unwilling to know the spiritual facts. They don't want to hear about the deception of temporal things and false laws. They even devote themselves a little longer to their material gods and

---

[1]   Matt. 13:4; Mark 4:4; Luke 8:5

cling to a mortal life and intelligence. They expect this error to do more for them than they are willing to admit the only living and true God can do. Impatient at your explanation, unwilling to investigate Science, they embrace false thinking more fully, and suffer the delusive consequences. Mind-Science however, could purge them of their problems.

Patience

Intent and action are not properly valued before they are understood. It is well to wait until those whom you would benefit are ready for the blessing. Science is working changes in personal character as well as in the temporal universe.

To obey the Scriptural command, "Come out from their midst and be separate,"[1] is to invite society's disapproval; but this disapproval, more than approval, enables one to be spiritual. Pope John Paul II said, "We cannot live for the future without intuiting that the meaning of life is greater than temporality and is above it. If the societies and the men of our continent have lost interest in such a meaning, they must rediscover it."[2] The Biblical Paul realized, "If God is for us, who can be against us?"[3]

Unimproved opportunities

To fall away from Truth in times of persecution, shows that we never understood Truth. The voice of wisdom calls a warning from the wedding banquet, "I don't know you."[4] Unimproved opportunities will rebuke us when we attempt to claim the benefits of an experience we have not made our own, or try to reap the harvest we have not sown Truth often goes ignored until we suffer severely from error and seek a spiritual remedy for human troubles.

Leaving all for Christ includes forsaking popularity and gaining true Christianity. Any attempt to engage society's friendship in order to gain dominion over humankind comes from worldly weakness.

---

[1]   II Cor. 6:17 (NASB)

[2]   Excerpt from *Day by Day with Pope John Paul II*, edited by Angelo Pisani, Copyright © 1980 by Piero Gribaudi.

[3]   Rom. 8:31

[4]   Matt. 25:12

Society and intolerance

Society is a foolish juror, listening only to one side of the case. Justice often comes too late to secure a verdict. People with mental work before them have no time for gossip about false law or testimony. To reconstruct timid justice and place the fact above the falsehood, is the work of time.

For Christianity, the cross is the central emblem of history. It is the guiding star in the demonstration of Christ-like healing—the demonstration by which sin and sickness are destroyed. The sects, who endured the abuse of their predecessors, in turn, may badly treat those who are in advance of creeds.

Right views of humanity

Material wealth, fame, and social organizations have no authority or influence in the presence of God. We attain clearer views of Principle as we break up cliques, level monetary wealth with honesty, and let worth be judged according to wisdom. We also get better views of humanity as we remove our self from biased personal perceptions.

Wicked human beings are not the rulers of upright neighbors. Let it be understood that success in error is defeat in Truth. The password of divine Science is Scriptural: "Let the wicked abandon their ways and the evil their thoughts."[1]

Standpoint revealed

To discover our progress, we must learn to what we are attached. What do we acknowledge and obey as power? If divine Love is becoming nearer, dearer, and more real to us, matter is then submitting to Spirit. The goals we pursue and the spirit we manifest reveal our standpoint and show what we are winning.

Antagonistic sources

Human mind is the acknowledged seat of human motives; it designs limited concepts and produces all bodily malfunctions. Action proceeding from erring human mind is inappropriate and ends in sin, sickness, and death. Appropriate action proceeds from the divine Mind. Those two opposite thought sources never mingle in cause or effect. Imperfect human mind projects outward its own resemblances

---

[1]   Isa. 55:7 (REB)

of which the wise man said, "Everything is meaningless."[1] The perfect Mind expresses perfection, for God is immortal Mind.

Some lessons from nature

Nature voices spiritual law and divine Love, but the human mortal mindset misinterprets nature. Arctic regions, sunny tropics, coral reefs, the Mid-Atlantic Ridge, flowering deserts, and galaxies—all point to Mind, the spiritual intelligence they reflect. The floral apostles are hieroglyphs of Deity. Quantum mechanics, gravity, and the cosmos teach grand lessons. The stars make night beautiful, and the leaf turns naturally toward the light.

Perpetual motion

In the order of Science, in which the Principle is above what it expresses, all is one grand agreement. Change this statement, suppose Mind to be governed by matter or assume that Soul is in the body and you will lose the keynote of being, and there is continual disagreement. Mind is perpetual motion. Its symbol is the sphere. The rotations and revolutions of the universe of Mind go on eternally.

Progress demanded

Humanity moves toward good or evil as time passes. If mortals are not progressive, past failures will be repeated until all wrong work is erased or corrected. If there is any satisfaction in wrongdoing, we must learn to loathe it. If we are now content with spiritual idleness, we must become dissatisfied with it. Remember that humankind must sooner or later, either by suffering or by Science, be convinced of the error that is to be overcome.

The effort to unlearn false perceptions includes forfeiting those views completely. Then error will be submissive to Truth. The divine method of becoming responsible for every thought and action, involves unwinding our snarls and learning from experience how to divide between the human and the spiritual.

"The Lord disciplines those he loves."[2] A person who refuses obedience to God is chastened by Love. People who know and obey

---

1   Eccl. 1:2

2   Heb. 12:6

God's will, or the demands of divine Science, will run up against the hostility of envy.

The doom of sin

Sensual treasures are stored "where moth and rust destroy."[1] Mortality is their doom. Sin breaks in and steals them away, carrying off their superficial joys. The sensualist's feelings are as imaginary, capricious, and unreal as their pleasures. Deceit, jealousy, hypocrisy, selfish ambition, hate, revenge, and so forth, steal away the treasures of Truth. Stripped of its coverings, what a mocking spectacle is sin!

Spirit transforms

The Bible teaches that Spirit renews and transforms the body. Take away the spiritual meaning of Scripture, and that collection of works can no more help human beings than moonbeams can melt a river of ice. The error of all generations is preaching without practice.

The substance of all commitment is the reflection and demonstration of divine Love. As we find progressive answers to problems and destroy sin and sickness, we are committed substantially. The Teacher said, "If you really love me, you will keep the commandments I have given you."[2]

The goal, a point beyond faith, is to find the footsteps of Truth, the way to health and spirituality. It is necessary to make a sincere effort to reach the Horeb height where God is revealed. The cornerstone of all spiritual building is purity. Spirit's baptism washes the body of all fleshly impurities and shows that the pure in heart see God. We approach spiritual Life and its demonstration through purity.

Spiritual baptism

It is "easier for a camel to go through the eye of a needle,"[3] than for materialist convictions to enter the kingdom of heaven, eternal harmony. Through repentance, spiritual baptism, and reformation, humanity advances past beliefs and false individuality. It is only a question of time when "they will all know me [God], from the least of

---

[1] Matt. 6:19, 20; Luke 12:33

[2] John 14:15 (Phillips NT)

[3] Matt. 19:24; Mark 10:25; Luke 18:25

them to the greatest."[1] Denying the claims of matter/energy is taking an important step toward the joys of Spirit, toward human freedom and the final triumph over the body.

The one only way

There is but one way to heaven, harmony, and Truth in divine Science shows us this way. It is to know no other reality—to have no other consciousness of life—than good, God and Spirit's reflection. Spiritual harmony, happiness, or Christ-likeness includes ascendancy over physical pain and pleasure.

Self-worship is denser than a solid body. In patient obedience to a patient God, let us labor to dissolve with the universal solvent of Love the congealed mass of error. Let us work to bankrupt selfish-will, self-justification, and self-worship, which are errors that compete against spirituality and are the investors in sin and death.

Divided clothing

The clothing of Life is Truth. According to the Bible, the facts of being are commonly misconstrued, for it is written: "They divided my garments among them and cast lots for my clothing."[2] The divine Science of person is woven into one garment of consistency without seam or rip. Mere speculation or superstition cannot divide the divine clothing, whereas spiritual inspiration can restore every fiber of the Christly garment of righteousness.

The sign-posts of divine Science show the way the Teacher walked. We are required to offer the same proof and not just talk about the walk. We may be able to hide from the world our neglect of putting into practice our spiritual power; however, negligence and hypocrisy have no part in the success of Science and in our demonstration of spiritual good.

Ancient and modern miracles

The divine Love, which made harmless the poisonous viper, which delivered men from the fiery furnace, boiling oil, and jaws of the lion, can also heal the sick in every era and triumph over sin and death. Love honored the demonstrations of Jesus with unsurpassed power

---

[1]   Jer, 31:34; Heb. 8:11 (Brackets added by Mary Baker Eddy)

[2]   Ps. 22:18; John 19:24

and compassion. But the same, "attitude . . . as that of Christ Jesus"[1] must always accompany the letter of Science in order to confirm and repeat the ancient demonstrations of prophets and apostles. That those wonders are not more commonly repeated today stems not so much from lack of desire as from lack of spiritual growth.

Mental communication

Computer software can't inform the programmer. The stomach, heart, colon, and lymph nodes don't inform us that they are nauseous, diseased, cancerous, or invaded by malignant tumors. If this information is conveyed, human mind conveys it. Negative information certainly doesn't come from immortal Mind and it can't come from inanimate matter/energy. God's "eyes are too pure to look on evil,"[2] and physicality has neither intelligence nor sensation.

Self-nihilistic error

Truth has no consciousness of error. Love has no sense of hatred. Life has no partnership with death. Truth, Life, and Love are a law of annihilation to everything unlike themselves, because they declare nothing except God.

Deformity and perfection

Sickness, sin, and death are not the merchandise of Life. They are simulations or virtual realities, which Truth destroys with immortal reality. Soundness does not animate defects. God is good and as the source of all being, God does not produce moral or physical deformity, therefore such deformity is not real, but is illusion—is the mirage of error. Divine Science reveals these grand facts. On their basis Jesus demonstrated Life, never fearing or obeying error in any form.

If we were to derive all our conceptions of people from what is seen between the cradle and the grave, happiness and goodness would have no home for us. Bacterium would rob us of the flesh. We would ultimately have no substance. However, Paul writes: "The law of the Spirit of life set me free from the law of sin and death."[3]

---

[1]   Phil. 2:5

[2]   Hab. 1:13

[3]   Rom. 8:2

Person never less than person

To undergo birth, maturity, and decay is like the beasts and vegetables—answerable to laws of deterioration. If man and woman were dust in the earliest stage of existence, we might admit the hypothesis that people eventually return to that primitive condition; but man and woman is not more or less than God's child.

If man and woman end in death or wait to come from dust, there must be instants when God is without the entire manifestation. There can't be one instant when infinite Mind isn't fully reflected.

Person not evolved

In Science, person is not young or old; we have no birth or death; we are not a beast, a vegetable, or an evolving mind; we do not advance from mortality to Mind, from the materialist to the spiritual. We do not rise from evil to good, or even shift from good to evil. Confessing to a state of mortality throws us headlong into darkness and dogma. Too much is written on that which advocates pictures of abnormal phases and helplessness. It is better to assign to humanity the everlasting grandeur and immortality of improvement, spiritual power, and prestige.

The error of thinking that we are growing old, and the benefits of destroying that illusion, has noticeable results. Most of us have met someone considered old, but very much young in mind/body/spirit. These people have been interviewed and questioned. Are they lucky? Is it their genes? Is it the food they eat? Maybe or maybe not, however, they usually always attribute their longevity to a positive and loving attitude.

Perpetual youth

The error of thinking that we are growing old, and the benefits of destroying that illusion make for a better life. Care-lined faces, wrinkles, and gray hair are not a law while youthfulness is an attribute of God.

Why not notice the manifestations of Spirit rather than the passing of years? Why not maintain a mental attitude of being young? As our consciousness of the eternal replaces the consciousness of time, we literally could grow no older.

From an empirical point of view, we know cell divisions take place in each living being continuously. Old cells in our bodies die and yield their place continuously to the new cells that are forming.

It is made plain that decrepitude is not according to law, nor is it a necessity of nature, but an illusion. There are many examples of perpetual youth, untouched by time, in the world. These examples furnish a useful hint to the ingenious mind that might work with more certainty than when Bill Gates[1] tapped into instantaneous and seamless communication and commerce around the globe by means of computers, unrestricted by the obstacle of time.

Impossibilities never occur. Years don't make us older. Our convictions manifest on our bodies, so why not have a sprightly conviction?

Man and woman reflects God

The infinite never began and it will never end. Mind and its formations can never be annihilated. God's child is not on a roller coaster, reeling between evil and good, joy and sorrow, sickness and health, life and death. Life and its faculties are not measured by calendars. The perfect and spiritual are the eternal likeness of their Maker. We aren't struggling to rise from an imperfect origin to Spirit. The stream rises no higher than its source.

Measuring life by solar years steals from our prime and gives ugliness to age. The radiant sun of virtue and truth coexists with being. Manhood and womanhood is its eternal noon, undimmed by a declining sun. As the physical and material, the transient sense of beauty fades, the radiance of Spirit illumines spiritual sense with bright and imperishable glories.

Undesirable records

Don't keep records of the aging process. Chronological data is no part of the vast forever. Albums that record births and deaths are so many conspiracies against manhood and womanhood. Measuring and limiting all that is good and beautiful is an age-old habit. If not for that routine, we would enjoy our advanced years and still be vigorous,

---

[1]   William Henry Gates III, philanthropist, author, and former CEO and current chairman of <u>Microsoft</u>, (1955—)

light-hearted, and full of promise. Governed by spiritual Mind, we are always graceful and noble. Each succeeding year unfolds wisdom, beauty, and holiness.

True life eternal

Life is eternal. We should find this out, and begin the demonstration thereof. Life and goodness are spiritual. Let us then shape our views of existence into loveliness, renewal, and consistency, rather than into decrepitude and loss.

Acute and chronic beliefs reproduce their own types. Acute beliefs of physical life come later on, and are not as disastrous as the chronic beliefs.

Eyes and teeth renewed

I have seen adults regain two of the elements they had lost, sight and teeth. A woman of eighty-five, whom I knew, had a return of sight. Another woman at ninety had new teeth, incisors, cuspids, bicuspids, and one molar. One man at sixty had retained his full set of upper and lower teeth without a decaying cavity.

Eternal beauty

Beauty, as well as truth, is eternal; but the beauty of material things passes away—fades and vanishes as mortal beliefs. Tradition, education, and fashion form the illusive standards of human beings. Spirituality, exempt from decline or decay, has a glory of its own—the radiance of Soul. People are models of spiritual sense. Our spirituality is designed by perfect Mind and reflects those higher conceptions of loveliness which transcend all false conceptions.

The divine loveliness

Good looks and poise are independent of matter. Being possesses its qualities before they are perceived humanly. Beauty is a thing of life. It dwells forever in the eternal Mind and reflects the living God in expression, form, outline, and color. It is Love which paints the petal with countless hues. It is Love that pours in the warm sunbeam, arches the cloud with the bow of beauty, blazons the night with starry gems, and covers the earth with loveliness.

Cosmetic surgery, botox, and body decoration are inadequate substitutes for the attractiveness of spirituality. Our spiritual nature is stunning and ongoing. It outperforms the aging process.

The recipe for beauty is to have less illusion and more Soul. Retreat from the belief of pain or pleasure in body and advance into the unchanging calm and glorious freedom of spiritual harmony.

Love's gift

Love never loses sight of loveliness. Its halo rests on its object. Isn't it amazing that a friend is always beautiful? Men and women of seasoned years and increased wisdom ought to advance in spirituality and health, instead of lapsing into gloom and doom. Spiritual Mind renews the body with nice features. God supplies the body with beautiful images of thought; which destroy the complaints of mortal sense bent on bringing us to the grave.

Mental sculpture

Sculptors turn from the marble to their model in order to perfect their conception. We are all sculptors, working at various forms, molding and chiseling thought. What is the model before human mind? Is it imperfection, joy, depression, sin, suffering? Have you accepted the human model? Are you reproducing it? Then you are haunted in your work by vicious sculptors and hideous forms. Don't you hear from all humankind of the imperfect model? The world is continually holding it before your observation. The result is that you are liable to follow those ruinous prototypes, limit your lifework, and adopt into your experience the angular outline and deformity of mortal models.

Perfect models

To remedy this, we must first turn our attention in the right direction and then walk that way. We must form exact God-like models in thought and look at them continually or we shall never carve them out in grand and noble lives. Allow unselfishness, goodness, mercy, justice, health, holiness, and love to control your mind and body. As the kingdom of heaven is found within, then sin, disease, and death will diminish until they finally disappear.

Let us acknowledge Science. Let us stop accepting theories based on temporal sense-testimony. Give up imperfect models and illusive icons. Let us have one God, one Mind, and that one perfect, producing Spirit's own models of excellence.

Renewed selfhood

Allow the "male and female"[1] of God's creating to appear. Let us feel the divine energy of Spirit, bringing us into newness of life and recognizing no human or material power as able to destroy. Let us rejoice that we are open to the divine "governing authorities."[2] Such is the true Science of being. Any other theory of Life, or God, is delusive and mythological.

Mind is not the author of delusive soulless substance. Either there is no omnipotence, or omnipotence is the only power. God is infinite substance, and infinity never began, will never end, and includes nothing unlike God. From what source then is soulless matter?

Illusive dreams

Life is, like Christ, "the same yesterday and today and forever."[3] Organization and time have nothing to do with Life. You say, "I dreamed last night." What a mistake! The "I" is Spirit. God never sleeps and never dreams, so, God's likeness is conscious and doesn't dream. Mortals are the Adam dreamers.

Sleep and apathy are dimensions of the dream that life, substance, and intelligence are temporal, measurable. Ironically, the human night-dream is sometimes closer to the fact of being than are the thoughts of human beings when they are awake. For example, the night-dreams present fewer limitations, less bulk. The dreamer can freely fly through the air.

Philosophical blunders

People are the reflection of Soul, the direct opposite of tactile matter, and Soul is the one Ego. We run into error when we divide Ego into egos or multiply Mind into minds. Misunderstandings occur when we suppose error to be mind, mind to be in matter and matter to be a lawgiver. We feel stuck between a rock and a hard place when we assume unintelligence is to act like intelligence or that mortality is the matrix of immortality.

---

1   Gen. 1:27

2   Rom. 13:1

3   Heb. 13:8

Spirit the one Ego

Mortal existence is a dream; mortal existence has no real entity, but mimics "I Am." Spirit is the Ego which never dreams, but understands all things. Spiritual Ego never mistakes and is always conscious. Spirit never believes or decides, but knows; Soul is never born and never dies. Spiritual person is the likeness of this Ego. We are not God, but we are the outcome of God. We reflect God.

Mortal existence a dream

Human body and mind are one, and that one is called man and woman, but a human is not person, for person is immortal. Depending on the dreams we entertain when asleep, human beings can find themselves in pain, afraid, in danger, enjoying or suffering. From an observer's point of view, our minds and bodies are sleeping, insensible. Moreover, when we wake up, the feelings vanish and we realize we are no longer experiencing those dream-sensations.

Is there any more reality in the waking dream of human existence than in the sleeping dream? There can't be, since whatever appears to be a human being is a mortal dream. Take away the mortal human mind and the body doesn't know if it is a person or a bird. The immortal, real person is spiritual.

Human existence is like a soap-opera. The human mind's performance consists of mortal thoughts chasing after each other only to always find disaster and heartache. Conversely, in the theater of divine Science, Life is revealed as not being at the mercy of mortality. Science cannot admit that happiness is ever the sport of circumstance.

Error self-destroyed

Error does not need to demand more and more attention as it accelerates toward self-destruction. Let's take an abscess. The sore does not need to become more painful before the pus is absorbed or drained. Or, in the case of a fever, the fever doesn't need to become severe or critical before it ends.

Illusion of death

Fear can be so great at certain points, that human thought will automatically be pushed into a new path. If thought takes the path of death, mortals wake to the knowledge of two facts: (1) that they are not dead; (2) that they only entered into a different or interim belief.

This is why those people who have been termed "clinically dead" come back with stories to tell. Truth works out the nothingness of error in just these ways. Sickness, as well as sin, is an error that Christ, Truth, alone can destroy.

Human mind's disappearance

We must learn how humankind governs the body—whether through faith in hygiene, in drugs, or in will-power. Does humankind govern the body through a belief in the necessity of sickness and death, sin and pardon? Or, does humanity govern it from the higher understanding that the divine Mind makes perfect? Divine Mind acts on the human mind through truth, leading it to relinquish its falsities. Our spiritual mindedness sees divine Mind to be the only Mind and the healer of bad-will, diseases, and fatality. This process of higher spiritual understanding improves humanity until error disappears, and nothing is left which deserves to perish or to be punished.

Spiritual unawareness

Lack of immortal awareness, which is identical to intentional wrong, is not Science. Ignorance must be seen and corrected before we can reach harmony. Chaotic and contradictory beliefs commit identity theft, giving matter the identity of Mind. These beliefs also set their own imaginations up as all-important (even as heroes), and thereby isolate themselves to, or confine themselves in, what they create. Beliefs are at war with Science, and as Jesus said, "Every city or household divided against itself will not stand."[1]

Any skepticism in regard to the pathology and theology of divine Science comes from being unfamiliar with Mind. Skepticism is also occasioned by an unawareness of the recuperative energies of Truth.

Eternal person recognized

Knowledge of error and how it operates must precede the understanding of Truth. When false human beliefs learn even a little of their own falsity they begin to disappear. Spiritual understanding then destroys error until the entire human, materialist error finally disappears. The eternal verity, man and woman created by and of Spirit, is understood and recognized as the true likeness of our Maker.

---

[1]   Matt. 12:25; Mark 3:24-25; Luke 11:17

The illusive evidence of physical sense certainly differs from the testimony of Spirit. Physical sense lifts its voice with the arrogance of reality and boasts: I am completely dishonest, and people don't know it. I can commit adultery, cheat, lie, steal, and murder. I evade detection by pretending to be a victim. My tendency is irrational, my feelings are deceitful, and my purpose is fraudulent, but I aim to make my short span of life one big fling. Resistance to spirituality is fantastic! How it succeeds, where the good purpose waits! The world is my territory. I am popular, surrounded by materialism. However, a reality check, an accident, or the law of God may at any moment annihilate my peace, for all my fancied joys are fatal. Like bursting lava, I increase but to my own despair, because the over-rated mortal life is a consuming fire.

The testimony of Spirit, Soul, maintains: I am Spirit. Man and woman, whose perceptions are spiritual, are my likeness, reflecting the infinite understanding, for I am Infinity. The beauty of holiness, the perfection of being, and imperishable glory—all are Mine, for I am God. I give spirituality, for I am Truth. I include and impart all happiness, for I am Love. I give life, without beginning and without end, for I am Life. I am supreme. I am an unlimited source of good ideas, for I am Mind. I am the substance of all, because "I AM WHO I AM."[1]

Heaven conferred prerogative

I hope, dear reader, I am leading you into the understanding of your divine rights, your heaven-bestowed harmony. I hope, as you read, you see there is no cause (outside of human imprints which are not power) able to make you sick, troubled, or sinful. I also hope that you are conquering human-egocentric thinking. Knowing the illusiveness of limited perceptions, you can assert your prerogative to overcome the belief in a worthless self, in disease, or mortality.

Right endeavor possible

If you believe in and practice wrong knowingly, you can at once change your course and do right. Matter can make no opposition to right endeavors against sin or sickness, for matter can't do anything on

---

[1]   Ex. 3:14

its own without mind. If you believe you have a disease, you can alter this wrong belief and action without hindrance from the body.

Do not believe in any supposed necessity for failure, adversity, or ruin, knowing (as you ought to know) that God never requires obedience to a physical law because no such law exists. Linear thinking is destroyed by the law of God, which is the law of Life eternal instead of death, the law of harmony instead of disorder, the law of Spirit instead of the flesh.

Patience and final perfection

The divine demand, "Be perfect, therefore, as your heavenly Father is perfect,"[1] is scientific, and the human footsteps leading to perfection are requisite. Individuals are consistent, who, watching and praying, can "run and not grow weary . . . walk and not be faint,"[2] who gain goodness rapidly and hold their position, or attain slowly and yield not to discouragement. God requires perfection, but not until the battle between Spirit and flesh is fought and the victory won. To stop eating, drinking, or being clothed materially before the spiritual facts of existence are gained step by step, is not legitimate. When we wait patiently on God and seek Truth righteously, Spirit directs our thought and action. Imperfect human beings grasp the ultimate of spiritual perfection slowly; but to *begin* aright and to continue the strife of demonstrating the great problem of being is doing much.

During the sensualist age, absolute divine Science may not be achieved prior to the change called death, for we have not the power to demonstrate what we do not understand. The human self must be evangelized. This task God demands us to accept gracefully today, and to abandon so fast as practical the temporal, and to work out the spiritual which determines the outward and actual.

If you float on the quiet surface of error and are in sympathy with error, what is there to disturb the waters? What is there to strip off error's disguise?

---

1   Matt. 5:48

2   Isa. 40:31

Reward of a fulfilled responsibility

If you dare to launch your ship on the ever-agitated but healthful waters of truth, you will encounter storms. The good you do will be spoken of as evil. This is the responsibility. Be accountable. For in answering to Spirit you will win and feel the honor. Stranger on earth, your home is heaven; foreigner, you are the guest of God.

CREATION

Your throne was established long ago; you are from all eternity.[1]

We know that the whole creation has been groaning as in the pains of childbirth right up to the present time. Not only so, but we ourselves, who have the firstfruits of the Spirit, groan inwardly as we wait eagerly for our adoption, the redemption of our bodies.[2]

Inadequate theories of creation

Eternal Truth is changing the universe, and physical forces are trying to keep up. Don't be impressed by materialist views that support physical forces, but instead, experience spiritual thought expanding into expression. "Let there be light,"[3] is the perpetual demand of Truth and Love, changing chaos into order and discord into the music of the spheres.[4] The mythical and scholarly theories of creation provide nothing to build on and are a far cry from views of creation as revealed by infinite Mind.

Limited views of God

Human beings habitually belittle divine Mind with immature perceptions. In league with physical sense, mortals take limited views of all things. That God is bodily or material, no person should affirm.

---

[1]   Ps. 93:2

[2]   Rom. 8:22-23 (TNIV)

[3]   Gen. 1:3

[4]   Music of the spheres is a concept frequently credited to Greek philosopher Pythagoras (569 B.C.—approximately 500 B.C.

The human form or physical structure can't be made the basis of any true idea of infinite God. Physical eyes and ears have not seen or heard Spirit.

No material creation

Progress removes the restraints imposed on human beings. The finite must yield to the infinite. Advancing to a higher level of activity, consciousness pierces the materialist view and discovers the spiritual view. Thought shakes off the scholastic and mortal and moves toward the inspirational and immortal. All things are created spiritually. Mind, not matter, is the creator. Love, the divine Principle, is the Father-Mother of the universe, including person.

Trinity

The theory of the Trinity as being three persons in one God suggests polytheism or multiple personalities, rather than the one ever-present I AM. "Hear, O Israel: The Lord our God, the Lord is one"[1]

No divine body form

The everlasting I AM is not bounded or compressed within the narrow limits of physical humanity, nor can Spirit be correctly understood through mortal concepts. The precise form of God is not very important. Ask rather; What is infinite Mind or divine Love?

Who is it that requires our obedience? God, who "controls the stars in the sky and everyone on this earth. When God does something, we cannot change it or even ask why."[2]

No form or physical organization can adequately represent Love. A materialist's sense of God leads to narrow-mindedness and formality in which Christianity loses its warmth and sincerity.

Limitless Mind

A limitless Mind will not be known through a limited human mind. Finiteness can't present the idea or the vastness of infinity. A mind which came from a limited source will be limited. Infinite Mind is the creator, and creation is the infinite image or idea emanating from this Mind. If Mind is within and without all things, then all is Mind, and this definition is demonstrable.

---

[1] Deut. 6:4

[2] Dan. 4:35 (CEV)

Material particles are not substance

If matter is shadow, and Spirit is substance, then matter can't produce substance any more than shadow can produce substance. The theory that Spirit is not the only real substance is pantheistic heterodoxy to those who worship Spirit. The belief that matter and spirit are a mixture leads to sickness, sin, and death. Measurable particles and waves produce measurable outcomes, but Spirit is immeasurable.

Mind creates the likeness of ideas, and the substance of an idea is polar opposite to the substance of non-intelligent matter. God did not create a physical universe as described through a materialist view. Materialist views confuse spiritual ideas with human conceptions and lean toward anthropomorphism. God is not anthropomorphic, but is divine Principle—in other words, divine Love—and brings "forth the constellations in their seasons,"[1] and leads "out the Bear with its cubs."[2]

Inexhaustible divine Love

A limited mind manifests all sorts of anomalies, and causes the mind-in-matter theory to be seen as a riddle. Who has found temporal mind sufficient to satisfy the demands of human lack and anguish? Our desires and aspirations ache to be fulfilled. We only feel a reward when we stop limiting infinite Mind to finite resources. Infinite Mind can't lose its character as inexhaustible Love, eternal Life, omnipotent Truth.

Infinite physique impossible

It would require an infinite form to contain infinite Mind, indeed the phrase *infinite form* is an oxymoron. Finite human beings cannot be the image and likeness of the infinite God. A mortal or finite conception of God cannot embrace the glories of limitless, bodiless Life and Love. It's no wonder we crave something better, higher, and holier than is afforded by the belief in a physical creator and creation. The insufficiency of a limited creation proves its falsity.

---

[1] Job 38:32

[2] *ibid*

Infinity's reflection

People are more than a material shell with a mind stuck inside. Spirituality is more than a soul trying to escape a human experience in order to be immortal. We reflect infinity, and this reflection is the true idea of God.

Spiritual selfhood is infinitely being expressed, broadening and ascending from a boundless basis. Mind manifests all that exists in the infinitude of Truth. The only way we will know our true self, is to know God properly.

The infinite Principle is reflected by the infinite idea and spiritual individuality, but the human ego and physical senses have no cognizance of either Principle or its idea. As spiritual mindfulness gains the true perception of God and creation, the human abilities are refined and sharpened.

Individual permanency

Mortals have an imperfect understanding of spiritual being and its infinite range of thought. Eternal Life belongs to spiritual being. Never born and never dying, it is impossible for people, under the government of God in eternal Science, to fall from an immortal status.

God's person perceived

Through spiritual perception we can discern the heart of divinity and thereby begin to understand the generic term *person*. Our spirituality is not absorbed in God. We do not become isolated or trapped in a vacuum. Our individuality goes on and on reflecting Life eternal. We each represent the totality of infinite Mind's substance.

In divine Science, person is the true image of God. The divine nature was skillfully personified by Christ Jesus, who shed light on a powerful concept of God. He shifted the people's thought to experience something better than what they had been trained to think was normal. Jesus served to remove the stereotypical view of people as sinners, destined to be sick and dying. The Christ-like understanding of scientific being and divine healing includes a perfect Principle and idea—complete God and complete person—as the basis of thought and demonstration.

The divine image is not lost

If person was once complete or perfect, but then lost his/her perfection, then the image of God was never known. The *lost* image is not an image. The true likeness can't be lost in divine reflection. Understanding this, Jesus said: "You shall be perfect, just as your Father in heaven is perfect."[1]

Immortal models

Human perceptions transmit their own images and form offspring after human illusions; whereas God, Spirit, works spiritually, not materially. The brain is an electrical device unable to originate a human concept, because electricity has no intelligence, no creative ability. Immortal ideas—pure, perfect, and enduring—are transmitted by the divine Mind through Science and demands spiritual thoughts to the end that they may produce harmonious results.

The study of divine Science helps eliminate a faulty thought process. Reasoning that begins with imperfection will end with imperfection. Reasoning that begins with perfection will arrive at perfection. A sculptor can't perfect her outlines while concentrating on an imperfect model. The painter can't depict the features and appearance of Jesus while thinking about the character of Judas Iscariot.

Spiritual discovery

The perceptions and realities of mortal thought either die or give way to the spiritual discovery of completeness and eternity. Through many generations, human beliefs reach diviner conceptions and the immortal model of God's revelation is finally seen as the only true conception of being.

Science not only reveals reasonable possibilities, but also prompts human beings to discover what God has already done. You must trust your ability to experience goodness and to bring out better and higher results. Don't become a sluggard. Be alert to Spirit so as to save yourself from the possibility of failure.

---

[1]   Matt. 5:48 (NKJV)

Requisite change of our ideals

A sick body evolves from sick thoughts. Illness, disease, and death proceed from fear. Debauchery causes hurtful physical and moral conditions.

Promiscuousness and self-centeredness are educated in mortal mind when humans repeat the same thoughts over and over. This education is at the expense of spiritual growth. Don't be surprised, when wrapping yourself up in mortal thinking, you will lose out wearing your immortal nature. It is better to stop talking constantly about the body or expecting pleasure or pain from it.

Thoughts are things

When we expect pleasure from the body, we get pain. When we look for life in the body, we find death. When we search for Truth or Spirit in material things, we find uncertainty. Now reverse this process. Look away from matter into Truth and Love, the Principle of all happiness, harmony, and immortality. Let your thought embrace the enduring, the honest, and the genuine, and you will bring these into your experience according to how often they occupy your thoughts. We are learning that the human mind affects our health and happiness.

Unreality of pain

There are innumerable accounts of people becoming preoccupied and as a consequence forgetting their body and its complaints. Our attention can be so focused on reaching a spiritual goal that pain is forgotten and shown to be powerless in the presence of good works. For example, after the September 11th, 2001 plane attacks on the Twin Towers in New York City, many people, especially firefighters performed miraculous feats saving lives while oblivious to their own bodies.

Our immutable identity

Detach feelings from the body, or matter, which is only a type of human belief. Learn the meaning of God, or good, and the nature of the immutable and immortal. Don't worry when breaking away from mutating time and feelings, because you will not lose your sense of reality, or your own identity. As you contemplate spiritual life, consciousness is purified and being groomed to experience the celestial; similar to a chick which has broken from the shell and preens its wings for a skyward flight.

Forgetting the temporal self

We can forget the body while remembering good and the human race. Good compels us to solve the problem of being. Commitment to good increases our dependence on a spiritual God and shows a paramount necessity to be responsible to Truth and Love. Divine Science does not claim the perfection of God, but ascribes to God the entire glory. By taking "off your old self with its practices,"[1] mortals are clothed "with immortality."[2]

Humans can't figure out the nature and quality of God's creation by diving into shallow materialist beliefs. The efforts to find life and truth in matter is tentative, therefore we must improve the effort and pay attention to spiritual sense and an immortal idea of substance. Spiritual, clearer, higher views inspire the Godlike person to reach the absolute center and circumference of reality.

The true perception

Job said: "My ears had heard of you but now my eyes have seen you."[3] Humans will echo Job's thought when the pain and pleasure of material bodies cease to predominate. People can learn to distinguish between fake happiness and true. We can feel the pleasure of loving unselfishly, working patiently, and conquering all that is unlike God as we highly value spiritual perceptions. "For where your treasure is, there your heart will be also."[4]

Mind the only cause

Where does the cacophony of life come from? Disorder comes when matter is considered to be a cause. Matter is not a cause or effect. Divine Mind is the only cause or Principle of existence. Your thought process, or mental treatment must begin with divine Mind, not the brain, not human mind, not physical form.

---

[1]   Col. 3:9

[2]   I Cor. 15:53

[3]   Job 42:5

[4]   Matt. 6:21; Luke 12:34

Human egotism

Human beings are egotists. They stroll around believing themselves to be independent workers, elite authors, or privileged originators of something God could in no way ever manifest. The creations of human mind represent the foibles of existence, whereas spiritual people represent the truth of creation.

Mortals are mis-creators

When human beings blend their thoughts of existence with the spiritual and work only as Truth and Love works, they will taste heaven and stop groping in the dark and clinging to the world. In his book, *The Power of Now,* Eckhart Tolle says, "You can still be active and enjoy manifesting and creating new forms, and circumstances, but you won't be identified with them. You do not need them to give you a sense of self. They are not your life—only your life situation."[1] It is important to remember to stay out of the dark beliefs that cheat us and make us involuntary hypocrites. Don't be induced to believe you are doing good when really you are producing evil, injuring others, and deforming goodness. People who think they are a semi-god will mis-create. In Bible language: "I cannot be good as I desire to be, and I do wrong against my wishes."[2]

No new creation

There can be but one creator, who has created all. Whatever seems to be a new creation is only the discovery of some distant idea of Truth; or else it is a self-division of mortal thought. The human mind is not an originator, but is a mime, attempting to mimic the divine infinite.

The multiplication of a human sense of persons and things is neither creation nor revelation. A temporal thought, like an atom of dust thrown into the face of spiritual immensity, is dense blindness instead of a scientific eternal consciousness of creation.

---

[1] *The Power of Now: A Guide to Spiritual Enlightenment* Copyright 1999 by Eckhart Tolle. Reprinted with permission of New World Library, Novato, CA www.NewWorldLibrary.com

[2] Rom. 7:19 (Moffatt)

Mind's true camera

The relativity of matter, the complex human body, and the turbulent earth are fleeting concepts of humans, trained to believe life is mortal. Fleeting concepts have their day before the permanent facts and their completeness in Spirit appears. The complicated creations of human thought must finally give place to the glorious forms which we sometimes glimpse through the eye of divine Mind when the mental picture is spiritual and eternal. Take the time to look past the fading, sensational pictures. Gain the true sense of life. Rest your gaze on the unsearchable realm of Mind. Look ahead and act as possessing all power from Truth and Love in whom you have your being.

Self-completeness

As humanity expands their correct views of God and creation, countless objects, which you did not see before, will be seen. When you realize that Life is Spirit, never in nor of matter, this understanding will develop into self-completeness, finding all in God, good, and needing no other consciousness.

Spiritual proofs of existence

What are the realities of being? Spirit and its formations. In other words, matter is not a reality of being, but is an incorrect or undeveloped view of reality which disappears as Spirit comes into view. Jesus overcame sickness and death and proved they were forms of error. Spiritual living and blessedness are the only evidences, by which we can recognize true existence and feel the unspeakable peace which comes from an all-engaging spiritual love.

The approach of divine Science is to recognize the spiritual identity of people and to see and understand God's creation—all the glories of earth and heaven and its inhabitants.

Gravitating toward God

The universe of Spirit is peopled with spiritual beings, and its government is divine Science. Man and woman are the offspring of the highest qualities of Mind. We understand spiritual existence in proportion to our understanding of Truth and Love. Humans must gravitate Godward. Humans will become more humane as their desires and aims grow spiritual. As sin and mortality are discarded, human

227

beings catch the broader interpretations of being and secure a lasting sense of the infinite.

This scientific sense of being, turning from matter to Spirit, by no means suggests we are absorbed into Deity or that we lose our identity. A scientific sense of being reveals a clearer distinct individuality, a wider sphere of thought and action, a more expansive inclusive love, and a more permanent peace.

Mortal birth and death

Mortal birth and death comes across as irresistible or untimely, however God's people aren't mortals. Mortals are unreal and obsolete. The truth of being is perennial. We are God's image and likeness.

Advancing from pain

When we feel the loss of human peace, the desire for spiritual joy gets stronger. This desire for heavenly good comes even before we discover what belongs to wisdom and Love. The loss of earthly hopes and pleasures can brighten the spiritual path. Pain in the body informs us that pleasure in the body is mortal, compelling us to discover spiritual joy.

Deleting error

The pains of the body can be salutary if they force the mind to dig itself out of false beliefs and transplant its affections in Soul, where the creations of God are good, "giving joy to the heart."[1] The sword of Science decapitates error with the blade of Truth. Materiality gives place to our higher individuality and destiny.

Uses of adversity

Would life without friends be empty? Then the time will come when you will feel alone, without sympathy, but this vacuum is filled with divine Love. When this time comes, even if you cling to a sense of personal joys, spiritual Love will force you to accept what best promotes your spiritual growth. Friends will betray and enemies will slander, until the lesson is learned, and you are exalted; for "man's extremity is God's opportunity."[2] I speak from experience. We are

---

[1]   Ps. 19:8

[2]   Quote attributed to John Flavel, (1627-1691) English Presbyterian.

learning to lay down our fleshliness and gain spirituality by ridding our self of a mortal identity. Universal Love is the divine way.

Wrongdoers make their own hell by doing things which avoid Life, Truth, and Love. Saints make their own heaven by embracing Life, Truth, and Love. Wrongdoers believe they are happier when being negative, but this is evil aiding evil. Do not be deceived by inverted human conclusions.

Presence that exalts

Following Jesus' sayings and demonstrations, we help our self to overcome the flesh. The sordid and narrow beliefs which originate in mortals are hell. Spiritual person is the idea of Spirit, reflecting the presence of virtue and illuming the universe with light. Spirituality is deathless, above sin or frailty. We do not cross over into the vast forever of Life, but we coexist with God and the universe. Complete and infinite Mind ordained, is heaven.

The infinitude of God

The objects of material thinking will be destroyed while the spiritual idea, whose substance is in Mind, is never destroyed. The offspring of God don't start from dust or a material gene. The offspring of God are in and of Spirit, divine Life, and so forever continue. God is one. The allness of Deity is God's oneness. Generally, person is one, yet person also means all people.

It is generally agreed upon that God is Father, eternal, self-created, infinite. If this is true, the forever Father must have had children prior to Adam. There is no linear life cycle that begins with Adam. We coexist with God. The great, I WILL BE WHAT I WILL BE[1] made all "that has been made."[2]

The Bible records Jesus saying, "For whoever does the will of my Father in heaven is my brother and sister and mother."[3] In a religious sense, the common name of mother, brother, and sister is identified with those doing God's will.

---

[1]   Ex. 3:14

[2]   John 1:3

[3]   Matt. 12:50; Mark 3:35; Luke 8:23

Signs to eternal Truth

When examined in the light of divine Science, we see beyond the surface of mortals and detect inverted thoughts and erroneous beliefs and learn not to be fooled by them. Or, in a circuitous manner, we borrow thought from a higher source than matter and reverse our thought process, to see celestial Truth replace error. Clothed in Spirit, appearance is "bright as a flash of lightning"[1]—like the garment of Christ. Even in this world, therefore, "always be clothed in white."[2] "Anyone who meets a testing challenge head-on and manages to stick it out is mighty fortunate. For such persons loyally in love with God, the reward is life and more life."[3]

---

[1] Luke 9:29

[2] Eccl. 9:8

[3] James 1:12 (*The Message*)

SCIENCE OF BEING

That which was from the beginning, which we have heard, which we have seen with our eyes, which we have looked at and our hands have touched—this we proclaim concerning the Word of life, . . . We proclaim to you what we have seen and heard, so that you also may have fellowship with us. And our fellowship is with the Father and with his Son, Jesus Christ.[1]

Here I stand. I can do no otherwise; so help me God! Amen![2]

In this world, *thought* rapidly brings to light many useful wonders. The force of thought also advances toward the spiritual cause of those things that give impulse to inquiry. Humanity is slowly yielding to the thoughts of Mind and looking away from physics to metaphysics as the cause of every effect. In this revolutionary period, physical hypotheses challenge metaphysics to meet in final combat. Like the shepherd-boy with his sling; we go forth to battle with the Goliath[3] of the human mind and its material world.

Confusion confounded

In this final struggle for supremacy, semi-metaphysical systems offer no substantial aid to scientific metaphysics. Arguments that try to integrate the inconsistent inventions of the human mind with the

---

[1]   I John 1:1, 3

[2]   Martin Luther, (1483-1546) Christian theologian and Augustinian monk whose teachings inspired the Reformation and influenced the culture of the Lutheran and Protestant traditions.

[3]   Referring to I Sam. 17

facts of Mind savor confusion, pandemonium, a house divided against its self.[1]

To suppose that eternal Mind and temporal human mind, or good and evil, coexist, is to agree with the philosophy of the serpent[2] as read about in the Bible. Jesus' demonstrations sift the chaff from the wheat,[3] and unfold the oneness and reality of good. The nothingness of evil becomes apparent in the presence of infinite good.

Divine mentality

Human philosophy has made God humanlike. Divine Science makes person Godlike. Human philosophy is error. Divine philosophy is truth. Metaphysics is above physics and the materialist thinking does not enter into metaphysical premises or conclusions. Metaphysics resolves things into thoughts and exchanges the objects of sense for the ideas of Soul.

Immortal ideas are perfectly real and tangible to spiritual consciousness and they have this advantage over the objects and thoughts of limited senses—they are good and eternal.

Biblical foundation as a means to reject theories

The testimony of human perceptions is neither absolute nor divine. I therefore stand unreservedly on the teachings of Jesus, of his apostles, of the prophets, and on the testimony of the Science of Mind. There are no other foundations. All other systems—systems based wholly or partly on knowledge gained through the physical senses—are reeds swayed by the wind,[4] not houses built on the rock.[5]

Divine Science rejects the following theories: (1) that all is matter or the human mind; (2) that matter or the human mind originates in Mind and is as real as Mind, possessing intelligence and life. The first theory, that matter is everything, is about as illogical as the second, that Mind and matter coexist and cooperate. One only of the following

---

[1] Matt. 12:25; Mark 3:25; Luke 11:17

[2] Gen. 3

[3] Matt. 3:12; Luke 3:17

[4] Matt. 11:7; Luke 7:24

[5] Matt. 7:24; Luke 6:49

statements can be true: (1) that everything is human mind; (2) that everything is divine Mind. Which one is it?

Human mind and divine Mind are opposites. One is contrary to the other in its very nature and essence. Consequently, they both can't be real. Only by understanding that there is but one power—not two powers—are scientific and logical conclusions reached. We must continue to admit that spiritual intelligence is apart from mortal beings and matter, and is expressing and controlling the universe. Spiritual intelligence is synonymous with the eternal Mind or divine Principle, Love.

Prophetic lack of knowledge

Prophets looked for something higher than the systems of their times; hence their foresight of the new dispensation of Truth, but they lacked a systematic teaching of God in Truth's more infinite meaning. The demonstration that destroys sin, sickness, and death is now presented in divine Science which establishes the definition of omnipotence while maintaining the Science of Spirit.

The arrogance of being a church official is the ruler of this world. Arrogance has nothing in Christ. Humility, honesty, and charity have divine authority. Mortals think wrongly; consequently they seem to work against themselves. They think sickly thoughts, and so become sick. If sin makes sinners, Truth and Love alone can unmake them. If a sense of disease produces suffering and a sense of ease antidotes suffering, disease is mental. Logic has it that the human mind suffers and is sick, and the divine Mind alone heals.

The life of Christ Jesus was not miraculous, but it was indigenous to his spirituality—the good soil wherein the seed of Truth is heard, understood, and producing a great crop.[1] Spirituality is the consistent link of scientific being, connecting all space/time in the design of Love. Illusion, chance, and depleted vitality do not exist in divine Science.

Jesus instructed his disciples to heal the sick through Mind instead of matter. He knew that the philosophy, Science, and proof of spirituality were in Truth, overcoming all disorders and confusion.

---

[1]   Matt. 13:23; Mark 4:20; Luke 8:15

Diligent students

In Latin the word *disciple* signifies student, a learner. The power of healing was not a supernatural gift to those learners, but the result of their cultivated spiritual understanding of the divine Science which their Teacher illustrated by healing the sick and sinning. Jesus' prayer includes us: "My prayer is not for them alone. I pray also for those who will believe in me [understand me] through their message."[1]

New Testament basis

Jesus was credited to say, "But the Counselor, the Holy Spirit, whom the Father will send in my name, will teach you all things."[2] When the Science of Christ-spirit appears, it will lead you into all truth. The Sermon on the Mount[3] is the essence of this Science, and the eternal life, not the death of Jesus, is its outcome.

Modern evangel

Those, who are willing to leave their nets,[4] or to cast them on the right side for Truth,[5] have the opportunity now, as aforetime, to learn and to practice Christ-like healing. Scriptures offer the opportunity of healing. The spiritual import of the Word imparts this power. But, as Paul says, "How can people call for help if they don't know who to trust? And how can they know who to trust if they haven't heard of the One who can be trusted? And how can they hear if nobody tells them? And how is anyone going to tell them, unless someone is sent to do it?"[6]

Spirituality of Scripture

The spiritual sense of truth must be gained before Truth can be understood. This sense is assimilated only as we are honest, unselfish, loving, and humble. In the soil of a "noble and good heart"[7] the seed must be sown, otherwise, the piggish element in human nature uproots

---

[1] John 17:20 (Brackets added by Mary Baker Eddy)

[2] John 14:26

[3] Matt. 5-7

[4] Matt. 4:20; Mark 1:18; Luke 5:11

[5] John 21:6

[6] Rom 10:14-15 (The Message*)*

[7] Luke 8:15

the seed making immortal progress negligible. Jesus said: "You are in error because you do not know the Scriptures."[1] The spiritual understanding of Scriptures brings out the scientific sense. The scientific meaning of the Bible is the new tongue referred to in the last chapter of Mark's Gospel.[2]

Jesus' story of "The Sower"[3] instinctively teaches us a lesson. We are cautioned not to teach spirituality to unresponsive ears and calloused hearts, since this density can't accept truth. Reading the thoughts of the people, Jesus said: "Do not give dogs what is sacred; do not throw your pearls to pigs. If you do, they may trample them under their feet, and then turn and tear you to pieces."[4]

Unspiritual contrasts

It is the spiritualization of thought and daily practice of Christ-likeness, in contrast with the results of the ghastly farce of mortal existence, which shows forth divine Science. It is integrity and purity, which attests to the divine origin and operation of divine Science. The triumphs of spiritual Science are recorded in the destruction of the errors and evils which propagate the dismal beliefs of senselessness, hopelessness, and loss.

God the Principle of all

The divine Principle of the universe must interpret the universe. God is the divine Principle of all that represents Spirit and of all that really exists. Divine Science, as demonstrated by Jesus, reveals the natural divine Principle of Science.

Human mind and its claims of sin, sickness, and death are contrary to God and cannot emanate from divine Mind. There is no *material* or mortal truth. Temporal, human perceptions can't cognize God and spiritual Truth. Human belief has sought out many inventions, but not one of them can solve the problem of being without the divine Principle of divine Science. Deductions from material hypotheses are

---

1   Matt. 22:29; Mark 12:24

2   Mark 16:17

3   Matt. 13; Mark 4; Luke 8

4   Matt. 7:6

not scientific. There is no complete unified human theory because material theories are not based on the divine law.

Science versus sense

Physical sciences analyze the testimony of the physical senses, constantly splitting it apart, breaking it down to nothing. This creates an aversion between physical sciences and divine Science, but as the errors of sense are eliminated, divine Science shows the possibility of attaining spiritual understanding.

The so-called laws of matter and of medical science have never made human beings whole, harmonious, and spiritual. Humanity is harmonious when governed by Soul. This is why it is so important to understand the truth of being, which reveals the laws of spiritual existence.

Spiritual law the only law

Mortal laws would counteract the supremacy of Spirit and contradict the wisdom of the creator. But, God never ordained a mortal law to annul the spiritual law. Jesus walked on the waves, fed the multitude, healed the sick, and raised the dead in direct opposition to mortal, physical laws. His acts were the demonstration of Science, overcoming the false claims of material law.

Knowledge of matter/energy is illusive

Science shows that conflicting convictions and opinions repeatedly transmit mixed signals. The signals symbolize confusion, but we can be safe from confusion when it is promptly and persistently tuned out. As we tune into divine Science, Truth and Love buffer confused mentalities and thereby invigorate and sustain existence. Knowledge picked up by the five senses is disposable. What we commonly call *natural science,* is not really natural, complete, or scientific, because it assumes matter is the basis of nature. Ideas, on the contrary, are from Spirit and are the true foundation of nature.

Spiritual senses are revelatory, physical sense are deceptive

The senses of Spirit remain in Love, and they manifest Truth and Life. Spirituality and the Science which explains it, is based on spiritual understanding which replaces the laws of matter. Jesus demonstrated this verity. When the five physical senses are misdirected, they manifest beliefs of human mind, which claims that life, substance, and intelligence are material, instead of spiritual. These false beliefs and their products constitute the flesh, and the flesh wars against Spirit.

Impossible partnership

Divine Science is absolute and permits to half-way position in learning its Principle and rule. It is established by demonstration. Bod never formed the conventional partnership, called mind and matter. In a manner, and at a period yet unknown, the mind/matter quandary will become outdated when examined in the light of divine metaphysics.

Spirit the starting-point

Matter has no life to lose, and Spirit never dies. Matter did not originate in God, it is not absolute; therefore, not substantial, stable, or intelligent. Collaboration between matter and Spirit would ignore omnipresent and omnipotent Mind. The starting-point of divine Science is that God, Spirit, is All-in-all, and that there is no other might nor Mind—that God is Love, and therefore Mind is divine Principle.

To become aware of the reality and order of being in its Science, you must begin by admitting Love as the divine Principle of reality. Spirit, Life, Truth, Love, combine as one—and are the Scriptural names for God. All substance, intelligence, wisdom, being, spirituality, cause, and effect belong to God. These are the attributes of the infinite divine Principle, Love. No wisdom is wise but Mind's wisdom; no truth is true, no love is lovely, no life is Life but the divine; no good is, but the good God gives.

The divine completeness

Divine metaphysics, as revealed to spiritual understanding, shows clearly that all is Mind, omnipotence, omnipresence, omniscience— that is, all power, all presence, all Science. Hence all is in reality the expressed thought of Mind.

Our material human theories are destitute of Science. The true understanding of God is spiritual and defeats mortality. Spiritual understanding destroys the false evidence that misleads thought and points to other gods or powers, such as genes, defects, and a dying mind disagreeing with the one Spirit.

Truth, spiritually discerned, is scientifically understood. Spiritual understanding banishes error and heals the sick.

Universal family

Having one God, one Mind, unfolds the power that heals the sick. These Scriptural sayings are then realized. "I am the Lord, who heals you,"[1] and "I have found a ransom (a price of redemption, an atonement)!"[2] When the divine precepts are understood, they reveal cooperation between creatures, because we all have one Spirit, God, one intelligent source, compatible to the Scriptural command: "Your attitude should be the same as that of Christ Jesus."[3] We, and our Maker have a reciprocal relationship in divine Science, and real consciousness is cognizant only of the things of God.

Once it is realized that disorder is illusory, a new perspective comes into light. Objects and thoughts are presented to the human view as beautiful and spiritually substantial. Harmony in us is as real and immortal as in music. Discord is unreal and mortal.

Perfection requisite

If God is admitted to be the only Mind and Life, there ceases to be any opportunity for sin and death. Our thoughts are turned into new and healthier channels as we learn in Science how to be perfect, even as our Maker in heaven is perfect. In perfection, we contemplate things spiritually and we naturally move away from materiality toward the Principle of the universe and God's harmonious people.

Materialist thinking never mingles with spiritual understanding. The latter destroys the former. Discord is the *nothingness* named error. Harmony is the *somethingness* named Truth.

Like evolving like

Nature and discovery inform us that life produces life. Divine Science does not gather grapes from thorns or figs from thistles.[4] Intelligence never produces non-intelligence. So, if matter is ever non-intelligent, it can't come from intelligence. To all that is unlike the

---

1   Ex. 15:26

2   Job 33:24 (Amplified)

3   Phil. 2:5

4   Matt. 7:16; Luke 6:44

perfect and endless Life, Mind said, "You will surely die."[1] We also read in Scripture, "You started out as dirt, you'll end up dirt."[2] In other words, the non-intelligent reverts back to unreality. Good can't result in evil. As God is good and is Spirit, goodness and spirituality must be immortal. Their opposites, evil and matter, are mortal error, and error has no creator. If goodness and spirituality are real, evil and materiality are unreal and cannot be the outcome of an infinite God, good.

Natural history presents vegetables and animals as preserving their original species—like producing like. Admittedly, a mineral is not produced by a potato; people are not produced by cats. Reproduction of the order of genus and species is preserved throughout the entire round of nature. The idea behind this evidence validates spiritual truth and the Science of being. Like produces like. Sin and error rely on a reversal of like producing like, asserting that eternal Spirit produces temporal matter which in turn produces all the ills of flesh. The vicious cycle of reversed thinking does not come from good and worse, leads one to believe that good is the source of evil.

Material error

The realm of the real is Spirit. Anything unlike Spirit is a human concept. Matter/energy and time/space are incomplete concepts. Being incomplete, they lead to incomplete statements. Nothing we can say or believe regarding matter is reliable, for matter is modifiable. Matter is a human phenomenon, a human invention, sometimes beautiful, always erroneous.

Is Spirit the source or creator of matter? Science reveals nothing in Spirit out of which to create matter. Divine metaphysics explains away matter. Divine Spirit is the only substance and consciousness recognized by divine Science. The materialist's convictions oppose Spirit, but there is no consciousness in matter to back up the convictions. In Spirit there are no human minds, even as in Mind there is no error, and in good there is no evil. It is deceptive to suppose that there are many minds. Spirit. Mind, is infinite, all. Spirit can have no opposite.

---

[1]   Gen. 2:17

[2]   Gen. 3:19; Ecc. 3:20 (The Message)

One cause supreme

That human mind is substantial or has life and sensation, is one of the false beliefs of human beings and exists only in a mortal perception. Therefore, as we approach Mind and Truth, we lose the sensation of mortal substance. Admitting that there can be a substantial human mind requires admitting that Spirit is not infinite and that human mind is self-creative, self-existent, and eternal. From this it would follow that there are two eternal causes warring forever with each other; and yet we say that Spirit is supreme and all-presence.

The thinking that matter or human mentality is eternal, contradicts the demonstration of life as Spirit. The logic that we originated in matter and will return to dust, leads to the conclusion that we will be annihilated.

Substance is Spirit

What we term sin, sickness, and death are convictions of the mortal human mind. We define matter as error, because it is the opposite of life, substance, and intelligence. Matter, with its mortality, can't be substantial if Spirit is substantial and eternal. We ask ourselves, what is substance to us—the flawed, the dying, the mutating and mortal? Or, is it that which is consistent, stable, and spiritual? A New Testament writer describes faith, a quality of mind, as "the assurance of *things* hoped for, the conviction of things not seen."[1]

With its doomed fate, human mind is basically insubstantial, mortal. The human mind's materialism could not have originated in the immortal Mind. The human mind was not created by Mind nor was it created to manifest and support Mind.

Spirit and mortality can neither coexist nor co-operate, and they do not create each other. Truth can't create error; error can't create truth. Look to ideas instead of things, because ideas are tangible and real to consciousness, and they have the advantage of showing us what is closer to reality.

As we stop thinking that life and intelligence are in human mind or matter, spiritual facts of being appear. The idea or intelligence of

---

[1]   Heb. 11:1 (NASB)

spiritual facts is in God. Spirit is reached through the understanding and demonstration of eternal Life and Truth and Love.

The systems of human philosophies, doctrines, and medicines are more or less infected with the thinking that matter has a life-code of its own—genes—but this thinking contradicts both revelation and right reasoning. Why would matter want a life with no mind? Logical and scientific conclusions are reached only through the knowledge that there are not two bases of being, matter and mind, but one alone—Mind.

Pantheism starts from a limited sense of God. It seeks to find cause in effect. Principle is not in its idea, and life and intelligence are not in matter.

The things of God are beautiful

Finite substance must be unknown to the infinite substance of Mind. Symbols, symptoms, and elements of disorder and decay are not products of the infinite, perfect, and eternal *All*. From Love and from Spirit's home of light and harmony, only reflections of good can come. All things beautiful and harmless are substantial ideas of Mind. Mind creates and multiplies them, and the product must be mental.

Thinking from the position of a beginning and an end will never do justice to Truth in any direction. Finite beliefs would compress Mind, which is infinite, into a skull bone. Such belief can't understand or worship the infinite. Moreover, in an effort to accommodate beginnings and endings, it breaks up Soul and substance. It tries to divide the one Spirit into persons and souls.

The mistake of trying to split Spirit causes human belief to have "many 'gods' and many 'lords'."[1] Moses declared the Lord's first command is: "You shall have no other gods before me,"[2] however in spite of this direction, human beings have an inordinate zeal to establish the opposite error of many spirits. The allegorical serpent argues, "You will be like God."[3] This argument is intent on persuading, through every avenue possible, the conviction that Soul

---

[1]   I Cor. 8:5

[2]   Ex. 20:3; Deut. 5:7

[3]   Gen. 3:5

is in body and that infinite Spirit, and Life, is in humanly defined forms—divided.

Non-sentient body

Instead of possessing our own sentient form, we reflect Soul-sense. God, the Soul of all existence, being perpetual in individuality, harmony, and spirituality, imparts and preserves harmony and spirituality in us—through Mind, not matter/energy. The only excuse for entertaining human opinions and rejecting the Science of being is our unawareness of Spirit—ignorance which vanishes as divine metaphysical Science is understood. Through spiritual understanding, we enter the universe of Truth on earth and learn that Spirit is infinite and supreme. Divine Mind and human mind do not join any more than the colors white and black join. When one appears, the other disappears.

Error assumes that God's children are both mind and matter. Divine Science contradicts the physical senses, refuses human assumptions, and asks: What is the Ego? Where is the source of Ego, and what is its destiny? The Ego-child is the reflection of the Ego-God; the Ego-child is the image and likeness of perfect Mind, Spirit, divine Principle.

The one Ego, the one Mind or Spirit called God, is infinite individuality. The one Ego supplies all form and attractiveness. Spirit reflects reality and divinity in our individual spirituality and in all things.

The mind supposed to exist in matter or a brain is a myth. The human mind is a misconceived sense and false conception as to us and Mind. When we put off the false for the true, and see that sin and mortality have neither Principle nor permanency and we shall learn that sin and mortality have no beginning and no rightful existence. Anything unlike God is native nothingness, out of which error would simulate creation through a human being formed from dust.

The true new idea

Divine Science does not put new wine into old wineskins.[1] It does not put Mind into human mind, or the indivisible into the divisible.

---

1   Matt. 9:17; Mark 2:22; Luke 5:38

The old views must be poured out or the new idea will be spilled, and the inspiration which is to change our standpoint, will be lost. Our false views of matter perish as we grasp the facts of Soul. Now, as always, Truth replaces mistaken teachings and heals the sick.

Using Symbols

The real Life, or Mind, and its opposite, the material life or mind, can be figured by a sphere and a straight line. The sphere represents the infinite without beginning or end; the straight line represents a beginning and end. The sphere represents good, the self-existent and eternal individuality; the straight line represents futility, a beginning and an end, a belief in a self-made and material existence. A straight line finds no conformance to a curve, and a curve finds no adjustment to a straight line. Similarly, matter has no place in Spirit, and Spirit has no place in matter. Truth has no home in error, and error has no foothold in Truth. Mind can't pass into non-intelligent matter, nor can non-intelligence become Soul. At no point can these opposites fuse or unite. Even though they seem to touch, one is still a curve and the other a straight line.

There is no inherent power in matter; for all that is material is a human mortal thought, always governing itself erroneously.

Truth is the intelligence of immortal Mind. Error is the so-called intelligence of human mind.

Truth is not inverted

Whatever indicates a fall from spirituality is the Adam-dream.[1] That which symbolizes an opposite to Spirit or an absence of Spirit is neither Mind nor us. We can overturn error and discover Truth. The light of Truth dispels the error. As human beings begin to understand Spirit, they give up the belief that there is any true existence apart from God.

Source of all life and action

Mind is the source of all movement, and there is no inertia to slow down, or stop, perpetual and harmonious action. Mind is the same Life, Love, and wisdom "yesterday and today and forever."[2] Matter

---

[1]   Gen 2:7

[2]   Heb. 13:8

and its effects—sin, sickness, and death—are conditions of human mind which act, react, and then come to an end. The human mind's conditions are not facts of Mind. The human minds imaginings are not ideas, but illusions. Principle is absolute. It admits of no error, but rests on understanding.

Prevalent theories insist that immeasurable Life, God, is the same as measurable life. Conventional systems speak of both Truth and error as *mind*, and of good and evil as *spirit*. Popular philosophies claim material structures to be the manifestation of the one Life, God, whereas material structures are only the objective state of material sense.

These false beliefs as to what really constitutes life, so detracts from God's character and nature that the true sense of Spirit's power is lost to all who embrace the falsities. The divine Principle, or Life, can't be practically demonstrated in length of days, as it was by the patriarchs, unless its Science is accurately stated. We must receive the divine Principle in understanding, and live it in daily life; otherwise, we can no more verify Science than we can teach and illustrate geometry by calling a curve a straight line or a straight line a sphere.

Are attitudes, spirituality, or consciousness, found in matter? It is irrational to say that Mind is infinite, but dwells in the finite. The incomplete, inconsistent matter/energy isn't the medium or product of Mind.

Mind never limited

God has no limiting factor. Spirit is not in us or in matter. Mind and Mind's expression, doesn't grow from a limited gene. Infinite Mind can have no starting-point, and can return to no limit. Spirit can never have borders nor be fully manifested through physicality.

Recognition of temporal substance is impossible

What is God's image and likeness? Is it matter or a fleshly human being? Is it collapse, complaint, and mourning? Can human mind recognize Mind? Can infinite Mind recognize human mind? Can the eternal dwell in the temporal or know anything unlike the infinite? Can Deity be known through the physical senses? Can the human perceptions, which receive no direct evidence of Spirit, give correct testimony as to spiritual life, truth, and love?

The answer to all these questions must forever be in the negative.
Physical sense cannot detect Spirit

The physical senses cannot secure proof of God. Spirit isn't tactile to flesh. Spirit isn't seen through the eye, isn't heard through the ear, isn't tasted or smelled by means of matter. Our physical senses are quite pathetic; they can't even cognize the microscopic particles of matter/energy, which are known only by the effects commonly attributed to them.

According to Christian Science the only real senses are Christlike and come from divine Mind. Thought passes from God to us. Sense and information do not go from material body to Mind. The intercommunication is always from God to existence. Wave/particles are not aware and have no consciousness of good or of evil, of pleasure or of pain. Our individuality is not directly or indirectly measurable. The Science of our spirituality doesn't come only in the hereafter in what is called heaven, but here and now. Christ-likeness, or spirituality, is the great fact of being for time and eternity.
The human counterfeit

What then is the human personality which suffers, sins, and dies? It is not God's image and likeness, but a counterfeit, an inversion, calling itself sin, sickness, and death. The incongruous natures of Spirit and matter, Mind and flesh, uncover the contradiction that human beings are the image of God, intelligence.
Material misconceptions

Is God a physical personality? Spirit is not physical. The mindset insisting a material body is person is advancing out of itself. The time comes when mindsets give way to a diviner sense of intelligence and its manifestations through the better understanding of the Supreme Being, or divine Principle, and idea.
Salvation is through reform

The interpretation of God as a Savior of the physical, instead of as the saving Principle or divine Love, triggers us to look for salvation through pardon and not through reform. We then resort to matter instead of Spirit for the cure of the sick. Knowledge of divine Science allows human beings to reach an improved sense of Spirit and seek to learn, not from matter, but from the divine Principle, God, how to demonstrate the Christ, Truth, as the healing and saving power.

It is essential to understand, instead of believe, what most nearly relates to the happiness of being. Someone who pursues Truth through reliance on a human doctrine does not understand the infinite. We can't find the absolute and spiritual in the relative and humanized. We must experience, or live, our spiritual understanding, because not doing so is fatal to knowledge of Science. The understanding of Truth gives full faith in Truth, and spiritual understanding is better "than all burnt offerings and sacrifices."[1]

Christ was proclaimed to say, "I am the way and the truth and the life."[2] The Teacher also exclaimed, "No one comes to the Father [the divine Principle of being] except through me," signifying the way of Christ, Life, Truth, Love. A physical cause is not the way. Jesus put aside physical causes. He must have known the divine Principle, Love, reveals and governs all that is real.

In the Saxon and twenty other tongues *good* is the term for God. The Scriptures declare all that He made to be good—good in Principle and in idea. Therefore the spiritual universe is good, and reflects God as God is.

Spiritual thoughts

God's thoughts are perfect, eternal, substance, and Life. Human thoughts are imperfect, temporal, frail, and doomed to death. Human thoughts lack a divine cause because God, Spirit, is the only cause and can only cause that which is eternal. The temporal and material are errors and are not creations of Spirit, but are imitations, opposites, or contradictions of the spiritual and eternal. Due to its contradicting nature, error must say, "I am true." But by this saying, error, or the lie, destroys itself.

Insanity, sickness, and destruction are comprised in human material belief, and do not belong to the divine Mind. They are without a real origin or being. They have neither Principle nor permanence, but belong with all that is relative and temporal. They

---

[1]   Mark 12:33

[2]   John 14:6

246

belong to the nothingness of error which feigns the creations of Truth. Creations of matter must return to dust, whereas Spirit's expression is substantial and eternal. Error surmises that God's child is both spiritual and material. Divine Science invalidates error and maintains our spiritual identity.

Divine allness

We call the absence of Truth, *error*. Truth and error are unlike. In Science, Truth is divine and the infinite God can have no unlikeness. Did God, Truth, create error? No! "Can both fresh water and salt water flow from the same spring?"[1] God being everywhere and all-inclusive, how can the all-presence be absent? How can the absence of omnipresence and omnipotence even be suggested? How can there be more than *all*?

Error unveiled

Error is not supplemented by understanding or truth. Error is not the outcome of Mind. Error calls itself something, when it is nothing. It says, "I am God's child, but I am not the image and likeness of God, Spirit;" whereas Scriptures declare that we were made in God's likeness.

Error is illegitimate, a mirage, and lacks spiritual identity or support. It has no real existence. The assumption that life, substance, and intelligence are *in* human thinking, or *of* it, is an error. Human thinking is neither a thing nor a person, but merely the objective assumption of Spirit's opposite. The five physical senses testify, saying that truth and error, good and evil, are united in a human mind. Their false evidence finally yields to Truth—to the recognition of Spirit and of spiritual reality.

Truth cannot be contaminated by error. The statement that *Truth is real* necessarily includes its correlation, that *error, Truth's unlikeness, is unreal.*

The great conflict

Truth and error seem to be in conflict. Remember though, the contention is only the mental conflict between the evidence of the spiritual perceptions and the testimony of the human imprints.

---

[1]   James 3:11

Through faith in, and the understanding of divine Love, the battle between Spirit and flesh will settle all questions.

Superstition and understanding can never unite. When the final physical and moral effects of divine Science are fully understood, the conflict between truth and error, understanding and belief, Science and material sense, will cease, and spiritual harmony will prevail. This harmony was predicted by the prophets and introduced by Jesus. The lightning and thunderbolts of error burst and flash, but the clouds will clear and the tumult will die away in the distance. Then the raindrops of divinity refresh the earth. As St. Paul says: "There remains, then, a Sabbath-rest for the people of God [of Spirit]."[1]

The chief stones in the temple

The underpinnings in the temple of Christian Science are to be found in the following postulates: that Life is God, good, and not evil; that Soul is sinless, not to be found in the body; that Spirit is not, and cannot be, humanized; that Life is not at risk to death; that the spiritual real person of God has no birth, no temporal life, and no death.

The Christ element

Science reveals the glorious possibilities of our spirituality, forever unlimited by the mortal senses. The Christ-element in the Messiah made him the Way-shower, Truth and Life.

The eternal Truth destroys what human beings have learned from error, and our real selfhood comes to light. Truth lived is eternal life. Human beings can never advance from the temporal debris of error—belief in sin, sickness, and death—until we learn that God is the only Life. We progress out of the thinking that life and sensation are in the body by understanding what constitutes ourselves as the image of God, and then Spirit will have overcome the flesh.

Wickedness is not person

A wicked human being is not the idea of God. Wickedness is little else than the expression of error. To suppose that stupidity, lust, hatred, envy, hypocrisy, revenge, have life abiding in them is a terrible

---

[1]   Heb. 4:9 (Brackets added by Mary Baker Eddy)

mistake. Life and Life's idea, Truth and Truth's idea, never made children who are sick, sinful, or mortal.

Death is an illusion

The fact that the Christ, Truth, overcame and still overcomes death proves the "king of terrors"[1] to be but a mortal belief, or error. The spiritual evidence of Life wipes out the mortal illusion of a final end. What appears to be death is an impression that can be overcome, for to the real man and woman and the real universe, there is no death-process.

The worldwide thinking that matter/energy has life, results in thinking death is a law. So, people, cells, jellyfish, and flowers are supposed to die. But the fact remains, that God's universe is spiritual and indestructible.

Spiritual offspring

The spiritual fact and the human perceptions are contradictions; but the spiritual is true and therefore the human must be untrue. Life is not in human perceptions, therefore it cannot be said to pass out of them. Human mind and even death are mortal illusions. Spirit and all things spiritual are the real and eternal.

We are not the offspring of flesh (nothingness), but of Spirit, of Life. Because Life is God, Life must be eternal, self-existent. Life is the everlasting I AM, the Being who was and is and will be; the Being whom nothing can erase.

Death offers no advantage

If the Principle, rule, and demonstration of our being is not in the least understood before what is termed death, we will not become more spiritual on account of the death experience. We are as narrow-minded or lacking after death as before. We can't pursue happiness through selfish and inferior motives. It is a blunder to suppose Life or Mind is manifest through brain and nerves. Hence Truth comes to destroy this blunder and its effects—sickness, sin, and death. To those pursuing Life, Scripture says: "The second death has no power over them."[2]

---

[1] Job 18:14
[2] Rev. 20:6

Future purification

If the change called *death* destroyed the complaining, hurting, and dying thinking, happiness would be won at the moment of demise; but this is not so. Cells are constantly dying in our bodies. They who are unrighteous shall be unrighteous still until Truth removes all ignorance and sin. Perfection is gained only by perfection.

The fear and negativity which possess us at the instant of death do not cease, but endure until the death of the fearful and negative consciousness. If a murderer died, the horrible murderous intent isn't forsaken just because the body died. Thought improves only when the cruel mind is disarmed by good. The body is as materialistic as the mind, and vice versa. To be wholly spiritual, we must be Godlike and we become that way only when we reach perfection.

Here are four serious mistakes: Supposing that sin is forgiven before the sin is abandoned; that happiness is genuine when connected to sin; that death of the body frees us from anything unspiritual; that God will forgive a sin without destroying it. We know that all will be changed "in the twinkling of an eye,"[1] when the last trumpet will sound; but this last call of wisdom can't come until human beings have taken every little step to yield to the whole spiritual character. Mortals do not need to delude themselves by thinking the experience of death will awaken them to glorified being.

Universal salvation rests on spiritual improvement and proof, and is unattainable without them. Heaven is not a locality, but a divine state of Mind in which all the manifestations of Mind are harmonious and immortal because sin is not there and God's person is found having no self-righteousness, but is in possession of "the mind of the Lord,"[2] as the Scripture say.

"Whether a tree falls to the south or to the north, in the place where it falls, there will it lie."[3] This text has been transformed into a popular proverb, as the tree falls, so it must lie. As we fall asleep, so we will wake up. As death finds human beings, so will human beings

---

[1]   I Cor. 15:52

[2]   I Cor. 2:16

[3]   Ecc. 11:3

be after death, until spiritual experience and advancement effects the needed change for the better. Mind never becomes dust. Mind, or Life, is not waiting to resurrect from the grave because the grave has no power over either.

Day of judgment

No final judgment awaits mortals. There is no time. The judgment day of wisdom comes thought by thought, by which human beings are deprived of all erroneous thoughts. As for spiritual error there is none.

When the last human fault is destroyed, then the final trump will sound and end the battle between Truth and mortality; but "no one knows about that day or hour."[1] Prophecy pauses at the trumpet sound. Divine Science alone can compass the heights and depths of being and reveal the infinite.

Primal error

Truth will be to us "the resurrection and the life"[2] only as it destroys all error. Truth dissolves the belief that Mind, the only source of our spirituality, can be shackled by a body. Life can't be controlled by death. A nihilistic, sick, or dying human is not the likeness of God, the perfect and eternal.

Matter/energy is the primitive belief of human mind. Because human perceptions are so limited and vague, the life of human beings is dependent on the limited and vague, on matter. The human mind can't discern Spirit, but can only repeat false imprints while believing evil is substantial and real.

Explaining the origin of human being and mind, Jesus said: "Why is my language not clear to you? Because you are unable to hear what I say. You belong to your father, the devil, and you want to carry out your father's desire. He was a murderer from the beginning, not holding to the truth, for there is no truth in him. When he lies, he speaks his native language, for he is a liar and the father of lies."[3]

The carnal human mentality, misnamed *mind*, is mortal. In his resurrection and ascension, Jesus showed that a mortal creature is not

---

[1]   Mark 13:32

[2]   John 11:25

[3]   John 8:43

our real essence. If it were not for the indissoluble immortal connection between God and spiritual identity, people would be annihilated. In divine Science, mortality disappears in the presence of reality.

Electricity is not a vital energy, but the least material form of illusive consciousness—a mindlessness that makes no connection between matter and Mind. Electricity is self-destructive. Matter and human mind are but different forms of the same stuff and mind is the least material form. The flesh and mind is the illusion called a human being, a mind in matter. In reality and in Science, illusive substance and intelligence are false representatives of the true person.

The material gases and forces are imitations of the spiritual forces of divine Mind, whose potency is Truth, whose attraction is Love, whose adhesion and cohesion are Life. They perpetuate the eternal facts of being. Electricity is the sharp surplus of materiality which counterfeits the true essence of spirituality or truth. The great difference between electricity and spirituality is that spirituality is intelligence while electricity is not. Spirituality, or truth, is Mind.

The counterfeit forces

The impressive fury of human mind—vented in earthquake, hurricane, supernovas, terrorism, famine, etc.—characterizes self-destruction. Calamities are sometimes referred to as "acts of God." Scriptures goes as far as to interpret God as saying, "And in anger and wrath I will execute vengeance on the nations that did not obey,"[1] but these catastrophes only counterfeit divine justice. In reality, the misfortunes point to the strength and permanency of Spirit. Science brings to light Spirit and its supremacy, universal harmony, the entireness of God, good, and the nothingness of evil.

Instruments of error

The five physical senses are the avenues and instruments of human error. The limited senses bear witness to the entrenched human belief that life, substance, and intelligence is a mixture of the temporal and the eternal. This thinking constantly campaigns for error and carries within itself the seeds of all error.

---

[1]   Micah 5:15, ESV

If a person has their own mind and substance, the loss of one finger would take away some quality and quantity of their self. Flesh and person are not the same.

The belief that matter thinks, sees, or feels is not more real than the belief that matter enjoys and suffers. Human mind invented itself and called itself man and woman. The invented scenario goes on to say: "Matter has intelligence. Neurotransmitters and hormones govern us. Nerves feel. Brain thinks and sins. The stomach can make people edgy. Injury can cripple and matter can kill us." These thoughts victimize human beings, taught, as they are by physiology, psychology, and pathology, to revere false testimony. Why do we respect the very falsities that are destroyed by Truth?

Mythical pleasure and pain

The disparity between our spirituality representing Spirit, and the materiality representing the error that life and intelligence are temporal, shows the pleasures and pains of temporal life to be myths. As humans believe in myths, there will be mythologies, in which matter is represented as divided into intelligent gods. Our genuine selfhood is recognizable only in what is good and true. We are neither self-made nor made by human beings. God revealed, and continues to reveal, us.

The inebriate believes that there is pleasure in intoxication. The thief believes something is gained by stealing, and the hypocrite thinks no one notices their deceit. The Science of Mind corrects such mistakes, for Truth proves the fallacy of error.

Nerves which have been amputated supposedly ache. Phantom limb is added proof of the unreliability of fleshly sense.

Mortal are unlike immortals

God creates and governs the universe, including us. The universe is filled with spiritual ideas, which Love evolves. Ideas are obedient to the Mind that makes them. Human mind would convert the unlimited into the limited and then think to recover the original self in order to escape from the mortality of the limited. Human beings are not like spiritual beings (created in God's own image). Infinite Spirit *is*, therefore human consciousness will succumb to the scientific fact and disappear. The real sense of being, perfect and forever intact, will appear.

Transparency of goodness

The manifestation of God through human beings is as light passing through the window. The light and the glass never mingle, but as matter, the glass is less opaque than the walls. The human mind through which Truth appears most vividly is that one which has lost much materiality—much error—in order to become a better transparency for Truth. Then, like a cloud melting into thin vapor, it no longer hides the sun.

Psychology and physiology are myths

The human consciousness, often named brain, is the exact opposite of real Mind, or Spirit. Mortal consciousness is made up of error. Biology or neuroscience teaches that mortals are created to suffer and die. Furthermore, we can be taught that when we die our human consciousness is resurrected from death and mortality. These erroneous theories are basically saying that spirit is born of matter and returns to matter, and that people have a resurrection from dust; whereas Science reveals the continuum of our spiritual selfhood, unaffected by the brain or death.

Progress comes from experience. Humanity is improved as the mortal is dropped for the immortal. Either here or hereafter, suffering or Science must replace all illusions regarding life and mind. Material sense and self must be regenerated. The old self with its practices must be dropped. Nothing fleshly or sinful is spiritual. The death of fleshly perceptions and habits, not the death of material organisms, is what reveals spirituality and Life, harmonious, real, and eternal.

Human pleasures and pains which come through mortal consciousness perish. They can't withstand the force of Truth. They can't withstand spiritual sense and the actuality of being. As people lose all satisfaction in error and in idle thinking, they find satisfaction in Soul-sense.

Whether mortals learn of Soul-sense sooner or later depends on the tenacity of mistaken mindsets. Until we learn of Soul-sense, we suffer from attachment to material based pleasures and pains.

Mixed testimony

The knowledge gained from logic based on physicality leads to sin and death. When the appearance of Spirit and matter, or Truth and error, seem to intermix, the appearance rests on foundations which time is wearing away. Mortal mind judges by the evidence of the physical senses, until Science wipes out this false evidence. A logic based on spirituality improves thought, takes a step out of error and encourages the next step in understanding the situation in divine Science.

Belief an autocrat

Human belief is a liar from the beginning, not deserving power. It says to human beings, "You are disgusting!" and they think they are. Nothing can change this state, until the mindset changes. Mortal belief says, "You are happy!" and human beings are; and no circumstance can alter the situation, until the thinking on this subject changes. Human belief says to mortals, "You are sick!" and this assertion manifests itself on the body as sickness. A change in either a health-belief or a belief in sickness affects the physical condition. Bear in mind, it is as necessary for a health-illusion, as for an illusion of sickness, to be instructed out of itself into the spiritual understanding of what constitutes health.

Self-improvement

The mere acquisition and retention of beliefs is destroyed by truth. Change the evidence to improve the human consciousness and that which before seemed real will disappear. As we attain the reality of spiritual evidence, we find our immortality. The only fact concerning any human belief is, that it is neither scientific nor eternal, but exposed to unrest and mutation.

Faith higher than belief

Faith is substantial and more advanced than belief. Faith is a chrysalis state of human thought in which metaphysical evidence, contradicting the testimony of physical sense, begins to appear, and Truth, the ever-present, becomes understood. Human thoughts have their degrees of comparison. Some thoughts are better than others. A belief in Truth is better than a belief in error, but no mortal belief is founded on the divine rock. Mortal testimony can be shaken. Until belief becomes faith, and faith becomes spiritual understanding, human thought has only a marginal connection to the actual or divine.

A human mindset carries out its own conditions. Sickness, sin, and death are the nebulous realities of human conclusions. Life, Truth, and Love are the realities of divine Science. Realities dawn in faith and glow full-orbed in spiritual understanding. Clouds hide the sun but they can't extinguish the sun, so false beliefs hide harmony, but can't destroy Science armed with faith, hope, and spiritual experience.

Truth's witness

What is termed physical sense can report only a mortal temporary sense of things, whereas spiritual sense can bear witness only to Truth. To human sense, the unreal is the real until this sense is corrected by Christian Science.

Physical sense flaunts the belief that mind is temporal. Human belief—shifting between feelings of satisfaction and dissatisfaction, hope and fear, life and death—never breaks through the limiting factors of the mortal or the unreal. Ah! But when the real is experienced, joy is no longer fragile and hope is no longer a con artist. Spiritual ideas, like numbers and notes, start from Principle, and admit no materialist beliefs. Spiritual ideas lead up to their divine origin, God, and to the spiritual sense of being. Spiritual perception, excelling over the material perception, involves intuition, hope, faith, understanding, spiritual experience, reality.

Thought-angels

Angels are not otherworldly human beings; angels are heavenly visitors traveling on metaphysical, not physical forces. Angels are pure thoughts from God, with diverse individualities, empowered by Truth and Love. Humans guess that angels are humanlike, marked with superstitious outlines, maybe even having wings, but this guesswork is only symbolism or fantasy. It has behind it no more reality than the sculptor's thought when carving the Statue of Liberty. Symbols embody a person's conception of an unseen quality or condition, but they have no physical antecedent reality except in the artist's own observation and "[secret] chambers of [idol] pictures."[1]

---

[1]   Ezk. 8:12 (Amplified)

One way to view angels is as exalted thoughts, appearing through a crack in the abyss of darkness where human thinking has buried its worthiest earthly hopes. Pure thoughts lead us to a new and glorified trust, to higher ideals of life and its joys. Angels are God's representatives. These ascending beings never lead toward selfishness, sin, or materiality, but guide to the divine Principle of all good, where every real individuality, image, or likeness of God, gathers. Resolved to pay attention to these spiritual guides they stay with us, and we entertain "angels without knowing it."[1]

Knowledge and Truth

Knowledge gained from limited senses or sciences is figuratively represented in Scripture as a tree yielding the fruits of chaos, unreliable health, and loss. The knowledge obtained through matter is thus judged dubious and dangerous, since "the tree is recognized by its fruit"?[2]

Truth never destroys God's idea. Truth is spiritual, eternal substance, which cannot destroy the true reflection. Temporal sense, or error, may seem to hide Truth, health, harmony, and Science—as the mist obscures the sun or the mountains—but Science, the sunshine of Truth, will melt away the shadow and reveal the celestial peaks.

Old and new

If people were exclusively a creature of the mortal perceptions, they would have no eternal Principle and would be unstable and temporal. Finite sense has no true appreciation of infinite Principle, or of God's infinite image or reflection. Mirages illustrate the illusion of mortal perceptions and of mortal people. Human logic is skewed when it attempts to draw correct spiritual conclusions from matter. People are the image of omnipresent God.

So far as the scientific statement as to God's child is understood, it can be proved. Spiritual understanding brings to light the true reflection of God—the real person, or the "new self."[3]

---

1   Heb. 13:2

2   Matt. 12:33; Luke 6:44

3   Eph. 4:24

The temporal and unreal never touch the eternal and real. The mutable and imperfect never touch the immutable and perfect. The inharmonious and self-destructive never touch the harmonious and self-existent. These opposite qualities are the weeds and wheat,[1] which never fuse, though to mortal sight they grow side by side until the harvest. Science separates the wheat from the weeds through the realization of God as ever present and person as reflecting the divine likeness.

The divine reflection

Spirit is God, Soul; therefore Soul is not the same as what we sometimes call a human soul. If Spirit were in a human soul, God would have no representative, and the human soul would be the same as God. Moreover, the impractical theory that Soul inhabits the human body is a misleading teaching. The universe reflects and expresses the divine substance or Soul; therefore God is seen only in the spiritual universe and in spirituality, as the sun is seen in the ray of light which goes out from it. Soul is revealed only in that which reflects Life, Truth, and Love. Our individual expression of Soul manifests God's attributes and power, just as the human likeness seen in a mirror repeats the color, form, and action of the person in front of the mirror. Our spirituality reflects Spirit.

Few persons grasp what divine Science means by the word *reflection*. To our trained thinking, the human person seems to be solid substance, rather than a likeness, but this sense of substance involves error and therefore is divisible, temporal.

On the other hand, our spirituality is substantial and reflects the eternal substance or Spirit which mortals hope for. The spiritual self reflects the divine, which constitutes the only real and eternal existence. This reflection seems to mortal sense transcendental, because our spiritual substantiality transcends human vision and is made known only through divine Science.

Inverted images and ideas

As God is substance and we are the divine image and likeness, we will wish for and in reality have, only the substance of good,

---

[1]   Matt. 13:24-30

the substance of Spirit, not mortality. Believing that we have any other substance, or mind, is not spiritual and breaks the First Commandment, You shall have one God, one Mind. Mortal substance seems to be the self of human beings, while real self is "image," idea. Delusion, sin, disease, and death come from the false testimony of physical sense, which, from a supposed standpoint outside the focal distance of infinite Spirit, presents an inverted image of Mind and substance with everything rearranged.

Mistaken systems suppose soul to be an unsubstantial occupant in a body, and therefore people seem to be confined and separate, instead of free and unified. Spirituality is not confined in mortality. Soul is not embraced by limitations. Principle is not to be found in fragmented ideas.

Identity not lost

The human body and consciousness are temporal, but the real substance and consciousness are spiritual and eternal. Spiritual consciousness is not lost, but found through this explanation; for the conscious infinitude of existence and of all identity is thereby discerned and remains unchanged. It is impossible for us to lose anything that is real, when God is all and eternally ours. The impulse to believe that mind is in flesh and that the fleshly pleasures and pains, birth, illnesses, defects, and death are real and can't be forgotten, is a human conviction and that conviction is all that will ever be lost.

Further defining person, let us remember that harmonious being has existed forever and is never connected to the mortal illusion of life, substance, and intelligence as existent in matter. The Science of being reveals spiritual beings as perfect, complete, even as the Father-Mother is perfect, because the Soul, or Mind, of our spirituality is God, the divine Principle of all being. We really are governed by Soul instead of sense, by the law of Spirit, not by the so-called laws of matter.

God is Love, the divine Father-Mother, infinite Principle, called Person. Our true consciousness is in the mental, not in any bodily or personal likeness to Spirit. Seriously, the human body is far from portraying a likeness to the divine, though humanity would gladly have us believe otherwise!

Mental propagation

Consider reproduction. In divine Science, individual spiritual ideas reproduce as they reflect Spirit's creative power. The reflection, through mental manifestation of the multitudinous forms of Mind which people the realm of the real, is controlled by Mind. The Principle governing the reflection, God's children do not multiply by propagating matter, but by reflecting Spirit.

The details of surrounding individualities reflect the one infinite individuality, God. Individual characteristics are understood in, and formed by, Spirit, not by mortal genes and environments. Whatever reflects Mind, Life, Truth, and Love, is spiritually conceived and brought forth, but the statements that person is conceived and evolved eternally *and* temporarily, or by both God *and* human beings, contradicts that eternal truth. All the vanity of the ages can never make contraries true. Divine Science lays obliterates the illusion that life or mind is formed by, or is in, the temporal body. As error self-destructs, Science removes the illusion of an incongruous life and mind through the spiritualized understanding of the Science of Life.

Error defined

A fatal error is to believe that we can experience a mingling of pain and pleasure, life and death, holiness and un-holiness. Another unfortunate error is to think that structural human beings are the likeness of God.

Spiritual entity

God, without the image and likeness of Mind's self, would be a nonentity, or Mind unexpressed. Spirit would be without a witness or proof of Spirit's own nature. We are the image or idea of God, an idea which can't be lost or separated from its divine Principle. As the evidence before the mortal perceptions evaporate in the presence of spiritual perception, nothing can estrange us from the sweet sense and presence of Life and Truth.

We are inseparable from Love

It is an unawareness of spirituality which hides real beauty. Limited mindsets are unable to reveal immortal goodness. Understanding this, Paul said: "Neither death nor life, neither angels nor demons, neither the present nor the future, nor any powers, neither height nor depth, nor anything else in all creation, will be able to separate us from the love of God."[1] This is the doctrine of Christian Science: that divine Love cannot be deprived of its manifestation or object; that happiness cannot be turned into sorrow, for sorrow is not the master of happiness; that good can never produce evil; that matter can never produce mind; and life cannot result in death. God's unspoiled child—governed by its perfect Principle—is sinless and eternal.

Harmony is natural

Harmony is not only produced and controlled by its Principle, but also remains with it forever. Divine Principle is our Life. Our contentment is not therefore at the disposal of physical sense. Truth is not contaminated by error. Harmony in our being is as beautiful as in music, and discord is unnatural, unreal.

The science of music governs tones. Abandoned to human conjecture, music is liable to be misapprehended and lost in confusion. Controlled by belief, instead of understanding, music is, must be, imperfectly expressed. So person, governed by the hard and soft sciences, is abandoned to guessing and liable to be misapprehended and lost in confusion. Controlled by belief, instead of spiritual understanding, person is, must be, imperfectly expressed. But, a discontented, disordered mortal is no more a *person* than discord is music.

Human reflection

An image on the television screen, or a face reflected in the mirror, is not the original, though resembling the original. Person, in the likeness of our Maker, reflects the original light of being, the invisible God. As there is no corporeality in the mirrored form, which is but the reflection, so man and woman, like all things real, reflects God, our divine Principle, not in a mortal body.

Gender is not a quality of God, but a characteristic of human mind. The fact that God's image is not a creator, though reflecting the creation of Mind, constitutes the underlying reality of reflection. "Jesus gave them this answer: 'I tell you the truth, the Son can do nothing

---

[1]   Rom. 8:38-39

by himself; he can do only what he sees his Father doing, because whatever the Father does the Son also does."[1]

While physical senses invert images, and matter deviates from the Science of spiritual reflection, the consequence is an unlikeness of Spirit. In the illusion of life that is here today and gone tomorrow, man and woman would be wholly mortal, were it not that Love destroys all error and brings spirituality to light. Because we are the reflection of our Maker, we are not subject to birth, growth, maturity, decay. These mortal projections are of human origin, not divine.

The Sadducees reasoned falsely about the resurrection. The Pharisees reasoned worse. They believed error to be as immortal as truth, and thought they could raise the spiritual from the material after resorting to death. Jesus taught, and faultlessly demonstrated, how death was to be overcome by spiritual Life.

Divinity not childless

Life demonstrates Life. Person reflects Life, Soul. The immortality of Soul makes person immortal. If God, who is Life, were parted for a moment from person, during that moment there would be no divinity reflected. The Ego would be unexpressed, and the Parent would be childless—not a Parent.

Guard against some common religious opinions, such as a breakable relationship with God. If Life or Soul and its representative, person, unite for a period and then are separated as by a law of divorce, to be brought together again at some uncertain future time and in manner unknown, we are left without a rational proof of immortality. We can't be separated for an instant from God, if reflecting God. Thus Science proves our spiritual being to be intact.

Thought forms

The plethora of human thought forms, apparently materialized, are not more distinct or real to the physical sense than are the Soul-created forms to spiritual sense. The senses of Spirit cognizes Life as permanent, and are undisturbed even amid the jarring testimony of the mortal senses. Christian Science is consistently revealing to

---

[1] John 5:19

human beings the perpetual divine Principle—is unfolding Life and the universe, ever present and eternal.

God's child, spiritually designed, is not illusive and mortal.

The serpent's whisper

The parent of all human disorder was the Adam-dream, the deep sleep, in which initiated the illusion that life and intelligence proceeded from and passed into matter. To the sleeper, error or the *serpent* is still insisting on the opposite of Truth, saying, "You will be like God, knowing good and evil."[1] In other words, keep dreaming and I will make error as real and eternal as Truth!

Evil, affirming itself to be mind, declares that there is more than one intelligence or God. It says: "There will be many lords and gods. I am telling you; not only does God make evil minds and evil spirits, but I help Him. You wait, because Truth will renege and become illusive, just like matter does. I will put the spiritual into what I call matter, and matter will seem to have life as much as God, Spirit, who *is* the only Life."

Bad results from error

Evil's erroneous affirmation has proved itself to be error. The life of error is found to have no resemblance to divine Life; it is only a fickle implication of an existence which ends in death. Ironically, error charges its lie to Truth and says: "The Lord knows falsities. God made unsettled mortal children out of matter instead of Spirit." Unquestionably, what's happening here is, that error is participating in its own nature, regurgitating its own nonsense. If we regard matter as intelligent, and Mind as both good and evil, every sin or supposed material pain and pleasure seems normal. If we believe the temporal is a part of God's creation, our spiritual path will be full of obstacles.

Higher laws

Truth has no starting point. Divine Mind is our Soul, and gives us dominion. We were not crafted from an untenable basis. We were not commanded to obey human laws which Spirit never made. Our sphere is in spiritual statutes, in the higher law of Mind.

---

[1]   Gen. 3:5

The great question

Piercing through the awful distractions, gloomy predictions, and chaos, mortals hear the voice of Truth calling: "Where are you?"[1] "Consciousness, where are you? Are you living in the thinking that mind is fragmented and flawed, and that evil is mind? Or, are you in the living faith that there is and can be but one God? Are you keeping Spirit's commandment?" Until the lesson is learned that God is the only Mind governing us, human mind will be timid and hide from the call. Or, the head, heart, stomach, cells, neurons, etc. will answer: "Here I am, looking for happiness and life in the body, but finding only an illusion, a blending of false claims, false pleasures, pain, sin, sickness, and death."

The Soul-inspired patriarchs heard the voice of Truth, and talked with God as consciously as people talk to one another.

Jacob's wrestling

Jacob was *alone,* wrestling with error—struggling with all his flesh was saying about pleasures and pains—when an angel, a message from Truth and Love appeared to Jacob and struck the sinew, or strength of the fleshly talk, until he perceived its unreality. Truth, being thereby understood, gave Jacob spiritual strength in this Peniel of divine Science. Then the angel said: "Let me go, for it is daybreak;"[2] that is, the light of Truth and Love dawns on you. But the patriarch, perceiving his faulty thinking and his need of improvement, did not loosen his hold on this glorious light until his nature was transformed. The angel asked Jacob what his name was. Jacob told him and the angel said, "Your name will no longer be Jacob, but Israel, because you have struggled with God and with men and have overcome."[3] Jacob asked his deliverer, "Please tell me your name."[4] However, a specific name was withheld. The messenger was not a corporeal being, but a nameless, bodiless communication of divine Love—giving a spiritual sense of being which rebuked a materialist sense. Likewise,

---

[1] Gen. 3:9

[2] Gen. 32:26

[3] Gen. 32:28

[4] Gen. 32:29

the Psalmist experienced this same touch of Love, and remarked that it restored his Soul.[1]

The result of Jacob's wrestling became apparent. He had conquered the human mindset with the new understanding of Spirit and of spiritual power. This changed the man. He was no longer called Jacob, but Israel—a prince of God, or a soldier of God, who had fought a good fight. He was to become the father of those who through earnest effort followed his demonstration of the power of Spirit over the human senses. The people who followed his example were to be called the children of Israel, until the Messiah should rename them. If people stray and forget that Life is God, they are brought back through great tribulation. Suffering compels us to deny the temporal life perceptions and understand un-humanized, unlimited Mind. Don't stray. We don't want to neglect the divine power which heals the sick and sinning.

Life is never structural

The Science of being shows it to be impossible for infinite Spirit or Soul to be in a finite body, or for person to have intelligence separate from our Maker. It is a self-evident error to suppose that there can be such a reality as biological animal or vegetable life, when such life always ends in death. Life is never for a moment extinct. Therefore Life is never structural. Life isn't established through levels of organization, and it is never absorbed or limited by its own formations.

Thought is seen as substance

The website designer is not in the website. The website is the designer's thought objectified. Human belief may imagine that it designs thought on an object, but what is this material object? Did websites exist prior to thought? Quantifiable objects can be traced back to the human mind-force. But, all might is divine Mind and Mind manifests spiritual thoughts. Thought will finally be understood and seen in all form, substance, and color, without material objectifications. The potter is not in the clay; else the clay would have power over the potter. God is self-acknowledged Mind, and expresses all.

---

[1]   Ps. 23:3

The central intelligence

The sun is not affected by the rotating earth. So Science reveals Soul as God, untouched by sin and death. Soul is the central Life and intelligence around which circle harmoniously all things in the systems of Mind.

Imperishable Soul

We are repeatedly taught that there is a human soul which sins and can be spiritually lost. To believe that soul may be lost and yet be spiritual doesn't make sense. If Soul could sin, Spirit, Soul, would be flesh instead of Spirit, because only flesh sins and is lost. Furthermore, if Soul sinned, Soul would die. Sin is the element of self-destruction, and spiritual death is oblivion. If there was sin in Soul, the annihilation of Spirit would be inevitable. The only Life is Spirit, and if Spirit should lose Life as God, then Spirit, which has no other existence, would be annihilated.

Mind is God, and God is not seen by physical sense. Because Mind is Spirit, physical sense is unable to discern it. Soul doesn't change. There is no growth, maturity, nor decay in Soul. The fleshly changes are mutations of human imprints, the shifting clouds of human thinking, which hide the truth of existence.

What we term mortal mind or human mind, dependent on a temporal materialization, is not Mind. God is Mind: all that Mind, God, is, or has made, is good, and all. Anything unlike Mind is not manifest and is not real.

Sin only of the flesh

Soul is immortal because it is Spirit and has no element of self-destruction. Is person lost spiritually? No, person can only lose an unspiritual sense. The unspiritual is of the flesh. It can't be spiritual. The unspiritual exists here or hereafter only so long as the illusion of mind in matter remains. It is a sense of sin, and not a sinful soul, which is lost. The unspiritual is destroyed by the sense of good.

Soul impeccable

To assess soul and mind as though they exist in matter, or in the human mindset, causes the thinker to stray into a feeling of loss. A false assessment believes Soul and spiritual truth could be absent. This state is the mortal dream of life and substance as existent in matter and is directly opposite to the immortal reality of being. So long as we believe that Soul can transgress or that spiritual Soul is in the human body, we can never understand the Science of being. When humanity does understand this Science, it will become our law of Life—even the supreme law of Soul, which prevails over temporal sense through harmony and spirituality.

The objects cognized by the physical senses do not have the reality of substance. They are only what human belief calls them. Flesh, imbalance, and mortality lose all supposed consciousness or claim to life or existence as human beings detach themselves from a false sense of life, substance, and intelligence. Remember: our spirituality and eternalness is not touched by the mortal phases.

How true it is that whatever is learned through human mind must be unlearned because such knowledge is replaced by the spiritual facts of being in Science. That which human sense calls intangible is found to be substance. That which seems to be substance becomes nothingness. Spiritual truths cause the sense-dream to vanish and reality to appear.

Think of a corpse. A corpse is admitted to be material particles, not a person. The death was the departure of a human's mind, not of matter. The human being died because the mindset believed it must die; yet it is said that matter/energy caused the death.

Vain ecstasies

People go into ecstasies over the sense of a humanistic Lord, though with scarcely a spark of love in their hearts; yet God *is* Love, and without Love, spirituality can't appear. Mortals try to believe without understanding Truth; yet God *is* Truth. Human beings claim that death is inevitable; but our eternal Principle is ever-present Life. Mortals believe in an outlined personal God; while God is infinite Love, which cannot be outlined.

Human theories are based on measurable components which cannot escape their own limitations. An anthropoid sense of God and an android sense of our own capabilities necessarily limit faith and delay spiritual understanding. Human-made theories divide faith and understanding between matter and Spirit, and as a result, turn to the inanimate drug and come short of tapping into the intelligent and divine healing Principle.

The anointed

Jesus' spiritual origin and his demonstration of divine Principle richly endowed and entitled him to his status as "Son" in Science. He was the son of a virgin. The term Christ Jesus, or Jesus the Christ (to give the full and proper translation of the Greek), may be rendered "Jesus the anointed," Jesus the God-crowned or the divinely royal man. "Therefore God, your God, has set you above your companions by anointing you with the oil of joy."[1]

Another passage in Hebrews agrees, referring to the Son as "the radiance of God's glory and the exact representation of his being [infinite Mind]."[2] The *Amplified Bible* version is noteworthy, saying the Son "is the sole expression of the glory of God [the Light-being, the out-raying or radiance of the divine], and He is the perfect imprint and very image of [God's] nature."[3] Using these words in their higher meaning, the author of this remarkable epistle appears to regard Christ as the Son of God, the royal reflection of the infinite. J. B. Phillips described the Son as the "radiance of the glory of God, flawless expression of the nature of God."[4] The reason given for the exaltation of Jesus as Mary's son was that he "loved righteousness and hated wickedness."[5]

Jesus the Scientist

Jesus of Nazareth was the most scientific human being that ever walked the earth. Jesus systematically looked past the superficial material cause, to discover and put into practice the spiritual cause. The people around him had immature ideas of spiritual cause. Even his disciples possessed a limited degree of spirituality. Therefore, Jesus used terms familiar to the people such as, "flesh and bones."[6] Jesus

---

[1] Heb. 1:9

[2] Heb. 1:3 (Brackets added by Mary Baker Eddy)

[3] Heb. 1:3 (Amplified*)*

[4] Heb. 1:3 (Phillips NT)

[5] Heb. 1:9

[6] Luke 24:39

meekly waited until his understanding advanced past believing in substance-matter. When he no longer felt attached to the world, Jesus proved conclusively that his substance was Spirit by raising his body from the dead. His body was no more perfect because of death and no less material until the ascension, when his consciousness was further spiritualized. Thus Jesus discovered the eternal Ego, and proved that he and the Father were inseparable as God and God's reflection. The Teacher gained the solution of being, demonstrating the existence of but one Mind without a second or equal.

The bodily resurrection

The people, looking to kill Jesus, showed that their materialist views were the parents of their wicked deeds. When Jesus spoke of reproducing his body—knowing as he did, that Mind was the builder—he said, "Destroy this temple, and I will raise it again in three days."[1] The people thought Jesus was talking about their church building instead of his body. To such materialists, a person's real spiritual identity seemed indefinite, unfamiliar, even preposterous, while the body which they laid in a tomb seemed to be the real deal. This materialism lost sight of the true Jesus; but the faithful Mary saw him, and he presented to her, more than ever before, the true idea of Life and substance.

Materialists try to oppose

Jesus was imperceptible to human sinful thinking. The higher his demonstration of divine Science carried the problem of Being, and the more distinctly he drove home the demands of divine Principle, the more he was hated. Because the materialist's law includes death, they thought they could make Jesus die. Jesus proved them wrong by his resurrection, and said: "Whoever lives and believes in me will never die."[2] Humans who are depending on doctrines and human laws, to save them from wrongdoing, death, and sickness, are offended by Jesus.

---

[1]   John 2:19

[2]   John 11:26

Human-made theology

That saying of the Teacher, "I and the Father are one,"[1] separated him from the scholastic theology of the ecclesiastical authorities. Jesus' better understanding of God discredited the authorities. He related to one Mind and didn't argue for material based power. Jesus must have known that the Ego was Mind instead of a bodily personality. He must have known that world energy and evil were not Mind. His understanding of scientific metaphysical fact provoked others to reject and curse him.

Sons and daughters of God

The contrary and illusory intentions of the people made it impossible for them to recognize Christ's relationship to God as God's child. They could not discern Christ's spiritual existence. Their thoughts were filled with human error instead of with God's spiritual idea as presented by Christ Jesus. Inhumane minds are hostile toward spirituality. Through wrong notions, we lose sight of God and the spiritual sense of Truth is eclipsed. We can however, realize God's likeness when we overcome the unspiritual and prove our spiritual heritage, when we prove the liberty of the children of God.

Jesus' spiritual origin and understanding enabled him to demonstrate the facts of being. Jesus proved irrefutably how spiritual Truth removes errors, heals sickness, and overcomes death. The divine conception of Jesus pointed to this truth and presented an illustration of creation. Jesus' history shows him to have been more spiritual than all other earthly personalities.

Jesus as mediator

Wearing in part a human form (that is, as it seemed to human view), being conceived by a human mother, Jesus was the mediator between Spirit and the flesh, between Truth and error. Explaining and demonstrating the way of divine Science, he became the way of salvation to all who accepted his word. From him, humanity may learn how to escape from negativity and mortality. We turn from the un-godlike and lose sight of the mortal self, before recognizing our relationship to God and our divine posterity. Our spirituality is linked

---

[1]   John 10:30

by Science to our Maker. Christ, Truth, was demonstrated through Jesus to prove the power of Spirit over the flesh—to show that Truth is experienced by its effects on the human mind and body, healing sickness and spiritualizing thought and action.

Jesus represented Christ, the true idea of God. The true idea of God causes a battle to flare. Perfunctory religion and the blindness of popular belief becomes determined to kill the true idea, and the only way they know how to, is by crucifying the flesh. However, spiritual clear-sightedness wins the battle. The Christ-like character takes on greater heights and proves that Truth is the master of death. Christ presents the indestructible person, whom Spirit forms, constitutes, and governs. Identifying our self with God, Christ, we feel our dominion to overcome worldliness.

The spiritual idea of God, as presented by Jesus, was scourged in person, and its Principle was rejected. Jesus was misinterpreted, even considered a criminal, but yet he proved God's divine power by healing the sick, driving out evils, and spiritualizing consciousness. He also raised the dead—those dead in trespasses and sins, satisfied with the flesh. When resting on the basis of matter, we are blind to the possibilities of Spirit and its interrelated truth.

Jesus brought to humanity's attention things "hidden since the creation of the world"[1]—since material knowledge overstepped the creative divine Principle. We don't have to buy into material knowledge which insists on the might of matter, the force of falsity, and the anthropomorphism of God.

While declaring the power of divine Spirit, we will feel haunted by a resistance to Truth. People who follow Christ will run up against the hatred of sinners, until "wisdom is proved right by her actions."[2] We can take to heart the blessed benedictions attributed to Jesus: "If the world hates you, keep in mind that it hated me first;"[3] "Surely I

---

[1] Matt. 13:35

[2] Matt. 11:19

[3] John 15:18

am with you always"[1]—that is, not only in all time, but in *all ways* and conditions.

Our individuality is no less tangible because it is spiritual. We are not at the mercy of matter. The understanding of our spiritual individuality makes us more real, more awe-inspiring in truth, and more able to conquer sin, disease, and death. Jesus presented himself to his disciples after his resurrection from the grave, as the self-same Jesus whom they had loved before the tragedy on Calvary.

Skepticism

The disciple Thomas looked for the ideal Savior in human mind instead of in holy Mind. Jesus was real only as a human structure in the flesh. The dull and doubting disciple had a difficult time acknowledging Jesus' proof that the crucifixion did not change him. Thomas was stuck on believing externalized human mind (matter) was reality. For him to believe in the material was no problem, but to grasp the substantiality of Spirit—and know nothing can destroy Mind—was more challenging. Looking to Soul, and not human evidence, we will become aware of people's true nature.

What the human perceptions originate

Scriptures declare God made all. Human experience defines diseases as realities even insisting that God cannot or will not heal problems. The human perceptions originate and support all that is unreliable, incomplete, selfish, or despicable. The material perceptions would put soul into soil, life into limbo, and doom all things to decay. With the truth of spiritual perceptions, we must silence this lie of unspiritual consciousness. We must stop the beliefs that attempt to efface the pure sense of omnipotence.

Sickness as disorder

Is the sick person more sinful than everyone else? No! But as long as the person is oppressed, he or she is not the image of God. Oppression wearies us. In our exhaustion, we can implicitly drift toward spirituality, and explicitly drop the beliefs of life in matter while consenting to the reality of spiritual Life.

---

[1]   Matt. 28:20

The Science of Mind denies conscious matter and heals with Truth, conscious Spirit. Medical science treats disease as though disease was real, therefore right, and then attempts to heal it. If disease is right, it is wrong to heal it. Inconsistent reasoning and methods of healing do not improve humanity.

Rhythm is not controlled by musical notes. Numbers don't regulate the rules of mathematics. Numbers did not originate mathematics, but is manifested through mathematics. In Science, person did not originate intelligence, but is manifested through intelligence. The appearance that there is intelligence or soul inside person has no relation to the Life reality.

Unscientific versus scientific thinking

Science depicts disease as error, as matter *versus* Mind. Reverse error, and the facts of health are witnessed. To forecast your future according to the world, infringes on spiritual law and misguides your hopes. We are sustained under all circumstances as we have faith in the divine Principle of health and as we spiritually understand God. The ordinary appeal to have faith in the world's ways and means must yield to faith in the all-might of infinite Spirit.

Throughout the infinite cycles of eternal existence, Spirit and matter never agree in person or in the universe.

God the only Mind

The variety of doctrines and theories which presuppose life, consciousness, and intelligence to exist in human mind are so many ancient and modern mythologies. Mystery, miracle, sin, and death will disappear when it becomes fairly well understood that the divine Mind controls us and we have no Mind but God.

Scriptures misinterpreted

The divine Science taught in the original language of the Bible came through inspiration and needs inspiration to be understood. Without inspiration, the spiritual meaning of the Bible is misinterpreted and people only repeat what an inspired teacher had said. An uninspired expression changes the intent and misstates the Science of the Scriptures. For example, to name love as merely an attribute of God, is uninspired, whereas, inspiration speaks as the beloved disciple spoke in one of his epistles, when he declared, "God is love."[1] Likewise, and with the use of capitalization, we can speak of the truth of Truth and of the life of Life, for Christ distinctly said, "I am the way and the truth and the life."[2]

Deeper meaning

Names are often expressive of spiritual ideas. Metaphors are plentiful in the Bible. It is reasonably agreed upon that Scriptures have both a spiritual and literal meaning. *Nelson's New Illustrated Bible Dictionary* says: "Interpreting the Bible correctly demands that we listen to what the text itself is saying, and then draw the meaning out of the passage."[3] Let's compare and contrast a verse, first from the King James Version, "And the Lord said My spirit shall not always strive with man, for that he also is flesh." Now from the New Revised Standard Version, "Then the Lord said, My spirit shall not abide in mortals forever, for they are flesh." We can interpret this today to mean, And the Lord said, My spirit shall not be humbled in human beings, seeing in their error they are but flesh. Notice, the different perspectives offer a clearer view of spiritual facts. Even though the thought of a non-fleshly person seems transcendental, we are image, idea, and this deeper thought or faith will not be humbled, or hidden, by error.

Job on the resurrection

The one important interpretation of Scripture is the spiritual. The text, "In my flesh I will see God,"[4] gives a profound idea of the divine power to heal the ills of the flesh, and encourages human beings to hope in Her who heals all our fleshly diseases. A literal interpretation of this passage assumes Job intended to say that even if disease and degradation destroyed his body, in latter days he should stand in celestial perfection before Elohim, decked out in material flesh. The literal interpretation opposes reason, as may be seen by studying the

---

[1]   I John 4:8

[2]   John 14:6

[3]   *Nelson's New Illustrated Bible Dictionary*, Ronald F. Youngblood, General Editor, Copyright 1995, 1986. Thomas Nelson Publishers, Inc., Nashville, Tennessee. All rights reserved.

[4]   Job 19:26

entire book of Job. Paul told the Corinthians, "Flesh and blood cannot inherit the kingdom of God."[1]

Fear of the snake is overcome

Moses, slow of speech, felt miserable knowing he had to make the people understand what should be revealed to him. When led by wisdom to throw his staff on the ground, he saw it become a snake. Moses ran from the snake; but wisdom told him to come back and overpower it, thus ending Moses' fear.[2] In this incident was seen the actuality of Science. Human perception was shown to be a belief only. The snake, under wisdom's command, was destroyed through the understanding of divine Science. This proof was a staff on which to lean. The illusion of Moses lost its power to alarm him when he discovered that what he apparently saw was really a phase of mortal belief.

Leprosy healed

When Moses obeyed God and put his hand inside his cloak, he took it out and the hand was leprous, proving that disease is a creation of human mind and not a condition of matter. As Moses again put his hand in his cloak and took it out, the dreaded disease was healed—restored to its natural condition by the same simple process. God reduced fear; Moses became aware of an inner voice, the voice of God which said: "If they do not believe you or pay attention to the first miraculous sign, they may believe the second."[3] It is through human experiences like these, that when scientifically viewed, our fear is decreased. So it was in the coming centuries, when the Science of being was demonstrated by Jesus who showed his students the power and supremacy of Mind by changing water into wine, healing the sick and driving out evils.

Changing our standpoints

When understanding changes the standpoints of life and intelligence from a material to a spiritual basis, we will gain the reality of Life. Spirituality allows us to experience the control of Soul over

---

[1] I Cor. 15:50

[2] Exodus 4:1-5

[3] Ex. 4:8

temporal sense and perceive Truth in its divine Principle. This must be the climax before our harmony and immortality is felt and our capabilities revealed. It is highly important—in view of the immense work to be accomplished before this recognition of divine Science can come—to turn our thoughts toward divine Principle, so that limited belief may be prepared to relinquish its error.

Saving the drunk

Our wisdom finds no satisfaction in misconduct, since God has sentenced negative behavior to suffer. The fascinations of yesterday, predicted today's obsessions or mesmerized thinking. The drunk thinks it is enjoyable to be intoxicated. You cannot make the inebriate leave the drunkenness until their temporal sense of pleasure yields to a better sense. A drunk will turn from the bottle, as the startled dreamer wakens from a nightmare due to the stress of distorted sense. A person who likes to do wrong—finding pleasure in it and refraining from it only through fear of consequences—is not moderate or reliable.

Uses of suffering

The sharp experiences of mortality, as well as our disappointments and constant troubles, turn us like tired children to the arms of divine Love. Then we begin to learn Life in divine Science. Without this process of weaning, "Can you fathom the mysteries of God?"[1] It is easier to desire Truth than it is to stop our bad habits. Human beings may seek the understanding of divine Science, but they will not be able to profit from Christian Science without applying the spiritual facts in their daily life. This endeavor consists of forsaking error of every kind and possessing no other consciousness but good.

A bright outlook

Love's discipline is wholesome. As Love corrects us, we advance toward justice, peace, and purity, which are the milestones of Science. Beholding the infinite tasks of truth, we pause—wait on God. Then we make every effort to improve for the better. Spiritualized thought feels creative, free, and inspired, touching the divine glory.

---

[1] Job 11:7

Need and supply

In order to understand more, we must put into practice what we already know. Truth is provable when understood, and good is not understood until proven. If "faithful with a few things,"[1] we will be put in charge of many things. However, the neglected or unused talent rots or is lost. When the sick or the sinning realize their need of what they don't have, they will be a receptor to divine Science. The human mind then thinks on things better than disease or negativity. Thought is attracted toward Soul and as a result, superficial perceptions and the body do not become distractions. The true idea of God gives the true understanding of Life and Love. Spiritual fact softens the hardness of death. Spiritual fact removes perversity and the delusion that there are other minds. Spiritual fact destroys mortality.

Childlike receptivity

The effects of spiritual Science are not so much seen as felt. It is the "gentle whisper"[2] of Truth expressing itself. We are either neglecting this expression or we are attentive to it and being improved by it. Willingness to become as little children[3] and to leave the old for the new, prepares thought to receive the advanced idea. To cheerfully leave behind the false imprints, and contentedly let them disappear, is the attitude that helps to precipitate the ultimate harmony. The purification of feelings and intent is a proof of progress. "Blessed are the pure in heart, for they will see God."[4]

Narrow way

Unless our harmony and spirituality are becoming more apparent, we are not gaining the true idea of God. Consequently, the body will reflect what governs it, whether it is Truth or error, understanding or belief, Spirit or matter. Therefore "submit to God and be at peace with him."[5] Be attentive, sober, and vigilant. The way is straight and narrow which leads to the understanding that God is the only Life. It is a fight

---

[1]   Matt. 25:23; Luke 19:17

[2]   I Kings 19:12

[3]   Matt. 18:3-4

[4]   Matt. 5:8

[5]   Job 22:21

with the flesh, in which we must conquer sin, sickness, and death, either here or hereafter—certainly before we can reach the realm of Spirit or life in God.

Paul's enlightenment

At first, Saul persecuted Jesus' followers. When Saul finally noticed the appearance of truth, he was made blind. After his eyes were healed by Ananias, spiritual light soon enabled Saul to change his name to Paul and follow the example and teaching of Jesus.[1] Paul healed the sick and preached Christianity throughout Asia Minor, Greece, and even in imperial Rome.

Paul writes, "If Christ [Truth] has not been raised, our preaching is useless and so is your faith."[2] That is, if the idea of the supremacy of Spirit doesn't come to your consciousness, you cannot be benefited by what I say.

Remaining in Life

Jesus said substantially, "He that believes in me will never die."[3] That is, those who perceive the true idea of Life lose their belief in death. People who have the true idea of good lose all sense of bad and by reason of this are being ushered into the undying realities of Spirit. Such a one abides in Life—life obtained not of the body incapable of supporting life, but of Truth, unfolding its own immortal idea. Jesus gave the true idea of being, which results in infinite blessings to humanity.

Indestructible being

Paul wrote in Colossians, "When Christ, who is your life, appears [is manifest], then you also will appear [be manifest] with him in glory."[4] When spiritual being is understood in all its perfection, continuity, and might, then person will be found in God's image. The absolute meaning of the apostolic words is this: Then will man and woman be found in God's likeness, perfect as the Father-Mother,

---

[1] Acts 9

[2] I Cor. 15:14 (Brackets added by Mary Baker Eddy)

[3] John 11:26 (John 6:47)

[4] Col. 3:4 (Brackets added by Mary Baker Eddy)

indestructible in Life, "hidden with Christ in God"[1]—with Truth in divine Love, where human sense has not seen man and woman.

Dedication required

Paul had a clear sense of the demands of Truth on mortals physically and spiritually. He said, "Offer your bodies as living sacrifices, holy and pleasing to God—this is your spiritual act of worship."[2] But the person who comes from, and serves fleshly beliefs, can never reach in this world the divine heights of our Lord. Jesus' human presence was accompanied by divine Science. We can similarly understand and demonstrate the spiritual origin.

When first spoken, in any era, Truth, like the light, "shines in the darkness, but the darkness has not understood it."[3] A false sense of life, substance, and mind hides the divine possibilities and conceals scientific demonstration.

Loving God supremely

If we wish to follow Christ, Truth, it must be in God's way. Jesus said, "The person who trusts me will not only do what I'm doing but even greater things."[4] Whoever would reach the source and find the divine remedy for every disorder must not try to climb the hill of Science by some other road. All nature teaches God's love to us, but we can't love God supremely and set our whole affections on spiritual things while loving the material or trusting in it more than in the spiritual.

We must continue to work our way out of human systems and theories, whether time-honored or not, if we would gain the Christ, Truth, as our only Savior. Not in part, but totally, the great healer of human mind is the healer of the body.

The purpose and motive to live spiritually can be achieved now. Getting off to the right start, you have taken the preliminary steps in divine Science, and nothing but wrong intention can obstruct your advancement. Working and praying with true motives, your Father

---

[1]   Col 3:3

[2]   Rom 12:1

[3]   John 1:5

[4]   John 14:12 (The Message*)*

will open the way. "Who cut in on you and kept you from obeying the truth?"[1]

Conversion of Saul

Saul of Tarsus turned his attention to the way of Christ, Truth— only when his uncertain sense of right yielded to a spiritual sense, which is always right. Then Saul was changed.[2] Thought took on a more decent attitude and his life was spiritualized. He learned the wrong he had done in persecuting followers of Spirit, whose religion he had not understood, and in humility he adopted the new name of Paul. The correct idea of Love dawned on him and he learned a lesson in divine Science.

Reform comes by understanding there really is no lasting pleasure in ill-will. Reform also comes by inclining one's self to good according to Science, revealing the immortal fact that pleasure, pain, appetite, and emotionalism cannot exist in or of human mind. Divine Mind can and does purge the false beliefs of pleasure, pain, or fear, and the destructive appetites of the human mind.

Image of the beast

Malice or hate, finding satisfaction in revenge, is pathetic. Evil is sometimes believed to our right, until we learn its self-destructiveness. As the pleasure in wickedness is lost, the wrongdoing becomes a torment. The way to escape the misery of sin is to stop sinning. There is no other way. Sin is the image of the beast to be wiped out through agonizing mental improvement. It is moral foolishness which rushes around chaotically, making annoying demands or loud complaints. We can become secure in civility and goodness.

Peremptory demands

To the physical senses, the strict demands of divine Science seem final. However, humanity is quickly learning that Life is God, faithful good. We also learn that the demand of mortal knowledge is harsh and has in reality no place or power in the human or the divine economy.

---

[1] Gal. 5:7

[2] Acts 9

Moral courage

Fear of punishment never made a person truly honest. Moral courage is requisite to meet the wrong behavior and proclaim the right. But how is the person, who has more animal courage than moral courage, reformed? How do we help a person who doesn't have the true idea of good? Through human consciousness, convince the person it is a mistake to look for power and happiness through material means. Reason is the most active human capability. Let rational thought guide the person's feelings and awaken their dormant sense of moral obligation. By degrees, they will learn the nothingness of the pleasures of human sense and the greatness and happiness of spiritual sense. This silences the corporeal and the person will not only be saved, but *is* saved.

Perpetual promise

Human beings assume that they can live without goodness, when God is good and the only real Life. What is the result? They understand little about the divine Principle which saves and heals, and they get rid of sin, sickness, and death only in the temporal imagination. These errors thereby are not really destroyed. All that is unlike God will taint mortals until, here or hereafter, they gain the true understanding of God in the Science which destroys human delusions and reveals the grand realities of Spirit's allness.

This understanding of our power when equipped by God has sadly disappeared from Christian history. For centuries it has been latent, a lost element of Christianity. Our missionaries carry the Bible around the world, but can it be said that they explain it practically, as Jesus did, when thousands of persons die annually from snake bites, famine, and disease? Understanding spiritual law and knowing that there is no temporal law, Jesus said: "These signs will accompany those who believe: . . . they will pick up snakes with their hands; and when they drink deadly poison, it will not hurt them at all; they will place their hands on sick people, and they will get well."[1] It would be better if Christians believed and obeyed this sacred saying.

---

[1]   Mark 16:18

Jesus' promise is perpetual. Had it been given only to his immediate disciples, the Scriptural passage would read *you*, not *they*. The purpose of his great life-work extends through time and includes universal humanity. Its Principle is unending and outreaches the boundaries of a particular period in time or a specific group of followers. As time moves on, the healing elements of pure spirituality will be honestly dealt with. Mind-healing will be researched and taught and will sparkle in all the elegance of universal goodness.

Imitate Jesus

A little yeast raises all the dough. A little understanding of Science proves the truth of all that I say of it. Because you can't walk on the water and raise the dead, you have no right to question the great might of divine Science in these directions. Be thankful that Jesus, who was the true demonstrator of Science, did these things and left his example for us. In Science we can use only what we understand. We must prove our faith by demonstration.

People should not linger in the storm if the body is freezing, nor should they remain in a contaminated environment. Until a person is able to prevent bad results, it is best to avoid adverse situations. To be discouraged is to resemble a student who is at an elementary level of mathematics and yet attempts to solve a problem of Euclid, only to deny the rule of the problem because the first effort brought failure.

Error destroyed, not pardoned

There is no hypocrisy in Science. Principle is imperative. You can't mock it by human will. Science is a divine demand, not human. Always right, its divine Principle never repents, but maintains the claims of Truth by quenching error. Divine mercy pardons a mistake when the error is destroyed. If people understood the blessedness of their real spiritual source, they would struggle to return to it and be at peace. However, the more entrenched human mind is in error, the more intense its resistance to spirituality, until error yields to Truth.

The hopeful outlook

Human mind's resistance to divine Science weakens in proportion as human beings give up error for Truth, and as the understanding of being supersedes mere belief. Until I learned the vastness of divine Science, the rigidity of mortal illusions and the human hatred of

Truth, I optimistically hoped that Christian Science would meet with immediate and universal acceptance.

When the following principles are understood and the letter and the spirit bear witness, the unfailing scientific divine Mind will be demonstrated.

The deific supremacy

1. God is infinite, the only Life, substance, Spirit, or Soul, the only intelligence of the universe, including person. Mortal eye has not seen Spirit or God's image and likeness. God and the perfect person can't be discerned by the physical senses. The individuality of infinite Spirit is unknown, consequently, knowledge of it is left either to human conjecture or to the revelation of divine Science.

The deific definitions

2. God is what the Scriptures declare Him to be—Life, Truth, Love. Spirit is divine Principle, and divine Principle is Love, and Love is Mind, and Mind is not both good and bad, for God is Mind; therefore there is in reality one Mind only, because there is one God.

Evil obsolete

3. The notion that both bad and good are real is a delusion of physical sense, which Science annihilates. Evil is nothing, no thing, mind nor power. As manifested by humankind, evil stands for a lie, nothing claiming to be something—claiming to be lust, fear, dishonesty, selfishness, envy, hypocrisy, slander, hate, theft, adultery, murder, dementia, insanity, idiocy, devil, hell, with all the etcetera that word includes.

Life the creator

4. God is divine Life, and Life is no more confined to the forms which reflect it than substance is in its shadow. If life were in human beings or material things, it would be open to their limitations and would end in death. Life is the creator reflected in Mind's creations. If Life existed inside its creation, God would not be reflected but absorbed. The Science of being would be forever lost through a mortal sense of a beginning and an end.

Allness of Spirit

5. The Scriptures imply that God is All-in-all. From this it follows that nothing possesses reality or existence except the divine Mind and its ideas. The Scriptures also declare that God is Spirit. Therefore in Spirit all is harmony and there can be no disorder; all is Life and there is no death. Everything in God's universe expresses Spirit.

The universal cause

6. God is individual, bodiless. Divine Principle, Love, is the universal cause, the only source, and there is no other self-expression. Being is all-inclusive, and is reflected by all that is real and eternal and by nothing else. God fills all presence (space), and it is impossible to conceive of such omnipresence and individuality except as infinite Spirit or Mind. Hence all is Spirit and spiritual.

Divine trinity

7. Life, Truth, and Love constitute the triumvirate Person called God—that is, the triad divine Principle, Love. They represent a trinity in unity, three in one—the same in essence though versatile in office: God the Father-Mother; Christ the spiritual idea of person; divine Science or the Holy Spirit (Counselor).

   These three express in divine Science the triply, essential nature of the infinite. The expression also indicates the divine Principle of scientific being, and the intelligent relationship between God, child, and the universe.

Father-Mother

8. Father-Mother is the name for Deity, which indicates Spirit's tender, committed affiliation to Mind's spiritual creation. As the apostle expressed it in words which he quoted with respect from a classic poet: "We are his offspring."[1]

The Child of God

9. Jesus was born of Mary. Christ is the true idea voicing good; the divine message from God to us, speaking to the human consciousness. The Christ is bodiless, spiritual—the holy

---

[1] Acts 17:28

image and likeness, dispelling the illusions of the senses; the Way, the Truth, and the Life, healing the sick and driving out evils, destroying sin, disease, and death. Paul said: "There is one God; there is also one mediator between God and humankind, Christ Jesus, himself human."[1] The physical Jesus was human.

Holy Spirit or Counselor

10. Jesus demonstrated Christ. Jesus proved that Christ is the correct impression or interpretation of God—the Holy Spirit, or Counselor, revealing the divine Principle, Love, and leading into all truth.

Christ Jesus

11. Jesus was the son of a virgin. He was appointed to speak God's word and to appear to human beings in such a form of humanity as they could understand as well as perceive. Mary's conception of him was spiritual, for only purity could reflect Truth and Love, which were plainly incarnate in the good and genuine Christ Jesus. He expressed the purest type of divinity, which a fleshly form could express in that age. Into the real and ideal child, the fleshly element can't enter. Thus it is that Christ illustrates the consistency or spiritual agreement, between God and our identity as the image of God.

Messiah or Christ

12. The word *Christ* is not properly a synonym for Jesus, though it is frequently used as such. Jesus was a human name, which belonged to him in common with other Hebrew boys and men, for it is identical with the name Joshua, the renowned Hebrew leader. *Christ* is not a name so much as the divine title of Jesus. Christ expresses God's immeasurable, eternal nature. The name is synonymous with Messiah and alludes to the spirituality which is taught, illustrated, and demonstrated in the life of which Christ Jesus embodied. The proper name of the Teacher in the Greek was Jesus the Christ; but Christ Jesus better signifies the Godlike.

---

[1] I Tim. 2:5 (NRSV)

The divine Principle and idea

13. The advent of Jesus of Nazareth marked the first century of the Christian era, but Christ-spirit is without beginning of years or end of days. Throughout all generations both before and after the Christian era, the Christ, as the divine idea— the reflection of God—has come with some degree of power and grace to all prepared to receive the Messiah, or Truth. Abraham, Jacob, Moses, and the prophets caught glorious glimpses of Christ, which baptized these insightful people in the nature, or essence of Love. The divine image, idea, or Christ was, is, and ever will be inseparable from the divine Principle, Truth. Jesus referred to this unity of his spiritual identity as so: "Before Abraham was born, I am!"[1] "I and the Father are one;"[2] "The Father is greater than I."[3] The one Spirit includes all identities.

Spiritual oneness

14. Jesus' sayings did not mean the human Jesus was or is eternal, but that the divine idea or Christ was and is so and therefore predated Abraham. The fleshly Jesus was not one with the Father, but the spiritual idea, Christ is. Christ dwells forever in the bosom of the Maker, God, from which it illumines heaven and earth. The Father is not greater than Spirit, which is God, but greater than the fleshly Jesus, whose earthly career was brief.

The Son's duality

15. Christ was imperceptible to the human personal senses, whereas Jesus appeared as a bodily existence. This dualistic personality of the unseen and seen, the spiritual and physical, the eternal Christ and fleshly Jesus, continued until his ascension. The human temporal concept, or Jesus, disappeared during his ascending transformation, while the spiritual self or Christ, continues to exist in the eternal order of divine Science.

---

[1] John 8:58

[2] John 10:30

[3] John 14:28

Christ-spirit takes away the sins of the world, as always, even before the human Jesus was incarnate to human eyes.

Eternity of the Christ

16. This was "the Lamb that was slain from the creation of the world"[1]—slain, that is, according to the testimony of the physical senses, but undying in the deific Mind. The Revelator represents the Son of man as saying: "I am the First and the Last. I am the Living One; I was dead [not understood], and behold I am alive for ever and ever [Science has explained me]!"[2] This statement not only symbolizes the eternity of Christ, Truth, but also references the human sense of Jesus crucified.

Infinite Spirit

17. Spirit being God, there is but one Spirit, for there can be but one infinite and therefore one God. There are neither spirits many nor gods many. There is no evil in Spirit, because God is Spirit. The theory that Spirit must pass through a human being to be individualized would reduce God to dependency on matter and establish a basis for pantheism.

The only substance

18. Spirit, God, has created all in and of Mind. Spirit never created human mortal mind. There is nothing in Spirit out of which a limited mind could be made, for, as the Bible declares, without the Logos, or Word of God, "nothing was made that has been made."[3] Spirit is the only substance, the invisible and indivisible infinite God. Things spiritual and eternal are substantial. Things changeable and temporal are insubstantial.

Soul and Spirit one

19. Soul and Spirit being one, God and Soul are one, and this one never included in a restricted mind or a limited body. Spirit is eternal, divine. Nothing but Spirit, Soul, can evolve Life, for Spirit is more than all else. Because Soul is immortal, it does

---

[1]   Rev. 13:8

[2]   Rev. 1:17-18 (Brackets added by Mary Baker Eddy)

[3]   John 1:3

not exist in mortality. Soul must be bodiless to be Spirit, for Spirit is not circumscribed. Only by losing the false sense of Soul can we gain the eternal unfolding of Life as immortality brought to light.

The one divine Mind

20. Mind is the divine Principle, Love, and can produce nothing unlike the eternal Father-Mother, God. Reality is spiritual, harmonious, unchangeable, indestructible, divine, and timeless. Nothing unspiritual can be real, euphonious, or eternal. Sin, sickness, and mortality are the presumptuous contradictions of Spirit and reality.

The divine Ego

21. Spirit's Ego is deathless and limitless, for limits would imply and impose ignorance. Mind is the I AM, or infinity. Mind never enters the measurable. Intelligence never passes into non-intelligence, or matter. Good never enters into evil. The unlimited never connects with the limited. The eternal never joins the temporal. Immortality never participates with mortality. The divine Ego, or individuality, is reflected in all spiritual individuality from the infinitesimal to the infinite.

The real person

22. Immortal person was and is God's image or idea, even the infinite expression of infinite Mind. Spiritual selfhood is coexistent and coeternal with that Mind. Spirituality has been forever in the eternal Mind, God. Mind is not in man and woman. Infinite Mind can only be reflected by person. The consciousness and individuality of person is the reflection of God; the emanation of Person who is Life, Truth, and Love. Immortal person is not and never was humanistic, but always spiritual and eternal.

Indivisibility of the infinite

23. God is indivisible. A part of God could not enter us; neither could God's inclusiveness be reflected by a single person. If God was divisible, God would be manifestly finite, would lose the deific character, and would then become less than God.

Allness is the measure of the infinite and nothing less can express God.

God the parent Mind

24. God, the divine Principle of our spirituality, and person in Mind's likeness are inseparable, harmonious, and undying. God is the parent Mind, and God's children are spiritual offspring.

People reflect the perfect God

25. God is individual and personal in a scientific sense, but not in any anthropomorphic sense. Therefore God's children can't lose their individuality. We lose sight of our spiritual individuality because of limited perceptions, or because blind mortals believe soul is in the body. Human personality is myth; it is not the reflection or likeness of Spirit. The thinking that flesh can tell us how to feel is not bliss, but bondage. For true happiness, man and woman must harmonize with Principle, divine Love. The child must synchronize with the Father-Mother, must be in conformity with Christ. According to divine Science, person is as perfect as the Mind that forms the perfect child. The truth of spiritual existence makes us harmonious and spiritual. The error of material existence makes us discordant and unspiritual.

Purity the path to perfection

26. Divine Science demonstrates that none but the pure in heart can see God, as the gospel teaches. Spirituality is directly proportionate to purity and perfection is the order of celestial being which demonstrates Life in Christ, Life's spiritual ideal.

True idea of people

27. The correct concept of person, as the reflection of the invisible God, is as incomprehensible to the limited senses as is infinite Principle. The visible universe and mortal persons are the poor counterfeits of the invisible universe and spiritual person, reflected in infinite individuality. Eternal things are God's thoughts as they exist in the spiritual realm of the real. Temporal things are the thoughts of human beings and are

unreal, being the opposite of the real or the spiritual and eternal.

Truth demonstrated

28. Expose disorder and impurity to the rule of health and holiness in divine Science and you will become aware of the truth of spiritual Science, for it heals the sick and sinning as no other system can. Divine Science, rightly understood, leads to eternal harmony. It brings to light the only living and real God, and person in God's likeness. To believe that we originate in human mind or from matter, with a beginning and end, and a good and bad demeanor, is to terminate in disorder and mortality. Error is destroyed by Truth. Mortality proves that error has been grafted into our premises and conclusions concerning humanity.

Adam is not the ideal person

29. The word *Adam* is from the Hebrew ādām, signifying the red earth. Divide the name Adam into two syllables, and it reads, a dam, or obstruction. This suggests the thought of human energy before it congealed to obstruct Spirit. It is pretending to be the "darkness . . . over the surface of the deep,"[1] but earthly dust was cursed by God. Dust is not the agent Deity uses to create person. Here *a dam* is not a mere play on words; it stands for obstruction, error, even the supposed separation of man and woman from God. It also represents the obstacle which the serpent, sin, would impose between God and God's children. However, The Lord did curse the ground[2] from which Adam came, but later said, "I will never again curse the ground because of humankind."[3] From this it follows that Adam was not the ideal person for whom the earth was blessed. The ideal person was revealed in due time, and was known as Christ Jesus. Note: The analysis and definition

---

[1] Gen. 1:2

[2] Gen. 3:17

[3] Gen. 8:21 (NRSV)

of words, aside from their metaphysical derivation, is not scientific.

Divine pardon

30. The divine method of pardon is to remove completely all that goes against Life, Truth, and Love. Divine Life replaces death, Truth removes error, and Love destroys hate. Being destroyed, sin needs no other form of pardon or forgiveness. Doesn't God's forgiveness, eliminating any one negative thought and action, prophesy and involve the final destruction of all negative thought and action?

Evil not produced by God

31. Since God is All, there is no dimension for something unlike Spirit. God alone designed all, and called it *good*.[1] Therefore evil, being contrary to good, is unreal, and can't be the product of God. A limited, contradictory mindset can receive no encouragement from the fact that Science demonstrates the unreality of limitation and sin, for the contradictor would make a reality of that which opposes Life, Truth, and Love; would make that real which is unreal, and store up "wrath *and* indignation."[2] Do not join in a conspiracy against yourself. Continue to recognize the awful unreality by which the human mind is deceived. Repent, think differently, abandon the unnatural and you can fully understand the unreality of that which argues against the infinite.

Basis of health and immortality

32. As the mythology of pagan Rome has yielded to a more spiritual idea of God, so will our human theories yield to spiritual ideas, until the finite gives place to the infinite, sickness gives way to health, sin to holiness, and God's kingdom comes "on earth as it is in heaven."[3] The basis of all health, purity, and spirituality is the great fact that God is the only Mind; and this Mind must be not merely believed, but

---

[1] Gen. 1:31

[2] Rom. 2:5 (Amplified)

[3] Matt. 6:10

it must be understood. To get rid of anything that opposes Love is to deprive the opposition of any supposed mind or reality, and never to admit the competitor can have intelligence or power, pain or pleasure. You conquer error by denying it validity. Our various theories will never lose their imaginary power for good or evil until we lose our faith in them and make life its own proof of harmony and God.

A text in the book of Ecclesiastes conveys the scientific mental thought, especially when the word *duty* is omitted. Quoting from *Moffatt*, "Stand in awe of God, obey his orders: that is everything, for every man."[1] In other words, love God and keep Mind's commandments: for this is the whole of man and woman in Soul's image and likeness. Divine Love is infinite. Therefore, all that really exists is in and of God and manifests Truth's love.

"You shall have no other gods before me."[2] The First Commandment is my favorite text. It demonstrates Christian Science. It inculcates the trinity of God, Spirit, Mind; it signifies that we will have no other spirit or mind but God, eternal good, and that all people will have one Mind. The divine Principle of the First Commandment bases the Science of spiritual being by which we demonstrate health, holiness, and life eternal. One infinite God, good, unites people and nations; constitutes good-will; ends wars; fulfills the Scripture, "Love your neighbor as yourself;"[3] annihilates false thinking and Christian idolatry—removes whatever is wrong in social, civil, criminal, political, and religious codes; equalizes the sexes; annuls the curse on us, and leaves nothing that can sin, suffer, be punished or destroyed.

---

[1] Ecc. 12:13 (Moffatt)

[2] Ex. 20:3

[3] Matt. 19:19, 22:39; Mark 12:31, 33; Luke 10:27; Rom. 13:9; Gal. 5:14; James 2:8

SOME OBJECTIONS DEBUNKED

Yet because I tell the truth, you do not believe me! Can any of you prove me guilty of sin? If I am telling the truth, why don't you believe me?[1]

And if the Spirit of him who raised Jesus from the dead is living in you, he who raised Christ from the dead will also give life to your mortal bodies through his Spirit, who lives in you.[2]

The restrictions on *Science and Health* would condemn to oblivion the truth which is strengthening the weak and elevating human consciousness from a theoretical to a practical Christianity. Criticisms are generally based on misquotes or phrases out of context. Even the Scriptures, which grow in beauty and consistency from one grand root, appear contradictory when torn apart and exposed to such usage. Jesus said, "Blessed are the pure in heart, for they will see God [Truth]."[3]

Supported by facts

In divine Science mere opinion is worthless. Sneers at the word *Science,* when applied to Christianity, can't prevent spirituality from being scientific. Spirituality is based on a divine Principle, demonstrated according to a given rule, and open to proof. The facts are so numerous in support of divine Science, that misrepresentation and denunciation cannot overthrow it. Paul warns about "quarreling over opinions."[4] This is an era when we live and think in terms of

---

[1] John 8:45-46

[2] Rom. 8:11

[3] Matt. 5:8 (Brackets added by Mary Baker Eddy)

[4] Rom. 14:1 (NRSV)

science, therefore proof and demonstration, instead of opinion and dogma, are called upon to support spirituality, "making wise the simple."[1]

Commands of Jesus

Unfounded attacks on scientific Mind-healing are a denial of Truth, and some may see with sorrow, this denial can produce sad effects on the sick. Finding fault with divine Science is done presumptuously, in the face of Bible history, and defies the direct instruction of Jesus, "Go into all the world and preach the good news to all creation."[2] To this instruction was added the promise that students will drive out evils and heal the sick. Jesus called upon the seventy-two[3] disciples, as well as the twelve, to heal the sick in any town where they should be kindly received.

If Godlike Christianity is not scientific, and Science is not of God, then there is no unified law, and truth becomes an accident. Shall it be denied that a system which works according to the Scriptures has Scriptural authority?

Argument of good works

Divine Science awakens the sinner, rehabilitates the self-deceived, and releases from pain the helpless sufferer. Science speaks the words of Truth to those who are lost, and they answer with rejoicing. It causes the deaf to hear, the lame to walk, and the blind to see. Who would be the first to disown the Christ-likeness of good works, when Jesus said, "By their fruit you will recognize them."?[4]

If Christian Scientists were teaching or practicing pharmaceutics or obstetrics according to the mainstream medical theories, little denunciation would follow them even if their treatment resulted in the death of a patient. The people are taught in such cases to say, it was God's will. Why then, am I maligned for healing, for teaching Truth as the Principle of healing, and for proving my word by my deed?

---

1   Ps. 19:7

2   Mark 16:15

3   Some documents say, seventy

4   Matt. 7:20

James said: "Show me your faith without deeds, and I will show you my faith by what I do."[1]

Personal experience

Isn't the human mind unaware of God's methods? This makes it doubly unfair for human beings to impugn and misrepresent the spiritual facts. In regard to the human mind's misrepresentations of God, eventually a person is able to say, "None of these things move me."[2] It is enlightened sense that understands God. Even though Truth is unjustly distorted, it will not forever be hidden from the enlightened sense of the people. The sick, the disabled, and the blind look to divine Science and receive blessing.

Proof from miracles

Jesus strips all disguise from error when his teachings are fully understood. By parable and argument he explains the impossibility of good producing evil. Jesus also scientifically demonstrates the allness of good, proving by what are wrongly called miracles, that sin, sickness, and death are beliefs—illusive errors—which he could and did destroy.

It would sometimes seem as if truth were rejected because humility and spirituality are the conditions of its acceptance, while Christendom generally demands so much less.

Example of disciples

The apostles who were Jesus' students, as well as Paul who was not his student, healed the sick and reformed the sinner by their religion. Hence the mistake which allows words, rather than works, to follow such examples! Whoever is first, humbly and conscientiously, to press along the line of gospel-healing, is considered a heretic.

Strong position

Christian Science is sometimes disapproved of because it claims God as the only absolute Life and Soul, and person to be God's idea— that is, Spirit's image. However, Scriptures confirm the claim, saying that God created "man" (a generic term for person given in many Bible

---

[1]   James 2:18

[2]   Acts 20:24 (KJV)

versions), "in our image, in our likeness."[1] Is it sacrilegious to theorize that God's likeness is not found in fleshly beings, sinful, sick, and dying? In reality, the person referred to as God's image represents the normal, healthful, and sinless condition of man and woman in divine Science.

Testing the effectiveness of spirituality

Were it more fully understood that Truth heals and error causes disease, maybe opponents of a demonstrable Science would mercifully withhold their harmful misrepresentations. Until the opponents of divine Science test its efficacy according to its rules, which reveal its usefulness or uselessness, it would be fair to observe the Scriptural precept, "Do not judge."[2]

The one divine method

Complementary and alternative medicines (CAM), osteopathy, chiropractic care, and conventional medicine are employed to treat disease. However, Jesus did not need any of these methods. The divine Science which he preached and practiced certainly healed and it should be presented to the whole world.

Why would a person refuse to investigate Jesus' method of treating disease when it was shown to work? Why default to the conventional mainstream systems when surgeries, harmful drug reactions, and substance abuse cause a number of complications? Is it because health insurance pays for those systems? Is it because orthodoxy is more fashionable?

Omnipotence set forth

In the Bible the word *Spirit* is so commonly applied to Deity that Spirit and God are often regarded as synonymous terms; and Spirit is exactly how God is understood in Christian Science. It is evident that the likeness of Spirit can't be material, therefore, doesn't it follow that God can't be in Spirit's unlikeness and work through matter to heal the sick? When the omnipotence of God is preached and Spirit's absoluteness is conveyed, the sick will be healed.

---

[1]   Gen. 1:26

[2]   Matt. 7:1; Luke 6:37; John 7:24

Contradictions not found

In his book, *Healing and Christianity*, Morton Kelsey presents a history of healing in the Christian church. Kelsey then points out this spiritual healing is often overlooked, because the connection between religion and healing is difficult to explain. Students of theology and philosophy may even criticize religious leaders who heal through Christ, Truth, in order to cover up their own lack of healing ability. Kelsey states, "There are some who, on the side, poke fun at the theological vagaries of Mary Baker Eddy."[1] A person who understands divine Science can heal the sick via divine Principle, and this practical proof is the only feasible evidence that one does understand this Science well enough to pass judgment on it. The theology of divine Science, including Christian healing, is consistent. In this volume there are no contradictory statements apparent to those who understand its propositions.

When we are able to perceive the inconsistency between mortal human beings and God's being, we can discern the distinction, made by Science, between the two.

The apostle says: "For if those who are nothing think they are something, they deceive themselves."[2] The thought of human material nothingness, enrages the human ego and is the main cause of its resistance to new ideas.

The distinction needs to be clear between God's ideal, person, and the human's idea of person. God's ideal is perfect, however, there is no perfect mortal human. In order to achieve the ideal of God, you must be careful not to fall into the human mind's tendency to believe that a particular human routine or lifestyle will guarantee spirituality. To insist on a particular human way of life as a means of achieving perfection, doesn't achieve God's ideal. For example, someone who thinks, "We do not seek sex; we do not try drugs; we do not take

---

[1] Kelsey, Morton T. *Healing and Christianity*. New York: Harper & Row, 1973.

[2] Gal. 6:3 (NRSV)

medicine; we do not go to doctors,"[1] will be disappointed. To avoid sex, drugs, medicine, and doctors, is the same as robotically having sex, taking drugs, and going to a doctor. Neither are a means of reaching the spiritual ideal. The imperative point is to understand God's ideal and let the divine understanding impel your thoughts and actions as a part of humanity. Our ideal directs our lifestyles, not vice versa. The teachings found in *Science and Health,* uncover spirituality and the understanding of God's ideal.

Thought must stay open to metaphysical ideas in science, theology, and medicine. Thought cannot obsess or fixate on lifestyles, symbols, or a favorite rule; otherwise people will lose touch with reason and develop a narrow and blurred view of reality—they will make mistakes, errors. Consider a successful math student. The student can't focus on only the rule of addition when working out a problem that also involves subtraction or division. Fixations cause confusion, the penchant to guess, and a lack of mental improvement. We must be receptive to all of the principles in Science and they need to be learned and applied in life's situations, otherwise error will be an unbroken head-wind.

Some critics think that Christian Scientists are deluded, or in some vacuum, because error is revealed as unreal. For instance, a Christian apologist, attempting to interpret the teachings of divine Science, says of Christian Scientists, "Their religious worldview teaches that sickness and pain are an illusion; they do not exist. But this belief is valid only by rejecting the fact that truth corresponds to reality."[2] The fact that truth corresponds to reality is not rejected in Christian Science. Instead, Christian Science reveals that much of the reality before the human perceptions is not actually true, for example the earth isn't a motionless solid mass, but consists of forces in constant

---

[1]   *The Unseen Shore* by Thomas Simmons. Copyright © 1991 by Thomas Simmons. Reprinted by permission of Beacon Press, Boston.

[2]   Taken from *Christianity on the Offense:Responding to the Beliefs and Assumptions of Spiritual Seeker* © 1998 by Dan Story. Published by Kregel Publications, Grand Rapids, MI. Used by permission of the publisher. All rights reserved.

motion. Truth, reality, has no error; therefore disbelief in error destroys error and leads to discernment of Truth.

We treat error through the understanding of Truth, because Truth is error's antidote. Error is like a dream, and when a dream stops, it is self-destroyed and the terror is over. Take pain. Many times over, pain disappears as dreams do. It may seem absurd to say pain is an illusion (dream), however, what else could it be? Human beings have forever been at odds when measuring pain levels. The same painful condition to one person isn't even noticed by another person. More bizarre is the fact that pain to one human being is actually pleasure to another. Pain has even been proven to be an error on the physical level. When a supposedly pained human mind is distracted, unconscious, or drugged, where is the pain? Pain is an error, sometimes a terror. Error has no part of Truth and this is an antidote that removes any terror.

Superstitions and a lack of knowledge within your own human framework must be expelled to make room for spiritual understanding. We cannot serve both the human and divine framework at the same time; but isn't this what frail mortals are trying to do? Paul says: "For the sinful nature desires what is contrary to the Spirit, and the Spirit what is contrary to the sinful nature."[1] Are you ready to admit this?

Critics who attack faith should be careful not to confuse spiritual faith with blind faith. Faith is necessary in science, medicine, and religion. Consider the researcher or scientist who is trying to find a cure for cancer; they obviously have faith that a cure exists; otherwise they would not even try. People who cannot distinguish between blind (ritualistic) faith and that of spiritual faith are easily misinformed. They can make unfortunate statements such as: "If your beliefs are those of a Christian Scientist, obliging you to forgo all medical interventions, you may even have collaborated with God by refusing to give your child antibiotics."[2] Christian Science does not "oblige" any particular human action as if people are androids. A student of Christian Science does not collaborate with God as if God is a separate

[1] Gal. 5:17

[2] Harris, Sam. *The End of Faith*. New York: W. W. Norton & Company, 2005.

mind. In Science, there is no attitude of give-and-take; there is no human element that says, "If you do this, I'll do that." Do physicists collaborate with the law of gravity in order to go to the moon? No. Scientists study the principles of physics, they have the faith those rules will work, they apply the principles, and they go to the moon. Comments and condemnations based on a lack of research obscure any good points being made.

Essential element of spirituality

Opponents should consider that the mortal human being is not the reality of God's child, and this consideration will allow the mind to receive new ideas that lead to progress and well-being. We can expect to receive more epiphanies, if you will, as a result of Christ in action. The Christ-spirit comes now as of old, preaching the good news to receptive minds, healing the sick, and destroying evils. Can error, human intellect, or any human invention, restore the essential element of spirituality—namely, apostolic, divine healing? No, the Science of Christ is restoring it, and is the light shining in darkness, a darkness that does not overcome the light.

If divine Science takes away the popular gods—sin, sickness, and death—it is Christ, Truth, who destroys these evils, and so proves their nothingness.

The dream that human mind and error are real or permanent must yield to reason and enlightenment. Then human beings will perceive the insubstantiality of sin and sickness, and sin and sickness will disappear from consciousness. The harmonious will appear real and the inharmonious will become extinct. Erroneous perceptions are seen as false gods, nonbeings; gods we do not desire to honor or fear.

When the medical field finds no biological or physical cause for symptoms of disease, various forms of psychotherapy have been known to improve the unhealthy condition. Psychosomatic illnesses or psychophysiological disorders are admitted to be problems caused by mental processes. They are problems in the mind, and once the mind is corrected, the symptoms vanish as illusions vanish. Mental conditions, such as severe stress, anger, anxiety, resentment, depression, and guilt have produced rashes, allergies, loss of hair, eating disorders, and pain, among other problems. So, why not approve of a cure which in effect makes any disease appear to be what it really is—an illusion?

Here is the difficulty: it is not generally understood how one disease can be just as much a delusion as another. It is a pity that the medical faculty and clergy have not learned this, for Jesus established this fundamental fact when devils (delusions) were driven to oblivion and the mute spoke.

Eliminating sickness

Are we irreverent toward sin, or assigning too much power to God, when we ascribe to Him almighty Life and Love? I deny God's cooperation with evil and I desire to have no faith in evil or in any power but God, good. Isn't it better to eliminate from so-called human mind that which, so long as it remains in human mind, will show itself in forms of sin, sickness, and death? Why complain of suffering while at the same time tenaciously defending the rights of disease? Wouldn't it be better to abandon the defense of dis-ease, especially when by doing so, our own condition can be improved and that of other persons as well?

More work to be done

I have never supposed the world would immediately leave everything for divine Science, or that people would instantly stop believing in sin, disease, and death. However, I do state that, as a result of teaching Christian Science in the late 19th century and early 20th century, ethics and moderation have received a stimulus, health has been restored, and people are living longer. If that was the fruit then, what will the harvest be, when this Science is more generally understood?

Paul asked the megalomaniacal leaders the same question we ask today concerning healing and teaching, "You who brag about the law, do you dishonor God by breaking the law?"[1] Jesus annulled fleshly law by healing contrary to those human laws. We have the gospel. We propose to follow Jesus' model, by obeying spiritual law which can overcome material law. Two essential points of Truth's law are

---

[1]   Rom. 2:23

that Life and spiritual being do not die, and God is not the author of sickness.

Language is inadequate

The major obstacle in conveying the teachings of divine Science accurately to human thought is that English, like all other languages, is inadequate to express spiritual concepts and intents. We have to use incomplete terms and symbols in dealing with spiritual ideas. The elucidation of Mind-science resides in its spiritual sense, and students need first to recognize their spiritual senses in order to grasp the meaning of divine Science. Out of this condition grew the prophecy concerning the apostles, "They will speak in new tongues."[1]

While dwelling on a physical plane, human terms must generally be employed to speak of the things of Spirit. It takes time for human thought to adjust to the higher meaning. Thought must be educated to perceive spirituality. To a certain extent, improved thought is necessary in all learning, even in that which is secular.

Substance spiritual

In divine Science, substance is understood to be Mind, while the disputer of Christian Science believes substance to be human mind and material things. Disputers believe the human mind and its projections are almost the only substance, and that the things which pertain to Spirit are next to nothing, or are very far removed from daily experience.

To understand all of Jesus' sayings as recorded in the New Testament, followers must advance into that stature of selfhood in Christ Jesus which enables them to interpret the ongoing vital spiritual meaning. Spiritual understanding knows how Truth dissolves error and heals the sick. Jesus' words were the offspring of his deeds, both of which must be understood. Unless the works are comprehended which his words explained, the words are blind.

Jesus often refused to explain his words. He said: "For this people's heart has become calloused; they hardly hear with their ears, and they have closed their eyes. Otherwise they might see with their eyes, hear with their ears, understand with their hearts and turn, and I would

---

[1]   Mark 16:17

heal them."[1] The materialist milieu has a difficult time understanding spiritual Truth.

The divine link to Life

"The Word became flesh."[2] Truth must be known by its effects on the body as well as on the human mind before the Science of being can be demonstrated. The idea of the Word becoming flesh was embodied in the incarnate Jesus. He was a life-link forming the connection through which the real reaches the unreal; through which Soul rebukes mortal impressions; and Truth destroys error.

Truth a present help

If the Word is explained through mortal convictions, the spiritual meaning will scarcely be perceived. Religion which stems from half-hidden history is pretentious and void of healing power. When we lose faith in God's power to heal or distrust the Principle of divine Science, we will project the belief that it is impossible to heal spiritually. It is difficult to heal metaphysically if we position ourselves on a material basis.

I became a member of the orthodox Congregational Church in early years. Later in life, I learned that my own prayers failed to heal me as did the prayers of my devout parents and the church. However, when the spiritual view of religion was discerned in Science, this view was a present help. The spiritual sense is the living, pulsating presence of Christ, Truth, which healed, and heals, the sick.

Fatal premises

We can't bring out the practical proof of spirituality which Jesus required while error seems as potent and real to us as Truth. We can't make a personal devil and an anthropomorphic God our starting points—especially if we consider Satan as a being coequal in power with, or superior to, the Almighty. Such starting points are neither spiritual nor scientific and they can't work out the metaphysical principles of divine healing, which prove the nothingness of error by demonstrating the all-inclusiveness of harmonious Truth.

---

[1]   Isa. 6:10; Matt. 13:15; Acts 28:27

[2]   John 1:14

Unproductive worship

Some worshipper's center thought on the material in an attempt to worship the spiritual. To these worshippers, the human perceptions, rituals, and worldly ways and means are substance and Spirit is insubstantial. But it is impossible to worship Spirit from the incongruous standpoint of human reverences and agendas. The people might appeal to their personal concepts or false gods, but their prayer brings no proof that it was heard, because they did not sufficiently understand God to be able to demonstrate His power to heal—to make harmony the reality and disorder the unreality.

Spirit is tangible

Jesus was known to say that his fleshly body was not spirit, evidently considering it a human and changeable belief of flesh and bones. People, even the religious leaders, did not share his view because the spiritual was the intangible and uncertain, if not the unreal.

Sin and disease are terrible bogeymen

Would a parent say to a child who is frightened by ghosts or sickened by fear of ghosts, "I know that ghosts are real. Ghosts exist and are to be feared, but you must not be afraid of them"?

It is absurd for children, or adults, to pretend not to be afraid of something scary. We have to understand the unreality of what scares us, otherwise, at any moment we may become a helpless victim. However, instead of increasing fears by declaring a bogeyman, or animal magnetism, or disease, to be real, merciless, and powerful, thus watering the very roots of helpless timidity, we should gain the spiritual understanding that assures us fear is groundless because ghosts and diseases are not realities, but are only a downward spiraling imagination that is erroneous and human-made.

Tell children not to believe in ghosts and explain the good that is worthy of respect and honor. If you destroy the thinking that ghosts are real, terror from the ghosts will fade and health will be restored. Objects of alarm will vanish and no longer seem worthy of fear or honor. To accomplish a good result, it is certainly not irrational to tell the truth about ghosts.

The spiritually scientific real goes unnoticed by the physical nervous system and cognitive ability. Likewise, negativity, confusion, erratic love/hate relationships, loss, whatever seems real to fleshly sense, is unreal in divine Science. The physical senses and Science have ever been antagonistic, and they will so continue until the physical senses entirely yield to scientific spirituality.

How can a person, who has glimpsed the evidence of Truth, any longer believe in the reality of error, either in the form of sickness or sin? All must admit that Christ, Truth, is "the way and the truth and the life,"[1] and that omnipotent Truth certainly does destroy error.

Getting past superstition

Human minds have not completely outgrown their superstitions. Human mindsets embody ghostly beliefs, and time is required before reaching eternity, spirituality, or complete reality. All the real is eternal. Perfection underlies reality. Without perfection, nothing is completely real. Temporal things will continue to be outgrown until perfection appears and reality is reached. Old-wives-tales, even new old-wives tales, need to become a thing of the past. We must not continue to be impressed by superstitious thinking, but we must be wise and let go of all misdirected reverences. When we learn that error is not real, we are ready for progress, "forgetting what is behind."[2]

Death will not banish the virtual reality of mortal existence. False perceptions and superstitions persist when humans limit Mind. Mind is limitless. Mind never was limited. The true idea of being is spiritual and immortal, and from this it follows that whatever is not of immortality is unreal. Human beliefs cannot demonstrate spirituality or comprehend the reality of Life.

Fighting the war

The teachings of Christian Science are grounded in Scripture, but yet critics warn people, that, "Christian Scientists profess a belief in God, but what kind of a God? Certainly not the same kind of God

---

[1] John 14:6

[2] Phil. 3:13

305

the Bible presents!"[1] To obey Scripture is to heal as Jesus healed—divinely. Why deny Christian Science, when it teaches divine healing? The words of divine Science find their immortality in deeds, for their Principle heals the sick and spiritualizes humanity.

Opponents of Christian Science neither give nor offer any proof that their Master's religion can heal the sick. Surely we need to do more than preserve unreliable and useless dogmas, derived from religious traditions and stamped with human approval or authorization.

Scientific consistency

Inconsistency is shown by words without deeds, which is like a car without an engine. If our words fail to express our deeds, God will redeem that weakness and out of the mouth of babes Soul will perfect praise. Consistency is seen in example more than in precept. The night of materiality is burning out, and Truth's glow wakens human beings spiritually to hear and to speak the new tongue.

Wrongdoing should become unreal to everyone. Sin is inconsistent, a divided kingdom with a realism that has no divine authority, and I rejoice in the understanding of this grand truth.

Spiritual meaning

The opponents of divine Science must be charitable if they would be Christian. If the letter of divine Science appears inconsistent, gain the spiritual meaning of Mind-science and the ambiguity will vanish.

Practical arguments

The charge of inconsistency in Christ-like scientific methods of dealing with disease is rendered pointless by the proof of the utility of these methods. Proofs are better than verbal arguments—better than prayers which don't manifest the spiritual power to heal.

As for sickness and unprogressive mindsets, divine Science says in the language of the Teacher, "Follow me, and let the dead bury their own dead."[2] In other words, let disorder of every name and nature be

---

[1]   MacGregor Ministries online. Examining Christian Science. http://mmoutreachinc.com/cult_groups/christian_science.html   Accessed 4/12/2014

[2]   Matt. 8:22; Luke 9:60

heard no more, and let the harmonious and true sense of Life and being occupy human consciousness.

There are two conflicting theories regarding Christian healing. One, according to the commands of Jesus, heals the sick now. The other, taught by mainstream religion, professes that Christian healing hasn't happened since the first century. What is the relative value of these differing theories?

Conditions of criticisms

Some people condemn Christian Science because *Science and Health* refers to God as Principle. Misleading comments are made such as, "It is therefore important to remember that Eddy never believed in a personal God nor does any true Christian Scientist today."[1] God doesn't have a human personality, but is the One Person, reflected uniquely by individual ideas, therefore, a very close personal relationship can be felt. Our personal relationship with Principle is higher and grander than human mortal friendships which are often selective, exclusive, or fickle.

Weakness of human theories

Strangely enough, we ask for physical theories to support spiritual and eternal truths, when the two are so antagonistic that the materialist thought must become spiritualized before the spiritual fact is attained. The material existence affords no evidence of spiritual being or immortality. Sin, sickness, and death do not prove the immortality of person. Discord can never establish the facts of harmony. Matter is not the threshold of Spirit.

Jesus reasoned practically on the subject of existence and controlled sickness, sin, and death on the grounds of spiritual existence. Understanding the insubstantiality of material things, he spoke of the flesh and Spirit as two opposites—as error and Truth, not contributing in any way to each other's happiness and being. It has been recorded that Jesus said, "The Spirit gives life; the flesh counts for nothing."[2]

---

1   Martin, Walter, and Zacharias, Ravi, *The Kingdom of the Cults*, Revised and Updated and Expanded Edition. Minnesota: Bethany House, 2003.

2   John 6:63

Partnership impossible

There is no immediate or on-going partnership between error and Truth, between flesh and Spirit. God is as incapable of producing wickedness, sickness, and mortality as Truth is of experiencing these errors. How then is it possible for Mind to create spiritual being, made in the divine likeness, capable of experiencing that which is unlike the divine?

Does evil proceed from good? Does God create a human out of Spirit? Does divine Love commit fraud by making man and woman free to do wrong, and then stand on the sidelines to punish the wrongdoer? Would anyone call it wise and good for God to create people and then condemn them to remain His enemy, prisoner, or an orphan?

Two infinite creators absurd

Subsequent follows its precedent. An intelligent sinless God precedes an intelligent sinless creation. God did not create sin and sin can't be self-creative, because God is the only Creator. There is not a second creator making people who need to be corrected.

God's "eyes are too pure to look on evil."[1] Truth is sustained, not by accepting, but by rejecting a lie.

Jesus was quoted to define anthropomorphic evil as, "a liar and the father of lies."[2] Truth does not materialize a lie, a capacity to lie, or a liar. If humankind would stop believing that God makes sickness, destruction, and death, or makes man and woman capable of suffering on account of this malevolence, the games of error would no longer be played and error's destruction would be guaranteed. Seriously, if we accept that disease and destruction are God's will, why do we try to fight or avoid disease and destruction? God isn't testing us, because God's will is good and can only produce goodness.

Anthropomorphism

Looking back at history, we can learn that the popular and misleading perceptions about the divine Being and character have originated in the human mind. Wrong notions about God do not

---

[1]   Hab. 1:13

[2]   John 8:44

originate in immortal Truth. As there is in reality but one God, one Mind, mistaken impressions of God eventually fade out according to St. John's vision in the book of Revelation.

One supremacy

If that which contradicts God is real, there must be two powers and then God would not be powerful and infinite. Can the Higher Power be Almighty if another mighty and self-creative cause exists and influences humankind? If the divine Parent has "Life in himself,"[1] as Scriptures say, could Life, or God, live in evil and create it? Can matter control Life, Spirit, therefore, and so defeat omnipotence?

Matter is impotent

Is the chainsaw, which destroys a tree's so-called life, superior to omnipotence? Can a bullet deprive consciousness of Life—that is, of God, who is the life of spiritual being? Clinically dead people have returned to life and said they still had a consciousness. God, Life, is not at the mercy of matter/energy. The doctrine that matter has power is "confusion worse confounded."[2] If two statements directly contradict each other and one is true, the other must be false. Is Science therefore contradictory?

Scientific and Biblical facts

Divine Science, understood, coincides with the Scriptures and sustains logically and demonstratively every point it presents, otherwise it would not be Science and could not present results. Mind-science is not made up of paradoxical clichés or of the inventions of those who ridicule God. Science presents the calm and clear verdict of Truth against error, voiced and illustrated by the prophets, by Jesus, and by his apostles—as recorded throughout Scripture.

Why are the words of Jesus more frequently cited for our instruction than his remarkable works? Is it because not many people know how important those works are to spirituality?

Is it likely that some people have more faith in a Christian Scientist, whom they have perhaps never seen and against whom they have been warned, than they have in their own accredited and

---

[1] John 5:26

[2] Milton, John, (1608-1974) *Paradise Lost.* Book 2, line 996.

orthodox leaders, whom they have seen and have been taught to love and to trust?

Let a member of the clergy try to cure a friend through personal faith in the clergy. Will that faith heal them? Yet Scientists will take the same case and cures can follow. Faith must be in God. I have healed unbelievers whose only objection to this method was, that I as a Christian Scientist believed in the Holy Spirit, while they, the patient, did not.

Even though you insist that the physical senses are indispensable to your existence or entity, you must change the human concept of life, and must extensively know yourself spiritually and scientifically. The evidence of the existence of Spirit, Soul, is substantial only to spiritual sense. Manifest Soul is not apparent to the limited senses because those senses are very busy accepting only that which opposes Spirit.

Author's parentage

True spirituality is to be honored wherever found, but when will we arrive at the goal which that word implies? From Puritan parents, I received my religious education. In childhood, I often listened with joy to these words falling from the lips of my saintly mother, "God is able to raise you up from sickness." I pondered the meaning of the Scripture: "And these signs will accompany those who believe: . . . they will place their hands on sick people and they will get well."[1]

Two different artists

A student of spiritual Science and a student of physical science are like two different artists. One says: "I have spiritual ideals, indestructible and glorious. When others see them as I do, in their true light and loveliness—and know that these ideals are real and eternal because drawn from Truth—they will find that nothing is lost and all is won, by a correct estimate of what is real."

The other artist replies: "You flaw my experience. My mind-ideals are both mental and material. It is true that materialization renders these ideals imperfect and destructible; yet I would not exchange mine for yours, for mine give me instant self-gratification, and they are not so shockingly transcendental. They don't require me to be unselfish.

---

[1]   Mark 16:17-18

They keep Soul well out of sight. Moreover, I have no notion of losing my old doctrines or human opinions."

Make a choice

Now then reader, which mind-picture or expressed thought will be real to you—the spiritual or the temporal? Both you cannot have. You are bringing out your own ideal. This ideal is either eternal or temporal. Either Spirit or matter is your model. If you try to have two models, then you practically have none. Like a yo-yo, you will spin and bounce between the unreal and the real.

Hear the wisdom of Job—

> Can mortals be righteous before God?
> Can human beings be pure before their Maker?
> Even in his servants he puts no trust,
> And his angels he charges with error.[1]

Jesus was put to death for the truth he spoke and demonstrated, while today, we have interfaith dialogue. Divine Science mediates to explain differing doctrinal points, cancel disagreements, and settle questions. Can doctrine and denomination come together on the very basis of Jesus' words and works? Rather than argue that the Messiah or Christ has not yet come, or that Christ is or isn't God, can we unite on the doctrine that God is One and is present now and forever? It is recognizable that Jesus Christ is not God, as Jesus himself declared, but is the Son of God. This fact understood, doesn't conflict with another statement: "I and the Father are one"[2]—because Christ and God are one in quality, not in quantity. As a drop of water is one with the ocean, a ray of light one with the sun, even so God and spiritual being, Parent and child, are one in being. The Scripture reads: "For in him we live and move and have our being."[3]

I have revised *Science and Health* only to give a clearer and fuller expression of its original meaning. Spiritual ideas unfold as we

---

[1]   Job 4:17-18 (MRSV)

[2]   John 10:30

[3]   Act. 17:28

advance. A human perception of divine Science, however limited, must be correct in order to be Science and subject to demonstration. A germ of infinite Truth, though least in the realm of heaven, is the higher hope on earth, but it will be rejected and hated until God prepares the soil for the seed. That which when sown produces immortal fruit, perfects humanity only when it is understood—consequently, the many readings given the Scriptures, and the requisite revisions of *Science and Health with Key to the Scriptures.*

CHRISTIAN SCIENCE PRACTICE

Why are you downcast, O my soul? Why so disturbed within me? Put your hope in God, for I will yet praise him, my Savior and my God.[1]

And these signs will accompany those who believe: In my name they will drive out demons; they will speak in new tongues; they will pick up snakes with their hands; and when they drink deadly poison, it will not hurt them at all; they will place their hands on sick people, and they will get well.[2]

A Gospel narrative

The seventh chapter of Luke's Gospel tells us that Jesus was once the honored guest of a certain Pharisee. The Pharisee's name was Simon (though he was quite unlike Simon the disciple). While they were at dinner, an unusual incident occurred, as if to interrupt the scene of Middle Eastern festivity. A "woman who had lived a sinful life"[3] came in. This woman's visit was made with no regard to the fact that she was excluded from such a place and such society, especially under the austere rules of that time period. She was looked upon as an outcast, intruding on the household of a high-caste religious authority. This woman easily approached the feet of Jesus, who was reclined on a couch with his head toward the table and his bare feet away from it, as was the custom of the day. The woman moistened Jesus' feet with her tears and wiped them with her long hair, which hung loosely about

---

[1]   Psalm 42:5, 11; 43:5

[2]   Mark 16:17-18

[3]   Luke 7:37

313

her shoulders as was common with women of her status. She carried an alabaster jar containing costly perfume. Perhaps it was sandalwood oil which was commonly used in the East. Breaking the seal of the jar, she anointed Jesus' feet with the oil.

Parable of the creditor

Did Jesus snub the woman? Did he reject her reverence? No! He regarded her compassionately, and this was not all. Jesus knew that the people around him were wondering why he, being a prophet and exalted guest, did not at once detect the woman's immoral status and tell her to leave. Knowing what they were thinking, Jesus reproached them with a short story or parable. He described two debtors, one with a large debt and one for a smaller, who were released from their obligations by the same creditor. He asked Simon "which of them will love him more?" Simon replied, "I suppose the one who had the bigger debt canceled." Jesus answered, "You have judged correctly." [1] The answer brought home the lesson to all, and Jesus followed it with that remarkable declaration to the woman, "Your sins are forgiven." [2]

Divine insight

Why did Jesus sum up the woman's debt to divine Love? Had she repented and reformed spiritually? Did his insight detect the unspoken moral improvement? She had bathed his feet with her tears before she anointed them with oil. In the absence of other proofs, was her grief sufficient evidence to warrant the expectation of her repentance, reformation, and growth in wisdom? Certainly there was encouragement in the mere fact that she was showing her affection for a man of undoubted goodness and purity, a man who has since been rightfully regarded as the best man that ever walked this planet. Her reverence was sincere. It was manifest toward one who was soon, though they knew it not, going to forfeit his human existence on behalf of all sinners, that through his words and works they might be redeemed from temporal perceptions and limited mortal thinking.

---

[1]   Luke 7:42-43

[2]   Luke 7:48

Penitence or hospitality

Which was the higher tribute to Jesus' ineffable affection? Was it the Pharisee's hospitality or the woman's perfected conscience? This query Jesus answered by rebuking self-righteousness and releasing the penitent from guilt. Jesus even pointed out that this poor woman had done what his wealthy host had neglected to do, anoint his guest's feet, a special sign of Middle Eastern courtesy.

Here is suggested a poignant question, a question indicated by a need of this and every era. Do Christian Scientists seek Truth as Simon sought the Savior, for material conservatism and for personal politics? Jesus told Simon that seekers like him were stingy, giving little in return for the spiritual reward that came through the Messiah. If Christian Scientists are like Simon, then it must be said of them also that they *love little.*

Genuine repentance

On the other hand, do students of Science show their regard for Truth, Christ, by their genuine repentance? Are they conscience-stricken and submissively expressing goodwill as the woman did? If so, then it may be said of them, as Jesus said of the unwelcome visitor, that they indeed love much, because much is forgiven them.

Compassion requisite

The careless doctor, the nurse, and the curt visitor may be sympathetic, but do they know the thorns they plant in the pillow of the sick and the heavenly homesick looking away from earth? Oh, why don't they know? Being aware of this unawareness would do much more toward healing the sick and preparing their helpers for the midnight call, than all cries of "Lord, Lord!" The benign thought of Jesus, found in such words as "Do not worry about your life,"[1] will heal the sick and so enable them to advance past the supposed necessity of taking thought for, and doctoring, the physical; however, the unselfish affections must be plentiful. Common sense and common humanity are to be highly regarded; otherwise, what mental quality remains, with which to call forth healing from the extended arm of righteousness?

---

[1]   Matt. 6:25; Luke 12:22

Quick healing

If the Scientist reaches the patient through divine Love, the healing work will be achieved at one visit. In the presence of Love, disease vanishes into its native nothingness like dew before the morning sunshine. In any case, it is necessary for the Scientist to have enough Christly intent to win their own pardon and to receive praise similar to that which Jesus gave the woman. Spirituality must be pure in order to practice scientifically and deal with patients compassionately. Results correspond to the spiritual intent.

Truth desecrated

The would-be healer is obligated not to bring hypocrisy, stupidity, inhumanity, or bad habits into the patient's environment. If these traits were present, the environment would be converted into a "den of robbers."[1] The un-Christ-like practitioner does not give to mind or body the joy and strength of Truth. Vanity and negativity desecrate the temple of the Holy Spirit, and the patient's spiritual power to resuscitate themselves is damaged. The poor suffering heart needs its spiritual nutriment, such as peace, patience in distress, and a priceless sense of the dear Father-Mother's loving-kindness.

Moral evils to be cast out

To cure a patient, the practitioner must first dismiss their own moral evils. Purification allows the practitioner to attain the spiritual freedom and ability to drive physical evils out of the patient. Healing will not radiate from someone who is so spiritually unproductive that they are unable to give drink to the thirsty or reach the patient's thought. Mental poverty alienates faith and understanding.

The true physician

The physician who lacks empathy for humanity is deficient in goodwill. The public then has the apostolic warrant for repeating: "Those who say, 'I love God,' and hate their brothers or sisters, are liars; for those who do not love a brother or sister whom they have seen, cannot love God whom they have not seen."[2] Not having spiritual goodwill, the physician lacks faith in the divine Mind, and can't

---

[1]   Jer. 7:11; Matt. 21:13; Mark 11:17; Luke 19:46

[2]   I John 4:20 (NRSV)

recognize infinite Love which alone confers the healing power. Such a so-called Scientist will "strain out a gnat"[1] while they swallow the camels of bigoted pompous learning.

Source of calmness

The physician must also pay attention so as not to be overwhelmed by either the hatefulness of sin or by the unveiling of wrong thinking (sin) in her or his own attitude. The sick are terrified by their sick beliefs and sinners should be frightened by their own sinful thinking; however, the Scientist of universal Truth and Love will be calm in the presence of both sin and disease, knowing that Life is God, and God is All.

Genuine healing

It takes effort not to bury the spirit of divine Science in the burial clothes of its letter. If we would open the prison doors for the sick, we must first learn to bind up the broken-hearted. If we would heal by the Spirit, we must not hide the talent of spiritual healing behind the glitz of worldly status, ritualistic activities or even somber piety. In the presence of a sick person, employ tender words and spiritual encouragement. Patiently remove all fears, without gushing theories, stereotyped clichés, and rigid arguments which are so many misrepresentations of divine Science, aflame with divine Love.

Gratitude and humility

We seek Truth, Christ, not for "the loaves"[2] and fishes, and not like the Pharisees with the arrogance of professional status and display of academia. Like the woman at Jesus' feet, we discover infinite Truth through the pure inner tendencies, with the oil of gladness and the perfume of gratitude, with tears of repentance and with those hairs all numbered by the Father-Mother.

The salt of the earth

At this time, Christian Scientists should strive to occupy the same place Jesus' disciples did. Jesus said, "You are the salt of the earth . . . You are the light of the world. A city on a hill cannot be hidden."[3] Let

---

1   Matt. 23:24

2   John 6:26

3   Matt. 5:13-14

us pay attention and participate in spirituality. Let us pray that this salt doesn't lose its saltiness, and that this light is not hidden, but radiates and glows into the glory of the sun at noon.

The infinite Truth of the Christ-cure has come to this age through a "gentle whisper."[1] The beneficial effects of spirituality accelerate and develop through silent communications and divine anointing. My hope is to see the student's increasing spiritual success in this line of light.

Real and counterfeit

Because Truth is infinite, error should be known as nothing. Because Truth is omnipotent in goodness; Truth's opposite, error, has no power. Evil is only the counterbalance of nonexistence. The greatest wrong is supposing that there is an opposite of the highest right. The confidence inspired by Science lies in the fact that Truth is real and Truth's opposite is unreal, is an error. Error is a coward before Truth. Divine Science insists that time will prove all this. Both truth and error have come nearer than ever before to the perception of human beings, and truth will continue to appear, as error is self-destroyed.

Results of faith in Truth

It is fatal to believe that error is as real as Truth or that evil is equal in power to good if not superior. Misperceptions not only work against the hope of being free from sickness and sin, but also depress the inspiration that encourages perfection. When we come to have more faith in the truth of being than we have in error, more faith in Spirit than in matter, more faith in living than in dying, more faith in spiritual being than in human beings, then no material suppositions can prevent us from healing the sick and destroying error.

Life independent of matter/energy

When we learn that life and people survive the body, we can prove Life is not dependent on bodily conditions. Evil, disease or death is not spiritual and these phantoms disappear as our spiritual awareness appears. Because matter has no consciousness or Ego, matter cannot act; its conditions are illusions, and these false conditions are the source of all seeming sickness. Admit the existence of temporal substance or mind, and you admit that mortality, and therefore disease,

---

[1]   I Kings 19:12

has a foundation in fact. Deny the existence of temporal substance and mind, and you can stop believing in delusive conditions. When fear disappears, the foundation of disease is gone. If under some circumstance, the mental physician believes matter/energy is solid fact, he or she becomes prone to also admitting the reality of all disturbing conditions. Thinking the unreal is real hinders the ability to destroy disorder and makes the healer unfit to treat disease successfully.

People's identity

We are able to master mortal characteristics as matter loses to human sense all entity as a person. Humanity then enters into a more spiritual sense of the facts, and comprehends the theology of Jesus as demonstrated in healing the sick, raising the dead and walking over the wave. Jesus' actions were proof that he had control over the thinking that matter or the human mind is substance. Matter, mortal consciousness, is not the determiner of life or the constructor of any form of existence.

The Christ treatment

We don't read that Luke or Paul made a reality of disease in order to discover some means of healing it. Jesus didn't discuss disease or ask whether it was acute or chronic. He never recommended attention to laws of health. He never gave drugs and never prayed to know whether God was willing that an individual should live. Jesus understood individuality, whose Life is God, to be spiritual. He knew that God's children do not have an outer shell and an inner being, one to be destroyed and the other to be made indestructible.

Matter not medicine

Preventative and curative arts belong emphatically to divine Science, as would be readily seen if the Science of Spirit, God, was understood. Unscientific methods are finding dead ends. Limited to matter by their own laws, what advantages do material methods have over unlimited Mind and spirituality?

No healing in sin

No one is physically healed in a willful lack of mindfulness, any more than she or he is morally saved in or by sin. It is a mistake even to complain or to be angry over sin. To be whole, people must be better spiritually as well as physically. To be spiritual, we must forsake the temporal sense of things, turn away from the lies of false beliefs, look to Truth, and gather the facts of being from the divine Mind. The body improves under the same plan which perfects the thought. If health is not made evident under the plan, this proves that fear is controlling the body. This is the law of cause and effect, or of like producing like.

Like curing like

The process of like curing like (e.g. homeopathy, vaccinations), involves different expectations, but the same medicine. The human mind expects the same drug to both cause and cure a disease. This confirms my theory that faith in the drug is the sole factor in the cure.

The moral and spiritual facts of health, whispered into thought, produce very direct and marked effects on the body. It stands to reason that a physical diagnosis of disease tends to induce disease, since human mind must be the cause of disease.

Transient potency of drugs

According to both medical knowledge and individual experience, a drug may eventually lose its power and do no more for patients. Diseases become drug resistant. Feel-good concoctions fail to inspire the unsuspecting minds, and patients cease to improve. These lessons are useful. They should naturally and genuinely change our basis from physical science to divine Science, from error to Truth, from human mind to Mind.

Diagnosis of matter

Physicians measure the pulse, blood pressure, temperature, respiratory rate, and intensity of pain in order to discover the physical condition of matter, when in fact all is Mind. The body is a figment of the imagination of the human mind. The false mind must succumb to the order of spiritual Mind.

Ghost-stories inducing fear

Discussions on disease have a mental effect similar to that produced when telling ghost stories in the dark. When we haven't been instructed in divine Science, nothing is really understood of temporal existence. Human beings are believed to be here without their consent and to be removed as involuntarily, not knowing why or when. As frightened children look everywhere for the imaginary ghost, so sick humanity sees danger in every direction, and looks for relief in all ways except the right one. Darkness stimulates fear. Adults who constantly refer to physical knowledge no more comprehend their real spiritual being than does the child. Adult and child must be taken out of their darkness before the illusive sufferings, which block the light, can be dissolved. The way in divine Science is the only way out of fearful conditions.

Mind imparts purity, health, and beauty

I would not transform the infant immediately into an adult, nor would I keep the infant a lifelong newborn. No impossible thing do I ask when urging the claims of Christian Science; but because this teaching is in advance of the times, we should not deny our need of its spiritual unfoldment. Humanity will improve through Science and spirituality. The necessity for spiritualizing humanity comes from the fact that Mind can do it. Mind, God, can impart purity instead of impurity, strength instead of weakness, and health instead of disease. Truth improves the entire system, and can heal "the whole body."[1]

Brain not intelligent, not consciousness

Remember, brain is not mind. Physical particles cannot be sick and Mind is everlastingly immortal. The human body is an erroneous conviction that mind is divisible and measurable. What is called matter/energy was originally error in solution, an immature human mind—likened by Milton to "Chaos, and old night."[2] One theory about this human mind is that its sensations can reproduce people—can form blood, flesh, and bones. If the generations had not been trained to believe matter is the medium of person, then the Science of being, in which all is divine Mind, or God and Love's idea, would be clearer. Science elucidates the fact that we cannot enter our own embodied thought, bind our self with our own limited thinking, call these bonds material, and then name them divine law.

True success

When Mind-Science is demonstrated absolutely, our spirituality will be recognized and seen to be perfect. Our immortal self, cannot

---

[1]   John 7:23 (REB)

[2]   Milton, John, (1608-1674) *Paradise Lost,* Book 1, line 540.

sin, suffer, be subject to mortality, nor disobey the law of God. The people "will be like the angels in heaven."[1] Divine Science and Christianity are one. How then, in Christianity any more than in Christian Science, can we believe in the reality and power of both, Truth and error, or Spirit and matter, and hope to succeed with contraries? Matter/energy, materialism, physicality is not self-sustaining. Its false supports fail one after another. Matter succeeds for a period only by falsely parading in the veneer of law.

Recognition of benefits

"Whoever denies me before men, I also will deny before my Father who is in heaven."[2] In divine Science, a denial of Truth is fatal, while a just acknowledgment of Truth and of what it has done for us is an effectual help. If arrogance, superstition, or any error prevents the honest recognition of benefits received, this will be a hindrance to the recovery of the sick and the success of the student.

Disease far more docile than iniquity

If we follow Christ on all moral questions, but are in darkness as to the physical exemption which spirituality includes, then we must have more faith in God on this subject and be more alive to Spirit's promises. It is easier to cure the most malignant disease than it is to cure sin. I have revitalized the dying, partly because they were willing to be restored, while I have struggled long, and perhaps in vain, to lift a student out of a chronic sin. Under all modes of pathological treatment, the sick recover more rapidly from disease than does the sinner from sin. Healing is easier than teaching, if the teaching is faithfully done.

Love frees from fear

The fear of disease and the love of sin are the sources of people's troubles. "The reverent and worshipful fear of the Lord is the beginning (the chief and choice part) of Wisdom."[3] Through the exalted thought of John, the Scriptures also declare, that "full-grown

---

1   Matt. 22:30; Mark 12:25
2   Matt. 10:33; Luke 12:9 (ESV)
3   Prov. 9:10 (Amplified)

(complete, perfect) love turns fear out of doors and expels every trace of terror!"[1]

The fear occasioned by ignorance can be cured. To remove the effects of fear produced by sin, you must overcome both fear and sin. Disease is expressed not so much by words as in the functions of the body. Establish the scientific spiritual perception of health, and you relieve the malfunctioning organ. A holy view of health stabilizes the body's equilibrium, and the body's internal environment is balanced as systems resume their healthy function.

Mind circulates blood

When the blood pressure is too high or too low, we call these conditions disease. This is a misperception. Mortal mind is producing the abnormal pressure, and we prove this to be so, when thought power changes blood pressure, and it returns to the standard which human mind has decided upon as essential for health. Topical pain relievers, anti-inflammatory drugs, and aspirin never reduce pain or inflammation scientifically, but the truth of being, whispered into the ear of human mind, will bring relief.

Mind can destroy all ills

Hatred and its effects on the body are removed by Love. Because human mind seems to be conscious, sick people say: "How could my mind cause a disease I never thought of and knew nothing about, until it appeared in my body?" I have answered this question in my explanation of disease as originating in human mind before it is consciously apparent in the body, which is in fact the objective state of human mind, though it is called physique or flesh. This human blindness and its sharp consequences show our need of divine metaphysics. Through immortal Mind, or Truth, we can destroy all ills which proceed from human mind.

Not understanding the cause or approach of disease is no argument against the mental origin of disease. You confess to ignorance of the future and incapacity to preserve your own existence, and this thinking helps rather than hinders disease. Such a mindset induces sickness. It is like walking in the darkness on a high narrow ledge. You cannot stop

---

[1]   I John 4:18 (Amplified)

suspecting danger, so your steps are insecure because of fear, and your unawareness of mental cause and effect.

Temperature is mental

Heat and cold are products of the human mind. Human mind produces bodily heat and then expels it by abandoning the thinking that caused it. Sometimes, human thinking is so extreme it increases bodily heat to the point of self-destruction, and calls the body dead. When the body is deprived of human mind, the body cools and then breaks down into simple atom structures. However, those very particles that make up the body don't produce heat or cold whether the body is alive or dead. It is human mind, not matter, which says, "I am hot," or "I am dying." Remove the thinking that inflammation and pain must accompany the separation of heat from the body. Heat can pass from the body as painlessly as vapor escapes water.

Science versus the power of mass suggestion

Chills and heat are often the form in which fever materializes itself. In regard to treatment for fever, people may manipulate the body or change their diet. This produces a change in the mental state, and the chills and fever may disappear. The patient says, "I am better," but the patient believes that matter, not mind, brought the relief. A hypnotist deprives people of their individuality in order to control them. No person is benefited by yielding his mentality to any mental authoritarianism or malpractice. All unscientific mental practice is erroneous and powerless, and should be understood and so rendered fruitless. The genuine spiritual Scientist is adding to the patient's mental and moral power, and is increasing his or her patient's spirituality while restoring the patient physically through divine Love. The Scientist of Truth demonstrates that divine Mind heals.

Cure for paralysis

Paralysis is a belief that matter or brain controls human beings and can palsy the body, making certain portions of it motionless. Destroy the belief, show human mind that muscles have no power to be lost, for divine Mind is supreme, and the palsy is cured.

Latent fear diagnosed

Cancer or tuberculosis patients often show great hopefulness and courage, even when they are supposed to be in hopeless danger. This state of mind seems strange except to the expert in divine Science. The attitude is misunderstood, simply because it is a stage of fear so excessive that it amounts to fortitude or human strength. The expectation of a horrific physical condition presents to human thought a hopeless state, an image more terrifying than that of most other diseases. The patient turns unintentionally from the contemplation of it, but without realizing it, the concealed fear and the despair of recovery remain in thought.

Insidious concepts

Along the same line, the greatest sin is most subtle and does its work almost self-deceived. The diseases considered dangerous sometimes come from the most hidden, undefined, and insidious thinking. The anemic invalid, whom you declare to be wasting away with a blood deficiency, should be told that blood never gave life and can never take it away. Understand and say, Life is Spirit, and there is more life and immortality in one good motive and act than in all the blood which ever flowed through mortal veins, mimicking a temporal sense of life.

Remedy for fever

If the body is material, it cannot for that very reason, suffer with a fever. Because the physical body is a mental concept and governed by human mind, it manifests only what that so-called mind expresses. Therefore the efficient remedy is to defeat the patient's misleading thought process, silently and audibly arguing the true facts in regard to harmonious being—representing the individual as healthy instead of diseased. Show that it is impossible for material atoms to suffer, to feel pain or heat, to be thirsty or sick. Destroy fear, and you end fever. Some people, wrongly taught as to Mind-Science, ask when it will be safe to check a fever. Know that in Science you cannot check a fever after admitting that fevers must finish their course. To fear and admit the power of disease is to paralyze mental and scientific demonstration.

If your patient believes in catching cold, mentally convince him or her that physical particles cannot get sick, and that thought governs this liability. If grief causes suffering, convince the sufferer that affliction often causes a mental shift, and joy is found in ever present Love.

Climate harmless

Sufferers may visit warmer climates in order to stay healthy, but they come back no better than before they went away. Then is the time to cure them through divine Science. When the fear of weather is exterminated it can be proven that people can be healthy in all climates.

Mind governs body

Through different mind patterns, the body becomes suddenly weak or abnormally strong, showing human mind to be the producer of strength or weakness. A sudden joy or grief has caused what is termed instantaneous death. Because thinking originates unseen, the mental state should be continually watched so that it may not unwittingly produce bad effects. I never knew a patient who did not recover when the belief in the disease was gone. Remove the leading error or governing fear of this lower mind, and you remove the cause of all disease as well as the morbid or excited action of any organ. Disease and functional difficulties can both be healed.

The cause of all so-called disease is mental, a human fear, a mistaken impression or certainty that ill-health is necessary and powerful. Dis-ease is also caused by the fear that Mind is not only helpless to defend our life, but also incompetent to control it. Unintentionally you sentence yourself to suffer; whereas, without the ignorant human mindset, any circumstance is of itself powerless to produce suffering. Disease has no intelligence. Disease is less than mind, and Mind can control it. It is latent belief in disease, as well as the fear of disease, which associates sickness with certain circumstances and causes the two to appear united. An example of this false association is when the two distinct entities of poetry and music are automatically reproduced as one entity in a song. Don't self-sentence yourself, meet every circumstance with truth.

Underlying power

Without the temporal mind, systems cannot break down or become inflamed. Remove the error in thought, and you destroy its effects. A person's gaze, fastened fearlessly on a ferocious beast, often causes the beast to retreat in terror. By meeting hateful prejudice with fearless love, Martin Luther King, Jr.[1] sent hate to its own defeat. These occurrences represent the power of Truth over error. Exercise the power of intelligence, to displace unintelligent behavior. The application of spiritual intelligence can also cause threatening situations to self-destruct. The cure of matter does not come from within itself. Temporal methods come from mortal attitudes, unintelligence. Remember: hypnotism, surgeries, and medicines, can counteract one another or create bad reactions. The antagonistic reactions are similar to one animal infuriating another by looking it in the eye, both fighting for nothing.

Disease powerless

Disease is not an intelligence to defy the administration of Mind or to overthrow Mind and take the government into its own hands. Sickness is not a God-given, nor a self-constituted material power, which shrewdly competes with, and finally conquers Mind. God never supplied matter with power to disable Life or to numb harmony with a long and cold night of misery. Such a power, without the divine permission, is inconceivable. If such an unbelievable power could be divinely directed, it would show less wisdom than we usually find in human governments.

Jurisdiction of Mind

If disease can attack and control the body without the consent of humans, sin can do the same. Disease and sin are errors, announced as partners in the beginning. The Christian Scientist finds only effects, where the ordinary physician looks for causes. The real jurisdiction of the world is in Mind, Spirit, controlling every effect and recognizing all causation as established in divine Mind.

Power of imagination

A felon, on whom certain English students experimented,[2] assumed he was bleeding to death, and died because of that assumption, when only a stream of warm water was trickling over his arm. His sense of bleeding and consequent death, prove the powers of

---

[1] Luther King Jr., Martin (1929-1968) American Civil Rights Leader.

[2] Yawger, N.S. Emotion as the cause of rapid and sudden death. *Archives of Neurology and Psychiatry* 36:875-879.

imagination or emotion. Had the felon known his sense of bleeding was an illusion, the results would have been different. Let today's hemorrhaging patient think of those English student's experiment, which caused the death of a man when not a drop of blood was shed. Instead of fearing blood as though it ultimately affects health, we can learn the opposite claim of spiritual Life as affecting health. The very results we expect or dread is manifest.

Fever and nausea the effect of fear

Fever and nausea are errors of various types. High temperatures, an abnormal pulse rate, delirium, pain, and nausea, are images imprinted on the body by a human mind. The images, held in this agitated mind tend to frighten conscious thought. Divine Science can replace the sick-image, which is produced by millions of human beings and imaged on the body because they believe that mind is in matter and sickness is as real as harmony. If the sick-image is not destroyed, some receptive thought may pick up on it and become sick itself. The case may even end in a belief called death, which must be finally conquered by eternal Life. Truth always triumphs. Sickness and sin fall by their own weight. Truth is the rock, the capstone of the corner, "and it will crush anyone on whom it falls."[1]

Misdirected contention

Insisting on the evidence or indulging the demands of wrongdoing, disease, or death, we virtually work against the control of Mind over body, and deny the power of Mind to heal. This misdirected method is as though the defendant should argue for the plaintiff in favor of a decision which the defendant knows will be turned against them.

Benefits of metaphysics

The physical effects of fear illustrate its illusion. A person should not be terrified when looking at a confined lion even if the lion is in the position to pounce. A person should not be terrified when looking at disease, chained by truth. Only the mind ignorant of truth is poorly affected. Nothing but the power of Truth can prevent the fear of disease and prove our dominion over it.

---

[1]   Matt. 21:44; Luke 20:18 (NRSV)

A higher discovery

Many years ago, I made a spiritual discovery, the scientific evidence of which has accumulated to prove that the divine Mind produces in us health, harmony, and spirituality. Gradually this evidence will gather momentum and clearness, until it reaches its culmination of scientific statement and proof. Nothing is more depressing than to believe that there is a power opposite to God, or good. God never allows or gives strength to an opposing power used against divine self, against Life, health, harmony.

Ignorance of our rights

Every law of physics or the body, supposed to govern people, is rendered null and void by the law of Life, God. Unaware of our God-given rights, we allow unjust decisions and make excuses for imperfection. Our education system is biased, expounding homogeny and marketing a resignation to poor choices. Become aware metaphysically. Be no more willing to suffer the illusion that you are sick or that some disease is developing in the system, than you are willing to suffer giving into a sinful temptation on the ground that sin has its necessities.

No laws of matter

When overstepping some supposed law, you say that there is danger. This fear is the danger and induces the physical effects. We cannot in reality suffer from breaking anything except a moral or spiritual law. The supposed laws of mortal thinking are destroyed by the understanding that the law of Soul is immortal, and that human mind cannot legislate the times, periods, and types of disease with which humans die. God is the lawmaker, but God is not the author of ruthless rules. In infinite Life and Love there is no sickness, no twisted good, no death, and Scriptures declare that in the infinite God "we live and move and have our being."[1]

God-given dominion

Think less of the human mind's ongoing melodrama, and you will more quickly know your spiritual God-given dominion. You must understand your way out of human theories relating to health,

---

[1]   Acts 17:28

or you will never believe that you are quite free from some affliction. Our harmony and spirituality will never be reached without the understanding that Mind is not in matter. Let us banish sickness as an outlaw, and abide by the rule of perpetual harmony—God's law. It is our moral right to nullify an unjust sentence, a sentence never inflicted by divine authority.

Begin right

Christ Jesus overruled the mistake which would impose penalties for transgressing physical laws of health. He annulled laws of physics which only have human approval for their validation. Laws of matter have no divine authority.

Mortal health care procedures excessive

If half the attention given to hygiene were given to the study of divine Science and to the spiritualization of thought, this alone would usher in the millennium. Skin exfoliates or scrubs used to remove unhealthy secretions or add a healthy look, receive a useful rebuke from Jesus' precept, "Do not worry . . . about your body."[1] We must beware of making clean merely the "outside of the cup and dish."[2]

Blissful ignorance

People who haven't been inundated with health laws are more receptive to spiritual power and faith in one God. People who are devoted to supposed health laws, and who think they need to teach others these contradictory laws, would be better off considering the health laws "more honored in the breach than the observance"?[3] A patient thoroughly booked in medical theories is more difficult to heal through Mind than one who is not. This verifies Jesus' saying: "Anyone who will not receive the kingdom of God like a little child will never enter it."[4]

I rescued a man from spiritual oblivion, who previously felt controlled by mortal senses. He wrote to me: "I should have died, but for the glorious Principle you teach—supporting the power of

---

[1]   Matt. 6:25; Luke 12:22

[2]   Matt. 23:25; Luke 11:39

[3]   Shakespeare, William (1564-1616) *Hamlet,* Act 1, iv.

[4]   Mark 10:15; Luke 18:17

Mind over the body and showing me the nothingness of the so-called pleasures and pains of sense. The essays I had read and the medicines I had taken only abandoned me to more hopeless suffering and despair. Adherence to hygiene was useless. Mortal mind needed to be set right. The ailment was not bodily, but mental, and I was cured when I learned my way in Christian Science."

A clean mind and body

We need a clean body and a clean mind—a body rendered pure by Mind as well as washed by water. One says: "I take good care of my body." Physical care requires the pure and spiritualizing influence of the divine Mind on the body. The body is best taken care of when it is left most out of thought. The Apostle Paul said, he "would prefer to be away from the body and at home with the Lord."[1]

A hint may be taken from the beggar whose filth does not affect his happiness, because mind and body rest on the same basis. To the mind equally gross, dirt gives no uneasiness. It is the native element of such a mind, which is symbolized, and not chafed by its surroundings. Impurity and foulness, which do not trouble the gross, could not be supported by the refined. A clean mind helps keep the body in proper condition.

Beliefs illusive

The tobacco-user, chewing or smoking poison for half a century, may tell you that the weed preserves his or her health, but does this make it so? Does that affirmation prove the use of tobacco to be a healthy habit, and the person to be better for it? Such instances only prove the illusive physical effect of mistaken thinking, and also confirm the Scriptural conclusion, "As he thinks in his heart, so is he."[2]

The movement cure—treating disease by manipulating the body's muscles or bones, to make it sensibly well when it ought to be insensibly so—is another traditional mistake, resulting from the common notion that health depends on inert matter instead of on Mind. Can the body either feel good or bad without its mind?

---

[1]   II Cor. 5:8

[2]   Prov. 23:7 (Amplified)

We should relieve our minds from the depressing thought that we have violated a human law and must of necessity pay the penalty. Let us reassure ourselves with the law of Love. God never punishes us for doing right. Love never penalizes us for honest labor or deeds of kindness, even if we are exposed to fatigue, cold, heat, contagion. If we seem to incur the penalty through matter, this is but the false-ego, or human mind's thinking. Unfair repercussions are not established by wisdom, and our nonconformity to injustice can nullify the penalty. Through this action of thought and its results upon the body, students will prove to themselves, by small beginnings, the grand verities of divine Science.

Not matter, but Mind

If you think weather affects health poorly, your Mind-remedy is safe and sure. If you are a scientist of Spirit, symptoms of sickness are not apt to follow exposure to certain weather. However, if you believe in laws of mortality and their fatal effects when transgressed, you are not fit to conduct your own case or to destroy the bad effects of what you believe. But you can pierce the façade of false laws. Your fear of weather subsides when you learn that people stay indoors during the cold weather, and pass around their local strains of illness. Now, reduce the fear of contagion and gain the spiritual conviction that you have broken no law, whether you go outdoors or stay inside. In Science, this is an established fact which all the evidence before the fleshly senses can never overrule.

Profit of philanthropy

Sickness, sin, and death must become obsolete before the divine rights of intelligence. Then the power of Mind over the entire functions and organs of the human system will be acknowledged. It is proverbial that Mother Teresa,[1] and other philanthropists engaged in humanitarian work have been able to undergo, without weariness and danger, that which ordinary people could not endure. The explanation lies in the support which they derived from the divine law, supreme to the human law. The spiritual demand crushes the material demand, and supplies not only energy but also endurance, which surpasses all

---

[1]   Mother Teresa (1910-1997) Albanian Roman Catholic nun.

other aid. Spirituality forestalls the penalty which our beliefs would attach to our best deeds. Let us remember that the eternal law of right, though it can never annul the law which makes sin its own executioner, exempts us from all penalties but those due for wrongdoing.

Honest work has not penalty

Hard work, deprivations, exposures, and all troublesome conditions, if without sin, can be experienced without suffering. Your true responsibility can be fulfilled without harm to yourself. If you sprain the muscles or wound the flesh, your remedy is at hand. Mind decides whether or not the flesh will be discolored, painful, and inflamed.

Our sleep and food

You say that you have not slept well or you have no self-discipline. You are a law to yourself. Saying this and believing it, you will suffer in proportion to your certainty and fear. Your sufferings are not the penalty for having broken a law of matter, for it is a law of human mind which you have disobeyed. You say or think, because you have eaten salty food, that you must be thirsty, and you are thirsty accordingly, while the opposite thought would produce the opposite result.

Doubtful evidence

Any information, coming from the body or from inert matter as if either were intelligent, is an illusion of human mind—one of its dreams. Realize that the evidence of the physical senses is not to be accepted in the case of sickness, any more than it is in the case of sin.

Climate and belief

Expose the body to certain temperatures and human conviction says that you may slide into a state of hypothermia or have heat stroke. However, no such result occurs without mind to demand and produce it. So long as human beings declare that certain weather instigates colds, fever, and other health difficulties, those effects will follow—not because of the climate or viruses, but on account of the belief. I have in too many instances healed disease through the action of Truth on the minds of human beings, and have seen the corresponding effect of Truth on the body, not to know that this is so.

Erroneous message

An irresponsible report, mistakenly announcing the death of a friend, occasions the same grief that the friend's real death would bring. You think that your anguish is occasioned by your loss. Another report, correcting the death announcement, heals your grief and you learn that your suffering was merely the result of your thinking. Thus it is with all sorrow, sickness, and death. You will eventually learn that there is no cause for grief, and divine wisdom will then be understood. Error, not Truth, produces all the suffering on earth.

Mourning causeless

If a Christian Scientist had said, while you were laboring under the influence of a grieving thought, "Your sorrow is without cause," you may misunderstand the meaning, although the correctness of the assertion might afterwards be proved to you. So, when our friends pass from our sight and we mourn, the mourning is needless and causeless. We will perceive this to be true when we grow into the understanding of Life, and know that there is no death.

Mind heals brain-disease

If human mind is kept active, must it pay a penalty by having a headache or becoming exhausted? Who dares to say that actual Mind can be overworked? When we reach our limits of mental endurance, we conclude that intellectual labor has been carried sufficiently far. On the other hand, when we realize that immortal Mind is ever active, we are able to rest in Truth. When we understand that our God-given spiritual energies and resources can't wear out, or be trespassed upon by mortal laws, we are refreshed by the assurances of immortality, opposed to mortality.

Right never punishable

People don't die young because they occupy the most important jobs and perform the most vital functions in society. If leading thinkers and doers die young, it's not because they occupied an important position. Think of Anglo-Irish explorer Ernest Shackelton,[1] and his expedition crew, who all survived overwhelming adversity in their 1914-1916 Antarctic expedition. Persons who act on integrity and

---

[1]   Ernest Shackleton (1874-1922) Irish explorer.

goodness do not pay severe penalties. By adhering to the realities of spirituality—instead of reading studies on the inconsistent assumption that death comes in obedience to the law of life, and that God punishes people for doing good—one cannot suffer as the result of any labor of love, but grows stronger because of it. It is a law of so-called human mind, misnamed matter, which causes all things discordant.

Christian history

The history of Christianity furnishes sublime proofs of the supporting influence and protecting power bestowed on us by our heavenly Father-Mother. Omnipotent Mind gives us faith and understanding whereby to safeguard our self, not only from temptation, but also from bodily suffering.

The Christian martyrs were prophets of divine Science. Through the encouraging and purifying power of spiritual truth, they obtained a victory over the bodily senses, a victory which Science alone can explain. A dull intellect, which is a resisting state of human mind, suffers less, only because it knows less of material law.

Spiritually minded people testify to the divine basis of Christian Science when dire inflictions fail to destroy their bodies. Spirituality is safe from tormenters. Tyrants are idolatrous; they believe in more than one mind, having "many gods,"[1] and think they can kill the body with matter, independently of mind.

Sustenance spiritual

What if we admit the common hypothesis that food is the nutriment of life? Then we will need to admit its opposite—that food has power to destroy Life, God, through a deficiency or an excess, a quality or a quantity. This is a specimen of the ambiguous nature of all material health-theories. Temporal theories in regard to health are self-contradictory and self-destructive, setting up a "kingdom divided against itself," which "will be ruined."[2] If food was prepared by Jesus for his disciples, it cannot destroy life.

---

[1]   I Cor. 8:5

[2]   Matt. 12:25; Mark 3:24; Luke 11:17

God sustains us

The fact is, food does not affect our absolute Life, and this becomes self-evident when we learn that God is our Life. Because sin and sickness are not qualities of Soul, or Life, we have hope in spirituality. Nevertheless, it would be foolish to stop eating a healthy balanced diet, or to stop exercising, until we gain perfection and a clear comprehension of the living Spirit. In that perfect day of understanding, we shall neither eat to live nor live to eat.

Diet and digestion

Human beings may think that food upsets the healthy functions of mind and body. If this is the case, either the food or this thought must be abandoned, for the penalty is connected to the thinking. Which shall it be? Leaving the decision to divine Science, the control of Mind will be given the advantage over the faulty thinking and every temporal condition. The less we know or think about diet and digestion, the less likely we are inclined to be sick. Remember, although we have been trained to believe otherwise, it is not the body, nerves, or organs, but human mind, which reports food as undigested or problematic. The human mind's report is a pseudo-mental testimony and can be destroyed only by the better results of Mind's opposite evidence.

Scripture keeps it straight

Our dietetic theories first admit that food sustains our life, and then they discuss the certainty that food can kill us. This illogical reasoning is rebuked in Scripture by the metaphors about the fountain and stream,[1] the tree and its fruit,[2] and the kingdom divided against itself.[3] If God has, as prevalent theories support, created laws that food shall support human life, God cannot nullify these regulations by an opposite law that food can kill us.

Ancient confusion

Materialists contradict their own statements. Their belief in material laws and in penalties for their infraction is the ancient error

---

[1] James 3:11

[2] Matt. 3:10, 7:17-19, 12:33; Luke 3:9, 6:43-44; James 3:12

[3] Matt. 12:25, Mark 3:24-26; Luke 11:17

that there is fraternity between pain and pleasure, good and evil, God and Satan. This belief totters to its falling before the ax of Science.

A case of convulsions, produced by indigestion, came under my observation. In her belief the woman had chronic liver disease, and was then suffering from a complication of symptoms connected with this belief. I cured her in a few minutes. One instant she spoke despairingly of herself. The next minute she said, "My food is all digested, and I should like something more to eat."

Ultimate harmony

We cannot deny that Life is self-sustained, and we should never deny the everlasting order of Soul, simply because to the temporal sense, there is seeming disorder. It is a disregard of God, the divine Principle which produces apparent imbalance, while a correct regard of God restores balance. Truth will ultimately compel us all to exchange the pleasures and pains of fleshly sensations for the joys of Soul.

Unnecessary prostrate

When the first symptoms of disease appear, resist the assertions of the fleshly impressions with divine Science. Let your higher sense of justice destroy the false process of human opinions which you name law, and then you will not be confined to a hospital room, or checked into a hospice facility, to suffer paying the last penalty demanded by error. "Settle matters quickly with your adversary who is taking you to court."[1] Do not let your thought become a captive audience to the demands of sin or sickness. Turn away from that which falsely pressures us, with the enduring conviction that those pressures are illegitimate. God is no more the author of sickness than of sin. You have no law of God to support the necessity either of sin or sickness, but you have divine authority for denying that necessity and healing the sick.

Treatment of disease

"Agree to disagree" with oncoming symptoms of chronic or acute disease, whether it is cancer, diabetes, or coronary artery disease. Meet the initial stages of disease with as powerful mental opposition as a legislator would employ to defeat the passage of an inhuman law.

[1]   Matt 5:25

Rise in the conscious strength of the spirit of Truth to overthrow the petition of human mind, alias matter, lobbying against the supremacy of Spirit. Exclude the images of mortal thought and its beliefs in sickness and sin. Then, when you are delivered to the judgment of Truth, Christ, the judge will say, "You are well!"[1]

Righteous rebellion

Instead of blind and calm resignation to the beginning or advanced stages of disease, confidently rebel against them. Evict the belief that you can possibly entertain a single intruding pain which cannot be ruled out by the might of Mind, and in this way you can prevent the development of pain in the body. No law of God hinders this result. It is a mistake to suffer for anything but your own irresponsibility and narrow-minded thinking. Christ, or Truth, will destroy all other suffering that has been accepted as true. Human suffering is escaped from as the wrong thinking is corrected.

Contradict error

Justice declares the presence of law. Injustice declares the absence of law. When the body is supposed to say, "I am sick," never plead guilty. Since matter can't talk, it must be human mind which speaks; therefore meet the implication with a protest. If you say, "I am sick," you plead guilty. Then your opponent will deliver you to the judge (human mind), and the judge will sentence you. Disease has no intelligence to declare itself something and announce its name. Human mortal mind alone sentences itself. Therefore, make your own terms with sickness and be just to yourself and to others.

Sin to be overcome

The only course is to take antagonistic grounds against all that is opposed to the health, holiness, and harmony of our spirituality, of God's image. Mentally contradict every complaint from the body. Evolve into the spiritual consciousness of Life as Love—as all that is pure, and bearing the fruits of Spirit. Fear is the source of sickness. You offset fear and negative desires through divine Mind; consequently, it is through divine Mind that you overcome disease. Only while fear or sin remains can it bring forth death. To cure a

---

[1] John 5:14

bodily ailment, every broken moral law should be taken into account and the error be rebuked. Fear, which is an element of all disease, must be driven out so you can focus better on God. With less fearful and ignorant thinking, you are able to see truth.

Illusions about nerves

The physical affirmation of disease should always be met with the mental negation. Whatever benefit is produced on the body must be expressed mentally and thought should be held fast to the improved ideal. If you believe in inflamed and weak nerves, you are liable to an attack from that source. You will call it neuralgia, but I call it a belief. If you think that cancer is hereditary in your family, you are liable to the development of that thought, unless Science shows you otherwise. If you decide that the weather or air quality is unhealthy, it will be so to you. Your decisions will control you, whichever direction they take.

Guarding the access

Improve the case. Safeguard, or firewall your thought. Admit only those conclusions that you wish realized in bodily results and you will control yourself harmoniously. When the condition is present which you say induces disease, whether it is air, exercise, heredity, contagion, or accident, than actively keep those unhealthy conclusions and fears out of thought. The issues of pain or pleasure must come through mind. Be on guard, do not abandon the mental post and do not forget that through divine help we can stop intruders. Exclude from human mind all offending errors; then the body cannot suffer from them.

The strength of Spirit

The body seems to be self-acting, only because mortal mind is ignorant of itself. The human mind is unaware of its own actions, and of their results—unaware that the inclining, outlying, and triggering cause of all bad effects is a law of so-called human mind, not of matter. Mind is the master of the physical senses and can vanquish sickness, sin, and death. Exercise this God-given power. Take possession of your body, and direct its feeling and action. Advance in the strength of Spirit to resist all that is unlike good. God has made you capable of this, and nothing can stop the ability and power divinely bestowed on your spirituality.

No pain in matter molecules

Be well-balanced in your understanding that the divine Mind governs, and that in Science person reflects God's government. There will be no fear that matter can ache, swell, and be inflamed as the result of a law of any kind, when it is self-evident that matter can have no pain or inflammation. If it wasn't for human mind, your body wouldn't suffer from wounds or strains anymore than the trunk of a tree or an electrical wire suffers from wounds or strains.

When Jesus declares that "the eye is the lamp of the body,"[1] he certainly means that light depends upon Mind, not upon the optic nerve, retina, muscles, the iris and pupil, constituting the visual organ.

No real disease

Person is never sick, for Mind is not sick. Material particles can't be sick. False thinking is the tempter and the tempted, the sin and the sinner, the disease and its cause. It is beneficial to be calm around sickness or when feeling sick; and to be hopeful is still better. However, understanding that sickness is not real and that Truth can destroy its seeming reality is best of all, for this understanding is the universal and perfect remedy.

Recuperation mental

By indisputably giving power to disorder, a large majority of doctors depress mental energy, which is the only real recuperative power. If we admit that some bodily condition is beyond the control of Mind, we become more vulnerable. Don't give the upper hand to matter, it's discouraging. It's similar to advising a person who is down in the world, not to bother overcoming their difficulties. The better approach is to apply the knowledge that we can accomplish the good we hope for. This stimulates the system to act in the direction which Mind points out.

Experience has proved the fallacy of material systems in general. The theories of temporal systems are sometimes destructive, and to deny them is better than affirming them. Will you urge people to let evils overcome them? Would you assure a person that all misfortunes are from God, against whom human beings should not fight? Will you

---

1   Matt. 6:22; Luke 11:34

tell the sick that their condition is hopeless, unless it can be aided by a drug, operation, or different climate? Are temporal means the only refuge from fatal chances? Is there no divine permission to conquer disorder of every kind with harmony, with Truth and Love?

Arguing wrongly

We should remember that Life is God, and that God is omnipotent. To forget that God is our Life, is too unconsciously enable suffering instead of contradict it. Not understanding divine Science, the sick usually have little faith in it until they feel its altruistic influence. This shows that faith is not the healer in such cases. The sick admit the reality of affliction, whereas, they should defy it. We should stand up against the testimony of the deceitful senses, while maintaining our spirituality and ongoing likeness to God.

Divine authority

Christ Jesus was an excellent example. Like him, the healer should speak to disease as having authority over it, leaving Soul to prevail over the false evidences of the physical senses and to assert Spirit's claims over mortality and disease. The same Principle cures both sin and sickness. When divine Science overcomes faith in a fleshly mind; and faith in God destroys all faith in temporal thinking and methods of healing, then sin, disease, and death will disappear.

Help in sickness

Prayers, in which God is not asked to heal but is asked to take the patient to Himself, do not benefit the sick. An ill-tempered, complaining, or deceitful person should not be a nurse. The nurse should be happy, orderly, conscientious, patient, full of faith—receptive to Truth and Love.

Mental quackery

It is mental quackery to make disease a reality and then attempt to cure it through Mind. In other words, those who pretend to be metaphysicians, hold disease as something seen and felt before undertaking its cure through Spirit. It is no less an illusion to believe in the real existence of a tumor, a cancer, or decayed lungs, while you argue against their reality, than it is for your patient to feel these ills in physical belief. Mental practice (malpractice), which holds disease as a reality, links disease to the patient and it may appear in a more alarming form.

Effacing images of disease

The knowledge that brain-lobes cannot kill people, or affect the functions of mind, would prevent the brain from becoming diseased. Remember though, a moral offence is indeed the worst of diseases. One should never keep in mind the thought of disease, but should erase from thought all forms and types of disease, both for one's own sake and for that of the patient.

Don't talk about disease

Avoid talking to the patient about illness. Make no unnecessary inquiries relative to feelings or disease. Never startle the patient with a discouraging remark concerning recovery. Don't draw attention to certain symptoms as unfavorable. Avoid speaking aloud the name of the disease. Never say beforehand how much you have to contend with in a case, and don't encourage in the patient's thought the expectation of growing worse before a crisis is passed.

False testimony refuted

Refuting or negating the testimony of temporal sense is not so difficult when the falsity of this sense is realized. The negation becomes arduous, not because the testimony of sin or disease is true, but solely on account of the obstinate, narrow mindset believing in its truth. This congealed habituated mindset is due to the force of education and the overwhelming weight of opinions on the wrong side—teaching that the body suffers, as if subatomic particles, though elaborately organized, could have sensation.

Healthful explanation

At the right time, explain to the sick the power which their thinking exercises over their bodies. Give them divine and wholesome understanding with which to defeat their erroneous sense and so obliterate the images of sickness from human mind. Keep clearly in thought that we are the offspring of God, not of human beings; that we are spiritual, not material; that Soul is Spirit, never inside matter. Matter never gives the body life and sensation. It breaks the dream of disease to understand that sickness is formed by the human mind, not by material energy, time, or divine Mind.

342

Misleading methods

We are misled in our conclusions and methods when we don't perceive vital metaphysical points. It is important to be aware of how the human mind can act beneficially or injuriously on bodily health, as well as on the morals and happiness of human beings. Perceiving the vital spiritual points, we find the mental influence on the right side and those whom we mean to help are blessed, instead of injured.

Remedy for accidents

Suffering is just as much a mental condition as enjoyment. You not only cause bodily suffering mentally, but you can also aggravate the suffering by admitting its reality and persistence. In the same way you enhance your joys by believing them to be real and continuous. When an accident happens, you think or exclaim, "Owe, I am hurt!" Your thought is more powerful than your words, more powerful than the accident itself, to make the injury real.

Now reverse the action. Affirm that you are not hurt and understand the reason why. You will then find the resulting good effects to be in exact proportion to your disbelief in physics and your fidelity to divine metaphysics, confidence in God as All, which the Scriptures declare Mind to be.

Independent mentality

To heal the sick, you must be familiar with the great truths of being. Humanity is no more material in their waking hours than when they act, walk, see, hear, enjoy, or suffer in dreams. We can never treat human mind and matter separately, because they combine as one. Give up the belief that mind is, even temporarily, compressed within the skull, and you will quickly become more manly or womanly. You will understand yourself and your Maker better than before.

Naming maladies

Sometimes Jesus called a disease by name, as when he said to the epileptic boy, "You deaf and mute spirit, I command you, come out of him and never enter him again." It is added that "the spirit [error] shrieked, convulsed him violently and came out. The boy looked so much like a corpse that many said, 'He's dead.'"[1] This is

---

[1]   Mark 9:25-26 (Brackets added by Mary Baker Eddy)

clear evidence that the affliction was not material. These instances show the concessions which Jesus was willing to make for those who were unfamiliar with spiritual Life-laws. Often Jesus gave no name to the infirmity he cured. To the synagogue ruler's daughter, whom they called dead, he said, "The child is not dead but asleep." Jesus then simply told the girl, "Little girl, I say to you, get up!"[1] To the sufferer with the shriveled hand he said, "Stretch out your hand," and "his hand was completely restored."[2]

The action of faith

Homeopathic remedies, sometimes not containing a particle of medicine, are known to relieve the symptoms of disease. What produces the change? It is the faith of the doctor and the patient which reduces self-inflicted sufferings and produces a new effect upon the body. Use this same faith to destroy the illusion of pleasure in intoxication, and the desire for strong drink is gone. Appetite and disease reside in human mind, not in matter or genes.

So also faith, cooperating with the trained thinking that time and medication produce a healing effect, will relieve fear and change the experience of disease to an experience of health. Even a blind faith removes bodily ailments for a season. Hypnotism changes one problem into new and more difficult forms of problems. The Science of Mind must come to the rescue and work a radical cure, and we then understand the process. The great fact remains that evil is not mind. Evil has no power, no intelligence, for God is good, and therefore good is limitless, is All.

Combining matter

You say that a combination of certain physical circumstances produce disease. If the physical body causes disease, can matter cure what matter has caused? Human mind prescribes the drug and administers it. Human mind plans the exercise and puts the body through certain motions. No gastric gas accumulates, not a cell function or chemical combination can operate, apart from the action of mortal thought, alias human mind.

---

1   Mark 5:39-41
2   Matt. 12:13; Mark 3:5; Luke 6:10

Automatic mechanism

The mechanisms of the human mind and body seem to talk to one another, but the mind is both the server and receiver. The human mind is a counterfeit. Nerves are unable to talk. Material atoms can return no answer to spiritual Mind. If Mind is all-acting, how can mechanism be automatic? Human mind perpetuates its own thought. It constructs a machine, manages it, and then calls it material. A computer at work or the action of a processor is but a derivative form, and continuation of, the primitive human mind. Without this human mind force, the body is devoid of action and this deadness shows that so-called human life is fleshly mind, not matter.

Mental strength

Scientifically speaking, there is no human mind out of which to make incomplete beliefs proceeding from illusion. This misnamed mind is not an entity. It is only a false sense of substance, since its substance called matter, has no sensitivity. The one Mind, God, contains no human opinions. All that is real is included in spiritual Mind.

Confirmation in a parable

The Teacher asked: "How can anyone enter a strong man's house and carry off his possessions unless he first ties up the strong man?"[1] In other words: How can I heal the body, without beginning with so-called fleshly mind, which directly controls the body? When disease is once destroyed in this ambiguous mind, the fear of disease is gone and the disease is thoroughly cured. Human mind is "the strong man," which must be held in subjection before its influence on health and morals can be removed. This error conquered, we can deprive "the strong man" of his goods—namely, of sin and disease.

Eradicate error from thought

Mortals receive the harmony of health only as they forsake disorder, abandon their imperfect thinking and acknowledge the supremacy of divine Mind. Eradicate the image of disease from the perturbed thought before it has taken tangible shape in conscious thought, alias the body, and you prevent the development of disease.

---

[1]   Matt. 12:29; Mark 3:27

This practice becomes easy, if you understand that every disease is an error, and has no identity or symptom, except what human mind assigns to it. By lifting thought above error or disease, and striving persistently for truth, you destroy error.

Mortal mind controlled

When we remove disease by addressing the disturbed mind, paying no attention to the body, we prove that thought alone creates the suffering. Human mind rules all that is temporal. We see in the body the images of this mind, even as in optics we see painted on the retina the image which becomes visible to the senses. The action of so-called human mind must be destroyed by the divine Mind to bring out the harmony of being. Without divine control there is disorder, manifest as sin, sickness, and death.

Human mind not a healer

The Scriptures plainly declare that the influence of unspiritual thought is harmful to the body. Even Jesus felt this. It is recorded that in certain localities he did not many mighty works because of "their unbelief"[1] in Truth. Any human error is its own enemy and works against itself. A human mistake does nothing in the right direction and much in the wrong. If human mind is cherishing wrong ambitions and malicious purposes, it is not a healer, but a procreator of disease and death.

Effect of opposites

Faith in the truth of being is communicated mentally and destroys error. If this communication causes chemicalization (as when an alkali is destroying an acid), it is because the truth of being must transform the error to the end of producing a higher manifestation. This chemical reaction should not aggravate the disease, but should be as painless to people as to a fluid, since matter has no sensation and human mind only feels and sees in belief.

What I term chemicalization is the upheaval produced when spiritual Truth is destroying erroneous materialistic thinking. Mental chemicalization brings unspiritual behavior and sickness to the surface, forcing impurities to pass away, as is the case with a fermenting fluid.

---

[1]   Matt. 13:58; Mark 6:6 (NRSV)

Medicine and brain

The effect produced by medicine is dependent on mental action. When the mind is gone from the dead body, could you produce any effect upon the brain or body by applying a drug? Would the drug remove paralysis, affect the system, or restore will and action to the cerebrum and cerebellum of a corpse?

Skillful surgery

Until the advancing age admits the supremacy of Mind and its power to produce an effect, it is better for Christian Scientists to leave surgery to the fingers of a skilled surgeon. Skillful surgery can also be appreciated in regard to the adjustment of broken bones and dislocations. The mental healer can restrict himself or herself chiefly to mental reconstruction and to the prevention of inflammation.

Divine Science is always the expert surgeon, but surgery is the branch of its healing which will be last acknowledged. However, it is but just to say that I have already in my possession well-authenticated records of the cure, by myself and my students through mental surgery alone, of broken bones, dislocated joints, and spinal vertebrae.

Indestructible life of man and woman

Sometime it will be learned that human mind constructs the human body with this mind's own mortal materials. The time approaches when human mind will swear off its temporal, structural, and physical basis, and spiritual Mind and its formations will be known in Science. We can realize that physical theories will not interfere with metaphysical facts. God's children are indestructible and spiritual. In Science, no breakage or dislocation can really occur. You say that accidents, injuries, and disease kill person, but this is not true. Our life is Mind. The physical body manifests only what human mind believes, whether it is a broken bone, a disease, or inappropriate behavior.

The evil of mesmerism (human suggestion)

We say that one human mind can influence another and in this way affect the body, but we rarely remember that we control our own bodies. The mesmerism, or hypnotism, illustrates the fact just stated. One human being would make another human being believe that they cannot act voluntarily and behave appropriately. If the misled human being allows this influence, it is because his or her faith is not better instructed by spiritual understanding. Hence the proof that hypnotism is not scientific; Science cannot produce both disorder and order. The involuntary pleasure or pain of the person under hypnotic control is proved to be blind faith without a real cause.

Wrongdoer suffers

Let us now examine the great difference between a wrong intention and a mistake. A wrong intention is induced consciously and should and does cause the perpetrator to suffer, while a mistake is induced unconsciously because human beings are badly instructed. In the first instance it is understood that the difficulty is a mental illusion, while in the second it is believed that the misfortune is a physical effect. The human mind is employed to remove the illusion in one case, but matter is appealed to in the other case. So the sick through their beliefs have induced their own diseased conditions. In reality, both have their origin in the human mind, and can be healed only by the divine Mind.

Error's power imaginary

You command the situation if you understand that temporal existence is a state of self-deception and not the truth of being. Fleshly mind is constantly producing on temporal body the results of false opinions; and it will continue to do so, until human error is deprived of its imaginary powers by Truth. Christ, Truth, sweeps away the gossamer web of temporal illusion. The most Christian state is one of integrity and spiritual understanding, and this is best adapted for healing the sick. Never conjure up some new discovery from dark premonitions regarding disease and then acquaint your patient with it.

Manufacturing disease

The fleshly mind produces all that is unlike the spiritual Mind. The human mind determines the nature of a case, and the practitioner improves or injures the case as either truth or error influences his or her conclusions. The mental conception and development of disease are not understood by the patient, but the physician should be familiar with mental action and its effect in order to judge the case according to divine Science.

Appetites to be abandoned

If a person is an alcoholic, a sex or drug addict, or has compulsive behavior, meet and destroy these errors with the truth of being. Point out to the person the suffering that comes along with indulging in bad habits. Convince him or her that there is no real pleasure in false appetites. A depraved mind is manifest in a depraved body. Lust, malice, and all sorts of evil are diseased beliefs, and you can destroy them only by destroying the wicked motives which produce them. If the evil is overcome in the repentant human mind, while its effects still remain on the individual, you can remove this disorder as God's law if fulfilled and reformation cancels the crime. The healthy sinner is the hardened sinner.

Reformation

Reformation and moderation are results of mental healing, which cuts down "every tree that does not produce good fruit."[1] The conviction, that there is no real pleasure in thinking and acting against Life, Truth, and Love, is one of the most important points in the theology of Christian Science. Awaken the self-indulgent to this new and true view of their self-destruction. Show the wrongdoer that negativity confers no pleasure, and this knowledge strengthens their moral courage and increases their ability to overcome evil and to love goodness.

Sin or fear the root of sickness

Healing the sick and reforming the sinner is one and the same thing in Christ's Science. Both cures require the same method and are inseparable in Truth. Hatred, envy, dishonesty, fear, and so forth, make human beings sick, and neither material medicine nor Mind can help them permanently, even in body, unless it makes them better mentally, and so delivers them from their destroyers. The basic error is human mind. Hatred ignites the cruel tendencies. To indulge in evil motives and aims makes any human being, who is above the lowest type of manhood or womanhood, a hopeless sufferer.

---

[1]   Matt. 3:10; Luke 3:9

Mental conspirators

Christian Science requires us to improve our intentions. Hatred is to become extinct through kindness. Lust is conquered with purity. Revenge is triumphed over with charity, and deceit is defeated with honesty. Starve errors in their early stages if you would not cherish an army of conspirators against health, happiness, and success. Mental traitors will deliver you to the judge, the arbiter of truth against error; the judge will deliver you to justice; and the sentence of the moral law will be executed upon human mind and body. Mind and body will be restricted until the last penny[1] is paid—until you have balanced your account with God. This is sin's necessity—to destroy itself. "You reap whatever you sow."[2] The goodness we live is the nemesis of negative inclinations. Spirituality in action, demonstrates the government of God, good, in which is no power to act against life, truth, and love.

Cumulative repentance

It would be better to be exposed to every plague on earth than to endure the amassed effects of a guilty conscience. The ability to do right tends to be damaged when continually conscious of wrongdoing. If sin is not regretted and is not lessening, then it is hurrying on to physical and moral doom. You are conquered by the moral penalties you invite and the ills they bring. The pains of sinful sense are less harmful than its pleasures. When human beings realize they no longer want to believe in physical suffering, they turn from the body to Spirit and call on divine sources outside of themselves.

The leaves of healing

The Bible contains the recipe for all healing. "The leaves of the tree are for the healing of the nations."[3] Sin and sickness are healed by the same Principle. The tree symbolizes our divine Principle, which is equal to every emergency. Love offers full salvation from sin, sickness, and death. Sin will submit to the Science of Christ when, in place of customs and routines, the power of God is understood and

---

1   Matt. 5:26 (NRSV)

2   Gal. 6:7 (NRSV)

3   Rev. 22:2

demonstrated in the healing of human beings, both mind and body. "Perfect Love casteth out fear."[1]

Sickness will abate

The Science of being uncovers the misperceptions, and spiritual perception assisted by Science, reaches Truth. Then error disappears. Sin and sickness will diminish and seem less real as we approach the scientific period, in which limited sense is subdued and all that is unlike the true likeness disappears. Moral human beings have no fear that they will commit a murder, and they should be as fearless on the question of disease.

Resist to the end

Resist evil—error of every kind—and it will cease to exist. Error is opposed to Life. We can, and ultimately will, so improve and make use in every direction the supremacy of Truth over error, Life over death, and good over evil. This spiritualization will go on until we arrive at the fullness of God's idea, and have no more fear that we shall be sick and die. Inharmony of any kind involves weakness and suffering—a loss of control over the body.

Morbid cravings

The depraved appetite for alcohol, tobacco, caffeine, methamphetamines, promiscuity, pornography, is destroyed only by Mind's control of the body. There is no enjoyment in getting drunk, in becoming a fool, or being an object of extreme disgust. There is actually a very sharp remembrance of idiocy, a suffering inconceivably terrible to one's self-respect. Morbid cravings are loathsome. Normal control is gained through divine strength and understanding.

Universal panacea

Humanity's dependence on the relentless passions, selfishness, envy, hatred, and revenge—is beaten only by a mighty struggle. Every hour of delay makes the struggle more severe. If someone can't stop the negative human elements from taking over their thought—happiness, health, and courage will be crushed. Here divine Science is the universal remedy, giving strength to the weakness of human mind. Spiritual and omnipotent Mind not only gives energy, but also lifts

---

[1]   I John 4:18 (KJV)

humanity above itself into purer desires, even into spiritual power and good-will to humankind.

Let the dupe of self-destructive desires learn the lessons of Christian Science. They then can get the better of those desires, and ascend a degree in the scale of health, happiness, and existence.

Immortal memory

Contradict the affirmations of delusion, such as, "I am losing my memory." No faculty of Mind is lost. In Science, all being is eternal, spiritual, perfect, and harmonious in every action. Let the perfect example be present in your thoughts instead of its demoralized opposite. This spiritualization of thought lets in the light and brings the divine Mind, Life not death, into your consciousness.

Sin a form of insanity

There are many categories of mental disease. Even sin is a mental disorder, just in a different degree. Sin is spared from the classification of insanity, only because its method of madness agrees with common human thinking. Every sort of sickness is error—that is, sickness is loss of harmony or balance. This view is not altered by the fact that sin is worse than sickness. Sickness is not acknowledged or discovered to be error by many who are sick.

There is a universal insanity concerning temporal health which mistakes fable for fact throughout the entire round of the human perceptions. However, this general craze cannot, in a scientific diagnosis, shield the individual case from the special name of say, Schizophrenia. Those unfortunate people who are committed to mental health institutions are only so many distinctly defined instances of the horrid effects of illusion on human minds and bodies.

Drugs and brain-lobes

To suppose that we can correct mental disorders by the use of medications and electroconvulsive therapy is in itself a mild species of insanity. The brain will only rewire itself after a "fix." On their own, can drugs go to the brain and destroy the so-called biochemical imbalances, thus reaching human mind through matter? Drugs and small electrical currents do not affect a corpse. Truth does not distribute antipsychotic medicines through the blood, and from them derive a supposed effect on intelligence and coping skills. Believe it or not, a dislocation of the knee joint would produce mental disorders if the human mind thought the knee joint was as intimately connected with the mind as the brain.

Matter and animate error

That condition of the body which we call sensation in matter is unreal. You may say: "But if disease comes through matter, why do you insist that disease is formed by human mind and not by matter?" Human mind and body combine as one. As matter approaches its final statement—animate error called nerves, brain, mind—the more prolific it is likely to become in wrongdoing and disease beliefs. Human mind is ignorant of itself—ignorant of the errors it includes and of their effects. This ignorance is evidenced by unconscious thoughts in the brain. Intelligent matter is impossible.

Dictation of error

Does a dead body become cancerous? Unconscious human mind— alias matter, brain—cannot dictate terms to consciousness or say, "I am sick." The mistaken thinking, that the unconscious substratum of human mind, termed the body, suffers and reports disease independently of this so-called conscious mind, is an error. This mistake prevents human beings from knowing how to control their bodies.

Bogus superiority

The so-called conscious human mind is believed to be superior to its unconscious substratum, matter, and the stronger never yields to the weaker, except through fear or choice. The animate should be governed by God alone. The real person is spiritual and immortal, but the human and imperfect so-called children of human beings are counterfeits from the beginning, to be laid aside for the pure reality. Mortality is put off and spirituality is put on in proportion as human beings realize the Science of true identity and seek the true model.

Death no benefactor

We have no right to say that life depends on matter now, but will not depend on it after death. We cannot spend our days here ignoring the Science of Life, and expect to find beyond the grave a reward for this ignorance. Death will not make us harmonious and spiritual as a recompense for ignorance. If here we do not pay attention to the

Science of Christ, which is spiritual and eternal, we shall not be ready for spiritual Life hereafter.

Life eternal and present

"Now this is life eternal," says Jesus—*now*, not later. Jesus then defined everlasting life as a present knowledge of his Father and of himself—the knowledge of Love, Truth, and Life. "Now this is life eternal: that they may know you, the only true God, and Jesus Christ, whom you have sent."[1] The Scriptures say, "It takes more than bread to stay alive. It takes a steady stream of words from God's mouth."[2] This shows that Truth is the actual life of person; but humankind objects to making this teaching practical.

Love casts out fear

Every test of our faith in God makes us stronger. The more difficult seems the fleshly condition to be overcome by Spirit, the stronger should be our faith and the purer our love. The Apostle John says: "There is no fear in love [dread does not exist], but full-grown (complete, perfect) love turns fear out of doors *and* expels every trace of terror! . . . he who is afraid has not reached the full maturity of love [is not yet grown into love's complete perfection]."[3]

MENTAL TREATMENT ILLUSTRATED

Don't be afraid

The Science of mental practice is susceptible of no misuse. Self-centeredness does not appear in the practice of Truth or Christ's Science. If mental practice is abused or is used in any way except to promote right thinking and doing, the power to heal mentally will diminish until the practitioner's healing ability is completely lost. Scientific practice begins with Christ's keynote of harmony, "Do not

---

1   John 17:3

2   Deut. 8:3; Matt. 4:4 (The Message)

3   I John 4:18 (Amplified)

be afraid!"[1] Job said: "Every terror that haunted me has caught up with me; what I dreaded has overtaken me."[2]

Naming diseases

My first discovery in the student's practice was this: If the student silently called the disease by name when arguing against it, as a general rule the body would respond more quickly. This is similar to people responding more readily when their name is spoken. The disease is called by named because we are not perfectly attuned to divine Science, and we need arguments of truth for reminders. If Spirit or the power of divine Love bears witness to the truth, this is the ultimatum, the scientific way, and the healing is instantaneous.

Evils cast out

It is recorded that once Jesus asked the name of a disease—a disease like dementia. The demon, or evil, replied that his name was "Legion."[3] Jesus sent the evil out, and the mentally disturbed man was changed and straightway became whole. The Scripture seems to signify that Jesus caused the evil to be self-seen and so destroyed.

Fear as the foundation

Fear, sin, and our neglect of spirituality is what brings on and feeds all sickness. Disease is always induced by a false sense mentally entertained, not destroyed. Disease is an image of thought externalized. The mental state is called a physical state. Whatever is cherished in human mind as the physical condition is imaged forth on the body.

Unspoken argument

Always begin your spiritual treatment by quieting the fear of patients. Silently reassure them as to their exemption from disease and danger. Watch the result of this simple rule of Mind-healing and you will find that it alleviates the symptoms of every disease. If you succeed in wholly removing the fear, your patient is healed. The great fact that God lovingly controls all—which naturally causes the self-punishment of anything that works against Life, Truth, and Love—is

---

1   Matt. 14:27, 17:7, 28:10; Mark 5:36, 6:50; Luke 12:32; John 6:20

2   Job 3:25 (REB)

3   Mark 5:9; Luke 8:30

your standpoint from which to advance and destroy the human fear of sickness. Mentally and silently plead the case scientifically for Truth. You may adapt the reasoning to meet the peculiar or general symptoms of the case you treat, but be thoroughly persuaded in your own mind concerning the truth which you think or speak, and you will be the winner.

Eloquent silence

You may call the disease by name when you mentally deny it; however in some circumstances, you are liable to impress disease on the thought by naming it audibly. The power of Christ's Science and divine Love is omnipotent, indeed adequate, to unlock the grip of and destroy disease, sin, and death.

Insistence requisite

To prevent disease or to cure it, the power of Truth, of divine Spirit, must break the dream of temporal convictions. To heal by argument, find the type of the ailment, get its name, and arrange your mental plea against the physical. Reason at first mentally, not audibly, that the patient has no disease, and conform the logic so as to destroy the evidence of disease. Mentally insist that harmony is the fact, and that sickness is a temporal dream. Realize the presence of health and the fact of spiritual being until the body agrees with the normal conditions of health and balance.

The cure of infants

If the case is that of a young child or an infant, it needs to be met mainly through the parent's thought, either silently or audibly on the aforementioned basis of divine Science. A single requirement, beyond what is necessary to meet the simplest needs of a baby is harmful. Mind regulates not only the condition of the stomach, bowels, organs, and cell division, but also the temperature of children and human beings; matter does not regulate. The wise or unwise views of parents and other persons on these subjects produce good or bad effects on the health of children. The Scientist also knows that there can be no hereditary disease, since matter is not intelligent and cannot transmit good or evil intelligence to man and woman. God, the only Mind, does not produce pain in matter. The act of allowing our thoughts to excessively contemplate physical wants or conditions induces those very conditions.

Cleanliness

"Cleanliness is next to godliness,"[1] but washing should only be for the purpose of keeping the body clean, and this can be done without scrubbing the whole surface every day. Water is not the natural habitat of humanity. To constantly wash an infant is no more natural or necessary than would be the process of taking a fish out of water every day and covering it with dirt in order to make it thrive more vigorously in its own element. Cleanliness within and without is good. Do not be patient with filth; however, in caring for an infant you don't need to wash his or her little body all over each day in order to keep it sweet as the newly-opened flower.

Adolescent problems

A mind loaded with illusions about disease, health-laws, and death should be careful around children. Giving drugs to infants, noticing every fart, and constantly directing the mind to what the body might be doing wrong will convey negative mental images to children's developing thoughts and often stamp them there; making it probable at any time that ills may be reproduced in the very ailments feared. A child may have allergies or ADHD (Attention Deficient Hyperactive Disorder) if you say so, or any other malady fearfully held in the beliefs concerning their mind and body. Thus are laid the foundations of the belief in disease and death, and thus are children educated into limitation.

Cure of insanity

The treatment of mental disorders is especially interesting. However stubborn the case, it gives up more readily than do most diseases to the healthful action of truth, which counteracts error. The arguments to be used in curing mental disorders are the same as in other diseases: namely, the impossibility that material particles (arranged as brain) can control or derange mind. Temporal particles cannot suffer or cause suffering. Know that truth and love will

---

[1] Quote attributed to John Wesley (1703-1791) 18th century Anglican Clergyman and Christian Theologian.

establish a healthy state, guide and control human mind or the thought of the patient, and destroy all error, whether it is called dementia, depression, autism, hatred, or any other disorder.

To keep truth firmly in your patient's thoughts, explain divine Science to them, but not too soon. Before explaining Science, first prepare your patients thought, or else you will trouble and confuse them by causing them to work against their own interests. The Scientist's argument rests on the Christ-like scientific basis of being. The Scripture declares, "The Lord is God [good]; besides him there is no other."[1] Even so, harmony is universal, and discord is unreal. Divine Science declares that Mind is substance, also that temporal substance neither feels, suffers, nor enjoys. Hold these points strongly in view. Keep in mind the reality of being—that everyone is the image and likeness of God, in whom all being is painless and permanent. Remember that our perfection is real and unimpeachable, whereas imperfection is blameworthy, unreal, and is not brought about by divine Love.

Matter is not inflamed

Matter cannot be inflamed. Inflammation is fear, an excited state of human beings which is not normal. Spiritual Mind is the only cause; therefore disease is neither a cause nor an effect. Mind in every case is the eternal God, good. Sin, disease, and death have no foundations in Truth. As a human belief, inflammation excites the system's action because thought is contemplating unpleasant things or some dreaded situation. Inflammation never appears in a part of the body which human thought does not reach. That is why narcotics relieve inflammation; quieting the thought by inducing insensibility, resorting to matter instead of relying on Mind. Narcotics do not remove pain in any scientific sense. They only render human mind temporarily less fearful until it can overcome its defensive, excited thinking.

Truth calms the thought

How can we be relaxed, and then all of a sudden break out in a nervous sweat? The thought of something frightening can quickly lead

---

1   Deut. 4:35; Mark 12:32 (Brackets added by Mary Baker Eddy)

to a disturbed body. In the same way thought increases or diminishes blood pressure, mutates the genes, or affects the action of the lungs, bowels, and heart. The muscles, moving quickly or slowly and impelled or palsied by thought, represent the action of all the organs of the human system, including brain and viscera. To remove the error producing disorder, you must calm and instruct human mind with spiritual Truth.

Effect of anesthetics

Anesthesia is a state of analgesia, reflex loss, narcosis, and relaxation. General anesthesia is most commonly achieved by inhalation or by intravenous techniques. When first administered, the patient may feel warm or have a feeling of detachment followed by excitement then unconsciousness. Anesthesia produces artificial insensitivity to pain, or a loss of consciousness. This process shows that the pain is in the mind, because as soon as the anesthesia (even local, epidural, or spinal anesthesia) wears off, the belief of pain will return, unless the mental image occasioning the pain is removed by recognizing the truth of being.

Sedatives valueless

Morphine is administered to a patient and in twenty minutes the sufferer is numb. To the patient there is no longer any pain. Yet any physician—allopathic, homeopathic, holistic—will tell you that the troublesome material cause is still present. Doctors and nurses know that when the influence of the pain reliever is exhausted, the patient will find their self in the same pain unless the belief which occasions the pain has meanwhile been changed. Where is the pain while the patient sleeps?

False human ego

The fleshly body, which you call *me*, is human mind, and this mind is limited in sensation. The body has originated and been developed by limited perceptions and is therefore material, limited. The materialism of parent and child is only in human mind, as the dead body proves; for when the human being has resigned the body to dust, the body is no longer the parent, even in appearance.

Evil thought depletes

The sick know nothing of the mental process by which they are weakened, and next to nothing of the metaphysical method by which they can be healed. If they ask about their disease, tell them only what is best for them to know. Assure them that they think too much about their ailments and have already heard too much on that subject. Turn their thoughts away from their bodies to better ideas. Teach them that their being is sustained by Spirit, not by matter, and that they find health, peace, and harmony in God, divine Love.

Helpful encouragement

Give sick people credit for sometimes knowing more than their doctors. Always support the patient's trust in the power of Mind to support the body. Never tell the sick that they have more courage than strength. Tell them rather that their strength is in proportion to their courage. If you make the sick realize this important principle, there will be no reaction from over-exertion or from excited conditions. Maintain the facts of divine Science—that Spirit is God, and therefore cannot be sick; that what is termed matter cannot be sick; that all cause is Mind, acting through spiritual law. Then take your stand with the unshaken understanding of Truth and Love, and you will win. When you silence the opposition against your prayer, you destroy the manifest disorder, for the disease disappears. The evidence before the physical senses is not the Science of our spirituality.

Disease to be made unreal

To the scientific metaphysical healer, sickness is a dream from which patients need to be awakened. Disease should not appear real to the physician, since it is demonstrable that the way to cure patients is to make disease unreal to them. To do this, the physician must understand the unreality of disease in Science.

Explain audibly to your patients, as soon as they can handle it, the complete control which Mind holds over the body. Show them how human mind seems to induce disease by certain fears and false conclusions, and how divine Mind can cure by opposite thoughts. Give your patients an essential understanding to support and shield them from the fatal effects of their own conclusions. Show the patient that the conquest over sickness, as well as over sin, depends on mentally destroying all belief in temporal pleasure or pain.

Christ-like pleading

Unite with the truth of being as opposed to the ingrained error that life, substance, or intelligence can be in matter. Pray with an honest conviction of truth and a clear perception of the unchanging, unmistaken, and certain effect of divine Science. Then, if your faithfulness is half equal to the truth of your prayer, you will heal the sick.

Truthful arguments

It must be clear to you that sickness is no more the reality of being than is sin. This mortal dream of sickness, sin, and death should cease through divine Science. Then one disease would be as readily destroyed as another. Whatever the un-Godlike thinking is, it must not be accepted. The belief must be rejected, and the rejection must extend to the supposed disease and to whatever decides its type and symptoms. Truth is affirmative, and confers harmony. All metaphysical logic is inspired by this simple rule of Truth, which governs all reality. By the truthful reasoning you employ, and especially by the spirit of Truth and Love which you entertain, you will heal the sick.

Morality required

Include moral as well as physical belief in your efforts to destroy error. Exclude all manner of evil. "Go into all the world and preach the good news to all creation."[1] Speak the truth to error in its every disguise. Tumors, ulcers, acne, inflammation, pain, deformed joints, are waking dream-shadows, dark images of human thought, which vanish in the light of Truth.

A moral issue may hinder the recovery of the sick. Lurking error, lust, envy, revenge, malice, or hate will perpetuate or even create the belief in disease. Errors of all sorts gravitate in this direction. Your true course is to destroy the foe and leave the field to God, Life, Truth, and Love, remembering that God and God's ideas alone are real and harmonious.

---

[1]   Mark 16:15

Relapse unnecessary

If your patient suffers a relapse, mentally and courageously treat whatever caused it. Know that there can be no reaction in Truth. Disease itself, sin, and fear have no power to cause disease or a relapse. Disease has no intelligence with which to move itself around or to change itself from one form to another. If disease moves, it is mind, not matter that moves it; therefore be sure that you move it out. Meet every adverse circumstance as its conqueror. Observe mind instead of body. Make sure nothing enters thought that is unfit for development. Think less of temporal conditions and more of spiritual.

Conquer beliefs and fears

Mind produces all action. If action proceeds from Truth, from spiritual Mind, there is harmony; whereas human mind is liable to any phase of belief. A relapse cannot in reality occur in human beings or so-called human minds, for there is but one Mind, one God. Never fear the mental mal-practitioner, the mental assassin, who, in attempting to rule humankind, tramples upon the divine Principle of metaphysics, because God is the only power. To succeed in healing, you must conquer your own fears as well as those of your patients and advance into spiritual, pure consciousness.

True government of people

If it is found necessary to treat against relapse, know that disease or its symptoms cannot change forms. The evidence of disease cannot go from one part of the body to another, for Truth destroys disease. There is no metastasis, no stoppage of harmonious action, and no paralysis in Science. Truth not error, Love not hate, Spirit not matter, governs us. If students do not readily heal themselves, they should soon call an experienced spiritual metaphysical Scientist to help them. If they are unwilling to do this, they need only to know that error cannot produce this unnatural reluctance.

Positive reassurance

Instruct the sick that they are not helpless victims. If they will accept Truth, they can resist disease and fight it off as positively as they can the temptation to sin. This fact of divine Science should be explained to invalids when they are in a fit mood to receive it. Otherwise, until the sick are ready to receive the new idea, they will turn against it. The fact that Truth overcomes both disease and sin reassures depressed hope. Truth imparts a healthy stimulus to the body, and regulates the system. Truth increases or diminishes the action as the case may require, better than any drug, bodily adjustment, or feel-good stimulant.

Proper stimulus

Mind is the natural stimulus of the body, but human thinking, taken at its best, does not promote health or happiness. Tell the sick that they can meet disease fearlessly, if they only realize that divine Love gives them all power over every physical action and condition.

Awaken the patient

If it becomes necessary to startle human mind in order to break its dream of suffering, urgently and forcefully tell your patient that they must wake up. Turn the patient's gaze from the false evidence of physical sense to the harmonious facts of Soul and spirituality. Tell them that they suffer only as the mentally ill suffer, from false beliefs. The only difference is, some mental health disorders imply belief in a pathological change in the brain, while physical ailments (so-called) arise from the thinking that other portions of the body are disordered. Disorder is a word which conveys the true definition of all human belief in ill-health or disturbed harmony. Should you thus startle human mind in order to remove its erroneous belief, afterwards make known to the patient your motive for this shock. Show the patient that the mental jolt was to facilitate recovery.

How to treat a crisis

If a crisis occurs in your treatment, you must treat the patient less for the disease and more for the mental disturbance. The patient's thoughts are reacting, and like some chemical reactions can be turbulent, so can mental reactions. Subdue the conviction that the reaction causes pain or disease. Insist fervently on the great fact which covers the whole ground, that God, Spirit, is all, and that there is one Soul. There is *no disease.* When the supposed suffering is gone from human mind, there can be no pain; and when the fear is destroyed, the inflammation will subside. Calm the excitement sometimes induced by this mental reaction, on the grounds that it is Truth's method of restoration and purification. Sometimes you can explain the symptoms and their cause to the patient.

No perversion of Mind-science

It is no more spiritually scientific to see disease than it is to experience it. If you would destroy the sense of disease, you should not build it up by wishing to see the forms it assumes or by employing a single material application for its relief. The perversion of Mind-science is like asserting that the products of eight multiplied by five, and of seven by ten, are both forty, and that their combined sum is fifty, and then calling the process mathematics. Wiser than his persecutors, Jesus said: "If I drive out demons by Beelzebub, by whom do your people drive them out?"[1]

If the reader of this book observes a great stir throughout his whole system, and certain moral and physical symptoms seem aggravated, these indications are favorable. Continue to read, and the book will become the physician, moderating the anxiety which Truth often brings to error when destroying it.

Disease neutralized

Patients, unfamiliar with the cause of mental reactions, and ignorant that it is a favorable sign, may be alarmed. If such be the case, explain to them the law of this action. As when an acid and alkali meet and bring out a third quality, so mental and moral chemistry changes the materialist thought and gives more spirituality to consciousness, causing it to depend less on material evidence. These changes which go on in human mind serve to reconstruct the body. Thus divine Science, by the alchemy of Spirit, destroys sin and death.

Example of bone healing

Let us suppose two parallel cases of bone disease, both similarly produced and attended by the same symptoms. A surgeon is employed in one case, and a Christian Scientist in the other. The surgeon, believing that matter forms its own conditions and renders them fatal at certain points, entertains fears and doubts as to the ultimate outcome of the disease. Not holding the control-instruments in his own hands, the surgeon believes that something stronger than

---

[1]   Matt. 12:27; Luke 11:19

Mind—controls the case. The surgeon's treatment is therefore tentative. This mindset invites defeat because it believes it has encountered a superior, called matter. The belief of a power opposing Mind increases fear and makes healing the bone more difficult. Yet this belief should not be communicated to the patient, either verbally or otherwise, for this fear greatly diminishes the tendency toward a favorable result. Remember that the unexpressed belief oftentimes affects a sensitive patient more strongly than the expressed thought.

Scientific corrective

The Christian Scientist, understanding that all is Mind, commences with mental causation, the truth of being, to destroy the error. This remedy has the power to correct positively, reaching to every part of the human system. According to Scripture, it searches the "joints and marrow,"[1] and restores the healthy functions of the body.

Coping with difficulties

The physical-physician deals with physicality as both the aggravator and the reliever. The ailment is regarded as weakened or strengthened according to the evidence which physical matter presents. Conversely, the metaphysical physician makes Mind the basis of his or her operation, in spite of matter. The truth and harmony of being are regarded as superior to error and disorder, and the metaphysician is rendered strong, instead of weak, to cope with the case. The mental scientist proportionately strengthens the patient with the stimulus of courage and conscious power. Both Science and consciousness are now at work in the economy of being according to the law of Mind, which ultimately asserts its absolute supremacy.

Formation from thought

Osteoporosis or any abnormal condition or derangement of the body is as directly the action of mortal mind as is functional or chemically based mental disorders, even depression. Bones have only the substance of thought which forms them. They are only phenomena of the mind of human beings. The so-called substance of bone is formed first by the parent's mind, through self-division. Soon the

---

[1] Heb. 4:12

child becomes a separate, individualized human mind, which takes possession of itself and its own thoughts of bones.

Accidents unknown to God

Accidents are unknown to God, or perpetual Mind. We must leave the worldly basis of thinking and unite with the one Mind, in order to change the notion of chance to the proper sense of God's perfect direction, and thereby bring out harmony.

Under divine Providence there can be no accidents, since there is no room for imperfection in perfection.

Opposing mentality

In the medical field, objections would be raised if one doctor administered a drug to counteract the working of a remedy prescribed by another doctor. It is equally important in metaphysical practice that the *minds* which surround your patient should not act against your influence by continually expressing such opinions as may alarm or discourage—either by giving antagonistic advice or through unspoken thoughts resting on your patient. While it is certain that the divine Mind can remove any obstacle, still you need the ear of your auditor. It is not more difficult to make yourself heard mentally while others are thinking about your patients or conversing with them, if you understand divine Science—the oneness and the allness of divine Love; but it is well to be alone with God and the sick when treating disease.

Mind removes cancer

To prevent or to cure cancer, leukemia and other hereditary diseases, you must destroy the belief in these ills and the false faith in the possibility of their transmission. The patient may tell you that they have tuberculosis and that their parents or distant ancestors believed the same. Human mind, not matter, triggers this conclusion and its results. You will have tuberculosis, just so long as you believe it to be an excuse, or to be ineradicable.

Nothing to consume

If the case to be mentally treated is tuberculosis, take up the leading points (according to belief) included in this disease. Show that it is not inherited or transmittable. Point out that inflammation, hemorrhage, and decay are beliefs, images of human thought superimposed upon the body. Show that false images are not the truth of man and woman. Bogus imprints should be treated as error and put out of thought. Then these ills will disappear.

If the body is diseased, this is but one of the evil spirits of mortal mind. Human beings will be less mortal when they learn that matter never sustained existence and can never destroy God, who is our Life. When this is understood, humanity will be more spiritual and know that there is nothing to become malignant or infected, since Spirit, God, is All-in-all. What if the belief is multiple sclerosis? God is more to an individual than the individual's belief, and the less we acknowledge matter or its laws, the more spirituality we possess. Consciousness constructs a better body when faith in matter has been conquered. Correct the human mortal convictions by spiritual understanding and Spirit will form you anew. You will never fear again except to offend God, and you will never believe that hormones, cells, heart, the central nervous system, or any portion of the body can destroy you.

Soundness maintained

If you want your colon, uterus, or lungs to stay healthy, with excellent capacity, be always ready with a mental protest against an unhealthy belief. Dismiss all notions about inflammation, inherited disease, weak lungs, or suffering, arising from any circumstance, and you will find that human mind, when instructed by Truth, allows the body to be guided into health by means of divine power.

Our footsteps heavenward

The path of divine Science is less difficult to follow when the high goal is always before the thoughts. This is in contrast to counting every single little footstep while endeavoring to reach the better goal. When the destination is desirable, expectation speeds our progress. The struggle for Truth makes one strong instead of weak, restful instead of weary. If the belief in death was obliterated, and the understanding obtained that there is no death, this would be a "tree of life,"[1] known by its fruits. Human beings should renew their energies and endeavors, and see the folly of hypocrisy while also learning the necessity of

[1]   Gen. 2:9; Rev. 22:2

367

working out their own salvation. When it is learned that disease cannot destroy life and that human beings are not saved from sin or sickness by death, this understanding will quicken into newness of life. This enlightenment will overcome the desire to die or a dread of the grave, and thus destroy the great fear that burdens mortal existence.

Standard

To relinquish all faith in death and the fear of its sting,[1] would raise the standard of health and morals far beyond its present elevation. Fearless spiritual understanding would enable us to hold the standard of spirituality high, with unflinching faith in God, in Life eternal. Sin and the neglect of spirituality brought death, and death will disappear with the disappearance of sin. Our identity is spiritual, and the body cannot die because matter has no life to surrender. The human perversions of good, named matter (limited substance), death, disease, sickness, and sin are all that can be destroyed.

Life not contingent on matter

If it is true that man and woman lives, this fact can never change in Science to the opposite belief that spiritual being dies. Life is the law of Soul, even the law of the spirit of Truth, and Soul is never without its representative. Our individual spirituality can no more die nor disappear in unconsciousness than can Soul, for both are immortal. If we believe in the death of good now, we must disbelieve in it when learning that there is no reality in death, since the truth of being is deathless. The belief that existence is dependent on that which passes away (matter) must be confronted and overturned by Science, before Life can be understood and harmony experienced.

Mortality vanquished

Death is but another facet of the dream that existence can be mortal, limited. In Science, nothing can interfere with the harmony of being nor end the existence of God's children. Human beings are the same after as before a bone is broken or the body executed. If we are never to overcome death, why do the Scriptures say, "The last enemy to be destroyed is death."?[2] The tenor of the Word shows that we will

---

[1]   I Cor. 15:55

[2]   I Cor. 15:26

CHRISTIAN SCIENCE PRACTICE

gain the victory over death in proportion as we overcome sin. However, defeating sin is complicated until we know what God is. God, Life, Truth, and Love make us undying. Immortal Mind, governing all, must be acknowledged as supreme in the physical realm, as well as in the spiritual.

No death, no inaction

When at the point of death, what material remedies do we have when all such remedies have failed? Spirit is turned to as the last resort, when it should have been the first and only action. The dream of death must be overcome by Mind here or hereafter. Thought will waken from its own materialistic declaration, "I am dead," to catch this trumpet-word of Truth, "There is no death, no inaction, diseased action, over-action, nor reaction."

Vision opening

Life is real, and death is the deception. A demonstration of the facts of Soul in Jesus' way resolves the dark visions of materialist sense into harmony and spirituality. Our privilege at this supreme moment is to prove the words of Jesus: "If you practice what I'm telling you, you'll never have to look death in the face."[1] To separate thought from false trusts and delusive evidence in order that the spiritual facts of being may appear—this is the great achievement by means of which we shall sweep away the false and give place to the true. Thus we may establish in truth the temple, or body, "with foundations, whose architect and builder is God."[2]

Intelligent consecration

We should consecrate existence, not "to an unknown God" whom we "worship as something unknown,"[3] but to the eternal builder, the everlasting Father, to the life which mortal sense or human logic cannot disable or destroy. We must realize the ability of mental might to offset human misconceptions and to replace them with the life which is spiritual, not limited.

---

1   John 8:51 (The Message)
2   Heb. 11:10
3   Acts 17:23

369

The present immorality

The great spiritual fact must be brought out that God's person *is*, not *will be*, perfect and spiritual. We must hold forever the consciousness of existence, and sooner or later, through Truth and Christian Science, we must break out of limited perceptions, out of sin and death. The evidence of our spirituality will become more apparent, as materialistic thinking is given up and the unending facts of being are admitted.

Careful guidance

I have healed hopeless physiological disease, and advanced the dying to life and health through the understanding of God as the only Life. It is backwards to believe that anything can overpower omnipotent and eternal Life. This Life must be brought to light by the understanding that there is no death, as well as by other graces of Spirit. We must begin however, with the more simple demonstrations of control, and the sooner we begin the better. The final demonstration takes time for its accomplishment. When walking, we are guided by the eye. We look before our feet, and if we are wise, we look beyond a single step in the line of spiritual advancement.

Clay replying to the potter

Science declares that we are under the power of Mind. Human knowledge claims that our body has dominance over our mind. Human logic affirms that the body dies, must be buried and decomposed into dust; but human mind's affirmation is not true. The corpse, deserted by thought, becomes cold and decays, but it never suffers. Human beings waken from the dream of death with bodies unseen by those who think that they bury the body.

Continuum of existence

If we did not exist before the fleshly organization began, we could not exist after the body is disintegrated. If we live after death and are spiritual, we must have lived before birth, for if Life ever had any beginning, it must also have an ending, even according to the calculations of natural science. Do you believe this? No! Do you understand it? No! This is why you doubt the statement and do not demonstrate the facts it involves. We must have faith in all the sayings of Christ Jesus, though they are not included in the teachings of the schools and are not generally understood by our religious and ethics instructors.

Life all-inclusive

Jesus said, "If you obey my words, you will never die."[1] That statement is not limited to spiritual life, but includes all the phenomena of existence. Jesus demonstrated this, healing the dying and raising the dead. Human mind must part with error, must put off itself with its deeds, and then spirituality, the Christ ideal, will appear. Faith should enlarge its borders and strengthen its foundation by resting on Spirit instead of matter. When we give up our belief in death, advancement toward God, Life, and Love, will be more rapid. Belief in sickness and death, as certainly as belief in sin, tends to shut out the true sense of Life and health. When will humankind wake to this great fact in Science?

I here present to my readers an allegory illustrative of the law of divine Mind and of the supposed laws of flesh and hygiene, an allegory in which the argument of Christian Science heals the sick.

A mental court case

Suppose a mental case to be on trial, as cases are tried in court. A man is charged with having committed liver disease. The patient feels ill, ruminates, and the trial commences. **Physical Sensation** is the plaintiff. **Human Being** is the defendant. **False Belief** is the attorney for **Physical Sensation**. Human Mortal Minds, Materia Medica, Anatomy, Psychotherapy, Physiology, Hypnotism, Envy, Greed and Ingratitude, constitute the jury. The court-room is filled with curious spectators, and **Judge Medicine** is on the bench.

The evidence for the prosecution being called for, a witness testifies thus:—

I represent Health-laws. I was present on certain nights when the prisoner, or patient, took care of a sick friend. Although I am in charge of human affairs, I was personally abused on those occasions. I was told to remain silent until called for at this trial, when I would be allowed to testify in the case. In spite of my rules to the contrary, the prisoner cared for the sick friend every night in the week. When the

[1] John 8:51 (CEV)

sick friend was thirsty, the prisoner gave him a drink. During all this time the prisoner still performed his own responsibilities, causing him to eat at irregular intervals, sometimes going to sleep immediately after an unhealthy dinner. His liver could not take the abuse and I considered it criminal, inasmuch as this offence is deemed punishable with death. Therefore I arrested **Human Being** in behalf of the state, Fleshly Body, and cast him into prison.

At the time of the arrest the prisoner summoned Physiology, Materia Medica, and Alternative Medicine to prevent his punishment. The struggle on their part was long. Materia Medica held out the longest, but at length all these assistants resigned to me, Health-laws, and I succeeded in getting **Human Being** into close confinement until I should release him.

The next witness is called:—

I am Coated Tongue. I am covered with a foul fur, placed on me the night of the liver failure. Morbid Secretion gripped the prisoner and took control of his mind, making him despondent.

Another witness takes the stand and testifies:—

I am Jaundiced Skin. I have been dry, hot, and chilled by turns since the night of the liver-attack. I have lost my healthy hue although nothing on my part has occasioned this change. The buildup of yellow pigment in the blood is to blame. I perform my functions as usual, but I am robbed of my good looks.

The next witness testifies:—

I am Nerve, the State Commissioner for **Human Being**. I am intimately acquainted with the plaintiff, **Physical Sensation** and know him to be truthful and upright, whereas **Human Being**, the prisoner at the bar, is capable of falsehood. I was witness to the crime of liver disease. I knew the prisoner would commit it, for I convey messages from my residence in matter, *alias* brain, to body.

Another witness is called for by the Court of Error and says:—

I am Mortality, Governor of the Province of Body, in which **Human Being** resides. In this province there is a statute regarding disease—namely, that he on whose person disease is found shall be treated as a criminal and punished with death.

The Judge asks, is it possible for man to become diseased and merit punishment because he did a good deed for his neighbor? Governor Mortality replies in the affirmative.

Another witness takes the stand and testifies:—

I am Death. I was called for shortly after the report of the crime by the officer of the Board of Health. The officer alleged that the prisoner had abused him, and that my presence was required to confirm his testimony. One of the prisoner's friends, Materia Medica, was present when I arrived, endeavoring to assist the prisoner to escape from the hands of justice, *alias* the Rule of Death. However, my appearance with a message from the Board of Health changed the purpose of Materia Medica, and it was decided at once that the prisoner should die.

Judge Medicine charges the jury

The testimony for the plaintiff, **Physical Sensation**, being closed, Judge Medicine arises, and with great ceremony addresses the jury of Human Mortal Minds. He analyzes the offence, reviews the testimony, and explains the law relating to liver disease. His conclusion is that laws of nature render disease homicidal. In compliance with a stern duty, his **Honor Judge Medicine**, urges the jury not to allow their judgment to be warped by the irrational, unchristian suggestions of Christian Science. The jury must regard in such cases only the evidence of **Physical Sensation** against **Human being**.

As the judge proceeds, the prisoner grows restless. His jaundiced face whitens with fear, and a look of despair and death settles on it. The case is given to the jury. A brief consultation ensues, and the jury returns a verdict of "Guilty of liver disease in the first degree."

Human Man sentenced

Judge Medicine then proceeds to pronounce the solemn sentence of death on the prisoner. Because he has loved his neighbor as himself, **Human Being** has been guilty of benevolence in the first degree, and this led him into the commission of the second crime, liver disease, which physical laws condemn as homicide. For this crime **Human Being** is sentenced to be tortured until he is dead. "May God have mercy on your soul," is the Judge's concluding remark.

The prisoner is then remanded to his cell (sick bed), and **Scholastic Theology** is sent for to prepare the frightened sense of Life, God—a sense which must be immortal—for *death*.

Appeal to a higher court

Ah! But Christ, Truth, the spirit of Life and the friend of **Human Being**, can open wide those prison doors and set the captive free. Swift on the wings of divine Love, there comes an appeal: "Delay the execution; the prisoner is not guilty." Consternation fills the prison-yard. Some exclaim, "It is contrary to law and justice." Others say, "The law of Christ supersedes *our* laws; let us follow Christ."

Counsel for defense

After much debate and opposition, permission is obtained for a trial in the Court of Spirit, where **Christian Science** is allowed to appear as counsel for the unfortunate prisoner. Witnesses, judges, and jurors, who were at the previous Court of Error, are now summoned to appear before the bar of Justice and eternal Truth.

When the case for **Human Being** *versus* **Physical Sensation** is opened, the counsel regards the prisoner with the utmost tenderness. The counsel's earnest, solemn eyes, kindling with hope and triumph, looks beyond circumstantial evidence. Then **Christian Science** turns suddenly to the supreme tribunal, and opens the argument for the defense:—

The prisoner at the bar has been unjustly sentenced. His trial was a tragedy, and is morally illegal. **Human Being** has had no proper counsel in the case. All the testimony has been on the side of **Physical Sensation,** and we shall unearth this foul conspiracy against the freedom and life of God's person. The only valid testimony in the case shows the alleged crime never to have been committed. There is "no charge against him that deserved death or imprisonment."[1]

Your Honor, the lower court has sentenced **Human Being** to die, but God made man and woman spiritual and amenable only to Life eternal. Denying justice to the body, that court commended a person's immortal Spirit to heavenly mercy—Spirit which is God and a person's only lawgiver! Who or what has sinned? Has the body or has **Human**

---

[1]   Acts 23:29

Mind committed a criminal deed? Attorney **False Belief** has argued that the body should die, while **Reverend Theology** would console conscious **Human Mind**, which alone is capable of sin and suffering. The body committed no offence. **Human Being**, in obedience to higher law, helped his neighbor, an act which should result in good to his self as well as to others.

The law of our Supreme Court decrees that whoever *sins* shall die; but good deeds are spiritual, bringing joy instead of grief, pleasure instead of pain, and life instead of death. If liver disease was committed by violating Laws of Health, this was a good deed, for the agent of those laws is an outlaw, a destroyer of **Human Being's** freedom and rights. Laws of Health should be sentenced to die.

Taking care of a friend in pain is the exercise of a love that "is the fulfillment of the law"[1]—doing "to others what you would have them do to you"[2]—this is not a violation of law. No demand, human or divine, renders it just to punish a person for acting justly. If humanity sins, our **Supreme Judge** in equity decides what penalty is due for the sin. **Human Being** can suffer only for his own sin and nothing else, as the law of Spirit, God, stands.

What jurisdiction had his Honor, **Judge Medicine**, in this case? To him I might say, in Bible language, "You sit there to judge me according to the law, yet you yourself violate the law by commanding that I be struck!"[3] The only jurisdiction to which the prisoner can submit is that of Truth, Life, and Love. If they condemn him not, neither will **Judge Medicine** condemn him. I ask that the prisoner be restored to the freedom of which he has been unjustly deprived.

The principal witness (the officer of the Health-laws) testified that he was an eye-witness to the good deeds for which **Human Being** is being sentenced to death. After betraying him into the hands of your law, the Health-agent disappeared, to reappear at the trial as a witness against **Human Being** and in the interest of **Physical Sensation**, a murderer. Your Supreme Court must find the prisoner on the night

---

[1]   Rom. 13:10

[2]   Matt. 7:12

[3]   Acts 23:3

of the alleged offence to have been acting within the boundaries of the divine law and in obedience thereto. Upon this statute hangs all the law and testimony. Giving a cup of cold water in Christ's name is a Christian service. Laying down his life while doing a good deed, **Human Being** should find it again. Such acts bear their own justification, and are under the protection of the Most High.

Prior to the night of his arrest, the prisoner summoned his professed friends, Materia Medica and Physiology, to prevent his committing liver disease, and thus save him from arrest. But they brought with them Sheriff Fear, to precipitate the result which they were called to prevent. It was Fear who handcuffed **Human Being** and would now punish him. You have left **Human Being** no alternative. He must obey your law, fear its consequences, and be punished for his fear. His friends struggled hard to rescue the prisoner from the penalty they considered justly due, but they were compelled to let him be taken into custody, tried, and condemned. Thereupon **Judge Medicine** sat in judgment on the case and substantially charged the jury, twelve Human Mortal Minds, to find the prisoner guilty. His Honor sentenced **Human Being** to die for the very deeds which the divine law compels us to commit. Thus the Court of Error construed obedience to the law of divine Love as disobedience to the law of Life. Claiming to protect **Human Being**, that court pronounced a sentence of death for doing right.

Another principal witness, Nerve, testified that he was a ruler of Body, in which province **Human Being** resides. He also testified that he was on close terms with the plaintiff and knew **Physical Sensation** to be truthful. **Physical Sensation** said that he knew man and woman, and that they were made in the image of God, but were criminals. This is foul slander on their Maker. It blots the fair insignia of omnipotence. It indicates malice aforethought, a determination to condemn man and woman in the interest of **Physical Sensation.** At the bar of Truth, in the presence of divine Justice, before the Judge of our higher tribunal, the Supreme Court of Spirit, and before its jurors, **Spiritual Perceptions**, I proclaim this witness, Nerve, to be destitute of intelligence and truth and to be assessed as a false witness.

Man and woman self-destroyed; the testimony of matter respected; Spirit not allowed a hearing; Soul a criminal though recommended to mercy; the helpless innocent body tortured—these are the terrible records of your Court of Error, and I ask that the Supreme Court of Spirit to reverse this decision.

This is when the opposing counsel, **False Belief,** called **Christian Science** to order for contempt of court. Various notables—Materia Medica, Anatomy, Physiology, Psychotherapy, Scholastic Theology, and Jurisprudence—rose to the question of expelling **Christian Science** from the bar for such high-handed illegality. They declared that **Christian Science** was overthrowing the judicial proceedings of a regularly constituted court.

But **Judge Justice** of the Supreme Court of Spirit overruled their motions on the ground that unjust usages were not allowed at the bar of Truth, which ranks above the lower Court of Error.

The attorney, **Christian Science,** then read from the supreme statute-book, the Bible, certain extracts on the Rights of God's child, remarking that the Bible was better authority than Sir William Blackstone:—[1]

> Let us make man in our image, after our likeness, and let them rule over all of the earth.[2]
>
> I have given you authority . . . to overcome all the power of the enemy; nothing will harm you.[3]
>
> I assure you that if anybody accepts my words, he will never see death at all.[4]

Then **Christian Science** proved the witness, Nerve, to be a perjurer. Instead of being a ruler in the Province of Body, in which **Human Being** was reported to reside, Nerve was an insubordinate citizen, putting in false claims although calling them official or

---

[1]   Blackstone, Sir William, (1723-1780) English jurist.

[2]   Gen. 1:26

[3]   Luke 10:19

[4]   John 8:51 (Phillips NT)

authorized, and bearing false witness against man and woman. Turning suddenly to **Physical Sensation**, by this time silent, **Christian Science** continued:—

I ask your arrest in the name of Almighty God on three distinct charges of crime: perjury, treason, and conspiracy against the rights and life of God's child.

Then **Christian Science** continued:—

Another witness, equally inadequate, said that on the night of the crime a garment of foul fur was spread over him by Morbid Secretion. The facts in the case show that this fur is a foreign substance, imported by **False Belief**, the attorney for **Physical Sensation**, who is in partnership with Error and smuggles Error's goods into market without the inspection of Soul's government officers. When the Court of Truth summoned Furred Tongue for examination, he disappeared and was never heard of again.

Morbid Secretion is not an importer or dealer in fur, but we have heard Materia Medica explain how this fur is manufactured, and we know Morbid Secretion to be on friendly terms with the firm of **Physical Sensation**, Error, & Co., receiving pay from them and introducing their goods into the market. Also, be it known that **False Belief**, the counsel for the plaintiff, **Physical Sensation**, is a buyer for this firm. He manufactures for it, stocks a warehouse, and advertises largely for his employers.

Death testified that he was absent from the Province of Body, when a message came from **False Belief**, commanding him to take part in the homicide. At this request Death resorted to the spot where the liver disease was progressing, frightening away Materia Medica, who was then manacling the prisoner in the attempt to save him. Yes, Materia Medica was a misguided participant in the misdeed for which the Health-officer had innocent **Human Being** in custody.

Christian Science turned from the humiliated witnesses, words flashing as lightning in the perturbed faces of these worthies, Scholastic Theology, Materia Medica, Physiology, blind Hypnotism, and the disguised **Physical Sensation**, and said:—

God will smite you, O whited walls, for injuring in your ignorance the unfortunate **Human Being** who sought your aid in his struggles

378

against liver disease and death. You came to his rescue, only to fasten upon him an offence of which he was innocent. You aided and abetted Fear and Health-laws. You betrayed **Human Being**, meanwhile declaring Disease to be God's servant and the righteous executor of spiritual laws. Our higher statutes declare you all, witnesses, jurors, and judges, to be offenders, awaiting the sentence which General Progress and Divine Love will pronounce.

We sent our best detectives to whatever locality was reported to be haunted by Disease, but on visiting the spot, they learned that Disease was never there, for he could not possibly elude their search. Your Material Court of Errors, when it condemned **Human Being** on the ground of not following the health rules, was manipulated by the suave scheming of the counsel, **False Belief**, whom Truth arraigns before the supreme bar of Spirit to answer for his crime. Morbid Secretion is taught how to make sleep befool reason before sacrificing mortals to their false gods.

Human Minds were deceived by your attorney, **False Belief**, and were influenced to give a verdict delivering **Human Being** to Death. Good deeds are transformed into crimes, to which you attach penalties; but no warping of justice can render disobedience to the so-called laws of Matter disobedience to God, or an act of homicide. Even penal law holds homicide, under stress of circumstances, to be justifiable. Now what greater justification can any deed have than for the good of one's neighbor? Wherefore, then, in the name of outraged justice, do you sentence **Human Being** for ministering to the wants of his neighbor in obedience to divine law? You cannot trample on the decree of the Supreme Bench. **Human Being** has his appeal to Spirit, God, who sentences only for sin.

The false and unjust reasoning of your human mental legislators compel them to enact wicked laws of sickness and so forth, and then render obedience to these laws punishable as crime. In the presence of the Supreme Lawgiver, standing at the bar of Truth, and in accordance with the divine statutes, I repudiate the false testimony of **Physical Sensation**. I ask that he be forbidden to enter against **Human Being** any more suits to be tried at the Court of Material Error. I appeal to the just and equitable decisions of divine Spirit to restore to **Human Being** the rights of which he has been deprived.

Here the counsel for the defense closed, and the **Chief Justice** of the Supreme Court, with benign and imposing presence, comprehending and defining all law and evidence, explained from his statue-book, the Bible, that any so-called law which undertakes to punish anything but sin, is null and void.

He also decided that the plaintiff, **Physical Sensation**, not be permitted to enter any suits at the bar of Soul, but be enjoined to keep perpetual silence, and in case of temptation to give heavy bonds for good behavior. Justice concluded the charge thus:—

The plea of **False Belief** we deem unworthy of a hearing. Let what **False Belief** utters, now and forever, fall into oblivion, "unknelled, uncoffined, and unknown."[1] According to our statute, Material Law is a liar who cannot bear witness against **Human Being**, neither can Fear arrest **Human Being** nor can Disease cast him into prison. Our law refuses to recognize spiritual being as sick or dying, but holds it to be forever in the image and likeness of our Maker. Reversing the testimony of **Physical Sensation** and the decrees of the Court of Error in favor of Matter, Spirit decides in favor of spiritual being, and against Matter. We further recommend that Materia Medica adopt **Christian Science** and that Health-laws, Alternative medicines, Hypnotism, Witchcraft, and Psychobabble be publicly executed at the hands of our sheriff, Progress.

The Supreme Bench decides in favor of intelligence, that no law outside of divine Mind can punish or reward **Human Being**. Your personal jurors in the Court of Error are myths. Your attorney, **False Belief**, is an impostor, persuading Human Minds to return a verdict contrary to law and gospel. The plaintiff, **Physical Sensation**, is recorded in our Book of books as a liar. The great Teacher of mental jurisprudence speaks of him also as "a murderer from the beginning."[2] We have no trials for sickness before the tribunal of divine Spirit. There, people are adjudged innocent of trespassing physical

---

[1]   Harold, Childe, (1788-1824) British Poet. *Ocean*, Pilgrimage.

[2]   John 8:44

laws, because there are no such laws. Our statute is spiritual, our Government is divine. "Will not the Judge of all the earth do right?"[1]

Divine verdict

The Jury of Spiritual Perceptions agreed at once upon a verdict, and there resounded throughout the vast audience-chamber of Spirit the cry, Not guilty. Then the prisoner rose up regenerated, strong, and free. We noticed, as he shook hands with his counselor, **Christian Science**, that all jaundice and debility has disappeared. His form was erect and commanding, his countenance beaming with health and happiness. Divine Love had cast out fear. **Human Being**, no longer sick and in prison walked forward, his feet "beautiful on the mountains"[2] and bringing a good report.

Christ the great physician

We cannot be mesmerized by the flesh or hypnotized by human mind while practicing the Science of Truth. Truth cannot be reversed, but the reverse of error is true. An improved conviction cannot retrograde. When Christ, Truth, changes a human mortal conviction of sin or sickness into a better conviction, then thought melts into spiritual understanding, and sin, disease, and death disappear. Truth, Love, gives human beings temporary food and clothing until the temporal, transformed with the ideal, disappears, and we are clothed and fed spiritually. St. Paul says, "Work out (cultivate, carry out to the goal, and fully complete) your salvation with reverence *and* awe and trembling (self-distrust, with serious caution, tenderness of conscience, watchfulness against temptation, timidly shrinking from whatever might offend God and discredit the name of Christ)."[3] Jesus said, "Do not be afraid, little flock, for your Father has been pleased to give you the kingdom."[4] This truth is divine Science.

Christian Scientists, be a law to yourselves that mental malpractice cannot harm you either when asleep or when awake.

---

1   Gen. 18:25
2   Isa. 52:7
3   Phil. 2:12 (Amplified)
4   Luke 12:32

TEACHING CHRISTIAN SCIENCE

Give instruction to the wise, and they will become wiser
still; teach the righteous and they will gain in learning.[1]

Study of medicine

As the discoverer of Christian Science, I was consulted about
the advantage of systematic medical study. I tried to show that under
ordinary circumstances, a resort to faith in temporal methods deters
those, who make such compromises, from entire confidence in
omnipotent Mind as possessing all power. While a course of medical
study is sometimes severely condemned by other Scientists, I feel, as
I've always felt, that all people are privileged to work out their own
salvation according to their own inspiration. Jesus' counsel, "Do not
judge, or you too will be judged,"[2] is an excellent motto.

Lessons from failure

If patients fail to experience the healing power of Christian
Science, and think they can be benefited by conventional treatment,
then the Mind-physician should respect the patient's decision and
let them freely choose whatever system they believe will offer relief.
Patients may thereby learn the value of the apostolic precept: "Correct,
rebuke and encourage—with great patience and careful instruction."[3]
If the sick find the mainstream treatments unsatisfactory, these very
failures may motivate their attention to look elsewhere. In some way,
sooner or later, people must overcome the temporal and suffering is

---

[1]   Prov. 9:9 (NRSV)

[2]   Matt. 7:1

[3]   II Tim. 4:2

often the divine agent. "In all things God works for the good of those who love him,"[1] is the dictum of Scripture.

Refuge and strength

Scientists may call on one another for metaphysical treatment. However, if the callers don't receive relief or help, they can be confident that God will guide them to use appropriately the temporary and eternal treatments. Step by step, as we trust Spirit, we will find that "God is our shelter, our strength, ever ready to help in time of trouble."[2]

Compassion to those opposed

I advise students to be charitable and kind, not only toward differing forms of religion and medicine, but to the very people who hold these differing opinions. Let us be faithful in pointing the way through Christ, as we understand it, but let us also be careful always to "stop judging by mere appearances, and make a right judgment."[3] Never condemn rashly. "If anyone strikes you on the right cheek, turn the other also,"[4] because if you refrain from retaliation, you will be struck again. If ecclesiastical sects or medical schools turn a deaf ear to the teachings of divine Science, then part from these opponents as did Abraham when he parted from Lot, and say in your heart: "'Let's not have any quarreling between you and me, or between your herdsmen and mine, for we are brothers."[5] Spiritual beings, or God's children in divine Science, are one harmonious family; but the children of human beings are discordant and oftentimes fake.

Conforming to explicit rules

Teachers must make clear to students the Science of healing, especially the moral and ethical principles—that all is Mind, and we measure up to the will of good. Teachers must thoroughly prepare students to defend themselves against sin and the attacks of the would-be mental assassin, who attempts to kill morally and physically.

---

1   Rom. 8:28

2   Ps. 46:1 (JB)

3   John 7:24

4   Matt. 5:39; Luke 6:29 (NRSV)

5   Gen. 13:8

No hypothesis as to the existence of another power should interject a doubt or fear to hinder the demonstration of divine Science. Teachers do not indoctrinate, but shed light on the student's hidden energies and capabilities for good.

Teach the great possibilities of man and woman equipped with divine Science. Enlighten the student's spiritual understanding and demonstration of Truth. Expose the dangerous possibility of minimizing spirituality by doing wrong or returning to quick-fixes for healing. The divine law of healing becomes obscure and void when you compare the human to the divine, or limit in any direction of thought the omnipresence and omnipotence of God. Share the humility and might of life "now hidden with Christ in God,"[1] and the desire for spiritual, eternal healing will expand.

Divine energy

Divine Science silences human will, disables fear with Truth and Love, and illustrates the unlabored motion of the divine energy in healing the sick. Self-indulgence, envy, emotionalism, arrogance, hatred, and revenge are dissolved by divine Mind which heals disease. The human will which makes and works a lie, hiding the divine Principle of harmony, is destructive to health and is the cause of disease rather than its cure.

Plague of greed

There is great danger in teaching Mind-healing indiscriminately, thus disregarding the morals of the student and caring only for the payments. Recall words that have been credited to Thomas Jefferson concerning slavery, "I tremble, when I remember that God is just."[2] I tremble whenever I see a person, for the petty reward of money, teaching his or her slight knowledge of Mind-power—increasing the probability of communicating the teacher's own bad morals. This sad state deals pitilessly with a community unprepared for self-defense.

---

[1] Col. 3:3

[2] Jefferson, Thomas (1743-1826) Political philosopher. Founding Father. Principal author of *Declaration of Independence*. The third President of the United States.

A thorough examination of my publications heals sickness. Sometimes the patient's condition seems to worsen when they read this book. The discomfort may come about because the physician is alarmed or the disease is reaching a crisis point. Perseverance in reading this book has generally completely healed such cases.

Exclude malpractice

Whoever practices the Science I teach, through which Mind pours light and healing on this generation, cannot practice from sinister or malicious motives. Dishonesty destroys not only the practitioner's power to heal, but also his or her own health. Good must dominate in the thoughts of healers, or their demonstrations are prolonged, perilous, and impossible in Science. A wrong motive involves defeat. In the Science of Mind-healing, it is imperative to be honest, for victory rests on the side of immutable right. To understand God strengthens hope, advances faith in Truth, and verifies Jesus' word: "Surely I am with you always, to the very end of the age."[1]

Iniquity overcome

Resisting evil, you overcome it and prove its nothingness. Not human clichés, but divine beatitudes, reflect the spiritual light and might which heal the sick. To insist on exercising the human will is to bring on a mesmerized attitude, detrimental to the health and integrity of thought. So, be observant, and guard against strong mortal mindedness. Do not protect or cover up iniquity, this only prevents prosperity and the ultimate triumph of any cause. If you are unaware of the error to be eradicated, you will sometimes be abused by it.

Do not intrude on human rights

The heavenly law is broken by trespassing on our neighbors individual right of self-government. We have no authority in divine Science and no moral right to attempt to influence the thoughts of others except to benefit them. In mental practice you must not forget that erring human opinions, conflicting selfish motives, and ignorant attempts to do good may render you incapable of knowing or judging accurately the real need of those who you are helping. Therefore the

---

[1]   Matt. 28:20

rule is to heal the sick when called on, and save the victims of the mental assassins.

Expose thinking that opposes Life, Truth, and Love, without believing in it

To say that there is no sickness does not heal the sick. You have to *know* there is no sickness. Ignorance, subtlety, or false charity does not forever conceal error; evil will in time uncover and punish itself. A balanced system and mind, mentally sustained by Truth, goes on naturally. When sin or sickness—the reverse of harmony—seems real to the fleshly sense, calmly and honestly encourage the patient with truth and spiritual understanding, which destroy disease. Expose and denounce the claims of evil and disease in all their forms, but realize no reality in them. Sinners are not reformed merely by assuring them that they cannot be sinners, because there is no sin. To put down the claim of sin, you must detect it, remove the disguise, point out the deception, and thus get the victory over sin and prove its unreality.

Unspiritual avoidances

A sinner is afraid to throw the first stone. Some sinners say, as a subterfuge, that evil is unreal, but to know it, they must demonstrate the statement. To assume that there are no claims of evil and yet to indulge them, is a moral offence. Close-mindedness and self-righteousness clamp onto iniquity. When the tax collector's confession[1] went out to the great heart of Love, it won his humble desire. Evil which prevails in the body's biology, but which the heart condemns, has no foundation. Remember though, if evil is not condemned or not denied, it is nurtured. Under such circumstances, to say that there is no evil is an evil in itself. When it is necessary to correct a lie with the truth, do so. Evasion of Truth cripples integrity, and sweeps you off the mountaintop.

Truth's grand results

Divine Science doesn't get caught up in worldly evidence. If you haven't advanced past sin yourself, don't congratulate yourself for being blind to evil or for not living the good you claim to know. A two-faced attitude is far from Christianly scientific. "No one who conceals

---

[1]   Luke 18:13

transgressions will prosper, but one who confesses and forsakes them will obtain mercy."[1] Every student's mind should be strongly impressed by divine Science; by an exalted awareness of the moral, social, and spiritual qualifications requisite for healing, well knowing it to be impossible for error, evil, and hate to accomplish the grand results of Truth and Love. Pursuing instructions opposite to absolute divine Science will always interrupt scientific demonstration.

Loyalty to righteousness

If the student stays true to the teachings of Christ's Science, not daring to break its rules, the person cannot fail to succeed in healing. It is divine Science to do right, and nothing short of right-doing has any claim to the name. To talk the right and live the wrong is foolish deceit, doing one's self the most harm. Captivated by sin yourself, it is difficult to rescue someone else from the prison of disease. If your own wrists are handcuffed it is hard to remove someone else's handcuffs. A little leaven causes the whole mass to ferment.[2] A grain of divine Science does wonders for human beings, so omnipotent is Truth, but more of Science must be gained in order to continue in well doing.

Right adjust the balance

Doing wrong to other people will react most heavily against yourself. Right adjusts the balance sooner or later. Think it "easier for a camel to go through the eye of a needle,"[3] than for you to benefit yourself by mistreating others. Your morals confirm your healing ability and fitness to teach. You should practice skillfully the good you know, and you will then advance to the extent of your honesty and fidelity—qualities which assure success in this Science. It requires a higher understanding to teach this subject correctly than it does to heal the most difficult case.

Inoculation of thought

The harmful effect of lousy friendships is less seen than felt. The inoculation of negative human thoughts ought to be understood and guarded against. The first impression, made on a mind, whether

---

[1]   Prov. 28:13 (NRSV)

[2]   Matt. 13:33; Luke 13:21; I Cor. 5:6; Gal. 5:9

[3]   Matt. 19:24; Mark 10:25

good or bad, is a capable detective of individual character. Certain minds meet only to separate through simultaneous repulsion. They are enemies without the preliminary offence. The impure are at peace with the impure. Only virtue is a rebuke to vice. A proper teacher of divine Science improves the health and morals of the student if the student practices what is taught, and unless this result follows, the teacher is a Scientist only in name.

Three classes of learners

There is a large class of thinkers whose excessive prejudice and conceit twist every fact to suit themselves. Their creed teaches belief in a mysterious, supernatural God, and a natural, all-powerful devil. Another class, still more unfortunate, are so depraved that they appear to be innocent. They repeat empty talk while looking you placidly in the face, and they never fail to stab their benefactor in the back. A third class of thinkers build with steel beams. They are honest, generous, noble, and are therefore open to the approach and recognition of Truth. Teaching Christian Science to this mindset is not a chore. Pure thought does not incline longingly to error, whine over the demands of Truth, nor play the traitor for place and power.

Some people respond slowly to the touch of Truth. Some people feel Truth's touch without a struggle. Many people are reluctant to admit that they have responded to Truth; however, if they don't admit their improvement, evils boasting will shout over good. The Mind scientist has enlisted to lessen evil, disease, and death. The Scientist will prove the nonbeing of all that opposed good by understanding the allness of Spirit. Sickness is no less a temptation than is sin and they are both healed by understanding God's power over them. The Christ-like Scientist knows that sickness and sin are errors of belief, which Truth can and will destroy.

False claims annihilated

Who, that has felt the perilous beliefs in life, substance, and intelligence separated from God, can say that there is no error of belief? The belief of life, substance, and intelligence in matter/energy, or in the fight-and-flight nature, or in morphing atoms, is flimsy propaganda, yet mesmerizing. So, we ask, who will deny that these are the errors which Truth must and will annihilate? Scientists of reality must live under the constant pressure of the apostolic command to come out from the material world and be dedicated. They must renounce aggression, oppression and the pride of power. Christianity, with the crown of Love on her brow, must be their queen of life.

Treasure in heaven

Students of divine Science, who start with its letter and think to succeed without the spirit, will either weaken their faith or get sadly off course. They must not only seek, but strive, to enter the narrow path of Life, "for the gate is wide and the road is easy that leads to destruction, and there are many who take it."[1] We walk in the direction toward which we look, and where our gratification is, there will our heart be also. If our hopes and inclinations are spiritual, they come from enlightenment, not from trained thinking, and they produce the fruits of the Spirit.[2]

Obligations of teachers

Every student of Science, every conscientious teacher of the Science of Mind-healing, knows that human will is not divine Science. This fact must be recognized in order to be immune to infectious human willfulness. All mental malpractice surfaces from ignorant or malicious intent. It is the injurious action of one human mind controlling another from wrong motives, and it is practiced either with a mistaken or a wicked purpose.

Indispensable defense

The teacher of Science feels morally obligated to open the student's eyes that they may perceive the tendencies and mechanics of every sort of error, deceived and deceiving. Teachers must show their students that mental malpractice tends to blast moral sense, health, and the human life. Instruct students on how to bolt the door of their thought against the seeming dark power of mental malpractice—a simple task, when the pupil understands that in reality evil has no power. It is favorable to arrest the wrong thought before it has a chance to manifest itself. Incorrect reasoning leads to practical error.

---

1   Matt. 7:13 (NRSV)

2   Gal. 5:22

Egotistic darkness

Walking in the light, we are accustomed to the light and require it; we cannot see in darkness. But eyes accustomed to darkness are pained by the light. When you outgrow the old, do not fear putting on the new. Your advancing course may provoke envy, but it will also attract respect. When error confronts you, do not withhold the rebuke or the explanation which destroys error. Never breathe an immoral atmosphere, unless in the attempt to purify it. Modest intellectual discoveries gained with contentment and virtue, are better than the luxury of learning with egotism and vice.

Unwarranted expectations

Right is revolutionary. Teachers must know the truth themselves; they must live it and love it, or they cannot impart it to others. We dirty our garments with conservatism, and afterward we must wash them clean. When the spiritual sense of Truth unfolds its harmonies, you take no risks in the policy of error. Expect to heal simply by repeating my words, by right talking and wrong acting, and you will be disappointed. Such a practice does not demonstrate the Science by which divine Mind heals the sick.

Reliable authority

Acting from bad motives destroys your power to heal from the right motive. On the other hand, if you had the inclination or power to practice destructively and then should adopt divine Science, the wrong power would be destroyed. We do not deny the mathematician's right to distinguish between correct and incorrect mathematical answers; we do not refuse to believe the musicians ability to distinguish harmony from discord; in like manner it should be granted that I understand what I am saying.

Winning the field

Right and wrong, truth and error will be at strife in the minds of students, until victory rests on the side of invincible truth. Mental weightlessness follows the explanation of Truth, and an improved state is won; but with some individuals the morbid moral or physical symptoms constantly reappear. I have never witnessed so decided effects from the use of temporary remedies as from the use of spiritual.

Knowledge and honesty

Teach your students that they must know their own self before they can know others and minister to human needs. Honesty is spiritual power. Dishonesty is human weakness, which forfeits divine help. You uncover sin, not in order to hurt, but in order to bless the human being; and a right motive has its reward. Hidden sin is spiritual wickedness in high places. The masquerader in this Science thanks God that there is no evil, yet serves evil in the name of good.

Mental treatment

Fear is the foundation of disease. Do not tell the patient that they are sick and do not give names to diseases, otherwise the wrong mind-picture will be more deeply impressed. The same manner of mental treatment is used in sickness as sin. A spiritual scientist's medicine is Mind, the divine Truth that makes people free. A Mind scientist doesn't recommend health care systems, and never manipulates. Scientists do not intrude on the rights of mind; in other words, mesmerism or hypnotism is not practiced. It need not be added that the use of tobacco or intoxicants are not in harmony with divine Science.

Powerlessness of hate

Teach your students the omnipotence of Truth, which illustrates the impotence of error. The understanding, even in a degree, of the divine All-power destroys fear, and aims the feet in the true path—the path which leads to "a house not made with hands, eternal in the heavens."[1] Human hate has no legitimate mandate and no kingdom. Love is enthroned. The doctrine of absolute divine Science, which strips all disguise from error, is the great truth that evil or human imprints do not have intelligence or power.

Love is the incentive

Teachers who understand in a sufficient degree the Principle of Mind-healing, point out error as well as truth, the wrong as well as the right practice. Love for God and humanity is the true incentive in both healing and teaching. Love inspires, illumines, designates, and leads the way. Right motives elevate thought, giving strength and

---

[1]   II Cor. 5:1 (NKJV)

freedom to speech and action. Love is priestess at the altar of Truth. Wait patiently for divine Love to move the human mind and form the perfect concept. "Perseverance must finish its work so that you may be mature and complete, not lacking anything."[1]

Continuity of interest

Do not dismiss students at the close of a class term, feeling that you have done enough. Let your compassionate care and sound counsels support their feeble footsteps, until your students walk firmly in the straight and narrow way. The superiority of spiritual power over sensuous power is the central point of divine Science. Remember, the letter and the mental affirmations only assist human beings, connecting thought with the spirit of Truth and Love, which heals the sick and the sinner.

Weakness and guilt

Mental states of self-condemnation and guilt, or a hesitant and doubting trust in Truth, are unsuitable for healing the sick. Such mindsets indicate weakness instead of strength. This is why it is necessary to be spiritually minded yourself to teach this Science of healing. You must utilize the moral might of Mind in order to walk over the waves of error and support your assertions by demonstration. If you are yourself lost in the belief and fear of disease or sin, and if, knowing the remedy, you fail to use the energies of Mind in your own behalf, you can exercise little or no power to help others. "First take the log out of your own eye, and then you will see clearly to take the speck out of your neighbor's eye."[2]

The trust of All-wise

Students, who receive their knowledge of Mind-Science or metaphysical healing from a human teacher, may be mistaken in judgment and demonstration, but God cannot mistake. God selects for the highest service people who have evolved into such a condition that they know any perversion of the mission is impossible. The All-wise does not grant trusts upon the unworthy. When Love commissions a

---

[1]   James 1:4

[2]   Matt. 7:5; Luke 6:41-42 (NRSV)

messenger, it is one who is spiritually near Soul. No person can misuse this mental power if they are taught of God to discern it.

Integrity assured

This strong point in divine Science is not to be overlooked—that "a spring doesn't gush fresh water one day and brackish the next."[1] The more expansive and inclusive your success is in the Science of mental healing and teaching, the more impossible it will become for you intentionally to influence humankind adverse to its highest hope and achievement.

Impostures impossible

Teaching or practicing in the name of Truth, but contrary to its spirit or rule, is most dangerous quackery. Strict adherence to the divine Principle and rules of the scientific method has secured the only success of the students of divine Science. Only this on-going integrity is worthy of prominence in the community, worthy of a reputation experimentally justified by the people's efforts. People who affirm that there is more than one Principle and method of demonstrating divine Science are mistaken, whether they do so ignorantly or intentionally. Whoever believes in more than one Principle, automatically separate themselves from the true conception of spiritual scientific healing and its possible manifestation.

No dishonest compromises

Any dishonesty in your theory and practice betrays a gross unawareness of the method of the Truth-cure. Science makes no concessions to persons or opinions. We must live in the morale of truth or we cannot illustrate the divine Principle. So long as fluctuating substance is the basis of practice, illness cannot be efficaciously treated by the divine mental process. Truth does the work and you must both understand and live up to the divine Principle of your demonstration.

This volume indispensable

A Mind-Scientist requires *Science and Health* as a textbook, and so do all students and patients. Why? First: Because it is the voice of Truth to this age, and contains the full statement of divine Science, or the Science of healing through immortal Mind. Second: Because

---

[1]   James 3:11 (The Message*)*

it was the first book known, containing a thorough statement of divine Science. Hence it gave the first rules for demonstrating this Science and registered the revealed truth uncontaminated by human hypotheses. Other works, which have borrowed from this book without giving it credit, have adulterated the Science. Third: Because this book, has done more for teacher and student, for healer and patient, than has been accomplished by other books.

Purity of science

Since the divine light of Christian Science first dawned on me, I have never used this newly discovered power in any direction which I feared to have fairly understood. Since entering this field of labor, the prime object has been to prevent suffering, not to produce it. That we cannot scientifically both cure and cause disease is self-evident. Suffering and mental malpractice always come up short, while Science prevails. A folktale from India tells of the day Akbar drew a line on the floor and told everyone to make it shorter without erasing any part of it. Everyone was stumped except Raja Birbal, who "at once drew a longer line next to the first line. He didn't touch the first line."[1]

Backsliders and mistakes

Divine Science is not an exception to the general rule that there is no excellence without labor in a direct line. We cannot scatter our fire and at the same time hit the mark. To pursue other vocations and advance rapidly in the demonstration of this Science is not possible. Advocating preventative medicine can detract the learner from divine Science. Students may even practice medical health care, intending thereby to initiate the cure which they mean to complete with Mind, as if the non-intelligent could aid Mind! The Scientist's demonstration rests on one Principle and there must and can be no opposite rule. Let this Principle be applied to the cure of disease without exploiting other means.

---

[1] *Folktales From India: A Selection of Oral Takes from Twenty-two Languages,* Make it Shorter. Edited by A. K. Ramanujan. New York: Pantheon Books, 1991.

Mental untruthfulness

Mental quackery rests on the same platform as all other quackery. Charlatanism is the doctrine that Science has two synergistic principles, one good and the other evil—one eternal, the other temporal—and that these two may be simultaneously at work on the sick. This theory is supposed to favor practice from both a mental and a physical standpoint. Another creed in quackery is that error will finally have the same effect as truth.

Divinity ever ready

It isn't spiritual to think we have to assist the divine Principle of healing, or try to sustain the human body until the divine Mind is ready to take the case. Divinity is always ready. Semper paratus is Truth's motto. Metaphysical impostures cause terrible suffering and the desire is to keep pretense out of Christian Science. The two-edged sword of Truth must turn in every direction "to guard the way to the tree of life."[1]

The protective covering of wisdom

Sin launches deadly attacks at the Scientist of Spirit as ritualism and creed are summoned to give place to higher law, but Science will ameliorate human malice. The spiritually scientific person reflects the divine law, thus becoming a law to self. The Scientist does violence to no person. A Scientist does not falsely accuse. Scientists wisely outline their possibilities, and are honest and consistent in following the leadings of divine Mind. Scientists must prove, through living as well as healing and teaching, that humane spiritual mindedness is the only mindset by which human beings are radically saved from sin and sickness.

Advancement by sacrifice

Spirituality causes people to turn naturally from temporal wave/particles to eternal Spirit, as the flower turns from darkness to light. People then secure those things which "no eye has seen, no ear has heard."[2] Paul and John realized that as human beings achieve worldly honor only by sacrifice, so they must gain heavenly riches by forsaking

---

[1]   Gen. 3:24

[2]   Isa. 64:4; I Cor. 2:9

all worldliness. Then people will have nothing in common with the worldly inclinations, goals, and outcomes. Do not judge the future advancement of divine Science by the steps already taken, unless you yourself will be condemned for failing to take the first step.

Dangerous knowledge

Any attempt to heal human beings with misbelieving mortal mind, instead of resting on the omnipotence of the divine Mind, must prove abortive. Conveying a threadbare process of mental healing to vulnerable humans, untaught and unrestrained by divine Science, is like putting a sharp knife into the hands of a blind raging maniac in the crowded streets of a city. Whether animated by malice or spiritual unawareness, a false practitioner will work mischief, and spiritual unawareness is more harmful than willful wickedness when the latter is distrusted and thwarted in its incipiency.

Certainty of results

To human perception Christian Science seems abstract, but the process is simple and the results are sure if the Science is understood. The tree that produces good fruit must be good itself. Guided by divine Truth and not guesswork, the theologian or the student—the spiritual and scientific expounder of divine law—treats disease with more certain results than any other healer on the planet. It is useful for the Scientist of Truth to understand and adhere strictly to the rules of divine metaphysics as laid down in *Science and Health*, resting their demonstration on this sure basis.

Ontology defined

Ontology is defined as "the branch of metaphysics dealing with the nature of being,"[1] and reinforces all mental practice. Our system of Mind-healing is supported by the understanding of the nature and essence of all being—by the divine Mind and Love's essential qualities. Its pharmacy is moral, and its medicine is intellectual and spiritual, though used for physical healing. Yet this most fundamental part of metaphysics is the most difficult to understand and demonstrate, for

---

[1] *The Oxford American Dictionary and Language Guide*, edited by Abate. F. s.v. "Ontology." New York: Oxford University Press, 1999. By permission of Oxford University Press, Inc. Recent edition. Copyright © 2007

to the flesh and blood mindset all is material, until such thought is rectified by Spirit.

Mischievous imagination

Sickness is real, is true that is, to the patient's frightened perception. Problems are more than imagination, but are solid convictions of fear or ignorance, and therefore need to be dealt with through an accurate comprehension of the truth of being. If Soul-healing is abused by those who are wise in their own conceit, treatment becomes an irksome trouble maker. Instead of scientifically affecting a cure, a dabbler in Science starts a petty crossfire over those who are disabled and sick. Humanity should not be knocked around with superficial and heartless remarks like, "It's all in your head. Matter is not real. Be more spiritual. You really are perfect."

Author's early instructions

When the Science of Mind was a newly tapped-into revelation, I had to impart the hue of spiritual ideas from my own spiritual condition. Teaching was done through the meager channel of the human language, both verbally and by means of a manuscript. As former beliefs were gradually expelled from my thought, the teaching became clearer, until finally the shadow of old errors was no longer cast on Christian Science.

Proof by induction

I do not insist that anyone can exist in the flesh without food and clothes; but I do believe that person is image, spiritual, and lives in Mind, not human mind. Divine Science must be accepted at this period by introduction. We admit the whole, because a part is proved and that part illustrates and proves the entire Principle. Divine Science can be taught only by those who are morally advanced and spiritually invested, for it is not artificial, nor is it discerned from the standpoint of human convictions. Only as spiritual perception is illumined can the light of understanding shine on this Science that reverses the evidence before the physical perceptions and furnishes the eternal interpretation of God and spiritual being.

If you believe that you are sick, is it better to say, "I am sick"? No, although you should sometimes responsibly tell other people you are sick in order to protect them. If you commit a crime, should you acknowledge to yourself that you are a criminal? Yes. Your responses differ because of the different effects they produce. Usually to admit that you are sick renders your case less curable, while to recognize your sin, helps destroy it. Both sin and sickness are error, and Truth is their remedy. The truth regarding error is that error is not true, hence it is unreal. To prove scientifically the error or unreality of sin, you must first see the claim of sin, and then destroy it. Whereas, to prove scientifically the error or unreality of disease, you must mentally stop perceiving the disease; then you will not feel it, and disease is destroyed.

Rapidity of assimilation

Systematic teaching and the student's spiritual growth and experience in practice are requisite for a thorough comprehension of the Science of Mind-healing. Some individuals realize truth more readily than others, but any student, who remains true to the divine rules of spiritual Science and becomes one with the spirit of Christ, can demonstrate Science, overcome error, heal the sick, and add continually to their supply of spiritual understanding, power, enlightenment, and success.

Divided loyalty

Some students may set out to practice Truth's teachings only in part, dividing their interests between God, and a preoccupation with worldly knowledge and wealth. Substituting their own views for Truth they will inevitably reap the error they sow. Whoever would demonstrate the healing of spiritual Science must precisely follow its rules, pay attention to every statement, and advance from the rudiments laid down. This task is not difficult or tiresome when the way is pointed out; but persistence, sincerity, spirituality, and denial of selfishness win the prize, as they usually do in every department of life.

Anatomy defined

Anatomy, when conceived of spiritually, is mental self-knowledge. Anatomy consists of dissecting thoughts in order to discover their quality, quantity, and origin. Are thoughts divine or human? That is the important question. This branch of study is indispensable to the excision of error. The anatomy of Christian Science teaches when and how to examine the self-inflicted wounds of ill-will, hostility, envy, and excuse making. It teaches the control of foolish ambition. It unfolds the sacred influences of honesty, philanthropy, spiritual love. It urges the government of the body both in health and in sickness. The Scientist of Spirit, through understanding mental anatomy, discerns and deals with the real cause of disease. The physical scientist explores symptoms or effects which constantly fluctuate under influences not embraced in the diagnosis, sometimes causing a stumble or a fall in the darkness.

Scientific obstetrics

It is important for both the teacher and student to be familiar with the obstetrics taught by this Science. To attend properly the birth of the new child, or divine idea, be sure to detach mortal thoughts from the human conceptions so that the birth will be natural and safe. As the child gathers new energy, the divine idea cannot injure its useful surroundings in its spiritual birth. There is not a single element of error in a spiritual idea and this truth properly removes anything that is offensive. The new idea, conceived and born of Truth and Love, is clothed in white garments and includes a humble beginning, a sturdy growth, and a renewing maturity. When this new birth takes place, the infant is born of the Spirit, born of God, and can cause the mother no more suffering. By this we know that Truth is here and has fulfilled its perfect work.

Unhesitating decision

To decide quickly as to the proper treatment of error—whether error is manifest in forms of sickness, sin, or death—is the first step toward destroying error. Jesus treated error through Mind. He never imposed obedience to the laws of nature, if by these are meant laws of matter. Jesus did not use drugs. There is a law of God applicable to healing, and it is a spiritual law instead of physical. The sick are not healed by inanimate matter or drugs, as they believe they are. Such seeming medical effect or action is that of so-called human mind.

Seclusion of the author

I have been told, "The world is benefited by you, but it feels your influence without seeing you. Why do you not make yourself more widely known?" Had my friends known how little time I have in which to make myself outwardly known except through my laborious publications—and how much time and toil are still required to establish the stately operations of Christian Science—they would understand why I am so secluded. Others could not take my place, even if willing to do so. I therefore remain unseen at my post, seeking no self-aggrandizement but praying, watching, and working for the redemption of humankind.

If from an injury or from any cause, a Christian Scientist were seized with pain so violent that the Scientist could not mentally treat their self—and other Scientists had failed to relieve them—the sufferer can get temporary help. Then, when the belief of pain is quieted, the Scientist can treat his or her own case mentally. In this way we "test everything; hold fast to what is good."[1]

The right motive and its reward

In founding a pathological system of spirituality, I have labored to expound divine Principle, and not to exalt personality. The weapons of bigotry, spiritual unawareness, and envy, will fall before an honest heart. The mindset that adulterates divine Science is the mindset trying to void out Science. Falsity has no foundation. "The hired hand runs away because a hired hand does not care for the sheep."[2] Dishonesty and a lack of spiritual experience do not establish, and cannot overthrow, a scientific system of ethics.

---

[1]   I Th. 5:21 (NRSV)

[2]   John 10:13 (NRSV)

REVIEW

For it is: do and do, do and do, rule on rule, rule on rule; a little here, a little there.[1]

This Chapter is from the first edition of my class book, copyrighted in 1870. After much labor and increased spiritual understanding, I revised that dissertation for this volume in 1875. Absolute Christian Science pervades its statements, to elucidate scientific metaphysics.

QUESTIONS AND ANSWERS

Question. What is God?
Answer. God is bodiless, divine, supreme, infinite Mind, Spirit, Soul, Principle, Life, Truth, Love.

Question. Are these terms synonymous?
Answer. They are. They refer to one absolute God. They are also intended to express the nature, essence, and fullness of Almighty God. The attributes of God are justice, mercy, integrity, wisdom, goodness, and so on.

Question. Is there more than one God or Principle?
Answer. There is not more than one God. Principle and its idea are one, and this one is God—omnipotent, omniscient, and omnipresent Being. *Omni* is adopted from the Latin adjective signifying *all*. Therefore God combines all-power or potency, all-science or true knowledge, all-presence. God's reflection is child (man and woman)

---

[1]   Isa. 28:10

401

and the universe. The diverse manifestations of divine Science indicate Mind, never matter, and have one Principle.

Real versus unreal

Question. What are spirits and souls?

Answer. To human belief, they are personalities composed of consciousness and unconsciousness, life and death, truth and error, good and evil. Divine Science reveals how those contrasting terms don't agree or conform to one another. Truth is immortal; error is mortal. Truth is limitless; error is limited. Truth is intelligent; error is non-intelligent. Moreover, Truth is real, and error is unreal. This last statement contains the point you will most reluctantly admit, although first and last it is the most important to understand.

Humankind redeemed

The terms *souls, spirits, or human beings* are as unsustainable as the term *gods.* Soul or Spirit signifies infinite Being and nothing else. There are not finite souls, spirits, or beings. Soul or Spirit means only one Mind, and cannot be rendered in the plural. Mythology and human philosophies have perpetuated the fallacy that intelligence, soul, and life can be divided and thus materialized. Idolatry and ritualism are the outcome of all human-made beliefs. The Science of spirituality comes with the tool in hand to separate the chaff from the wheat. Science will declare God aright, and Christianity will demonstrate this declaration and its divine Principle, making humankind better physically, morally, and spiritually.

Two important commands

Question. What are the requirements of the Science of Soul?

Answer. The first requirement of this Science is, "You shall have no other gods before me."[1] This *me* is Spirit. Therefore the command means this: You shall have no intelligence, no life, no substance, no truth, and no love, except the spiritual. The second command, you shall "love your neighbor as yourself"[2] is like the first.

---

[1]   Ex. 20:3; Deut. 5:7

[2]   Matt. 19:19, 22:39; Mark 12:31; Luke 10:27; Rom. 13:9; Gal. 5:14; James 2:8

It should be thoroughly understood that all people have one Mind, one God and Father, one Life, Truth, and Love. The perfection of person will be realized as this fact is understood. War will cease and the true sisterhood and brotherhood will be established. When we have no other gods and turn to no other but the one perfect Mind to guide us, we then experience our God-likeness, pure and eternal, having that Mind which was also in Christ.

Soul not confined in body

Science reveals Spirit, Soul, as reflected by spiritual beings. God is not *in a* body, but God is reflected by spiritual beings. The belief that the eternal can be constrained in the temporal is an error that creates problems. A leading point in the Science of Soul is that Principle is not controlled by its idea. Spirit, Soul, has never been confined to human beings, and is never in matter. If we reason from effect to cause, we will believe God created matter, and sure enough, material existence becomes a mystery. We cannot interpret Spirit, Mind, through matter, because matter does not really see, hear, or feel. So, improve the thought process; reason from cause to effect and Spirit will be found giving the true mental idea.

Sinlessness of Mind, Soul

Reasoning from cause to effect in the Science of Mind, we begin with Mind, which must be understood through the idea which expresses it and cannot be learned from matter. Thereby, we arrive at Truth, or intelligence, which evolves its own perfect idea and never can equate with human illusions. If Soul sinned, it would be mortal. Sin is mortal because it kills itself. If Truth is immortal, error must be mortal, because error is unlike Truth. Because Soul is immortal, Soul cannot sin, for sin is not the reality of being.

Question. What is the scientific statement of being?
Answer. There is no life, truth, intelligence, nor substance in matter. All is infinite Mind and its infinite manifestation, for God is All-in-all. Spirit is divine Truth; matter is human error. Spirit is the real and eternal; matter is the unreal and temporal. Spirit is God, and we are Spirit's image and likeness. Therefore person is not mortal, but is immortal.

403

Spiritual synonyms
Question. What is substance?
Answer. Substance is that which is eternal and incapable of disorder and decay. Truth, Life, and Love are substance, as the Scriptures use this word in Hebrews: "The substance of things hoped for, the evidence of things not seen."[1] Spirit, the synonym of Mind, Soul, or God, is the only real substance. The spiritual universe, including individual person, is a united idea, reflecting the divine substance of Spirit.

Eternity of Life
Question. What is Life?
Answer. Life is divine Principle, Mind, Soul, Spirit. Life is without beginning and without end. Eternity, not time, expresses the thought of Life, and time is not a part of eternity. You know Life when you stop knowing time. Time is finite; eternity is forever infinite. Life has nothing to do with boundaries of any kind. Spirit doesn't know the stuff called matter. Soul includes in itself all substance and is Life eternal. Matter is a human concept or invention. Life is divine Mind. Life is not limited; death and limitation are unknown to Life. If Life ever had a beginning, it would also have an ending.

Question. What is intelligence?
Answer. Intelligence is omniscience, omnipresence, and omnipotence. It is the primal and perpetual quality of infinite Mind, of the all-inclusive Principle—Life, Truth, and Love—named God.

True sense of infinitude
Question. What is Mind?
Answer. Mind is God. The exterminator of error is the great truth that God, good, is the *only* Mind. To suppose there is an opposite to infinite Mind—called devil or evil—is not Mind, is not Truth, but error, without intelligence or reality. There can be but one Mind, because there is but one God; and if human beings claimed no other Mind and accepted no other, all that opposes infinite Mind would be unknown. We can have but one Mind, if that one is infinite. We bury the perception of infinitude, when we admit that, although God

---

[1]   Heb. 11:1 (NKJV)

is infinite, evil has a place in this infinity, for evil can have no place where all presence is God.

The sole governor

We lose the exalted significance of omnipotence, when after admitting that God, or good, is omnipresent and has all-power, we still believe there is another power, named *evil*. To think that there is more than one mind is pernicious, destructive to divine theology, and on par with ancient mythology and pagan idolatry. With one Parent, God, all people would be family, with one Mind, good. The family would consist of Love and Truth, and have unity of Principle and spiritual power which constitute divine Science. The supposed existence of more than one mind was the basic error of idolatry. This error assumed the loss of spiritual power, the loss of the spiritual presence of Life as infinite Truth without an unlikeness, and the loss of Love as ever present and universal.

The divine standard of perfection

Divine Science explains the abstract statement that there is one Mind by the following self-evident proposition: If God, or good, is real then the unlikeness of Life, Truth, and Love is unreal. Any unlikeness to God can only seem real by giving reality to the unreal. The children of God have but one Mind. How can good lapse into bad, when God, the Mind of person, never falters? The standard of perfection was originally God and God's image, or offspring. Has God's standard been lowered, and has God's image fallen?

Indestructible relationship

God is the creator of person, and, the divine Principle of person remaining complete, the divine idea or reflection, person, remains complete. Person is the expression of God's being. If there ever was a moment when person did not express the divine perfection, then there was moment when person did not express God, and consequently a time when God was unexpressed—that is, without entity. If spiritual being has lost perfection, then God's idea has lost his or her perfect Principle, the divine Mind. If people existed without a complete Mind, then their existence was a myth.

The relationship between God and person, divine Principle and idea, is indestructible in Science, and Science knows no drifting from, nor return to harmony, but holds the divine order or spiritual law, in which God and all that He creates is complete and eternal, to have remained unchanged in its eternal history.

Celestial evidence

The unlikeness of Truth—named *error*—the opposite of Science, and the evidence before the five corporeal senses, offer no sign of the grand facts of spiritual being. But don't fret, because even though our human senses feel no evidence that our earth is spinning rapidly through space, we still can learn the truth through science and break through limitations.

The facts of divine Science should be admitted, although the evidence as to these facts is not supported by evil, by matter, or by corporeal sense. The evidence that God and people coexist is fully sustained by spiritual sense. Person is, and forever has been, God's reflection. God is infinite, therefore ever present, and there is no other power, no other presence. The spirituality of the universe is the only fact of creation. "Let God be found true though every human being is false *and* a liar."[1]

The test of experience

Question. Are doctrines and creeds a benefit to human beings?

Answer. I subscribed to an orthodox creed when young, and tried to adhere to it until I caught the first view of that which interprets God as above human mortal perceptions. The new view rebuked human beliefs and gave the spiritual interpretation, expressed through Science, of all that proceeds from the divine Mind. Since then my highest creed has been divine Science, which, reduced to human comprehension, I named Christian Science. This Science teaches us that God is the only Life, and that this Life is truth and love; that God is to be understood, compassionately respected, and demonstrated; that divine Truth drives out supposed errors and heals the sick.

God's law destroys evil

The way which leads to Christian Science is straight and narrow. God has put Her mark on Science, making it equal to all that is real and only with that which is harmonious and eternal. Sickness, sin,

---

[1]   Rom. 3:4 (Amplified*)*

and death, being inharmonious, do not originate in God nor belong to His government. God's law, rightly understood, destroys all that contradicts Life, Truth, and Love.

Short-lived materiality

Question. What is error?

Answer. Error is the theory that pleasure, pain, intelligence, substance, and life, are existent in human mind/body. Error is not Mind and is not one of Mind's forces. Error is the contradiction of Truth. Error is a belief without understanding. Error is unreal because untrue. Error is that which seems to be and is not. If error were true, its truth would be error, and we should have a self-evident absurdity—namely, erroneous truth. If an erroneous truth were real, there would be no such thing as Truth.

Unrealities that seem real

Question. What about sin?

Answer. All reality is in God and God's revelation, harmonious and eternal. That which Truth creates is good, and Truth makes all that is made. Therefore the only reality of sin, sickness, or death is the awful fact that unrealities seem real to human, erring belief, until God strips off their disguise. Sin, sickness, and death are not true, because they are not of God. We learn in Christian Science that all inharmony of human mind (or body) is a false impression, possessing no reality or identity, although it seems to be real and identifiable.

Christ the ideal Truth

The Science of Mind disposes of sin—of all that goes against Life, Truth, and Love. Truth, God, is not the parent of error. Sin, sickness, and death are to be classified as effects of error. Christ comes to destroy the belief of sin. The God-principle is omnipresent and omnipotent. God is everywhere, and nothing apart from Principle is present or has power. Christ is the ideal Truth, which comes to heal sickness and sin through divine Science and attributes all power to God. Jesus is the name of the human being who, more than all other human beings, has presented Christ, the true idea of God, healing the sick and the sinning and destroying the power of death. Jesus is the human person, and Christ is the divine idea; hence the duality of Jesus the Christ.

Jesus is not God

In the age of religious tyranny, Jesus introduced a teaching and practice that was later termed Christianity. He gave the proof of Christianity's truth and love; however, to reach his example and to test its unerring Science according to his rule, healing sickness, sin, and death, a better understanding of divine Principle, rather than the human personality of Jesus, is required.

Jesus needs to be understood

Jesus established what he said by demonstration, consequently making his acts of more importance than his words. Jesus proved what he taught. This is the Science of Christianity. Jesus *proved* the Principle, which heals the sick and casts out error, to be divine. Few people, however, except his students understood in the least his teachings and their glorious proof—namely, that Life, Truth, and Love destroy all error, evil, disease, and death.

Miracles rejected

Truth is received today as well as it was in the early Christian period. Whoever introduces the Science of Christianity will also be ridiculed and vindictively burdened. To the people unaware of spirituality, Science at first appears to be a mistake, and it is consequently misinterpreted and badly treated. Miracles are misunderstood and misused by many until the glorious Principle of these marvels is gained.

Divine fulfillment

If sin, and its morphing expressions, is as real as Life, Truth, and Love, then it must all be from the same source; God must be its author. Jesus came to destroy sin, sickness, and death and we read in Scripture, "I did not come to abolish, but to complete."[1] Is it possible, then, to believe that the evils which Jesus lived to destroy are real, or are the offspring of the divine will?

---

[1]   Matt. 5:17 (NEB)

Truth destroys falsity

In his book, *The Four Agreements: Wisdom Book*, Don Miguel Ruiz[1] presents a reasonable view of sinlessness based on the word "Impeccability." Differing views of falsity help us grasp the fact that to infinite Spirit there is no sin, because all is sinless Spirit, all is divine Principle and its idea. The sacred influence of Truth is to abolish error and sin, so, can error be immortal? Truth spares all that is true. If evil is real, Truth must make it so, but error, not Truth, is the author of the unreal. The unreal vanishes, while all that is real is eternal. The apostle says that the mission of the divine idea, called Christ, is to "destroy the works of the devil."[2] Truth wipes out falsity and error, for light and darkness can't dwell together. Light extinguishes the darkness—there is "no night there."[3] To Truth there is no error, all is Truth.

Fleshly factors unreal

Question. What is person?

Answer. Person is not physical particles. God's offspring is not made up of the temporal brain, blood, bones, and other mortal elements. The Scriptures inform us that God's offspring is made in the image and likeness of Spirit. Physical human beings are not the likeness of Spirit. The likeness of Spirit cannot be so unlike Spirit. Person is spiritual and perfect. Christian Science helps us understand spiritual being, immortal and perfect. Man and woman are spiritual beings, the image of Love. Spiritual being is not a physique but is the compound idea of God, including all right ideas. Spiritual being is the term for all that reflects God's image and likeness; the conscious identity of existence as found in Science, reflecting God, Mind. Man and woman do not have a mind separate from God. We do not have a single quality that didn't come from divine Being. We do not possess a life, intelligence, or creative power of our own, but reflect spiritually all that belongs to our Maker.

---

1 Ruiz, Don Miguel, *The Four Agreements: Wisdom Book*. California: Amber-Allen Publishing, 1997.

2 I John 3:8 (NASB)

3 Rev. 21:25, 22:5

God said: "Let us make man [*humane* being, person, God's posterity] in our image, in our likeness, and let them rule over the fish of the sea and the birds of the air, over the livestock, over all the earth, and over all the creatures that move along the ground."[1]

Man and woman have not fallen

Man and woman are incapable of sin, sickness, and death. The substantiating idea of person cannot fall from holiness. God, from whom person evolved, cannot bring about the capacity or freedom to sin. A mortal sinner is not God's image. Mortals are the counterfeits of immortals; they are the heirs of the one evil, which insists that we begin in dust and have a detached physical identity. In divine Science, God and our spiritual identity are as inseparable as divine Principle and idea.

Mortals are not immortals

Error, urged to its final limits, is self-destroyed. Error will cease to hypothesize that soul is in body, that life and intelligence are in human mind, and that this human mind is person. God is the Principle of spiritual being, and person is the idea of God; therefore, spiritual being has no mortal pattern or relationship. Mortals will disappear, and immortals—the children of God—will appear as the only and eternal fact of existence. Human mortal beings are not fallen children of God; they never had a perfect state of being, which may subsequently be regained. They were, from the beginning of mortal history, "brought forth in [a state of] iniquity;"[2] and conceived in sin. Mortality is finally swallowed up in immortality. Destructiveness, incapability, and dying must disappear to give place to the facts which belong to spiritual being.

Imperishable identity

Earnestly seek the immortal status of person, which is outside the illusion of mortal human men and women. "Men and women don't live very long; like wildflowers they spring up and blossom, but a storm snuffs them out just as quickly."[3]

---

1   Gen. 1:26 (Brackets added by Cheryl Petersen)
2   Ps. 51:5 (Amplified*)*
3   Ps. 103:15-16 (The Message)

The kingdom within

When speaking of God's children, not the children of human beings, Jesus said, "The kingdom of God is within you;"[1] that is, Truth and Love prevail in the real man and woman, showing that spiritual being in God's image is eternal and not fallen. Jesus perceived in Science the flawless person, who appeared to him where flawed mortals appeared to worldly thinkers. In the perfect person, the Savior saw God's own likeness, and this correct view of man and woman healed the sick. Consequently, Jesus taught that the realm of God is intact, universal, and that person is pure and holy. People are not a material habitation for Soul, because people are spiritual and have no relationship to imperfection or matter.

Physical body never God's idea

Anything in the human mind is mortal. To the five physical senses, a person appears to be matter and mind united. Divine Science reveals man and woman as the idea of God. Science supports the fact that the physical senses are capricious and illusory. Divine Science shows that it is impossible for congealed atoms to be person even though interwoven with matter's higher echelon called brain (misnamed mind). The genuine and total person, the spiritual idea of being is indestructible and eternal. If it were otherwise, person would be annihilated.

Reflection of Spirit

Question. What are body and Soul?

Answer. Identity is the reflection of Spirit, the reflection in many, many forms of the living Principle, Love. Soul is the substance, Life, and intelligence of spiritual being, which is individualized, but not in matter. Soul can never reflect anything inferior to Spirit.

We are inseparable from Spirit

The expression of Soul is person. We can capture the underlying reality of Soul through expression. It is recorded that Mahatma Gandhi[2] said, "When I admire the wonder of a sunset or the beauty of the moon, my soul expands in worship of the Creator." Spirit would be

---

[1] Luke 17:21

[2] Gandhi, Mahatma, (1869-1948) Political and religious leader of India.

a nonentity if it was separated from spiritual being. Similarly, people would lose their entity if divorced from Spirit, however there is, there can be, no such division, for spiritual being is coexistent with God.

What evidence of Soul or of immortality do you have within mortality? Even the sciences taught in the schools have never seen Spirit or Soul leaving a body or entering it. What warrants the theory of an indwelling spirit, except the argument of human sentiment? What would be thought of the hypothesis that a house was inhabited by a certain class of persons, when no such persons were ever seen going into or coming out of the house? Who can see a soul in the body?

Question. Does the nervous system think or feel, and does the human mind have intelligence?
Answer. No. Not when the human senses are so unreliable. God is true, and interprets reality to us. The assertion that there can be pain or pleasure in matter is erroneous. How can intelligence dwell in matter when matter is non-intelligent and brain-lobes can't think? Matter can't perform the functions of Mind. Erroneous human mind says, "I am man and woman;" but this belief lacks actuality. From beginning to end, whatever is mortal is composed of limited human beliefs and of nothing else. Only that which reflects God is real. St. Paul said, "But when it pleased God, who separated me from my mother's womb, and called me by his grace . . . I conferred not with flesh and blood."[1] Our body is most harmonious when we don't fixate on its every function.
Immortal birthright
Human being is really a self-contradictory phrase, for spiritual being is not a mortal human and has no flesh. Mortality and corporeality "neither can nor will follow his Law."[2] A human origin designates the offspring of physical sense, not of Soul. The picture of a weak, unbalanced, or mortal person did not come from God. All that comes from God is immortal and spiritual.

---

[1]   Gal. 1:15-16 (KJV)

[2]   Rom. 8:7 (Philips NT)

Matter's supposed selfhood

Human flesh is neither self-existent nor a product of Spirit. The physical eye only sees an image of human thought reflected on the retina. Matter cannot see, feel, hear, taste, or smell. Matter/energy is not self-cognizant—cannot feel itself, see itself, nor understand itself. If you take away the human mind, which constitutes mortal selfhood, matter can take no cognizance of matter. Does the comatose patient ever see, hear, or feel? Why doesn't a corpse use any of the physical senses?

Darkness and chaos are the imaginary opposites of light, understanding, and eternal harmony. In the vast forever, in the Science and truth of being, the only facts are Spirit and its innumerable expressions. "In the beginning God created the heavens and the earth. Now the earth was formless and empty, darkness was over the surface of the deep, and the Spirit of God was hovering over the waters."[1]

Spiritual reflection

Black doesn't reflect light. If there is no spiritual reflection then there remains only darkness, without a trace of heavenly tints. Evil doesn't have identity or power, because it doesn't reflect any of the divine colors (e.g. health, decency, stamina . . .). Paul says: "Since the creation of the world God's invisible qualities—his eternal power and divine nature—have been clearly seen, being understood from what has been made, so that men are without excuse."[2] When the substance of Spirit appears in divine Science, the emptiness of matter is recognized. Evil is absent where the spirit of God **is**. There is no dimension where God is gone.

Harmony from Spirit

Nerves are an ingredient in the concoction of sensation in matter, but that mixture is a fiasco because matter is void of sensation. Physical sense has its realm in the unreal, apart from Science. Consciousness, as well as action, is governed by Mind. Consciousness is in God, the source and governor of all that Science reveals. Balanced action proceeds from Spirit, God. Imbalance has no Principle; its

[1] Gen. 1:1-2

[2] Rom. 1:20

action is erroneous and assumes people are in the fluctuating elements of the human mind. Imbalance would make human mind the cause as well as the effect of intelligence, thus attempting to separate Mind from God.

Evil is non-existent

Man and woman is not Mind, and Mind divine is not the created. God, or good, never made us capable of insanely chasing after illusions. The misinterpretations and egotistic human views have no real basis. Contorted perceptions instigate wrongdoing. God is not the cause of illusions. The presumed parent of evil is a lie.

The Bible declares: "All things were made through Him, and without Him nothing was made that was made."[1] This is the eternal truth of Christian Science. If human transgressions, vulnerabilities, and losses were understood as nonbeing, they would disappear to the reality of good which naturally banishes evil, just as acts of kindness make self-pity go away. One must hide the other. How important, then, to choose good as the reality! We are secured by God, Spirit, and by nothing else. God's being is infinity, freedom, balance, and boundless happiness. "Where the Spirit of the Lord is, there is freedom."[2] Like the archpriests of long ago, we are free "to enter the Most Holy Place"[3]—the realm of God.

Forbidden fruit

Physical sense never helps human beings understand Spirit. Through spiritual sense only, we comprehend and love the Almighty. Physical sense convolutes the Science of Mind, however, the unseen, intact Truth is unchanged. The forbidden fruit of knowledge, against which wisdom warns us, is the testimony of error declaring existence to be at the mercy of death, and good and evil to be capable of intertwining. This is signified in Scripture concerning the "tree of the knowledge of good and evil," the energy of temporal belief, of which it is said: "When you eat of it you will surely die."[4] Human hypotheses

---

[1]   John 1:3 (NKJV)

[2]   II Cor. 3:17

[3]   Heb. 10:19

[4]   Gen. 2:17

first assume the reality of sickness, sin, and death, and then assume the necessity of these evils because of their admitted actuality, when in fact these assumptions are the procurers of all disorder.

Sense and pure Soul

If Soul uses, or has, temporal sense, it must be mortal. Soul is not self-destructive, but is self-sustaining, therefore Soul is immortal. Human perception or intelligence includes the building blocks of self-destruction and they are not able to sustain themselves. God does not support, sustain, or uphold error. In Science we learn that mortal senses are senseless. You will find that it is the sense of senselessness which is lost, and not a senseless soul. When reading the Scriptures, the substitution of the word *sense* for *soul* gives the exact meaning in a majority of cases.

Soul defined

Human thought has adulterated the meaning of the word *soul* through the hypothesis that soul is both an evil and a good intelligence, resident in matter. The proper use of the word *soul* can always be gained by substituting the word *God*, where the divine meaning is required. In other cases, use the word *sense*, and you will have the scientific meaning. As used in divine Science, Soul is the synonym of Spirit, or God; but outside of Science, soul is identical with sense, with mortal sensation or perception.

Question. Is it important to understand the explanations of divine Science in order to heal the sick?

Answer. Since the ideal Truth is "the way,"[1] to overcome all error, it is important to comprehend the explanation of divine Science in order to heal. Divine Science is the law of Truth, which heals the sick on the basis of the one Mind or God. It can heal in no other way, since the human, mortal mind is not a healer, but actually causes the belief in disease. Sickness is part of the error which Truth replaces. Error will not expel error.

---

[1]   John 14:6

True healing is transcendent

Then comes the question, how do drugs, time, surgery, and hypnotism heal? They do not heal, but only relieve suffering temporarily, exchanging one problem for another. We classify disease as error, which nothing but Truth or Mind can heal. Mind is holy, not human. Mind transcends all other power and will ultimately supersede all other means in healing. In order to heal by Science, you must be aware of, and obey, its moral and spiritual principles. Moral ignorance or sin affects your demonstration and hinders your approach to the paradigm in divine Science.

For this sacred discovery, I adopted the term Christian Science. I applied the name "error" to fleshly senses or mortal human perceptions. I applied the name "substance" to Mind. Science is compelling the world to battle over the subject of divine Mind and its demonstration, which heals the sick, destroys error and reveals the universal harmony. To the natural students of Christian Science, to the ancient worthies, and to Christ Jesus, God certainly revealed the spirit of divine Science, if not the absolute letter.

Sonship of Jesus

Jesus called himself "the Son of Man," but not the son of Joseph. As woman is but a species of the genera, he was literally the Son of collective humanity. Jesus exemplified the human mind's highest understanding of spiritual person. Jesus was in harmony with Christ, inseparable from the Messiah—the divine idea of God outside the flesh but with us now. This enabled Jesus to demonstrate his control over matter. Angels announced to the wise men this dual appearing, and angels whisper it through faith, to the hungering heart in every age.

Science the way

Christianity will never be based on a divine Principle and so found to be unerring, until its absolute Science is reached. The Science of Mind seems to dishonor the ordinary scientific schools, which wrestle with human observations alone; therefore, this Science has met with opposition. However, any system honoring God ought to receive support, not resistance, from all thinking persons. Divine Science honors God as no other theory and it does this in the way of

Soul's appointing, by doing many wonderful works through the divine name and nature. All persons must fulfill their own mission without timidity and without putting on a show. Spiritual goals are successfully achieved when our work is done unselfishly, and as a result, arrogance, prejudice, bigotry, and envy cannot wash away its foundation, for it is built on the rock, Truth.

Mindless methods

Question. Are medications, hypnotism, quantum-touch, and New Age remedies included in Christian Science or divine metaphysical healing? *Answer.* Not one of them is included in scientific mental treatment. In divine Science, the supposed physical laws yield to the law of Mind. What are termed natural science and physical laws are the objective states of human mind. The physical universe expresses the conscious and unconscious thoughts of human beings. Physical force and human mind are one. Drugs and quantum dynamics oppose the supremacy of the unquantifiable divine Mind. Drugs and inert matter are unconscious, mindless. Certain results, supposed to proceed from drugs, are really caused by the faith in them which the false human consciousness is educated to feel.

Hypnotism, quantum energy, and New Age remedies are human—are conditional and oftentimes unpredictable. They are the voluntary or involuntary action of error. Science must triumph over limited knowledge. Truth must prevail over error and put an end to the suggestions involved in all insufficient theories and practices.

Error only ephemeral

Question. Is the material linked to spiritual, and is a material sense of things first necessary before understanding and expressing Spirit? *Answer.* If error is necessary to define or to reveal Truth, the answer is yes; but not otherwise. *Material sense* is an absurd phrase, for material molecules have no consciousness, no sense. Science declares that divine Mind, not material mind, sees, hears, feels, and speaks. Anything that contradicts this statement is the false sense which betrays human beings into sickness, sin, and death. Why slam Christian Science for instructing human beings how to make sin, disease, and death appear more and more unreal? If the unimportant and evil appear, only soon to disappear because of their uselessness or their iniquity, then these ephemeral views of error ought to be obliterated by Truth.

Advance naturally from matter into Spirit. Don't try to frustrate the spiritual ultimate of all things by ignoring, or forcing, spirituality. Sincere spiritual growth is wise and brings about better health and improved morals.

Not death, but the understanding of Life, makes us spiritual. Christ, Truth, destroys the human error resulting from the thinking that life can be in molecules or DNA, or that soul can be in the body. The spiritual law of being is fulfilled by Christ as persons manifest perfection, even as "your heavenly Father is perfect."[1] Be aware: if unspiritual powers dominate in your thinking, then thought is unable to outline on the body its own beautiful images. Negative thinking hides the beautiful and then proceeds to delineate dreadful agents called disease and self-destructive habits.

The gods of mythology controlled the weather and war as much as nerves control sensation, or muscles measure strength. To say that strength is in matter is like saying that the power is in the lever. The notion of intelligence in matter/energy is without foundation in fact, and you can have no faith in falsehood when you have learned falsehood's true nature.

Sense versus Soul

Suppose an accident happens to the eye, then the ear has a problem, then the taste buds can't be stimulated, and so on, until every physical sense is lost. What is the remedy? To die, that we may regain these faculties? Even then we must gain spiritual understanding and spiritual sense in order to possess indestructible consciousness. In reality, spiritual beings never die. The belief that we die will not establish scientific harmony. Death is not the result of Truth but of error, and one error will not correct another. Every day on earth we must improve, discover, and utilize our spiritual faculties.

Permanent sensibility

Spiritual sight, hearing, and so on, are eternal. Immortal senses cannot be lost. The reality and immortality of spiritual sense are in

---

[1]   Matt. 5:48

Spirit and understanding—hence their permanence. The senses are not in mutating matter/energy. If the body's physical senses were the medium through which to understand God, then paralysis, disabilities, blindness, and deafness would place people in a terrible situation, "Without hope and without God in the world."[1] These calamities however often drive human beings to seek and to find a more secure sense of happiness and existence in Spirit.

Death is an error

To prove that his body was the same immediately after death as before, Jesus showed the nail prints in his hands. If death restores sight, sound, and strength to man and woman, then death is not an enemy but a better friend than Life, but this is not so.

Sad day for the blindness of belief, which makes harmony conditional on the human mind or death, and supposes Mind unable to produce harmony! So long as this error of belief remains, human beings will continue fleshly in belief and susceptible to mortality and change.

Exercise of Mind-faculties

Life is deathless. Life is the origin and ultimate of spiritual being, never attainable through death. Life is discovered by breaking human thought barriers with Truth both before and after that which is called death. There is more spirituality in seeing and hearing objectively, than seeing and hearing with the bias of human experiences. There is more Science in the perpetual exercise of the Mind-faculties than in their loss. The true perceptions cannot be lost while Mind remains. This comprehension gave sight to the blind and hearing to the deaf centuries ago, and it will repeat the wonder.

Understanding versus belief

Question. You speak of belief. Who or what is it that believes?

Answer. Spirit is all-knowing and this rules out the need of believing. Divine Mind understands. Quantifiable matter/energy doesn't believe. Matter is unintelligent and sensationless. The believer and belief are one and are mortal. The human mind is the believers and the belief. Mere belief is blindness without Principle from which to explain the

---

[1]   Eph. 2:12

419

2ND CENTURY SCIENCE & HEALTH WITH KEY TO THE SCRIPTURES

reason of its hope. Evidence established on Science or demonstrable Truth, and flowing from immortal Mind, is Christ-like.

The Apostle James said, "Show me your faith without your works, and I will show you my faith by my works."[1] The understanding that Life is God, Spirit, extends our days by strengthening our trust in the deathless reality of Life, its almightiness and immortality.

Confirmation by healing

Genuine faith relies on an understood Principle. An understood Principle releases people from problems, and reveals the self-perpetuating and harmonious phases of everything. These teachings are confirmed by healing. When, on the strength of these instructions, you are able to banish a severe illness, the cure shows that you understand this teaching and therefore you receive the blessing of Truth.

Belief and firm trust

The word *belief,* translated from the Hebrew and Greek differs somewhat in meaning from the English verb *believe*. The biblical word *believe* is defined: to be faithful, trustworthy, reliable, firm, entrusted. It's significant to keep this discrepancy in mind when reading Scripture. Otherwise, it may appear as though Scripture is approving and endorsing a belief system, when it actually is enforcing the necessity of *understanding.*

All faculties from Mind

Question. Do atoms, in the form of chemicals, or the five senses, constitute person?

Answer. Divine Science sustains, with immortal proof, the impossibility of atoms having perception or consciousness. Divine Science defines the sensory and motor systems as human beliefs or inventions. If we were humanly programmed to believe it, we would believe the veins in a plant could feel stimuli like nerves. The bodily senses can take no cognizance of spiritual reality and immortality. God, Mind alone possesses all sensation, perception, and interpretation. Therefore, mental perception or awareness is not at the mercy of physical organization and decay—otherwise bacteria could

---

[1]   James 2:18 (NKJV)

undo us. If it were possible for our real senses to be injured, Soul could reproduce them in all their perfection, but they cannot be disturbed or destroyed, since they exist in immortal Mind, not in matter.

Possibilities of Life

When the unthinking salamander loses its limb, the limb grows back. If the Science of Life were understood, it would be found that the senses of Mind are never lost and that human mind has no sensation, then the human limb would be replaced as readily as the salamander's limb—not with an artificial limb, but with the genuine one. Any hypothesis that assumes life is in human mind is an educated belief. Beliefs, in their infancy are like an infant, not able to guide the hand to the mouth. As spiritual consciousness develops, belief goes out, yielding to the reality of everlasting Life.

Physical senses defraud and lie; breaking the Ten Commandments to meet their own demands. How then can measurable, chemically-based perceptions be the God-given channel of divine blessings or understanding? How can we, reflecting God, be dependent on human mortal mind as a means for knowing, hearing, and seeing? Who dares to say that the senses of person can be at one time the medium for sinning against God and at another time be the medium for obeying God? An affirmative reply would contradict Scripture, for the same fountain does not send forth both fresh and salt water.[1]

Mortal perceptions (or rather misperceptions) are the only source of evil or error. Divine Science shows that physical senses are false, because matter can't hear or see or be consciousness. Beyond the limited mortal impressions of things, all is harmony. A mysterious sense of spiritual being, and revelation, is *nonsense*, no sense. Human belief would make the physical senses sometimes good and sometimes bad. Human mindedness swears that there is real pleasure in sin, but the beautiful truths of divine Science dispute this error.

Will-power is an animalistic propensity

Will-power is only a product of belief, and this belief makes human beings desperate. Human will is an untamed inclination, not a propensity of Soul. Consequently, mortal will-power does not properly

---
[1] James 3:11

govern. Human will—selfishly exclusive, negligent, and head-strong—cooperates with idleness and hyperactivity. From this cooperation arises the evil of human willfulness. From this also comes the powerlessness of mortal will-power, since all power belongs to God, good. Christian Science reveals Truth and Love as our motive-powers.

The Science of Mind needs to be understood. Until it is understood, human beings are more or less deprived of truth. Human theories are helpless to make people harmonious or spiritual. In divine Science we already are harmonious and spiritual. Our only need is to know this and reduce to practice our divine Principle, Love.

"Do not put out the Spirit's fire; do not treat prophecies with contempt."[1] Human belief (knowledge gained from the physical senses) would by fair logic, annihilate people along with the disintegrating elements of matter. The scientifically Christian explanations of the nature and origin of spiritual being destroys all mortal sense with immortal testimony. This immortal testimony ushers in the spiritual sense of existence, which can't be obtained in any other way.

Sleep is an illusion

Sleep shows that physical sensations can quickly enter oblivion—nothing, an illusion, or dream. Sleep and hypnotism point to the mythical nature of the human sensory and motor systems. Under the mesmeric illusion of belief, a person will think they are freezing when they are warm. Worse yet, a hypnotic personality can temporarily alter the human consciousness of other people, making them do something that goes against their nature. We can't help but learn from these instances. Human feelings are a belief without actual foundation or validity. Change the belief, and the feelings change. Destroy the belief, and the human sensations or feelings disappear.

We are linked with Spirit

Human beings are made up of involuntary and voluntary error, of a negative right and a positive wrong, the latter calling itself right. The individuality of spiritual person is never wrong. Our spirituality is the likeness of God, Truth. Matter cannot connect humans with spiritual being. The demands of matter are annulled as we acknowledge the

---

[1] I Thes. 5:19-20

supremacy of Spirit. It is only in this way that human beings can advance out of mortality and find the indissoluble spiritual link which establishes us forever in the divine likeness, inseparable from divine Mind.

Material people are as a dream

The belief that matter and mind are one—that matter is awake at one time and asleep at another, fluctuating between the mindful and the mindless—is the kind of thinking that culminates in death. When we are asleep, memory and consciousness are lost from the body, and they wander around apparently with their own separate embodiment. Science reveals the fact that mortal personality has nothing to do with our real personhood. We call the human character a personality. Human personality is a dream, and the dream or belief goes on whether our eyes are closed or open. A wicked person may have an attractive personality; therefore, human personality is not the true character of spiritual person.

Spiritual existence the one fact

When we are awake, we dream of the pains and pleasures of matter. Who will say, even though Christian Science is not understood, that the dream—rather than the dreamer—may not be mortal human person? Who can rationally say otherwise when the dream leaves human beings intact in body and thought, although the so-called dreamer is unconscious? For right reasoning there should be but one fact before the thought, namely, spiritual being. In reality there is no other existence, since Life cannot be united to its unlikeness, mortality.

Being is holiness, harmony, immortality. It is already proved that knowledge of this, even in a small degree, will improve the physical and moral standard of human beings, will increase longevity, will purify and elevate character. Progress will finally destroy all error and bring immortality to light. Spiritual progress is truthful. New thoughts are constantly breaking human laws. The two contradictory theories— that human mind is something, or that all is Mind—will fight each other until one is acknowledged to be the victor. Calling the people to arms, Winston Churchill said: "Our task is not only to win the battle—but to win the war."[1] Science says: All is Mind and Mind's idea. You must fight it out to the end. Matter, human mind, is of no help in this war.

Scientific ultimatum

The notion that mind and matter can mix in the human illusion of sin, sickness, and death must eventually submit to the Science of Mind which denies the notion. *God is Mind, and God is infinite; and so all is Mind.* On this statement rests the Science of being, and the Principle of this Science is divine, demonstrating harmony and spirituality.

The conservative theory, embedded into society's belief system, is that there are two factors, matter and mind, uniting on some impossible basis. This theory would keep truth and error always at battle, however victory for either side would never come. On the other hand, divine Science efficiently shows Truth to be triumphant. All the evidence of, and all the knowledge obtained from physical sense must yield to Science, to the immortal truth of all things. The misguiding physical senses are yielding whether they want to admit it or not. Physical sense can no longer contradict the heliocentric theory even though they see and feel it not.

Mental preparation

Question. Will you explain sickness and show how it is to be healed?

Answer. The method of divine Science Mind-healing is touched on in a previous chapter titled Christian Science Practice. A full answer to the above question involves teaching, which enables healers to demonstrate and prove for themselves the Principle and rule of divine Science or metaphysical healing.

Mind destroys all ills

Divine Mind must be found superior to all that the human mind/body has been convinced to believe. Spirit must be discovered as able to destroy all ills. Sickness is a materialized mortal conviction, which must be annihilated by the divine Mind. Disease is an experience

---

[1] Churchill, Winston. "Be ye men of valour," BBC Radio, 1940. *Twentieth-Century Speeches*, edited by Brian MacArthur. London: Penguin Books, 1992. Reproduced with permission of Curtis Brown Ltd, London on behalf of The Estate of Winston Churchill. Copyright Winston S. Churchill.

of so-called human mind. Disease is fear made manifest on the body. Divine Science takes away this physical sense of disorder, just as it removes any other sense of moral or mental imbalance. The propositions that people are mortal, or that organized atoms can suffer, only seems real and natural in illusion. Any appearance of soul in a measurable energy field is not the reality of being.

If Jesus awakened Lazarus[1] from the dream (appearance) of death, this proved that the true idea of Life could improve on a misconception of life. Why doubt this consummate test of the power and willingness of divine Mind to hold us forever intact in our perfect state? Why doubt God's inclination and ability to govern our entire action? Jesus said: "Destroy this temple [body], and I [Mind] will raise it again in three days;"[2] and he did this for tired humanity's reassurance.

Inexhaustible divine Love

Isn't it a species of unbelief to believe that so great a work as the Messiah's was done for himself or for God? God did not need Jesus' example to preserve the eternal harmony, however human beings did, and Jesus pointed the way. Divine Love always has met and always will meet every human need. Do not imagine that Jesus demonstrated the divine power to heal only for a select number of people or for a particular period of time, since to all humankind and in every hour, divine Love supplies all good.

Reason and Science

The miracle of grace is not a miracle to Love. Jesus demonstrated the inability of the human body, as well as the infinite ability of Spirit. This helps the inconsistent human consciousness abandon its own convictions and seek safety in divine Science. Reason, rightly directed, serves to correct the errors of fleshly sense. Sin, sickness, and death will continue to seem real (even as the experiences of the sleeping dream seem real) until the Science of man and woman's harmony breaks their illusion with the unbroken reality of scientific being.

What can we believe and accept concerning a person? Can we accept the mortal testimony, changing, dying, and deceptive? Or,

---

1 John 11
2 John 2:19 (Brackets added by Mary Baker Eddy)

can we accept the good and real evidence, bearing Truth's mark and flourishing with spiritual results?

Followers of Jesus

Jesus cast out devils (evils) and healed the sick. Followers can also drive fear and all evil out of themselves and others and heal the sick. God will heal the sick through us whenever we are governed by God. Truth banishes error now as surely as it did twenty centuries ago. All of Truth is not understood; that is why its healing power is not fully demonstrated.

If sickness is true or the idea of Truth, you cannot destroy sickness, and it would be absurd to try. Then classify sickness and error as Jesus did, when he spoke of the sick, "whom Satan has kept bound."[1] Find a sovereign antidote for error in the life-giving power of Truth acting on human belief. Truth's power opens the prison doors to those who are bound, and sets the captive free physically and morally.

When the curse of sickness or sin tempts you, cling steadfastly to God and Spirit's idea. Allow nothing but Soul's likeness to prevail in your thought. Do not let fear or doubt eclipse your clear sense and calm trust in Truth. The recognition of life harmonious—as Life eternally is—can destroy any painful sense of, or belief in, that which Life is not. Let divine Science, instead of fleshly sense, support your understanding of being and this understanding will exchange error for Truth, replace physicality with spirituality, and silence complaint with harmony.

Fundamentals and growth

Question. How can I make consistent, rapid progress in my understanding of Christian Science?

Answer. Study thoroughly the letter, receive and retain the spirit. Unite with the divine Principle of spiritual Science; practice the intent of Spirit; and remain sincere in wisdom, Truth, and Love. In the Science of Mind, you will eventually figure out that error cannot destroy error. You will also learn in Science, that the transfer of negative suggestions from one human being to another can be proven unreal, for there is but one Mind. This ever-present omnipotent Mind expresses the

---

[1]   Luke 13:16

entire universe and is reflected by us. The first responsibility in divine Science is to adapt to Soul, to have one Mind, and to love another as yourself.

Condition of progress

We all must learn that Life is God. Ask yourself: Am I living the life that advances with supreme good? Am I manifesting the healing power of Truth and Love? If so, then the path will be "shining ever brighter till the full light of day."[1] Your accomplishments will prove what the understanding of God brings to person. Hold perpetually this thought—that it is the spiritual idea, the Holy Spirit and Christ, which enables you to demonstrate with scientific certainty, the rule of healing, based on its divine Principle, Love, underlying, overlying, and encompassing all true being.

Triumph over death

"The sting of death is sin, and the power of sin is the law."[2] The law of mortal belief is at war with the facts of immortal Life. Spiritual law says to the grave, "Where, O death, is your victory?"[3] "When the perishable has been clothed with the imperishable, and the mortal with immortality, then the saying that is written will come true: 'Death has been swallowed up in victory.'"[4]

Question. Do Christian Scientists have any religious policy or creed? *Answer.* They do not, if by that term is meant doctrinal beliefs. The following is a brief exposition of the important points, or religious tenets, of divine Science:

1. As followers of Truth, we take the inspired Word of the Bible as our sufficient guide to eternal Life.
2. We acknowledge and respect one supreme and infinite God. We acknowledge God's child, one ideal; we admit the Holy

---

[1]   Prov. 4:18

[2]   I Cor. 15:56

[3]   I Cor. 15:55

[4]   I Cor. 15:54

Spirit or divine Counselor; and we recognize person in God's image and likeness.

3. We acknowledge God's forgiveness of sin in the destruction of sin with the spiritual understanding that drives out evil as unreal. But sin will continue to be self-punished as long as the belief lasts.

4. We acknowledge Jesus' atonement as the evidence of divine, healing Love, unfolding our unity with God through Christ Jesus the Way-shower. We acknowledge that our salvation is through Christ, through Truth, Life, and Love as demonstrated by the Galilean Prophet in healing the sick and overcoming sin and death.

5. We acknowledge that the crucifixion of Jesus and his resurrection served to advance faith to the understanding of eternal Life, to the allness of Soul, Spirit, and the nothingness of matter/energy.

6. And we solemnly promise to be mindful, to pray for that Mind to be in us which was also in Christ Jesus; to do to others as we would have them do to us;[1] and to be merciful, just, and pure.

---

[1] Matt. 7:12

GENESIS

I appeared to Abraham, to Isaac and to Jacob as God Almighty, but by my name the LORD I did not make myself known to them.[1]

Through him all things were made; without him nothing was made that has been made. In him was life, and that life was the light of men.[2]

Spiritual interpretation

Scientific interpretation of the Scriptures starts with the first chapter of the Old Testament, mainly because the spiritual meaning of the Word often seemed smothered by the immediate context and requires explanation. The New Testament narratives, however, are clearer and nearer the heart. Jesus illumines the illustrations. He shows the poverty of mortal existence and the richness of spirituality as a remedy for human needs and questions. The incarnation of Truth, the amplification of wonder and glory which angels could only whisper and which God illustrated by light and harmony, is consonant with ever-present Love. So-called mystery and miracle serve the unfolding of good. The supernatural is explained by that Love which gives rest to the weary. Love does comfort the people who are yearning for something more than the history of perpetual evil.

Spiritual introduction

Minus the first chapter, the book of Genesis includes the history of an untrue image of God, signified as a super-, yet dubious, human being. Spiritually interpreted, this deviation of being can indirectly

---

[1]   Exodus 6:3

[2]   John 1:3-4

point to the proper understanding of God and the spiritual actuality of man and woman, as presented in the first chapter of Genesis. When scientific divine views of the universe appear, the crude forms of human thought take on higher symbols and significations, and time is illuminated with the glory of eternity.

Deviation of being

A second reason for beginning with Genesis is that the living and real prelude of the older Scriptures is so brief that it would almost seem as though the unreal material creation is dominant. However, this is not the case. Spiritual being predominates over the material as light predominates over darkness and the eternal over the temporary.

In the following exegesis, each text is followed by its spiritual interpretation according to the teachings of Christian Science.

> *Genesis 1:1.* In the beginning God created the heavens and the earth.

Ideas and identities

The infinite has no beginning. This word *beginning* is employed to signify *the only*—that is, the eternal truth and unity of God and spiritual being, including the universe. The creative Principle—Life, Truth, and Love—is God. The universe reflects God. There is but one creator and one creation. The one creation consists of the unfolding of spiritual ideas and their identities, which are embraced in the infinite Mind and forever reflected. These ideas range from the infinitesimal to infinity, and the highest ideas are the sons and daughters of God.

> *Genesis 1:2.* Now the earth was formless and empty, darkness was over the surface of the deep, and the Spirit of God was hovering over the waters.

Spiritual harmony

The divine Principle and idea constitute spiritual harmony—heaven and eternity. In the universe of Truth, unpredictability and error are unknown. Finiteness and limitation (matter/energy) have no universe. Divine Science, the Word of God, says to the darkness over the face of error, "God is All-in-all," and the light of ever-present Love illumines the universe. Hence the eternal wonder—that infinite space is peopled with God's ideas, reflecting Being in countless spiritual forms.

> *Genesis 1:3.* And God said, "Let there be light," and there was light.

Mind's idea faultless

Immortal and divine Mind presents the idea of God: first, in light (enlightenment), second, in reflection, third, in spiritual and immortal forms of beauty and goodness. This Mind creates no element or symbol of disorder and decay. God did not create a thought that can go wrong. Spirit did not order a life of mortality. Truth did not design a truth that can mutate into something untrue, and did not reveal a love that can be uncertain.

> *Genesis 1:4.* God saw that the light was good, and he separated the light from the darkness.

God, Spirit, expressing infinite light and harmony from which emanates the true idea, is never reflected by anything but the good.

> *Genesis 1:5.* God called the light "day," and the darkness he called "night." And there was evening, and there was morning—the first day.

Light preceding the sun

The question as to whether or not the divine creation includes matter/energy is answered in this passage, for although solar beams are not yet included in the record of creation, still there is light. This light is not from the sun, not from a nuclear fusion reaction, not from electromagnetic radiation, not from bioluminescence, but is the revelation of Truth and of spiritual ideas. God's light is always available, since Truth, Life, and Love fill immensity and are ever-present. Wasn't this a revelation instead of a creation?

Evenings and mornings

The successive appearing of God's ideas is represented as taking place on so many *evenings* and *mornings*. Evening and morning—separate from the human invention and definition of time—signifies spiritually clearer views of Life, Truth, and Love, views which do not imply the comings and goings of darkness and dawn. Here we have the explanation of another passage of Scripture, that "with the lord a day is like a thousand years."[1] The rays of infinite Truth, when gathered into the focus of ideas, bring light instantaneously. A thousand years of human doctrines, hypotheses, and vague speculations don't emit that kind of brilliance.

Spirit versus darkness

Did infinite Mind create matter, and call it *light?* Spirit is light, and the contradiction of Spirit is matter, darkness, and darkness obscures the light. Material sense is nothing but a supposition of the absence of Spirit. The revolution of the planet does not form a day of Spirit. Spiritual light is always present—is presence—and is not dependent on what humans call time, photons, or sunbeams. Immortal Mind makes its own record, but mortal mind, sleep, dreams, sin, disease, and death have no record in the first chapter of Genesis.

> *Genesis 1:6.* And God said, "Let there be an expanse between the waters to separate water from water."

Spiritual expanse

Spiritual understanding, by which human conception, material sense, is separated from Truth, is the expanse. The divine Mind, not human mind, creates all identities, and they are forms of Mind. The ideas of Spirit are apparent only as Mind, never as mindless matter, never as the so-called material physical senses.

---

[1]   II Peter 3:8

Genesis 1:7. So God made the expanse and separated the water under the expanse from the water above it. And it was so.

Understanding imparted

Soul imparts the understanding which spiritualizes consciousness and leads into all truth. The Psalmist said: "Mightier than the thunder of the great waters, mightier than the breakers of the sea—the LORD on high is mighty."[1] Spiritual perception is the discernment of spiritual good. Understanding is the line of demarcation between the real and unreal. Spiritual understanding unfolds Mind—Life, Truth, and Love—and demonstrates the divine sense, giving the spiritual proof of the universe in divine Science.

Original reflected

Spiritual understanding is not academic, is not the result of scholarly book learning, but is the reality of all things brought to light. God's ideas reflect the immortal, unerring, and infinite. The mortal, erring, and finite are human beliefs, appointing themselves to the impossible task of distinguishing between the false and the true. Objects utterly unlike the original do not reflect that original. Therefore matter, not being the reflection of Spirit, has no real entity. Understanding is a quality of God, a quality which separates divine Science from theories, and makes Truth final.

Genesis 1:8. God called the expanse "sky." And there was evening, and there was morning—the second day.

Exalted thought

Through divine Science, Spirit, God, unites understanding to eternal harmony. The calm and enlightened thought, or spiritual perception, is at peace. Thus the dawn of ideas goes on, forming each successive stage of progress.

---

[1]   Ps. 93:4

Genesis 1:9. And God said, "Let the water under the sky be gathered to one place, and let dry ground appear." And it was so.

Unfolding of thoughts

Spirit, God, gathers unformed thoughts into their proper channels, and unfolds these thoughts, even as Love opens the petals of a holy purpose in order that the purpose may appear.

Genesis 1:10. God called the dry ground "land," and the gathered waters he called "seas." And God saw that it was good.

Spirit names and blesses

In this verse, the human concept and divine idea seem confused by the translator, but they are not so in the scientifically spiritual meaning of the text. In metaphor, the *dry ground* illustrates the absolute formations instituted by Mind. *Water* symbolizes the elements of Mind, such as beauty and grace. Spirit appropriately feeds and clothes every object, as it appears in the line of spiritual revelation, thus tenderly expressing the motherhood and fatherhood of God. Spirit names and blesses all. Without natures particularly defined, objects and subjects would be obscure and creation would be full of nameless offspring—wanderers from the parent Mind, strangers in a tangled wilderness. Even the pleasing task of finding names for all material things was supposedly passed down to Adam; however, Adam hasn't yet appeared in the narrative.

Genesis 1:11. Then God said, "Let the land produce vegetation: seed-bearing plants and trees on the land that bear fruit with seed in it, according to their various kinds." And it was so.

Divine propagation

The universe of Spirit reflects the powerful creativity of the divine Principle, or Life, which reproduces the multitudinous forms of Mind and governs the increase of the multifaceted idea of spiritual being. The tree and vegetation do not yield fruit because of any propagating power of their own, but because they reflect the Mind which includes all. A material world implies a human mind and person as creator. The scientific divine creation declares immortal Mind and the universe created by God.

Ever-appearing creation

Infinite Mind creates and governs all, from the mental molecule to infinity. This divine Principle of all expresses Science and art throughout Spirit's entire work including the immortality of spiritual being and the universe. Creation is always appearing, and must always continue to appear from the nature of its inexhaustible source. Mortal sense inverts this appearing and calls ideas material. Thus misinterpreted, the divine idea seems to fall to a level of human or material belief, called mortal human being. The seed is in itself, only as the divine Mind is All and reproduces all—as Mind is the multiplier, and Mind's infinite idea, person and the universe, is the result. The only intelligence or substance of a thought, a seed, or a flower is God, the creator of it. Mind is the Soul of all. Mind is Life, Truth, and Love which governs all.

> *Genesis 1:12.* The land produced vegetation: plants bearing seed according to their kinds and trees bearing fruit with seed in it according to their kinds. And God saw that it was good.

Mind's pure thought

Kind (sort) does not necessarily refer either to a masculine or feminine gender. *Kind* is not confined to sexuality, and grammars usually recognize a neuter gender, neither male nor female. God determines the gender (kind) of Soul's ideas. Gender is mental, not physical. The seed within itself is the pure thought emanating from divine Mind. The intelligent individual idea, ever-ascending, unfolds the infinitude of Love.

> *Genesis 1:13.* And there was evening, and there was morning—the third day.

Rising to the light

The third stage in the order of divine Science is important to human thought, letting in the light of spiritual understanding. This stage parallels the resurrection, when Spirit is discerned to be the Life of all, and that the deathless Life, Mind, is not dependent on material organization. To the comprehension of his students, Jesus rose from the grave, or rather, on the third day of his ascending thought, Jesus reappeared, and so presented to them the certain sense of eternal Life.

> *Genesis 1:14.* And God said, "Let there be lights in the expanse of the sky to separate the day from the night, and let them serve as signs to mark seasons and days and years.

Expansion of thought

Spirit creates no other than heavenly or celestial bodies, but outer space is no more celestial than our earth. This text gives the idea of the diffusion of thought as it expands. Divine Mind forms and peoples the universe. The light of spiritual understanding gives glints of the infinite, even as black holes indicate the immensity of space.

Divine nature appearing

Mineral, vegetable, and animal substances are no more contingent now on time or material structure than they were "while the morning stars sang together."[1] Mind made the "plant of the field"[2] before it appeared on the earth. The events of spiritual ascension are the days and seasons of Mind's revelation, in which beauty, magnificence, purity, and holiness (the divine nature) appear in spiritual beings and the universe, never to disappear.

Spiritual ideas comprehended

Knowing the Science of creation, in which all is Mind and its ideas, Jesus rebuked the materialist thought of the people: "You

[1] Job 38:7
[2] Gen. 2:5 (NASB)

hypocrites! You know how to analyze the appearance of the earth and the sky, but why do you not analyze this present time?"[1] We may be able to sequence the human genome, but wouldn't we rather seek and know the thoughts behind the genes? To discern the rhythm of Spirit and to be holy, thought must be purely spiritual.

> *Genesis 1:16.* God made two great lights—the greater light to govern the day and the lesser light to govern the night. He also made the stars.

Geology a failure

The sun metaphorically represents Soul, outside the body, giving existence and intelligence to the universe. Love alone can impart the limitless idea of infinite Mind. Geology, chemistry, physics, astronomy, cosmology, or biology, do not really explain nature's patterns and relationships. There is no Scriptural hint that solar light preceded time. The allusion to liquids (Genesis 1:2) indicates a supposed formation of matter by the congealing of energy into matter, analogous to the supposed resolving of thoughts into material things.

Spiritual subdivision

Light symbolizes Mind, Life, Truth, and Love. Light is not a vitalizing property of matter. Science reveals only one Mind, and this one shining by its own light and governing the universe, including spiritual beings, in perfect harmony. Spirit, Mind forms its own images, subdivides and radiates their borrowed light or intelligence, and so explains the Scripture paraphrase, the seed is in itself. Thus God's ideas "increase in number" and "fill the earth."[2] Divine Mind supports the resplendency, magnitude, and infinitude of Her spiritual work.

> *Genesis 1:17-18.* God set them in the expanse of the sky to give light on the earth, to govern the day and the night, and to separate light from darkness. And God saw that it was good.

---

[1] Matt. 16:3; Luke 12:56 (NASB)
[2] Gen. 1:28

Darkness scattered

In divine Science, which is the signature of Deity and has the impression of heaven, God is revealed as infinite light. In the eternal Mind there is no darkness.

> *Genesis 1:19.* And there was evening, and there was morning—the fourth day.

The progressive brilliance and intense radiance of God's infinite ideas, or images, mark the periods of progress.

> *Genesis 1:20.* And God said, "Let the water teem with living creatures, and let birds fly above the earth across the expanse of the sky."

Soaring aspirations

To human mind, the universe is ether, liquid, and dense. Spiritually interpreted, rocks and mountains stand for solid and grand ideas. Animals and mortals metaphorically present the development of human thought, advancing in intelligence, taking form in neuter, androgynous, masculine, or feminine gender. The birds, which fly above the earth in the open expanse of heaven, correspond to aspirations soaring beyond and above limited concepts to the understanding of the unlimited and divine Principle, Love.

> *Genesis 1:21.* So God created the great creatures of the sea and every living and moving thing with which the water teems, according to their kinds, and every winged bird according to its kind. And God saw that it was good.

Angelic symbols

Spirit is symbolized by strength, presence, power, and also by holy thoughts, winged with Love. These angels of Soul's presence, which have the holiest responsibility, abound in the spiritual atmosphere of Mind and consequently reproduce their own characteristics. Their individual forms we know not, but we do know that their natures are allied to God's nature; and spiritual blessings, thus typified, are the externalized, yet subjective, states of faith and spiritual understanding.

> *Genesis 1:22.* God blessed them and said, "Be fruitful and increase in number and fill the water in the seas, and let the birds increase on the earth."

Multiplication of pure ideas

Spirit blesses the multiplication of its own pure and complete ideas. From the infinite elements of the one Mind emanate all form, color, quality, and quantity, and these are mental, both primarily and secondarily. Their spiritual nature is discerned only through the spiritual senses. On the other hand, mortal mind skews the true likeness, and then attaches demeaning names and natures upon its own misconceptions. Ignorant of the origin and operations of mortal mind—that is, ignorant of itself—this so-called mind puts forth its own qualities and claims God as their author. The haughty human mind, however, can only pretend to interfere with infinity. God's infinite nature precludes knowing measurable. God is so completely aware of the infinite that even a hint of ignorance, pretense, or mortal mentality is impossible.

> *Genesis 1:23.* And there was evening, and there was morning—the fifth day.

Spiritual spheres

Again, in the narrative, time is still not measured by solar revolutions, but by spiritually clearer views of Truth (evenings and mornings). The motions and reflections of deific power cannot be comprehended until divine Science becomes the interpreter. Advancing spiritual steps in the teeming universe of Mind, leads to spiritual spheres and beings, however, the divine universe is hidden and mysterious to materialist sense. Metaphysical Science lifts the curtain and the scene shifts into light.

Genesis 1:24. And God said, "Let the land produce living creatures according to their kinds: livestock, creatures that move along the ground, and wild animals, each according to its kind." And it was so.

Continuity of thoughts

Spirit diversifies, classifies, and individualizes all thoughts, which are as eternal as the Mind conceiving them. The intelligence, existence, and continuity of all individuality remain in God, who is the divinely creative Principle thereof.

Genesis 1:25. God made the wild animals according to their kinds, the livestock according to their kinds, and all the creatures that move along the ground according to their kinds. And God saw that it was good.

God's thoughts are spiritual realities

God creates all appearances of reality. God's thoughts are spiritual realities. The human mind cannot simulate God's power by inverting the divine creation and afterward recreating persons or things in its own dimensions. The human mind has no real existence, since nothing exists beyond the expanse of all-inclusive perpetuity, infinite God. In humble contentment, Mind's infinite ideas manifest Life, happily realizing fulfillment.

Qualities of thought

Moral courage is "the Lion of the tribe of Judah,"[1] the king of the mental realm. Free and fearless it roams in the forest. Spiritual courage rests in the open field, undisturbed in "green pastures . . . beside quiet waters."[2] In the figurative transmission from the divine thought to the human, diligence, promptness, and perseverance are likened to "the cattle on a thousand hills."[3] They carry the baggage of stern resolve, and keep pace with the highest purpose. Patience is symbolized by the

---

[1] Rev. 5:5

[2] Ps. 23:2

[3] Ps. 50:10

tireless worm, creeping over lofty summits, persevering in its intent. The snake of God's creating is not subtle or poisonous, but is a wise idea, delightful in its dexterity. Love's ideas are subject to the Mind which constructs them—the power which changes the snake into a staff.[1]

Tenderness accompanies all the might imparted by Spirit. The individuality created by God is not carnivorous, as witness the millennial estate pictured by Isaiah:

> The wolf will live with the lamb,
> The leopard will lie down with the goat,
> The calf and the lion and the yearling together;
> And a little child will lead them.[2]

God's creatures are useful

Daniel felt safe in the lion's den[3] because he understood the control which Love held over all ideas. Paul proved the viper to be harmless.[4] All of God's creatures, moving in the harmony of Science, are harmless, useful, and indestructible. A realization of this excellent truth is a source of strength. It supports Christ-like healing, and enables its possessor to emulate the example of Jesus. "God saw all that he had made, and it was very good."[5]

> *Genesis 1:26.* Then God said, "Let us make man in our image, in our likeness, and let them rule over the fish of the sea and the birds of the air, over the livestock, over all the earth, and over all the creatures that move along the ground."

---

[1] Ex. 7:10

[2] Isa. 11:6

[3] Dan. 6

[4] Acts 28:3-5

[5] Gen. 1:31

Elohistic plurality

The eternal Elohim includes the forever universe. The name Elohim is in the plural, but this plurality of Spirit does not imply more than one God. It also does not imply three persons in one. It relates to the oneness, the singleness of Life, Truth, and Love. The idiom *man* is used as a generic name for all people, or ideas; however, the term *man* is becoming obsolete. Gender-inclusive language predominates. The terms man and woman, spiritual being, living being, or person, are today more commonly used to denote the child of God, expressing countless attributes and moving in accord with Spirit, reflecting goodness and power. "Let them rule."[1]

Reflected likeness

Your mirrored reflection is your own image or likeness. If you lift a weight, your reflection does this also. If you speak, the lips of this likeness move in sync with yours. Now call the mirror divine Science, and call person the reflection. Compare spiritual being (man and woman) to divine Principle, God. How close, in Science, is the reflection to the original? As the reflection of yourself appears in the mirror, so you, being spiritual, are the reflection of God. The substance, Life, intelligence, Truth, and Love, which constitute Deity, are reflected by Mind's creation. When we subordinate the false testimony of the bodily senses to the facts of Science, we will see this true likeness and reflection everywhere.

Love imparts beauty

All things are fashioned by, and after, God's own likeness. Life is reflected in existence, Truth in truthfulness, God in goodness. They impart their own peace and permanence. Love, fragrant with unselfishness, bathes all in beauty and light. The grass beneath our feet silently exclaims, "Happy are those who claim nothing, for the whole earth will belong to them!"[2] The sturdy trumpet vine sends her sweet breath to heaven. The great rock gives shadow and shelter. The sunlight flows into the church and prison cell, glides into the sick room, brightens the earth, beautifies the landscape and blesses the

---

[1] Gen 1:26
[2] Matt. 5:5 (Phillips NT)

galaxy. Not human beings, but living beings, made in Soul's likeness, possess and reflect God's dominion to bless the environment. In glorified quality, man and woman as coexistent and eternal with God forever reflect the infinite Father-Mother God.

> *Genesis 1:27.* So God created man in his own image, in the image of God he created him; male and female he created them.

Ideal man and woman

Again: the word m*an* has a generic meaning, signifying the one perfect nature of person or spiritual being. Today's common use of *man*, defined as human males, narrows and confuses the original meaning. However, we can recapture a broader perspective, where the word *man is* connected with the root **men*—"to think" (cognate to *mind*). The life-giving quality of Spirit is Mind, not human mind. The ideal thoughtful person corresponds to intelligence, to reality, Truth, Life, and Love, not to mortal males. In divine Science, we have no more authority to consider God male as we have to consider God female, for Love imparts the clearest idea of Deity. We can interpret Genesis one, verse twenty-seven, as repeating the momentous thought that God made man and woman (person, spiritual being) in Spirit's image.

The generic term *man* has not only been restricted in its definition, but it also has been weakened by anthropomorphism or humanization of God. The word *anthropomorphic* is derived from two Greek words, signifying *human* and *shape*. Biblical literalism has mentally attempted to reduce God to a physical anatomy, with fleshly organs, and human passions. This picture of a humanlike God is naturally resisted by our inner being; therefore, gender-neutral alternatives to the word *man* have been demanded. (See also: *Definitions of person,* page 450)

Divine personality

The world believes in many persons, but if God is personal, there is only one person, because there is only one God. Soul's personality can only be reflected, not sent from one person to another. God has countless ideas, and they all have one Principle and parentage. The only proper symbol of God as person is Mind's infinite ideal. What is this ideal? Who will behold it? This ideal is God's own image, spiritual and infinite. Eternity cannot even reveal the whole of God, since there is no limit to its infinite reflections.

> *Genesis 1:28.* God blessed them and said to them, "Be fruitful and increase in number; fill the earth and subdue it. Rule over the fish of the sea and the birds of the air and over every living creature that moves on the ground."

Our birthright

Divine Spirit blesses its own ideas, and causes them to multiply— to manifest Love's power. We are not made subordinate to matter/ energy. We also are not made to dominate. Our dominion is to respect and care for all the symbols of God, the Maker; this is the Science of being.

> *Genesis 1:29-30.* Then God said, "I give you every seed-bearing plant on the face of the whole earth and every tree that has fruit with seed in it. They will be yours for food. And to all the beasts of the earth and all the birds of the air and all the creatures that move on the ground—everything that has the breath of life in it—I give every green plant for food." And it was so.

Brotherhood and sisterhood

Love is the source of might, immortality, and goodness, which shine through all as the blossom shines through the bud. God's ideas are simple, yet great, and through a sharing process these ideas are strengthened, and found to be interconnected, as they have the same Principle, or Parent. Happy is the person who sees the need of others and supplies it, seeking his or her own supply in someone else's good. All the diverse expressions of God reflect health, holiness, immortality—infinite Life, Truth, and Love.

Genesis 1:31. God saw all that he had made, and it was very good. And there was evening, and there was morning—the sixth day.

Perfection of creation

The divine Principle, or Spirit, comprehends and expresses all, and all must therefore be as perfect as the divine Principle is perfect. Nothing is new to Spirit. Nothing can be novel to eternal Mind, the author of all things, who from all eternity knows His own ideas. Love is satisfied with Truth's work. How could the Perfect be unsatisfied? The spiritual creation is the result, the outflow of Father-Mother's infinite self-containment and immortal wisdom.

Genesis. 2:1. Thus the heavens and the earth were completed in all their vast array.

Infinity measureless

Science reveals infinity and the fatherhood and motherhood of Love, therefore, the ideas of God in universal being are complete and forever expressed. Human ability is slow to perceive and realize God's creation and the divine power and presence which go with it (demonstrating its spiritual origin). Mortals can never know the infinite until they throw off the old self and reach the spiritual image and likeness. What can fathom infinity! How can we describe God, Life, "Until we all reach unity in the faith and in the knowledge of the Son of God and become mature, attaining to the whole measure of the fullness of Christ"?[1]

Genesis 2:2. By the seventh day God had finished the work he had been doing; so on the seventh day he rested from all his work.

---

[1] Eph. 4:13

Resting in holy work

God rests in action. Imparting has not impoverished and can never impoverish the divine Mind. As understood in divine Science, no exhaustion follows the action of this Mind. The most satisfying and sweetest rest, even from a human standpoint, is in holy work.

Love and man and woman coexistent

Immeasurable Mind is expressed. The depth, breadth, height, might, majesty, and glory of infinite Love fill all space. That is enough! Human language can repeat only an infinitesimal part of what exists. The absolute ideal, person, is no more seen or comprehended by mortals than is the infinite Principle, Love. Principle and its idea, spiritual being, are coexistent and eternal. The numbers of infinity, called seven days, can never be computed according to calendar time. Spiritual days will appear as mortality disappears, and they will reveal eternity, newness of Life, in which all erroneous conclusions forever disappear and thought accepts the divine infinite calculus.

> *Genesis 2:4-5.* This is the account of the heavens and the earth when they were created. When the Lord God made the earth and the heavens—and no shrub of the field had yet appeared on the earth and no plant of the field had yet sprung up, for the Lord God had not sent rain on the earth and there was no man to work the ground.

Growth is from Mind

Here is the emphatic declaration that God creates all through Mind, not through matter (human mind). The plant grows not because of seed or soil or bioengineering, but because growth is the eternal rule of Mind. The immortal creative thought is from Mind, not from the ground of mortal thinking. Mind makes all, so there is nothing left to be made by another power. Spirit acts through the Science of Mind, never causing people to cultivate mortal thinking. Knowing this fact, we can overcome physical limitations and a mortal view of earth and its environments, and discover conscious spiritual harmony and eternal being.

Here the inspired record closes its narrative of being that is without beginning or end. All that was made is the work of God, and all is good. This brief glorious history, the spiritual creation, is left in the hands of God, not of man or woman, in the keeping of Spirit, not matter. Now and forever, we joyfully acknowledge God's supremacy, omnipotence, and omnipresence.

The harmony and immortality of person are intact. We should keep our gaze on the spiritual record and not become entranced by the material creation. It is best to keep turning our attention to the spiritual record of revelation, to that which should be engraved on the understanding and heart, "with the point of a diamond"[1] and the pen of an angel.

If the reader asks for more than the spiritual record, another record is also found in Genesis. But the continued account is mortal, temporary, involving confusion and limitation. Let's take a look at it.

Genesis 2:6. But streams came up from the earth and watered the whole surface of the ground.

The story of error

The Science and truth of the divine creation have been presented in the verses already discussed, and now an erroneous view of creation is considered. The second chapter of Genesis contains a fateful view of God and the universe. Its statement opposes the scientific truth as previously recorded. The history of error or matter, if true, would negate the omnipotence of Spirit, but it is only an illusory history in contradistinction to inescapable reality.

The two records

The Science of the first record proves the falsity of the second. If one is true, the other is false, for they contradict one another. The first record assigns all might and government to God, and establishes person by God's perfection and power. The second record chronicles man and woman as changeable and mortal—as able to outwit God and live in some dimension separate from Mind, revolving in an orbit

---

[1]   Jer. 17:1, KJV

of its own. Science explains as impossible an existence divorced from God.

This second record unmistakably gives the history of error in its externalized forms called living matter/energy. This state of things and people is declared to be temporary—dust returning to dust. Basically, it's a record of pantheism, challenging the supremacy of Spirit.

Erroneous representation

In the erroneous theory where matter takes the place of Spirit, matter is represented as the life-giving principle of the earth. Spirit is represented as entering matter in order to create man and woman. However, people are denounced when not found in the likeness of Spirit, and this indirectly convinces reason and coincides with revelation to declare this material creation false.

Hypothetical reversal

This latter part of the second chapter of Genesis, which portrays Spirit as supposedly cooperating with matter in constructing the universe, is based on some hypothesis of error. Scripture already declared God's work to be finished. Does the infallible Principle of divine law change or repent? Does the Maker condemn its own likeness? Do Life, Truth, and Love produce death, error, and hatred? An unintelligent reading of this Scriptural account may say so, however, Principle can't deviate.

Mist or false claim

Error evolves a stream, or mist, or fog, which obscures God's perfect creation, thereby leading to an unsound infrastructure which declares that God knows error and that error can improve Truth's creation. Although error is presenting a distorted picture, it claims to be truth. The creations of matter come from a mist or false assertion. Temporal things do not come from the expanse of understanding, which God established between the true and false. In error everything comes from that which is fallible, not infallible. Whatever is not the reflection of Spirit is myth.

Distinct documents

It may be worthwhile here to remark that there is evidence of two distinct documents in the early part of the book of Genesis. One is called the Elohistic, because the Supreme Being is therein called

Elohim. The other document is called Yahwistic, because the Supreme Being is called the Lord God, as many of our Bible versions have translated it.

Elohim versus Yahweh

Throughout the first chapter of Genesis and in three verses of the second—in what we understand to be the spiritually scientific account of creation—it is Elohim (Almighty) who creates. From the fourth verse of chapter two to chapter five, the creator is called the Lord, or Yahweh. The distinctions become harder to recognize up to chapter twelve, after which the difference is not traceable. In the historic parts of the Old Testament it is usually the Lord, a divine sovereign, who is referred to.

Gods of mythology

The idolatry which followed this material mythology is seen in the Phoenician worship of Baal, in the Moabitish god Chemosh, in the Molech of the Amorites, in the Hindu Vishnu, in the Greek Aphrodite, and in a thousand other so-called deities.

Yahweh a tribal (ethnicity) deity

Idolatry caused some people to go after "foreign gods."[1] They called the Supreme Being by the national name of Yahweh. In that name of Yahweh, the true idea of God seems almost lost. God becomes "a warrior,"[2] a tribal god to be worshipped, rather than Love, the divine Principle to be lived and honored.

> *Genesis 2:7.* The Lord God formed the man from the dust of the ground and breathed into his nostrils the breath of life, and the man became a living being.

Creation reversed

Did the divine and infinite Principle become a separate super-power or finite deity, that He should now be called the Lord God? With a single command, Mind had made spiritual being with both feminine and masculine qualities. How then could a physical

[1] Deut. 32:16
[2] Ex. 15:3

organization become the basis of person? How can non-intelligence be the medium of Mind, or error be the announcer of Truth? The human mind is not the reflection of Mind, yet God is reflected in Mind's entire creation. Is this historical account in chapter two, real or unreal? Is it the truth, or is it a lie concerning person and God? It must be a lie, for in the next chapter the Lord will curse the ground.

Could Spirit evolve an opponent, matter? Can Mind give human mind the ability to sin and suffer? Is Spirit, God, injected into dust, and eventually ejected at the demand of matter/energy? Does Spirit enter dust, and lose therein the divine nature and omnipotence? Does Mind enter human mind to become there a mortal sinner, animated by the breath of God? In this second narrative, the validity of matter is opposed. The legitimacy of Spirit or Spirit's work is affirmed. Person (even the essence of humanity) reflects God; mortal humankind represents the fleshly race and is a mortal creation, not a divine revelation.

Definitions of person

In the late 20th century, society began using the words *person* or *people* as a gender-neutral alternative to *man. Person* is defined as a *human being,* or *individual.* One train of thought goes from human being to a physical mortal being. Another train of thought, keeping in the metaphysical track, goes from human being to humane being to spiritual being. A human being is of the species *Homo sapiens* (Lat. *Sapiens,* to be wise, rational). The term *human* is identified with the word *humane,* indicating a humane person. Some Bible versions, in the first chapter of Genesis, say God created "human beings," not meaning self-centered egotistical mortals, but a humane person. "A person is defined by philosophers as a being who is in possession of a range of psychological capacities that are regarded as both necessary and sufficient to fulfill the requirements of personhood. These are, in general, that it is capable of reasoning, that it is self-conscious, and that is has an identity that persists through time."[1] The humanity of human beings is valid. Reader, keep in mind, that human terminology and definitions change, but we have the capacity to reason correctly,

---

[1]   http://en.wikipedia.org/wiki/Person Accessed 11/3/2006.

adjust, and identify with the spiritual meaning.¹ For example, referring back to Genesis chapter one, we could contemplate this interpretation: So Mind created consciousness in his own image, reflecting Mind, he created them male and female.

No harmful creation

In the Gospel of John, it is declared that all things were made through the Word of God, "without him [the *logos,* or *word*] was not anything made that was made."² Everything good or worthy, God made. Spirit did not make whatever is worthless or destructive and therefore we can prove its unreality. In the Science of Genesis we read that Mind saw everything "and it was very good."³ If we give the same attention to the history of error as to the record of truth, the Scriptural documentation of sin and death will appear to favor the flawed logic of the human perceptions. However, sin, sickness, and death are as void of reality as they are void of good, God.

> *Genesis 2:9.* And the Lord God made all kinds of trees grow out of the ground—trees that were pleasing to the eye and good for food. In the middle of the garden were the tree of life and the tree of the knowledge of good and evil.

Contradicting first creation

The previous and more scientific record in Genesis chapter one, declared that "the land produced vegetation."⁴ This scientific teaching is being contradicted with a declaration that life comes from matter, "out of the ground." This belief in intelligent matter, then theorizes that hearing, sight, touch, taste, and smell originate in molecular compounds, thereby making the product automatically vulnerable to mutation, to unsatisfied appetites and passions, and to crime, bad health, and death, as it Belief is less than understanding.

---

1 Updated "definition of person" by Cheryl Petersen
2 John 1:3 (KJV) (Brackets added by Mary Baker Eddy)
3 Gen. 1:31
4 Gen. 1:12

Record of error

All that Spirit made was pronounced good and Spirit created all. The "tree of life"[1] stands for the idea of Truth. The sword which guards this tree represents divine Science. The "tree of knowledge"[2] stands for the erroneous doctrine that the knowledge of evil is as real, therefore as God-given, as the knowledge of good. Was evil established through God, Love? Did Soul create this sin producing tree to contradict the "trees bearing fruit with seed in it according to their kinds"[3]—that God saw as good? Evil is not mentioned in the legendary Scriptural text until the second chapter of Genesis. This second biblical account is a picture of error throughout.

> *Genesis 2:15.* The Lord God took the man and put him in the Garden of Eden to work it and take care of it.

Garden of Eden

In this text "Eden" stands for the mortal, material body. God could not put Mind into matter. God could not put infinite Spirit into finite forms, to domesticate it—to make it beautiful or cause it to live and grow. The name Eden, according to *Nelson's New Illustrated Bible Dictionary*[4] and *HarperCollins Dictionary*,[5] means "delight." Eden is also identified with the Hebrew word meaning "luxury" or "pleasure." God could not put life into unstable matter to make it pleasing or cause it to live and grow. Spiritual being, as God's reflection, doesn't need sophistication, but is always beautiful and complete.

> *Genesis 2:16-17.* And the Lord God commanded the man, "You are free to eat from any tree in the garden; but you

---

1 Gen. 2:9
2 Gen. 2:9
3 Gen. 1:12
4 *Nelson's New Illustrated Bible Dictionary.* General Editor, Ronald F. Youngblood. Tennessee: Thomas Nelson, Inc., 1995.
5 *The HarperCollins Bible Dictionary.* General Editor Paul J. Achtemeier. New York: HarperCollins, 1996.

must not eat from the tree of the knowledge of good and evil, for when you eat of it you will surely die."

No temptation from God

The metaphor now represents God, Love, as tempting people, but the Apostle James says: "God cannot be tempted by evil, nor does he tempt anyone."[1] It is the knowledge of evil which would make us into mortal human beings. Mortal perception, gathered from human education and experiences, make up evil and mortal knowledge. Can it be true that God, good, made "the tree of life"[2] to be the tree of death to Spirit's own creation? Does evil have the reality of good? Evil is unreal because it is a lie—false in every statement.

> *Genesis 2:19.* Now the Lord God had formed out of the ground all the beasts of the field and all the birds of the air. He brought them to the man to see what he would name them; and whatever the man called each living creature, that was its name.

Existence's counterfeit

Here the lie represents God as repeating creation, but doing so materially, not spiritually, and asking a prospective sinner to help. Is the Supreme Being regressing, and is God's child giving up dignity? Was it requisite for the formation of beings that dust should become sentient? Beholding the creations of his dream, calling his inventions real and God-given, Adam—alias error—gives them names. Afterward he is supposed to become the basis of the creation of woman and of his own kind, calling them humankind—that is, a kind of human. That Adam provided the name and nature of animals is solely mythological and material. It also cannot be true that man was ordered to partner up with God and create new people. A Maker other than Spirit is a fiction, a fabrication. God already made and knows every identity.

---

[1]   James 1:13
[2]   Gen. 2:9

Genesis 2:21-22. So the Lord God caused the man to fall into a deep sleep; and while he was sleeping, he took one of the man's ribs and closed up the place with flesh. Then the Lord God made a woman from the rib he had taken out of the man, and he brought her to the man.

Hypnotic surgery

Here error credits Mind, God, with inducing a sleep or hypnotic state in order to perform a surgical operation, thereby creating woman from man. This is the first record of hypnotism, beginning creation with darkness instead of light, materially rather than spiritually. Error, darkness, is attempting to simulate the work of Truth, mock Love, and announce what great things error has done.

Mental midwifery

Interestingly, the idea of mental surgery is introduced here, an idea that may be useful to the medical field. A rib was removed and the flesh was closed up without instruments. But notice, how later in human history, as the knowledge of good and evil replicated itself, instruments became more widely used to assist with the birth of human beings. Obviously, the method of multiplication changes throughout history and will continue to change until our true nature and origin is realized and the dream-existence is destroyed. Revelation reinstates reality, introduces Science and the glorious fact of being, that person proceeds from God. People are God's eternal children, belonging to no lesser parent.

Genesis 3:1-3. Now the serpent was more crafty than any of the wild animals the Lord God had made. He said to the woman, "Did God really say, 'You must not eat from any tree in the garden'?" The woman said to the serpent, "We may eat fruit from the trees in the garden, but God did say, 'You must not eat fruit from the tree that is in the middle of the garden, and you must not touch it, or you will die.'"

Mythical snake

Where does this talking conniving serpent come from? The serpent enters into the metaphor only as evil. We have nothing in the animal kingdom which represents the species described—a talking serpent. So be glad that evil, by whatever figure presented, contradicts itself and has no origin or support in Truth and good. Seeing this, we should have faith to fight all claims of evil because they are worthless and unreal.

Error or Adam

Adam, synonymous with error, stands for a belief of mortal mindedness. Error starts ruling the thinking somewhat mildly and subtly. Human mind then covers a lie with more lies, until its days become shorter. In this confused frame of mind, human beings perceive the spiritual law of Truth as an opposition or threat.

Divine providence

In divine Science, heavenly beings are sustained by God, the divine Principle of being. The earth, at God's command, provides food for our use. Knowing this, Jesus once said, "Do not worry about your life, what you will eat or drink."[1] Jesus didn't tell us not to worry, as if he had some special authority to tell others what to do. He clearly recognized God, the Father-Mother, as able to feed and clothe everyone, just as the lilies are cared for.[2]

> *Genesis 3:4-5.* "You will not surely die," the serpent said to the woman. "For God knows that when you eat of it your eyes will be opened, and you will be like God, knowing good and evil."

Error's assumption

Error is shown to be always asserting its superiority over truth. A liar will always try to make Christian Science look like the liar. Error talks through the human limited perceptions saying: "I can open your eyes. I will do for you what God has not. Serve me and have

---

[1]   Matt. 6:25, 31

[2]   Matt. 6:28; Luke 12:27

another god. Go ahead, admit that I am real. Admit that sin, flesh, and temporal life are more desirable than Truth and I will know you and you will be mine." As long as mistaken concepts are regarded as solid fact, Spirit and flesh have a conflict.

Scriptural allegory

The history of error is a dream-narrative, Adam never woke up. The dream has no reality, no intelligence, and no mind; therefore the dreamer and dream are one, but not true or real. Think about it. *First,* this narrative supposes that something comes from nothing (dust), that matter precedes mind. *Second,* it supposes that mind enters matter, and matter becomes living, substantial, and intelligent. The order of this allegory—everything starting from dust instead of Mind— is maintained in all the subsequent forms of belief. It is a mistake to assume we started materially, or that non-intelligence becomes intelligence, or that mind and soul are right and wrong simultaneously.

Higher hope

It is better for hope to prophesy that the human mind will sometime ascend above all limited and physical sense. As dimensional and unreliable views are exchanged for spiritual perception, human concepts are advanced. The divine consciousness is experienced and person recognizes their God-given dominion and being.

Biological inventions

If the first person did originate in non-intelligent dust, and mind was afterward put into body, then why isn't this divine order still maintained? Who will say that atoms, cells, or mammals have a propagating property of their own? How can we say that God is in matter or that matter exists without God? Did people seek out other creative inventions and so change the method of our Maker?

What establishes Life? Does matter/energy, or Mind, establish Life? Does Life begin with human mind or with Mind? Is Life sustained by material molecules or by Spirit? Certainly not by both, since flesh wars against Spirit and the flesh can take no cognizance of Spirit. At no point does the theory of material life resemble the scientific record of spiritual beings as described in the first chapter of Genesis. Did God at first create one person unaided, but afterward require Adam, or the union of the two sexes, or biotechnology, in order to create the rest of the human family? No! God made and governs all.

Progeny cursed

All human knowledge and perception must be acquired through the five fleshly senses. Is this knowledge safe, when eating its first fruits brought death? "For when you eat of it you will surely die,"[1] was the prediction in the story under consideration and Adam and his progeny felt cursed, not blessed. In the presence of divine Spirit (Father-Mother), the dream existence feels condemned and reverts back to dust.

> *Genesis 3:9-10.* But the Lord God called to the man, "Where are you?" He answered, "I heard you in the garden, and I was afraid because I was naked; so I hid."

Shame the effect of sin

Knowledge and pleasure, evolved through physical sense, produce the immediate mindset of fear and shame. Uncomfortable in the presence of Truth, human knowledge becomes confused, and people cower and hide when they hear the divine voice calling for their attention. The spiritual call may be paraphrased: "People, where are you? Is Mind restricted to human mind or the brain? Is Mind capable of error as well as of truth, of evil as well as of good, when God is All and is Mind? Is there more than one God, one Mind?"

Fear comes of error

Fear was the first experience of physical awareness. This is how error begins, and this is how the dream of matter will end. Reviewing the allegory, before taking in material knowledge, Adam had no idea his body was naked. The knowledge of good and evil demands that mind will see and feel through matter, the five senses. The first impression human beings had of themselves was one of nakedness and guilt. Can we cover up error? Can we lose our rich inheritance and God's gifts? No! Perfection and dominion were never given to mortal human beings.

---

[1]   Gen. 2:17

Genesis 3:11-12. And he said, "Who told you that you were naked? Have you eaten from the tree that I commanded you not to eat from?" The man said, "The woman you put here with me—she gave me some fruit from the tree, and I ate it."

The beguiling first lie

Adam is attempting to trace all human errors directly or indirectly to God, as if good was the creator of evil. The allegory shows that the talking serpent spun the first lie which beguiles the woman and demoralizes the man. Adam, (alias mortal error) accuses and blames God and woman with his own abandon, basically saying, "The woman you gave me is responsible." According to belief, the rib taken from Adam's side has grown into an evil mind, named woman, who helps man to make sinners more rapidly than he can alone. Is this any kind of help?

The belief in material life and intelligence is growing worse at every step. Error will inflate and morph until it self-destructs. Materiality deteriorates. Materiality is obnoxious. Materiality is found in the decaying flesh which came from Adam to form Eve.

False womanhood

Truth, cross-questioning human beings as to their knowledge of error, finds woman the first to confess her fault. She says, "The serpent deceived me, and I ate."[1] Or, in other words, God and another person are not to blame for my fault. Woman has already learned that the physical perceptions are the serpent. Her humble confession allows her thought to leave behind the belief in a material origin and discern spiritual revelation. This improved consciousness enabled woman to be the mother of Jesus and to see at the tomb the risen Savior, who was soon to manifest the deathless child of God's creating. Humility and a perception of spiritual existence also enabled woman to interpret the Scriptures in their true sense, which reveals the spiritual origin of God's children.

---

[1]   Gen. 3:13

Genesis 3:14-15. So the Lord God said to the serpent, "Because you have done this, 'Cursed are you above all the livestock and all the wild animals! You will crawl on your belly and you will eat dust all the days of your life. And I will put enmity between you and the woman, and between your offspring and hers; he will crush your head, and you will strike his heel.'"

Spirit and flesh

This prophecy has been fulfilled. The Son of the Virgin-mother revealed the remedy for Adam, or error. The Apostle Paul explains the enmity, or warfare, between the idea of divine power which Jesus presented, and human thought which diverts attention away from Spirit.

Paul says in his epistle to the Romans: "The sinful mind is hostile to God. It does not submit to God's law, nor can it do so. Those controlled by the sinful nature cannot please God. You, however, are controlled not by the sinful nature but by the Spirit, if the Spirit of God lives in you."[1]

Bruising sin's head

There will be greater mental opposition to the spiritual, scientific meaning of the Scriptures than there has ever been since the Christian era began. The serpent, limited sense, will strike the heel of the woman—will struggle to destroy the spiritual idea of Love; and the woman, this idea, will crush the head of lust. The spiritual idea has given the understanding a foothold in divine Science. The offspring of Truth and the offspring of error, of understanding and of belief, of Spirit and of matter, are the wheat and weeds which time will separate, the one to be gathered into heavenly places and the other to be burned.

Genesis 3:16. To the woman he said, "I will greatly increase your pains in childbearing; with pain you will give birth to children. Your desire will be for your husband, and he will rule over you."

[1] Rom. 8:7-9

Judgment on error

Divine Science deals its chief blow at the supposed material foundations of life and intelligence. It dooms idolatry. The thinking that we are a god, a creator, or a co-creator must be spiritualized by divine Science. Science unveils the results of sin as materialized in sickness and death. When will we pass through the open gate of divine Science into the heaven of soul, into the heritage of the eternal being? Truth is indeed "the way."[1]

> *Genesis 3: 17-19.* To Adam he said, 'Because you listened to your wife and ate from the tree about which I commanded you, "You must not eat of it," 'Cursed is the ground because of you; through painful toil you will eat of it all the days of your life. It will produce thorns and thistles for you, and you will eat the plants of the field. By the sweat of your brow you will eat your food until you return to the ground, since from it you were taken; for dust you are and to dust you will return."

New earth and no more sea

The way of error is awful to consider. The illusion of sin is without hope or God. If our spiritual gravitation and attraction to the one Father-Mother, in whom "we live and move and exist,"[2] should be lost, and if we should be governed by physical principles instead of divine Principle, by body instead of by Soul, we would be annihilated. Created by flesh instead of by Spirit, starting from matter instead of from God, human beings would be governed by mortality's self. The blind leading the blind, both would fall.

The fall of error

Mortal passions and appetites must end in pain. They are "of few days and full of trouble."[3] Their temporal joys cheat us.

---

[1]   John 14:6
[2]   Acts 17:28 (NASB)
[3]   Job 14:1

Emotionalism and cravings belittle their satisfactions and surround their achievements with thorns.

Mortal mind accepts the erroneous, material conception of life and joy, but the true idea is gained from the immortal side. Humanity may ask, What on earth do we gain through this toil, struggle, and sorrow? We gain by giving up our belief in perishable life and happiness. We gain when the mortal and material return to dust and the immortal is reached.

In the first chapter of Genesis we read: "God called the dry ground 'land,' and the gathered waters he called 'seas.'"[1] In Revelation it is written: "I saw a new heaven and a new earth, for the first heaven and the first earth had passed away, and there was no longer any sea."[2] In St. John's vision, heaven and earth stand for spiritual ideas, and the sea—a symbol of storm-tossed human concepts advancing and receding—is represented as having passed away. The divine understanding is *all*, and there is no other consciousness.

> *Genesis 3:22-24.* And the Lord God said, "The man has now become like one of us, knowing good and evil. He must not be allowed to reach out his hand and take also from the tree of life and eat, and live forever." So the Lord God banished him from the Garden of Eden to work the ground from which he had been taken.

Justice and recompense

Knowledge of evil was never the essence of divinity or the essence of manhood and womanhood. In the first chapter of Genesis, evil has no absolute or relative space, no position, no name (nature). Creation is represented as spiritual, entire, and good. Truth guards the gateway to harmony. "You reap whatever you sow."[3] Sin is its own punishment. Error excludes itself from harmony. Error cultivates its own barren soil and buries itself in the ground, since ground and dust stand for nothingness.

---

[1]   Gen. 1:10

[2]   Rev. 21:1

[3]   Gal. 6:7 (NRSV)

461

Inspired interpretation

No one can reasonably doubt that the purpose of this allegory—the account of human history—is to depict the falsity and the effects of error. Subsequent Bible revelation, when spiritually interpreted, synchronizes with the Science of revelation as recorded in the first chapter of Genesis. Inspired writers interpret the Word spiritually, while the ordinary historian interprets it literally. When the text is literally taken, contradictions appear and divine Love, which blessed the earth and its inhabitants, is represented as changeable. The literal meaning also implies that God withheld from people the opportunity to reform, unless people should improve it and become better. However, that is not the nature of God, who is Love always—Love infinitely wise and altogether lovely, who "is not self-seeking."[1]

Spiritual gateway

Truth should, and does, drive error out of all mortal selfhood. Truth is a two-edged sword, guarding and guiding. Truth places the Cherubim wisdom at the gate of understanding to acknowledge the proper guests. Radiant with mercy and justice, the sword of Truth shines far. It also cannot help but indicate the infinite distance between error and Truth, between the material and spiritual—the unreal and the real.

Contrasted testimony

Before continuing, we can quickly summarize the first three chapters of Genesis. The sun, giving light and heat to the earth, is a figure of divine Life and Love, enlightening and sustaining the universe. The "tree of life"[2] is significant of eternal reality or being. The "tree of knowledge"[3] typifies unreality. The serpent illustrates the illusiveness of error and all that misrepresents God, good. Sin, sickness, and death have no record in the Elohistic introduction of Genesis, in which God creates the heavens, earth, and heavenly beings, or us. Until that which contradicts the truth of being comes

---

[1] I Cor. 13:5

[2] Gen. 2:9

[3] Gen. 2:9

onto the scene, evil has no history. Evil is brought into view as the unreal because it goes against the real and eternal.

> *Genesis 4:1.* Adam lay with his wife Eve, and she became pregnant and gave birth to Cain. She said, "With the help of the Lord I have brought forth a man."

Erroneous conception

This account concerns mortals and the human theory of creation (not immortals or spiritual beings). Human beings and sin have a beginning; therefore they must have an end. The sinless, real person is eternal. Eve's announcement, "With the help of the Lord I have brought forth a man," supposes God to be the author of temporal life or sin. Believing God to be the maker of evil or sin is the illegitimate thinking that commits atrocities. Jesus said evil (devil) is "a murderer from the beginning."[1] Error begins by thinking life is separate from Spirit. This thinking attempts to undermine the stability of immortality, as if life and immortality were something which matter could give and take away.

Only one standard

The high standard of good, of Spirit, of Life, or of Truth, could not be sustained if God produced an opposite such as evil, matter, error, or death. God could never impart an element of evil, and we possess nothing which we have not derived from God. Where then can we find a reason for wrongdoing? Where could we obtain the inclination or power to do evil? Has Spirit handed the government of the universe over to matter, human mind?

A type of falsehood

The Scriptures say that the lie of a material origin and materialistic character, epitomized by the serpent, was condemned—never able to stand with God's creations. It doesn't make sense to say that a lie can integrate with Truth. In parable and argument, the sham of a united good and bad was exposed by the Teacher as self-evidently wrong. Disputing these points with the Pharisees and arguing for the Science

---

[1] John 8:44

of creation, Jesus said: "Do people pick grapes from thornbushes?"[1] Paul asked: "What do righteousness and wickedness have in common? Or what fellowship can light have with darkness? What harmony is there between Christ and Belial?"[2]

Scientific offspring

The divine origin of Jesus gave him more than human power to expound the facts of creation and demonstrate the one Mind which makes and governs person and the universe. The Science of creation, so conspicuous in the birth of Jesus, not only inspired his wisest and least understood sayings, but was also the basis of his marvelous actions. Christ is the offspring of Spirit, and spiritual existence shows that Spirit does not create a wicked person or a human being who lapses into sin, sickness, and death.

Cleansing upheaval

In Isaiah we read: "I bring prosperity and create disaster; I, the Lord, do all these things."[3] The prophet refers to divine law dawning on human consciousness, causing evil and wrong thinking to surface before being reduced to its common denominator, nothingness. The infected system needs to be scanned entirely in order to clean the hard-drive. During moral purification, when the symptoms of evil and illusion are aggravated, we might ignorantly think that the Lord brought about the evil. Thinking it through metaphysically, we ascertain that the discovery of God's law uncovers so-called sin and its effects in order for Truth to annihilate all sense of evil and all power to sin.

Allegiance to Spirit

Science provides "to Caesar what is Caesar's, and to God what is God's."[4] Science says, to the human sense of destructiveness, disease, and fatality, that God never made you. God never made a perception that lacks knowledge of the unlimited God. The purpose of the Hebrew allegory of creation, representing error as assuming a divine character, is to teach human beings never to believe a lie.

---

[1]   Matt. 7:16
[2]   II Cor. 6:14-15
[3]   Isa. 45:7
[4]   Matt. 22:21; Mark 12:17; Luke 20:25

Genesis 4:3-4. In the course of time Cain brought some of
the fruits of the soil as an offering to the Lord. But Abel
brought fat portions from some of the firstborn of his flock.

Spiritual and material

Cain typifies a person who is humanly limited in origin and sense;
he is not the model of Truth and Love. He is the sort of self-absorbed
and shallow person conceived in error and "brought forth in iniquity,"[1]
bringing "some" superficial offering to God. Cain's brother, Abel,
offers to God from the firstborn—offers that which was considered to
have a higher status or prominence—a mind-offering. Jealous of his
brother's gift, Cain seeks Abel's life instead of making his own gift a
higher tribute to the Most High.

Genesis 4:4-5. The Lord looked with favor on Abel and his
offering; but on Cain and his offering he did not look with
favor.

Did God have more favor for the reverence offered through a
gentle animal than for the worship expressed by Cain's fruit? No.
Abel's mind-offering was a more spiritual type of the human concept
of Love than was Cain's tribute.

Genesis 4:8. Cain attacked his brother Abel and killed him.

Brotherhood and sisterhood rupture as soon as we think that life,
substance, and intelligence can be unstable, divided.

Genesis 4:9. Then the Lord said to Cain, "Where is your
brother Abel?" "I don't know," he replied, "Am I my
brother's keeper?"

---

[1] Psm. 51:5 (NASB)

Repudiating brotherhood and sisterhood

Here the serpentine lie changes its story. At first it oversteps divine power, telling us "You will be like God."[1] Now the lie recants, refusing to acknowledge even the human responsibility of brotherhood or sisterhood.

> *Genesis 4:10-11.* The Lord said . . ."Your brother's blood cries out to me from the ground. Now you are under a curse and driven from the ground."

Murder brings its curse

Sin multiplies when we believe life is in matter. If thinking doesn't shift out of the vicious cycle of believing in a temporal life, life is very disheartening and we feel cursed. Error hides behind a lie and excuses guilt, but can't be concealed forever. Even the attitude that tries to justify or hide guilt is punished. People who avoid justice and deny truth tend to perpetuate sin, bring on crime, jeopardize self-control, and mock divine mercy. This human mindset tries to eliminate the spiritual idea, or improved thought, whenever and wherever it appears. It is that same mindset which tried to kill Jesus in order to get rid of Truth. However, Truth, through eternal laws, causes error and sin to betray itself.

> *Genesis 4:15.* The Lord said to him, "Not so; if anyone kills Cain, he will suffer vengeance seven times over." Then the Lord put a mark on Cain so that no one who found him would kill him.

Retribution and remorse

"All who draw the sword will die by the sword."[2] Let Truth uncover and destroy error in God's own way, and let human justice imitate the divine. Sin will receive its full penalty, both for what it is and for what it does. Justice marks the sinner, and teaches human

---

[1]   Gen. 3:5

[2]   Matt. 26:52

beings not to remove the ways and means of God. Cain was envious. To envy's own hell, justice consigns the lie which, to advance itself, breaks God's commandments.

> *Genesis 4:16.* So Cain went out from the Lord's presence and lived in the land of Nod, east of Eden.

Climax of suffering

The misperception of Life as something less than God, with no truth to support it, collapses. This misperception will reach the climax of suffering, yield to Truth and return to dust. However, it is only a mortal person, and not the real person who dies. The image of Spirit can't be effaced, since it is the idea of Truth. The image of Truth doesn't change, but becomes more beautifully apparent at error's demise.

Dwelling in dreamland

In divine Science, the mortal identity is shut out from the presence of God. The fleshly senses can't cognize Spirit. The knowledge filter of human mind—filtering out what doesn't fit into its personal paradigm—can't come into the presence of God, and must live in fantasyland until mortals arrive at the understanding that limited life, with all its sin, sickness, and death, is an illusion, against which divine Science is engaged in a warfare of extermination. The great verities of existence are never excluded by falsity.

We spring from Mind

All error proceeds from what the physical senses have been convinced to accept as real evidence. If people originate from molecules, then someone can say we are primarily dust. May Darwin's theory be correct in thinking apes preceded mortal humans? Morphing minerals and vegetables are found, according to divine Science, to be the creations of erroneous thought, not of matter. Did people then, whom God created with a word, originate in an egg? If Spirit, Mind, made all, what was left for matter to create? Ideas of Truth alone are reflected in the many manifestations of Life, and consequently, we perceive that person is solely from Mind. The belief that matter supports life actually makes Life (God) a human, mortal.

467

Material inception

The text, "The Lord God made the earth and the heavens,"[1] introduces the history of a problematical existence which followed the spiritual revelation. Spirit did not participate in the material creation, wholly apart from God. In God's existence, ideas are productive, obedient to Mind. There is no rain and "no man to work the ground."[2] Life is self-sustained because Mind, not matter, is the Maker. Birth, decay, and death are a spin-off of human limited sense. Spiritual Life doesn't consist of mortal feelings. Life consists of spiritual feelings, and matter can't change the eternal fact that we exist because Life exists. There is no new discovery to the infinite Mind.

First evil suggestion

In Science, Mind doesn't produce matter and matter doesn't produce mind. No human mind has the might or right or wisdom to create or to destroy. All is under the control of the one Mind, God. The first statement about evil—the first suggestion of more than one Mind—is in the fable of the serpent. The facts of creation, as previously recorded in Chapter One, include no suggestive statements.

Material personality

The allegorical serpent is supposed to say, "You will be like God,"[3] but this God must be evolved from the same stuff as dirt. Human-made gods deny immortal and spiritual being. People are the likeness of Spirit. A changeable human personality is not the likeness of Spirit. Therefore, this allegorical person who listens to an allegorical serpent is neither a lesser god nor the image and likeness of the one Almighty God.

Material, erroneous belief reverses understanding and truth. Mistaken thinking declares mind to be in and of matter, so-called mortal life to be Life, and infinity to enter the nostrils so that matter/ energy becomes spiritual. Meanwhile erroneous thinking begins with corporeality as the producer instead of divine Principle, and explains Deity through mortal and finite conceptions.

---

1   Gen. 2:4

2   Gen. 2:5

3   Gen. 3:5

The statement that person "has now become like one of us,"[1] was voiced by the human-made god, not voiced by Truth or Science. Truth and Science are unaware of a fast degenerating material person that had never been divinely conceived.

Mental cultivation

The condemnation of human beings to toil in the ground symbolizes the process where we must mentally work to spiritualize thought until all mortal thinking is destroyed. Heavenly beings, created by God were given dominion over earth bound notions. The notion of a material universe is diametrically opposed to the theory of person as evolved from Mind. Fundamental errors, claiming that which is finite to be a cause, send falsity into all human doctrines and conclusions, and do not credit infinity to Spirit. If error toils in the ground of material theories, existence and happiness are destroyed. Outside of divine Science all is unstable and hypothetical, the opposite of Truth. Yet this false view of God and God's child defiantly demands a blessing.

Erroneous standpoint

Translators of the scientific record of creation often entertain a misinterpretation of being. They believe in the existence of matter, its propagation and power. From that erroneous standpoint, they have a difficult time understanding the nature and operation of Spirit, and sure enough, Scripture seems to be contradictory, when really it is glorious in its spiritual signification. Truth has but one reply to all error—to sin, sickness, and death: "Dust [nothingness] you are and to dust [nothingness] you will return."[2]

Mortality mythical

"As in Adam [error] all die, so in Christ [Truth] all will be made alive."[3] Mortality is a myth, spirituality is real. To imagine that spirit is trapped in matter and at some future time is set free, is mortal belief. Spirit, God is not metamorphic, but is "the same yesterday and

---

1   Gen. 3:22
2   Gen. 3:19; Ecc. 3:20 (Brackets added by Mary Baker Eddy)
3   I Cor. 15:22 (Brackets added by Mary Baker Eddy)

today and forever."[1] If Mind, God, creates error, that error must exist in divine Truth and this assumption of error would overthrow the perfection of God.

No truth from a material basis

Is Christian Science contradictory? Is the divine Principle of creation misstated? Has God no Science to declare Mind, while matter is governed by unerring intelligence? "A mist went up from the earth."[2] This represents error as starting from a good idea but then accumulating false information from mortal standpoints, thereby creating a fog of complications. It supposes God and spiritual being to be manifested only through the bodily senses, although the bodily senses are unable to cognize Spirit or Mind's reflection.

Genesis and Revelation seem more ambiguous than other Scripture because they can't possibly be interpreted from a human standpoint. However, they are transparent because they contain the deep divinity of the Bible.

Dawning of spiritual facts

The Science of Truth and Love is penetrating hard-set beliefs, like rays of light shining "in the darkness, but the darkness has not understood."[3] The proof that the system stated in this book is spiritually scientific resides in the good this system accomplishes, for it cures on a divine demonstrable Principle which may be understood by everyone.

Proof given in healing

If mathematics should present a thousand different examples of one principle, the proof of one example would validate the others. A simple statement of divine Mind's Science, if demonstrated by healing, contains the proof of all here said of Christian Science. If one of the statements is true, every statement must be true, for none depart from the stated system and principle. You can prove for yourself, dear reader, the Science of healing, and so ascertain if I have given you the correct interpretation of Scripture.

---

[1]   Heb. 13:8

[2]   Gen. 2:6 (NKJV)

[3]   John 1:5

Evolution versus creationism

Contradictions are found in both the theories of creationism (Intelligent Design) and evolution. James Watson, in his book, *DNA: The Secret of Life,* wrote, "There are those who will continue to believe humans are creations of God, whose will we must serve, while others will continue to embrace the empirical evidence indicating that humans are the product of many millions of generations of evolutionary change." [1] However, the First Cause did not create something out of nothing, did not create human fleshly beings that must serve a super-humanlike God. Mortal humanity is not the real identity of people. Also, the First Cause did not become changeable only to pass through temporal phases before returning to nothingness. Spirit and spiritual being is reality, is the unified theory.

True theory of the universe

The Scriptures are sacred. Our aim must be to have them understood spiritually, for only by this understanding can truth be gained. The true theory of the universe, including person, is not in material history but in spiritual development. Mental evolution, or ascension, inspires thought to expand to a higher awareness and relinquish a changeable, superficial, mortal theory of the universe. The spiritual and immortal are then adopted through metaphysical improvement.

Scriptural perception

It is this spiritual perception of Scripture, which lifts humanity out of disease and death and inspires faith. "The Spirit and the bride say, 'Come' . . . And let the one who is thirsty come; let the one who wishes take the water of life without cost."[2] Divine Science separates error from truth, and breathes through the sacred pages the spiritual sense of life, substance, and intelligence. In this Science, we discover person in the image and likeness of God. We see that people have never lost their spiritual estate and eternal harmony.

---

[1]   Watson, James, *DNA: The Secret of Life. (*Alfred Knoff, Distributed by Random House, New York: 2003)

[2]   Rev. 22:17 (NASB)

471

The clouds dissolving

When the clouds are heavy, they block the sun's light and heat from our earth. But clouds can disappear. Likewise, as the clouds of physical knowledge dissolve, then spiritual Science will reach our consciousness and experience. Earth has little light or joy before Life is spiritually learned. Every agony of mortal error helps error to destroy itself and we can perceive immortal Truth. This is the new birth going on hourly, by which human beings may entertain angels, the true ideas of God, the spiritual sense of being.

Dynamic research has provided an incredible amount of information and evidence that contradicts the predominant conventional scientific theories concerning our origin. This research as portrayed in films, books, and articles would bless the human race more, if the diviner side was gained, instead of continually debating or questioning only the limited physical sense of animal growth and organization.

Reproduction methods

Natural history is richly endowed by the labors and genius of great people. Modern breakthroughs, biotechnology, in vitro fertilization, and cloning, have brought to light important facts in regard to supposed embryonic life. But, to suppose life germinates in anything other than Mind is a blunder. All theories within the material realm never reach past the temporal. They will finally give place to higher theories and demonstrations.

The lower forms of organisms apparently reproduce sexually or asexually—including binary fission, grafting, and budding. There are even viruses which take control of host cells to reproduce more viruses. Next, there are the plants, animals, and humans which reproduce sexually or originate in a laboratory, proving that sexual activity is detachable from life, love. Biotechnological discoveries will continue to conform to the spiritual fact that life doesn't germinate in an egg, chemical, or atom, before maturing to death. Our theories and experiences will continue to change as programmed human thinking is replaced by spiritual reality.

Should we look at a cell, or DNA, as the starting point of the most complicated bodily structures, including those which we call human? Unless this question is answered with some metaphysical consideration, material research will be random and open to vulnerability.

Don't fall back on material law

The many different ways of reproduction, the genetic modifications, and all the other systems that rely on physics, are endlessly vague and sometimes frightening. Bruce Lipton, Ph.D. uses common sense to move thought into a new biology, saying, "Genes are not destiny! Environmental influences, including nutrition, stress and emotions, can modify those genes, without changing their basic blueprint."[1] We can't be our DNA because it is constantly renewing and dying. Every day, DNA falls off us as dead skin, or it hangs around in our skeleton after we die, so, where is our life? Our individuality and life is metaphysical, known in Mind, in thought.

Deep reaching interrogations

If we came from genes, how did Mind come to human beings? DNA surely does not possess Mind or a consciousness. God is the life or intelligence which forms and preserves the individuality, consciousness, and identity of the universe, of people, and of animals. Spirit cannot become a finite human mind nor be limited to human perceptions. Spirit cannot be developed through something which would resist it. Of what advantage is it then to only investigate material human life, which ends as it begins, in nameless nothingness? The true sense of being and its eternal perfection should appear now, even as it will hereafter.

Stages of existence

Error of thought is reflected in error of action. The obsessive study of material existence—of a beginning and end, with birth, decay, and dissolution as its component stages—hides the true and spiritual Life, and causes our standard to drag behind. If Life has any starting point whatsoever, then the great I AM is a myth. If Life is God, as the Scriptures imply, then Life, Mind, isn't embryonic, isn't a primordial

---

[1] Lipton, Bruce, Ph.D. *The Biology of Belief: Unleashing the power of Consciousness, matter, and miracles.* California: Mountain of Love/Elite Books, 2005. www.brucelipton.com

explosion of dense matter. A particle or physical force is an impossible enclosure for infinite Spirit.

Embryology supplies no instance of one species producing its opposite. A serpent never produces a bird, and a lion doesn't originate a lamb. Hybridization can be freakish and is sometimes fruitful, but it is not so hideous and absurd as supposing that Spirit—the pure, immutable and immortal—can produce the impure and mortal and then live in it. It is only the human perspectives which come up with such absurdities, which are unnatural, impossible, and unreal. Divine Science rejects self-evident impossibilities

The real producer

Either Life produces, or it is produced. If Life is first, it cannot produce its opposite in quality and quantity, and call it mortal humanity. If mortality is first, it cannot breed immortal Life. Like produces like. In natural history, the bird is not the product of a wart hog. In spiritual history, matter is not the progenitor of Mind.

The ascent of species

We are taught that mortals come from cells. Charles Darwin admitted this, but he added that human beings have evolved through all the lower grades of cell organization. Physical evolution can be seen to describe the evolving stages of human thinking, but it still does not acknowledge the method of divine Mind. Evolving human stages are impossible in divine Science. All Science is of God, not of human beings.

How does DNA control all of life's developments? The question amounts to this: How can matter originate or transmit mind? We answer that it can't. Materialists also say that the physical seed must decay in order to propagate its species, while the resulting seed is doomed to the same routine. Deficiency and doubt surround thought as long as it bases creation on physics, biology, time, or space. From a human standpoint, "Can you fathom the mysteries of God?"[1] Everything must be unchangeable Mind, or else everything must be changeable matter. Neither can produce the other. Mind is immortal.

---

[1] Job 11:7

No one knows if the first chicken was created as a chicken or if it came from an egg. What about the beginning of the universe? Did the big bang blow life into being? If so, who or what produced the big bang? Idolatrous philosophies, modern geology, synthetic biology, and all other material hypotheses deal with causation as contingent on matter/energy or time. Cause is also treated as necessarily apparent to the physical senses, even when the evidence to sustain their assumptions is undiscovered. Mortal theories make friends of sin, sickness, and death; whereas the spiritual scientific facts of existence include no aspect of this depressing trio.

Emergence of mortal human beings

Human experience in mortal life, which starts from a cell, corresponds with that of Job, when he says, "Man born of woman is of few days and full of trouble."[1] Human beings must break out of this mental cycle of thinking that material life is all-in-all. They must think outside of the box with divine Science, and look to the infinite cosmos. Be aware though, that thought which escapes the box and has not yet been instructed by the Science of Truth and Love, may become wild with freedom and so be self-contradictory.

Persistence of species

No remedy for depression, sin, and death comes from the bottom-up. The redeeming power is not in a cell, a physical force, chemicals, or human mind. Matter/energy is a materialization of mortal mind. The process of mortal mind is such that it manifests itself but is eventually urged to its furthest limits, only to return to its original stance. Hybrid plants are a good illustration. A hybrid pushed out of its boundaries, will revert back to the parent plant. Matter will always surrender its claims when the perfect and eternal Mind is understood.

Better basis than embryology

K. C. Cole, in her book, *Mind over Matter: Conversations with the Cosmos,*[2] challenges readers to expand their thinking away from

---

[1]   Job 14:1

[2]   *Mind Over Matter: Conversations with the Cosmos,* by K. C. Cole. (Harcourt Books, Florida: 2003)

limited concepts. Biologists and astrophysicists describe the origin of human and material existence in various ways. They accompany their descriptions with important observations such as the mapped genome or the string theory. But why don't these observations awaken thought to a higher and purer contemplation of our origin? Genetic modification doesn't cure the cause of disease. Human thought must obtain a better basis, get nearer the truth of being, or health will never be universal, and harmony will never become the standard. A clearer consciousness must precede an understanding of the harmony of being.

Origin is in thought

Whatever theory is adopted by the mass human thinking, that theory is sure to signal its appearance in form and operation. Take the analogy of Adam and Eve. Adam came from dust. Eve came from a rib. Adam and Eve had sex—joined together and shared information—and this then was believed to be the point of emergence for humans. Centuries later, mass human consciousness changes. Now, biotechnology says multiplication can result in the laboratory. These theories will keep changing; however, matter and materialism began and will end with the human mind.

Being is spiritual

You may say that human beings are formed before they think or know anything of their origin. You may also ask how belief can affect a result which precedes the development of that belief. It can only be replied that divine Science reveals what "No eye has seen"[1]—even the cause of all that exists. The universe, inclusive of person, is as eternal as God, who is their divine immortal Principle. There is no such thing as mortality, nor are there properly any mortal beings, because being is immortal, resembling Spirit—or, rather, spiritual being and Spirit are inseparable.

Our conscious development

Error is always error. It is *no thing.* Any conclusion regarding life as based on a misconception of life is erroneous. False conclusions are destitute of any knowledge of life, destitute of any knowledge of its origin or existence. Human beings are unconscious of their fetal

---

[1]   I Cor. 2:9

and infant states. As they grow into another false claim, that of self-conscious matter, they learn to say, "I am somebody, but who made me?" Error replies, "God made you." The first effort of error has been and is to charge God with the creation of whatever is ultimately doomed. Infinite Mind corrects the mistaken affirmations.

Jesus defined the mendacity of error "as a liar and the father of lies."[1] He also said, "Have I not chosen you, the Twelve? Yet one of you is a devil!"[2] This he said of the human Judas. Jesus never hinted that God made a devil, but he did say, "You belong to your father, the devil."[3] He said these things in order to show that human mortal mind is the producer of itself and a hollow mind, falsely self-justified.

Ailments of animals and pets

It is interesting to note that animals (primates, hominids) who are trained in human knowledge are also more sickly, especially those of the human form. A fair deduction from this observation might be that it is the human thinking, and not divine decision or physical susceptibility, which brings the physical organism into the clutches of disease. There is less disease as the force of mortal mind is less intense or sensitive. Health attends the absence of mortal mind.

Ignorance the sign of error

An inquirer once told me: "I like your explanations of truth, but I do not comprehend what you say about error." This is the nature of error; the mark of ignorance is on its forehead, for it neither understands nor can be understood. Error would have itself received as mind, as if it were as real and God-created as truth, but Christian Science attributes neither entity nor power to error, because error is neither mind nor the effect of Mind.

The origin of divinity

Searching for the origin of people, who are the reflection of God, is like inquiring into the origin of God, the self-existent and eternal. In order for error, sin, disease, and death to have power and existence, they have to try and unite Spirit with matter, good with evil,

---

[1] John 8:44
[2] John 6:70
[3] John 8:44

477

immortality with mortality. Error then calls this sham unity *man and woman,* as if they were the offspring of both Mind and matter, of both Spirit and structural humanity. We lose our standard of perfection and throw out the proper concept of the Almighty when we admit that the perfect is the cause of anything that can become imperfect, that God bestows the power to sin, or that Truth confers the ability to err. Creation rests on a spiritual basis; and this fact allowed Jesus to restore the individualized manifestation of existence which seemed to vanish in death. Knowing that God was the Life of person, Jesus was able to present himself unchanged after the crucifixion. Truth fosters the idea of Truth, displacing the belief in illusion or error. That which is real, is sustained by Spirit.

Genera classified

Athropoda, Chordata, Mollusca, vertebrates, and so on, are human and material concepts classified, supposedly possessing life and mind. These human classifications will disappear when the energy of Spirit destroys forever all belief in intelligent matter. Then will the new heaven and new earth appear, for the former things will have passed away.

The Christian's privilege

Human belief involves the conditions of the unspiritual. Mortal belief dies to live again in renewed forms, only to end forever; for life everlasting is not to be gained by dying. Divine Science may absorb the attention of the intellectual and philosopher, but only the spiritually minded can fathom it. Divine Science is made known most fully to the people who understand best the divine Life. Sleep is darkness, but God's creative mandate was, "Let there be light."[1] In sleep, cause and effect are mere illusions. They seem to be something, but aren't. Did the origin and the enlightenment of human beings come from the deep sleep which Adam never woke up from? Oblivion and dreams, not realities, come with sleep and so goes the Adam-belief of which human and material life is the dream.

---

[1] Gen. 1:3

Metaphysics versus physics

The science of metaphysics receives less attention than physics. Why? My experience has been that the human mind must wake up to the spiritual essence of life before it cares to solve the problem of existence metaphysically. When mental enlightenment is received, existence is on a new standpoint.

Recognizing the power of thought is valuable. Parents can develop their children properly with spiritual thoughts and knowledge.

The curse removed

Mind controls the birthing process in the lower realms of nature, where birth is without suffering. Vegetables, minerals, and many animals do not suffer when giving birth. Human multiplication has its suffering because human mind believes suffering is a law. Divine Science reveals harmony as proportionately increasing as the line of creation rises toward spiritual being—toward enlarged understanding and intelligence. We have less pain and sorrow as we have more love and spirituality. When the haze of human mind clears, the curse will be removed which says to woman, "With pain you will give birth to children."[1] Divine Science rolls back the clouds of error with the light of Truth, and reveals person as never born and as never dying, but as coexistent with the Almighty.

Popular theology takes up the history of people as though they began materially right, however, immediately fell into mental sin. Revealed theology proclaims the Science of Mind and its formations as being in accordance with the first chapter of the Old Testament, when God, Mind, spoke and it was done.

---

[1]   Gen. 3:16

REVELATION

Blessed is the one who reads the words of this prophecy, and blessed are those who hear it and take to heart what is written in it, because the time is near.[1]

Great is the Lord, and most worthy of praise, in the city of our God, his holy mountain.[2]

John the Revelator writes in the tenth chapter of the book of Revelation:

> *Revelation 10:1-3.* Then I saw another mighty angel coming down from heaven. He was robed in a cloud, with a rainbow above his head; his face was like the sun, and his legs were like fiery pillars. He was holding a little scroll, which lay open in his hand. He planted his right foot on the sea and his left foot on the land, and he gave a loud shout like the roar of a lion. When he shouted, the voices of the seven thunders spoke.

The new Evangel

The "mighty angel," or message, which comes from God, represents divine Science. To human perception, divine Science seems at first obscure, abstract, and dim, but a bright promise crowns its brow. Divine Science understood, is the prism and praise of Truth. An honest view of divine Science enables you to heal by its means. Science

---

[1] Rev. 1:3
[2] Ps. 48:1

has for you a light greater than the sun, for God "is its lamp."[1] Its fiery legs are the foundations of Love and Truth. It brings the baptism of the Holy Spirit, whose flames of Truth were prophetically described by John the Baptist as consuming error.

Truth's scroll

The angel was holding a scroll which "lay open"[2] for everyone to read and understand. Did this scroll contain the revelation of divine Science? The angel's right foot illustrates Truth's prevailing power over hidden, not yet materialized, error. The left foot represents Truth's continuing power over visible error and audible sin. The calm voice of Truth sounds like a lion's roar to the human mind; Love is heard in the desert and in dark places of fear. The "still small voice"[3] of scientific thought reaches over continents and oceans. Truth triggers the seven thunders of evil to be self-exposed. With evil out in the open, the power of Truth is then made manifest in the destruction of error.

> *Revelation 10:9.* So I went to the angel and asked him to give me the little scroll. He said to me, 'Take it and eat it. It will turn your stomach sour, but in your mouth it will be as sweet as honey.'

A voice from harmony encourages us to let in the Science of Life, Truth, and Love. Read the scroll—understand Principle—study and think about it. Yes, at first it will be sweet, when you are healed. However, be warned: the digestion of spiritual understanding may be sour. Don't be surprised or dissatisfied when you come closer to divine Principle and a bitter experience tries to spoil your spiritual progress. The progression out of limitation seems very challenging; as it was when the Israelites escaped the ruling Egyptians, but you can escape from bondage to the paragon of faith and hope.

The opening of the sixth seal in the twelfth chapter of Revelation suggests a connection to the nineteenth century.

---

1   Rev. 21:23
2   Rev. 10:2
3   I Kings 19:12 (NKJV)

481

Revelation 12:1. A great and wondrous sign appeared in heaven; a woman clothed with the sun, with the moon under her feet and a crown of twelve stars on her head.

Spiritual sunlight

Heaven represents harmony. Divine Science interprets the Principle of heavenly harmony. The great miracle, to human sense, is divine Love, and the grand purpose of life is to gain the true idea of what constitutes the kingdom of heaven in us. This goal is never reached while we hate our neighbor or get hung up on a person whom God has appointed to voice His Word. The message, not the messenger is the point, and this correct sense allows us to see the highest visible idea and understand its divine Principle.

Abuse of the motives and religion of St. Paul hid from view the apostle's character, which made him equal to his great mission. Persecution of all who have spoken something new and better of God has not only obscured the light of the ages, but has been fatal to the persecutors. Why? Because persecutors can't see the true idea even if right in front of them. Misunderstandings show an ignorance of the divine idea taught by the enlightened thinker. Ignorance of the divine idea betrays at once a greater ignorance of the divine Principle of the idea—ignorance of Truth and Love. The understanding of Truth and Love works out the ends of eternal good and destroys both faith in evil and the practice of evil. It leads to the discernment of the divine idea.

John the Revelator, using spiritual vision, saw an "angel standing in the sun."[1] Purity was the symbol of Life and Love. The spiritual ideal as a woman clothed in light was also linked to a bride coming down from heaven, wedded to the Lamb of Love. "The bride" and "the Lamb" represented the correlation of divine Principle and spiritual idea, God and His Christ, bringing harmony to earth.

John saw the human and divine parallel in the man Jesus. It was a sign of divinity embracing humanity in Life and its demonstration. In divine revelation the material wasn't reduced, but was vanished as the spiritual idea was reduced to human understanding.

---

[1] Rev. 19:17

As for the metaphor, the woman symbolizes all people, the spiritual image of God, agreeing with divine Principle, Love. The Revelator illustrates Spirit as the sun. The spiritual idea is clothed with the radiance of spiritual truth, and matter is put under her feet. The light portrayed has nothing to do with photons, but everything to do with spiritual Life, "the light of all people."[1] "There came a man who was sent from God . . . as a witness to testify concerning that light."[2]

John the Baptist prophesied the coming of the immaculate Jesus, baptizing with Spirit, who, along with Elijah, presented the spiritual idea of God's fatherhood. John the Revelator completes the picture with woman, typifying the spiritual idea of God's motherhood. The moon under her feet reveals the universe as secondary and attributable to Spirit, from which the universe borrows its reflected light, substance, life, and intelligence.

> *Revelation 12:2.* She was pregnant and cried out in pain as she was about to give birth.

The process of advancing the spiritual idea is typified by a woman in hard labor, waiting to be delivered of her sweet promise. The idea is great and the birth is ominous, however, the stress doesn't linger because the birth goes on and includes joy.

> *Revelation 12:3.* Then another sign appeared in heaven: an enormous red dragon with seven heads and ten horns and seven crowns on his heads.

Breaking down the dragon
The enormous red dragon symbolizes a lie—the belief that substance, life, and intelligence can be restricted, separated, or fleshly. This dragon stands for the sum total of human error. The ten horns typify the belief that matter/energy has a power of its own, an evil mind which can break the Ten Commandments.

---

[1] John 1:4 (NRSV)

[2] John 1:6-7

Know the dragon for what it is

Fear and hatred lifts its hydra head and shows its horns in the many inventions of evil, including sickness, vice, and destruction. We may be afraid, confused or shocked at the chaos, as human perceptions struggle to keep their identity. However, to our spiritual perception, harmony is real and the chaos is unreal, so why do we stand aghast at the sight of limitation and evil, or attempt to cope with it? Don't be immobilized by the different disguises of fear and hatred. The Revelator uncovers and explains the embodiment and awful character of all evil, but he also sees its nothingness, or in other words, he sees the allness of God, good.

> *Revelation 12:4.* His tail swept a third of the stars out of the sky and flung them to the earth. The dragon stood in front of the woman who was about to give birth, so that he might devour her child the moment it was born.

Neanderthal tendency

The dragon is subtle; it cunningly maneuvers around in the name of good. It is the ancient serpent holding tireless watch, fiercely striving to impede the spiritual idea, which is prolific in health, holiness, and immortality. Pay attention: it is the brutish, animal instinct in human beings which triggers them to devour each other.

The spiritual idea isn't devious, but evil will habitually impose its own shifty nature and methods on the true idea. Error's malicious cruel instinct incites humans to kill each other morally and physically, and worse yet, to blame the innocent for the crime. This last weakness of sin will pull its perpetrator into the black hole of oblivion.

Dragon is doomed

From Genesis to Revelation, the snake or dragon represents revenge, hatred, envy, death, and disease—all evil. From beginning to end, the dragon pursues the spiritual idea with malice. The snake is perpetually close on the heel of harmony. In Genesis, the allegorical talking snake illustrates mortal human mind "more cunning than any beast of the field."[1] In Revelation, the error increases and becomes the great red dragon, swollen with negativity, inflamed with war against spirituality, and near its doom. Error is full of greed and spite, detesting the brightness of divine glory.

Maliciousness

I am convinced that the accusations against Jesus were instigated by the criminal instinct described by John the Revelator. The dragon wars against innocence, the Lamb of God. Since Jesus must have been tempted at all points, he met and conquered error in every form. Jesus repeated, "They hated me without reason."[2] The brutality of his enemies could come from no source except the highest degree of depravity. Jesus "did not open his mouth,"[3] because it was futile. When human beings exhibit the level of depravity that his accusers did, they won't listen to goodness. The spiritual idea was put on trial in a biased courtroom, but only so the human mind might uncover its own crime of denying and defying immortal Mind.

> *Revelation 12:5.* She gave birth to a son, a male child, who will rule all the nations with an iron scepter. And her child was snatched up to God and to his throne."

The conflict with purity

Christ, God's idea, of which "his kingdom will never end,"[4] will ultimately rule all nations and peoples—imperatively, absolutely, finally—with divine Science. This pure idea, embodied first by man, and according to the Revelator, last by woman, will baptize with fire and burn up the impurities of error with the fervent heat of Truth and Love. The gold of human character will be melted and purified. The lies of the world conflict with harmony. However, Truth and Love win the war. Notice: at the time of Jesus' birth, King Herod decreed the death of every male child so that Jesus would not be a threat to the

---

1 Gen. 3:1 (NKJV)
2 Ps. 35:19, 69:4; John 15:25
3 Isa. 53:7; Acts 8:32
4 Luke 1:33

king's position.[1] Herod's actions were induced by the most deplorable element of human mind, but it could not touch the spiritual idea which will be understood expansively and be snatched up to God—be found in its divine Principle.

> *Revelation 12:6.* The woman fled into the desert to a place prepared for her by God.

Spiritual guidance

Here we have a comparison to when the children of Israel were being guided triumphantly through the sea into the wilderness.[2] A promise of joy was anticipated while wearily walking through the desert of human hopes. Even so now, the spiritual idea will guide all right desires from limited perception to Soul perception, to the glory prepared for us who love God. Science is the guide, never pausing, but leading to divine thoughts with a pillar of cloud by day and fire by night. In *War and Peace,* Leo Tolstoy depicts the guiding presence found in consciousness. The main character, Pierre Bezúkhov, "felt like a man who, after straining his eyes to peer into the remote distance, finds what he was seeking at his very feet. All his life he had been looking over the heads of those around him, while he had only to look before him without straining his eyes . . . He had learned to see the great, the eternal, the infinite in everything . . . And the closer he looked, the happier and more serene he was."[3]

> *Revelation 12:7-8.* And there was war in heaven. Michael and his angels fought against the dragon, and the dragon and his angels fought back. But he was not strong enough, and they lost their place in heaven.

---

[1]   Matt. 2:16

[2]   Exodus 16

[3]   Tolstoy, Leo, *War and Peace,* translated by Ann Dunnigan. New York: Penguin Books, 1968.

Angelic offices

The Old Testament assigns different functions to the angels, or God's divine messages. Michael's characteristic is spiritual strength. He leads the troops of heaven against the power of sin (Satan), and fights the holy wars. Gabriel has the quieter task of imparting a sense of the ever-presence of ministering Love. These angels deliver us from the depths. When strong faith or spiritual strength wrestles and prevails through the understanding of God, Truth and Love are tangibly felt, even in times of anguish. There is no contest for Gabriel. To infinite, ever-present Love, all is Love and there is no error, no sin, sickness, or death. The dragon can't war for long against Love because it is killed by divine Principle. Truth and Love prevail and the conflict between flesh and Spirit is ended.

> *Revelation 12:9.* The great dragon was hurled down—that ancient serpent called the devil, or Satan, who leads the whole world astray. He was hurled to the earth, and his angels with him.

Dragon cast down to earth

The ancient belief, that old serpent whose name is devil (Satan), falsely claims that there is intelligence in matter either to benefit or to injure people. This belief is pure delusion, the red dragon. It is hurled out by Truth and proved to be powerless. "Hurled to the earth" is analogous as dust to dust, showing the dragon to be nothingness. The dragon was a lie from the beginning, when it pretended to be a talking snake. The liar's angels (suggestions) were hurled to the earth with their author. The beast and the false prophets are lust and hypocrisy. These wolves in sheep's clothing are detected and killed by innocence, the Lamb of Love.

War with error

Divine Science shows how the Lamb slays the wolf. Innocence and Truth overcome guilt and error. Ever since the foundation of the world, ever since error would establish rut thinking, evil has tried to kill the Lamb, but Science is able to destroy this lie called evil.

Note: The narrative in chapter twelve of the Apocalypse follows the same order used in Genesis. The first verses present the clearest human concept of existence, and then an unspiritual human concept is presented. The more spiritual perspective typifies not only the divine scientific method of warfare, but is also shows the glorious results of this warfare. The following verses depict the fatal effects of trying to meet error with error.

> *Revelation 12:10-12.* Then I heard a loud voice in heaven say: Now have come the salvation and the power and the kingdom of our God, and the authority of his Christ. For the accuser of our brothers, who accuses them before our God day and night, has been hurled down. They overcame him by the blood of the Lamb and by the word of their testimony; they did not love their lives so much as to shrink from death. Therefore rejoice, you heavens and you who dwell in them! But woe to the earth and the sea, because the devil has gone down to you! He is filled with fury, because he knows that his time is short.

Inclusive song

For victory over a single sin, we give thanks and magnify the Lord of Hosts. What will we say of the mighty conquest over all that is unspiritual? A louder song, sweeter than has ever before reached high heaven, now rises clearer and nearer to the great heart of Christ; for the accuser is not there, and Love expresses Her primal and everlasting symphony. A rule in Science is to fight against error and negate the human finite self with infinite Truth. This rule clearly interprets God as divine Principle—as Life, epitomized by the Father; as Truth, represented by the Child; as Love, represented by the Mother. Every human being at some point, here or hereafter, must battle with and overcome the mortal belief in a power opposed to God.

The garment of Science
The Scripture, "You have been trustworthy in a few things, I will put you in charge of many things,"[1] is literally fulfilled when we are conscious of the supremacy of Truth. The nothingness of error (which is in proportion to its wickedness) is seen as we are conscious of Truth. People, who touch the fringe of Christ's garment[2] and master their illegitimate convictions, their angers, and their fight-or-flight reactions, will rejoice in the proof of healing—in a sweet and certain sense that God is Love. It is a sad day for the person who professes to practice and be faithful to divine Science but fails to strangle the serpent of sin as well as of sickness! They are still living in their self-sabotaging comfort-zones and human passions. They are in the turbulent sea of error, not struggling to lift their heads above the drowning wave.

Payback by suffering
What happens when we don't fight and destroy sin? What happens when we don't destroy finite convictions or mortal status quos? Our mental and physical state will perceive suffering. The sin, which you think you love or is a part of you, comes back with accelerated force, for the devil knows its time is short. The Scriptural reference to time reaffirms the fact that evil is temporal, not eternal. The dragon is at last stung to death by its own malice. Paul refers to its sting as, "spiritual forces of evil in the heavenly realms."[3] How many periods of torture are required to remove all sin will depend on sin's stubbornness.

> *Revelation 12:13.* When the dragon saw that he had been hurled to the earth, he pursued the woman who had given birth to the male child.

Esoteric apathy
Mind's constant movement, along with honest investigation, will bring the hour when people will stop in some way, the mysteriousness

---

[1] Matt. 25:21; Luke 19:17 (NRSV)
[2] Matt. 9:20
[3] Eph. 6:12

that increases with material knowledge. Apathy toward the tendency of certain active yet unseen mental agencies will finally be shocked into another extreme mortal mood—into human indignation, for one extreme follows another.

> *Revelation 12:15-16.* Then from his mouth the serpent spewed water like a river, to overtake the woman and sweep her away with the torrent. But the earth helped the woman by opening its mouth and swallowing the river that the dragon has spewed out of his mouth.

Receptive hearts
Millions of unprejudiced minds are waiting and looking for rest and drink. They are simple seekers for Truth, weary wanderers thirsty in the desert. Give them a cup of cold water[1] with Christ's attitude and never fear the consequences. Watch out, because the old dragon may cause a torrential uproar to drown the Christ-idea. However, the dragon can't destroy "an instrument through which only truth can speak."[2] The truth of being will be understood. The earth will help. People who are ready for the blessing will give you thanks. The river will be calmed, and Christ will command the wave.

Hidden ways of wrong thinking
When God heals the sick or the sinning, it is better if the people know what Mind has done. It is also progressive to know how the human mind dupes us to make us sick or sinful. Once we've learned human mind's tactics, we can expose its unconscious and subconscious ways in which it accomplishes iniquity. Paradoxically, many of us are willing to tell people about the power of good resident in divine Mind, but we hesitate to point out the evil in human thought.

Christ-like warning
Exposing error is necessary to guarantee not making more mistakes. Why are we reluctant to expose the human mind's

---

[1]   Matt. 10:42

[2]   *Peace Pilgrim, Her Life and Work in Her Own Words.* New Mexico: Ocean Tree Books, 1982.

deficiencies? Why are we unwilling to point out wrong-thinking? We hesitate because people like us better when we tell them their virtues than when we tell them their vices. It requires the spirit of Truth and Love to point out miscalculated thinking. We risk human disapproval for the sake of doing right and benefiting humanity. Who is telling humankind of the enemy in ambush? Does the informant see a foe? Listen and be wise. You can escape from error. You can also detect the unfaithful people who saw the danger and gave no warning.

At all times and under all circumstances, overcome evil with good. Know yourself, and God will supply the wisdom and the occasion for a victory over evil. Love is a protective covering. Wear it! Wrapped up in love, human hatred can't reach you. The confirmation of a higher humanity will unite all interests in the one divinity.

Through symbolism and metaphor, the Revelator, immortal scribe of Spirit and of a true idealism, furnishes the mirror in which mortals may see their own image. In significant figures he depicts the thoughts held in human mind. The conceit of sin is rebuked and its doom is characterized beforehand. With his spiritual strength, the Revelator has opened wide the gates of glory and illumined the night of religious opinions with the sublime grandeur of divine Science, outshining the lust, sin, and hypocrisy. The Revelator removes from office all idolatry; advances pure and undefiled religion; and lifts on high only those who have washed their robes white in obedience and suffering.

We have now seen, in both the first and last books of the Bible—Genesis and Revelation—that sin is to be spiritually and scientifically reduced to its native nothingness. "Love one another,"[1] is the simplest and most profound counsel of the inspired writer. In Science we are children of God, but whatever is of human cognizance doesn't belong to us, for materiality or mortality is the misinterpreted image of spirituality.

Love fulfills the law of divine Science and nothing short of this divine Principle, understood and demonstrated, can ever furnish the vision of the Apocalypse, open the seven seals of error with Truth,

---

[1]   I John 3:23

or uncover the myriad illusions of sin, sickness, and death. Under the supremacy of Spirit, it will be seen and acknowledged that matter (limited mind) must disappear.

> *Revelation 21:1.* Then I saw a new heaven and a new earth, for the first heaven and the first earth had passed away, and there was no longer any sea.

The Revelator had not yet passed the transitional stage in human experience called death, but he already saw a new heaven and a new earth. How did this vision come to John? The spiritual interpretation of heaven and earth didn't come through the physical visual organs for seeing, for human optics is inadequate to take in so wonderful a scene. Was the new heaven and new earth physical or mental, relative or absolute, quantum or infinite? The human mind's sense of space/time, wave/particle is unable to grasp the spiritual view. The Revelator was on our plane of existence, while yet perceiving what the eye cannot see—that which is invisible to the uninspired thought. This testimony of Holy Writ sustains the fact in Science that the heavens and earth to one human consciousness, that consciousness which God gives, are spiritual, while to another, the unenlightened human mind, the vision is material. This shows that what the human mind defines as matter and spirit indicates states and stages of consciousness.

Accompanying this scientific consciousness was another revelation, even the declaration from heaven, supreme harmony, that God, the divine Principle of harmony, is always with men and women, and they are the people of Soul. Therefore, people are no longer regarded as miserable sinners, but as the blessed reflection of God. Why? Because St. John's corporeal sense of the heavens and earth had vanished, and in place of this limited sense was the spiritual sense, the subjective state by which he could see the new heaven and new earth which involve the spiritual idea and consciousness of reality. This is Scriptural credibility for concluding that such a recognition of being is, and has been, possible in this present state of existence—that we can become conscious, here and now, of a cessation of death, sorrow, and pain. This is indeed a foretaste of absolute Christian Science. Take heart, dear sufferer, for this reality of being will surely appear sometime and in some way. There will be no more pain and all tears will be wiped away. When you read this, remember Jesus' words, "The kingdom of God is within you."[1] This spiritual consciousness is therefore a present possibility.

In chapter twenty-one, the Revelator takes up another view, adapted to console the struggling soul, overwhelmed with "horror and exhaustion."[2]

> *Revelation 21:9.* One of the seven angels who had the seven bowls full of the seven last plagues came and said to me, "Come, I will show you the bride, the wife of the Lamb."

This ministry of Truth, this message from divine Love, carried John away in spirit. It exalted him until he became conscious of the spiritual facts of being and the "New Jerusalem, coming down out of heaven from God"[3]—until he became aware of the spiritual outpouring of bliss and glory, which he describes as the city which "was laid out like a square."[4] The beauty of this text is that the sum total of human misery, represented by the seven angelic vials full of seven plagues, has full compensation in the law of Love. Note this, that the very message, or swift-winged thought which poured forth hatred and torment, brought also the experience which at last lifted the seer to behold the great city, the four equal sides of which were heaven-given and heaven-giving.

Think of this, dear reader, for it will lift the sackcloth from your eyes, and you will experience the soft-winged dove descending on you. The very circumstance, which your suffering sense thinks is horrible and distressing, Love can make you entertain "angels without knowing

---

[1] Luke 17:21

[2] Hugo, Victor. *Les Miserables.* Translated from the French by Charles E. Wilbour. New York:The Modern Library.

[3] Rev. 21:2

[4] Rev. 21:16

it."[1] Then thought gently whispers: Come on! No more attention on narrow-minded conclusions; experience now the true sense of Love. Observe the Lamb's wife—Love wedded to its own spiritual idea. Then comes the marriage reception, for this revelation will destroy forever the physical plagues imposed on human beings by material perceptions.

This sacred city, described in Revelation as one "laid out like a square"[2] and "coming down out of heaven from God,"[3] represents the light and glory of divine Science. The "architect and builder" of this New Jerusalem is God, and it is "the city with foundations."[4] Yes, the description is metaphoric. Spiritual teaching must always be by symbols. Didn't Jesus illustrate the truths he taught by the mustard seed[5] and the Lost Son?[6] Taken in its allegorical sense, the description of the city as foursquare has a profound meaning. The four sides of our city are the Word, Christ, spirituality, and divine Science; "on no day will its gates ever be shut, for there will be no night there."[7] The four sides indicate this city is wholly spiritual.

As the Psalmist said, "Beautiful in elevation, the joy of the whole earth, Is Mount Zion in the far north, The city of the great King."[8] It is indeed a city of the Spirit, fine-looking, noble, and symmetric. Northward, its gates open to the North Star, the Word, the polar magnet of Revelation; eastward, to the star seen by the wise men of the Orient who followed it to the manger where Jesus was born; southward, to the genial tropics, with the Southern Cross in the skies—the Cross of Calvary, which binds human society into solemn union; westward, to the grand realization of the Golden Shore of Love and the Peaceful Sea of Harmony.

---

[1]   Heb. 13:2

[2]   Rev. 21:16

[3]   Rev. 21:10

[4]   Heb. 11:10

[5]   Matt. 13:31, 17:20; Mark 4:31; Luke 13:19, 17:6

[6]   Luke 15:11-24

[7]   Rev. 21:25

[8]   Ps. 48:2 (NASB)

This heavenly city, lighted by the Sun of Righteousness—this New Jerusalem, this infinite All, which to us seems hidden in the mist of remoteness—reached John's vision while he yet lived with mortals.

> *Revelation 21:22.* I did not see a temple in the city, because the Lord God Almighty and the Lamb are its temple.

There was no temple—that is, no material structure in which to worship God, for Principle must be worshipped in spirit and in love. The word *temple* also means *body*. The Revelator was familiar with Jesus' use of this word, as when Jesus spoke of his physical body as the temple to be temporarily rebuilt. What further indication than this do we need of our spirituality? John saw heaven and earth, but "did not see a temple [body] in the city."[1] This kingdom of God "is within you,"[2] is within reach of people's consciousness here, and the spiritual idea reveals it. In divine Science, people consciously possess this recognition of harmony as they continue to understand God.

The term Lord, as used in the Old Testament, is often synonymous with Yahweh, and expresses a rudimental human concept, not yet elevated to spiritual understanding through transfiguration. Yet the word Lord gradually approaches a higher significance as the human mind's concept of God extends to a diviner meaning. The human mind's linear thinking is obliged to admit a more expansive thought. God and the children of the Almighty are discovered as the infinite Principle and infinite idea—as one Father-Mother with a universal family held in the gospel of Love. The Lamb's wife presents the unity of male and female as no longer two wedded individuals, but as two individual natures in one; and this compounded spiritual individuality reflects God as Father-Mother, not as a physical being. In this divinely united spiritual consciousness, there is no impediment to eternal happiness—to the perfectibility of God's creation.

---

[1]   Rev. 21:22 (Brackets added by Mary Baker Eddy)
[2]   Luke 17:21

This spiritual, holy habitation has no boundary or limit, but its four cardinal points are: first, the Word of Life, Truth, and Love; second, the Christ, the spiritual idea of God; third, spirituality, which is the outcome of the divine Principle of the Christ-idea in Christian history; fourth, divine Science, which today and forever interprets this great paradigm and the great Exemplar. This city of our God has no need of sun or moon, for Love is the light of it, and divine Mind is its own interpreter. All who are saved must walk in this light. Administrators and commanders will lay down their honors within the heavenly city. Its gates open toward light and glory both within and without, for all is good, and "Nothing impure will ever enter it, nor will anyone who does what is shameful or deceitful."[1]

My feeble sense of Christian Science closes with John's Revelation as recorded by the great apostle, for his vision is the acme of this Science as the Bible reveals it.

In the following Psalm one word shows, though faintly, the light which divine Science throws on the Scriptures by substituting for the physical sense, the spiritual sense of Deity:

[Divine Love] is my shepherd, I shall not be in want.

[Love] makes me lie down in green pastures,

[Love] leads me beside quiet waters,

[Love] restores my soul [spiritual sense]. [Love] guides me in paths of righteousness for his name's sake.

Even though I walk through the valley of the shadow of death, I will fear no evil, for [Love is] with me; [Love's] rod and [Love's] staff, they comfort me.

[Love prepares] a table before me in the presence of my enemies. [Love anoints] my head with oil; my cup overflows.

Surely goodness and love will follow me all the days of my life, and I will dwell in the [consciousness] of [Love] for ever.[2]

---

[1] Rev. 21:27

[2] Ps. 23 (Brackets added by Mary Baker Eddy)

GLOSSARY

These are the words of him who is holy and true, who holds
the key of David. What he opens no one can shut, and what
he shuts no one can open. I know your deeds. See, I have
placed before you an open door that no one can shut.[1]

In Christian Science we learn that substituting the spiritual
for the material definition of a Scriptural word often elucidates the
meaning of the inspired writer. On this account this chapter is added.
It contains the metaphysical interpretation of Bible terms, giving their
spiritual sense, which is also their original meaning.

Abel. Attentiveness; self-offering; surrendering to the creator the early
fruits of experience.

Abraham. Perseverance; faith in the divine Life and in the eternal
Principle of being.
 This patriarch illustrated the purpose of Love to create trust in
good. Abraham also showed the life-preserving power of spiritual
understanding.

Adam. Error; a falsity; the belief in "original sin," sickness, and death;
evil; the opposite of good—of God and Soul's existence; a curse; a
belief in intelligent matter, finiteness, and mortality; "dust you are
and to dust you will return;"[2] red earth; nothingness; the first god of
mythology; not God's child, who represents the one God and is Spirit's
own image and likeness; the opposite of Spirit and spiritual being; that

---

1   Rev. 3:7-8
2   Gen. 3:19; Ecc. 3:20

which is not the image and likeness of good, but a changeable belief, opposed to the one Mind, or Spirit; a so-called finite human mind, producing other minds, thereby making "many gods and many lords;"[1] A product of nothing as the mimicry of something; an unreality as opposed to the great reality of spiritual existence and creation; a so-called person, whose origin, substance, and mind are found to oppose God, or Spirit; a perverted image of Spirit; the image and likeness of what God has not created, namely, matter, sin, sickness, and death; the adversary of Truth, termed error; Life's counterfeit, which ends in death; hate; a coup d¢ état against Spirit's creation by that which is called self-creative matter; mortality; that of which wisdom says, "you will surely die."[2]

The name Adam represents the false supposition that Life is not eternal, but has beginning and end; that the infinite enters the finite, that intelligence passes into non-intelligence, and that Soul dwells in material sense; that immortal Mind results in matter, and matter in human mind; that the one God and being entered what Mind expresses and then disappeared in the atheism of matter.

Adversary. An adversary is one who resists, denies, or argues, not one who constructs and sustains reality and Truth. Jesus said of the devil, "He was a murderer from the beginning . . . he is a liar and the father of lies."[3] This view of Satan is confirmed by the name often conferred in Scripture, the "adversary."

Almighty. All-power; infinity; omnipotence.

Angels. God's thoughts passing to people; spiritual intuitions, pure and perfect; the inspiration of goodness, purity, and immortality, counteracting all evil, brute-like inclinations, and mortality.

---

[1]   I Cor. 8:5 (NASB)

[2]   Gen. 2:17

[3]   John 8:44

Ark. Safety; the idea, or reflection, of Truth, proved to be as immortal as its Principle; the understanding of Spirit, destroying belief in matter.

God and spiritual beings coexistent and are eternal; Science shows that the spiritual realities of all things are created by Soul and exist forever. The ark indicates temptation overcome and followed by exaltation.

Asher (Jacob's son). Hope and faith; spiritual compensation; the ills of the flesh rebuked.

Babel. Self-destroying error; a kingdom divided against itself which cannot stand;[1] knowledge of material, mortal life.

As false knowledge accumulates from the evidence gained from the five physical senses, the more confusion and the more certain is the downfall of its structure.

Baptism. Purification by Spirit; submergence in Spirit.

"We have confident *and* hopeful courage and are pleased rather to be away from home out of the body and be at home with the Lord."[2]

Believing. Firmness and constancy; not a wavering or blind faith, but the perception of spiritual Truth. Human thoughts, illusion.

Benjamin (Jacob's son). A physical belief as to life, substance, and mind; human knowledge or human mind devoted to matter; arrogance, envy; fame; illusion; a false belief; error masquerading as the possessor of life, strength, purpose, motivation, and the power to act.

Renewal of affections; self-offering; an improved state of human mind; the introduction of a more spiritual origin; a gleam of the infinite idea of the infinite Principle; a spiritual type; that which comforts, consoles, and supports.

---

1 Matt. 12:25; Mark 3:24; Luke 11:17
2 II Cor. 5:8 (Amplified)

Bride. Purity and innocence, conceiving man and woman in the idea of God; a sense of Soul, which has spiritual happiness and enjoys but cannot suffer.

Bridegroom. Spiritual understanding; the pure consciousness that God, the divine Principle, creates person as the spiritual image of Father-Mother, and that God is the only original power.

Burial. Corporeality and physical sense put out of sight and hearing; annihilation. Submergence in Spirit; immortality brought to light.

Canaan (the son of Ham). A belief in physical sensuality; the testimony of what is termed material sense; the error which would make humanity mortal and would make human mind a slave to the body.

Children. The spiritual thoughts and representatives of Life, Truth, and Love.

Thinking the body can be gratified and mortal; counterfeits of being, whose better originals are God's thoughts, not immature, but mature; material suppositions of life, substance, and intelligence, opposed to the Science of being.

Children of Israel. The representatives of Soul, not mortal mind; the offspring of Spirit, who, having wrestled with error, sin, and dead end logic, are governed by divine Science; some of the ideas of God thought of as people, destroying error and healing the sick; Christ's offspring.

Christ. The divine manifestation of God, which comes to the flesh to destroy incarnate error.

Church. The structure of Truth and Love; whatever leans on and progresses from divine Principle.

The Church is that organization which gives proof of its usefulness and is found spiritualizing humanity; which rouses dormant understanding from limited thinking to the understanding of infinite ideas and the demonstration of divine Science, consequently driving out devils, or error, and healing the sick.

Creator. Spirit; Mind; intelligence; the animating divine Principle of all that is real and good; self-existent Life, Truth, and Love; that which is perfect and eternal; the opposite of matter and evil, which have no Principle; God, who made all that was made and could not create a particle or element to oppose unbounded Mind.

Dan (Jacob's son). Hypnotism; alleged human mind controlling human mind; error, working out the designs of error; one belief preying on another.

Day. The illumination of Life; light, the spiritual idea of Truth and Love. "And there was evening, and there was morning—the first day."[1] The objects of space/time, wave/particle, and temporal impressions disappear in the illumination of spiritual understanding, and Mind measures time according to the good that is revealed. This unfolding of good is God's day, and "there will be no night there."[2]

Death. An illusion, the lie of life in human finite mind; the unreal and untrue; that which is contrary to Life.
Human mind has no life; therefore it has no real existence. Mind is immortal. The flesh wars against Spirit; human mind worries itself out of one belief only to be captivated by another until every belief of life where Life is not yields to eternal Life. Any material evidence of death is false, for it contradicts the spiritual facts of being.

Devil. Evil; a lie; error; not corporeality or mind; the reverse of Truth; a belief in sin, sickness, and death; the power of suggestion, hypnotism; the lust of the flesh, which cries out: "I am living and intelligent matter. There is more than one mind, for I am mind—a

---

[1]   Gen. 1:5
[2]   Rev. 21:25

501

fickle mind, self-made or created by a tribal god and put into the opposite of mind, termed energy, afterward to reproduce a mortal universe, including human beings who are not the image and likeness of Spirit, but images of themselves."

Dove. A symbol of divine Science; purity and peace; hope and faith.

Dust. Nonbeing; the absence of substance, life, or intelligence.

Ears. Not organs of the purported bodily perceptions, but spiritual understanding.

Jesus said, referring to spiritual perception, "Having ears, do you not hear?"[1]

Earth. A sphere; an example of eternity and immortality, without beginning or end.

To physical sense, earth is matter; to spiritual sense, it is a compound idea.

Elijah. Prophecy; spiritual evidence contradicting limited perspectives; Christian Science, with which can be discerned the spiritual fact of whatever the material senses behold; the basis of immortality.

"To be sure, Elijah comes and will restore all things."[2]

Error. See Review chapter, page 407.

Euphrates (river). Divine Science encompassing the universe and humanity; the true idea of God; a type of glory which is to come; metaphysics taking the place of physics; the control of righteousness. The milieu of human belief before it accepts sin, sickness, or death; a human attitude, the only error of which is limitation; finitude; the opposite of infinitude.

---

[1] Mark 8:18 (Amplified)
[2] Matt. 17:11

Eve. A beginning; mortality; that which does not last forever; a restricted view concerning life, substance, and intelligence in matter; error; the thinking that people began materially instead of spiritually—that people started first from dust, second from a rib, and third from an egg.

Evening. Mystification of human thought; weariness of human mind; obscured views; peace and rest.

Expanse (firmament). Spiritual understanding; the scientific line of demarcation between Truth and error, between Spirit and so-called matter.

Eyes. Spiritual discernment—not physical but mental.
  Jesus said, thinking of the outward vision, "Do you have eyes but fail to see?"[1]

Father. Eternal Life; the one Mind; the divine Principle, commonly called God.

Fear. Heat; inflammation; anxiety; spiritual unawareness; error; desire; caution.

Fire. Fear: remorse; lust; hatred; destruction; affliction purifying and elevating humanity.

Flesh. An error or mistake of physical belief; misinterpretation of life, substance, and intelligence; a false impression; a belief that matter has sensation.

Gad (Jacob's son). Science; spiritual being understood; acceleration toward harmony.

---

[1]   Mark 8:18

Gethsemane. Patience overcoming misery; the human yielding to the divine; love meeting no response, but still remaining love.

Ghost. An illusion; a belief that mind is outlined and limited; a theory that spirit is finite.

Gihon (river). The rights of woman acknowledge morally, civilly, and socially.

God. The great "I AM;"[1] the all-knowing, all-seeing, all-acting, all-wise, all-loving, and eternal; Principle; Mind; Soul; Spirit; Life; Truth; Love; all substance; intelligence.

Gods. Mythology; the trained reaction to think that life, substance, and intelligence are both mental and material; the hypotheses that matter can be conscious; the rationale that infinite Mind is in finite forms; the various theories that hold mind to be a temporal cognition, existing in brains, nerves, chemicals; supposititious minds going in and out of matter, mistaken and mortal souls; the serpents of error, which say, "You will be like God."[2]

God is one God, infinite and perfect, and cannot become finite and imperfect.

Good. God; Spirit; omnipotence; omniscience; omnipresence; omni-action.

Ham (Noah's son). Bodily beliefs; sensuality; slavery; tyranny.

Heart. Human feelings, motives, inclinations, joys, and depressions.

Heaven. Harmony; the rule of one Spirit; government by divine Principle; spirituality; happiness; the atmosphere of Soul.

---

[1] Ex. 3:14

[2] Gen. 3:5

Hell. Mortal belief; error; lust; regret; hatred; revenge; sin; sickness; death; suffering and self-destruction; self-imposed agony; effects of sin; that which "is shameful or deceitful."[1]

Holy Spirit. Holy Ghost; divine Science; the development of eternal Life, Truth, and Love; that which interprets divine Mind.

Human mind. Mortal mind; nothing claiming to be something, for Mind is immortal; mythology; error generating other errors; a suppositional material perception, alias the belief that sensation is in matter, whereas matter is sensation-less; the unreliable conviction that life, substance, and intelligence are in and of matter/energy; that which contradicts Spirit, and therefore contradicts God, good; a false perception that life has a beginning and therefore an end; the limited knowledge that person is the offspring of human beings; the thinking that there can be more than one creator; idolatry; the subjective states of error; speculative perceptions; that which neither exists in Science nor can be recognized by spiritual sense; sin; sickness; death.

I, or Ego. Divine Principle; Spirit; Soul; incorporeal, unerring, immortal, and eternal Mind.

There is but one I, or Us, but one divine Principle, or Mind, governing all existence; people unchanged forever in their individual characters, even as numbers which never blend with each other, though they are controlled by one Principle. All the objects of God's existence reflect one Mind, and whatever doesn't reflect this one Mind, is illusive and erroneous, even the belief that life, substance, and intelligence are both mental and material.

I Am. God: bodiless and eternal Mind; divine Principle; the only Ego.

In. A term obsolete in Science if used with reference to Spirit or Deity.

---

[1] Rev. 21:27

Intelligence. Substance; self-existent and eternal Mind; that which is never unconscious or restricted. See Review chapter, page 404.

Issachar (Jacob's son). An embodied belief; the offspring of error; envy; hatred; selfishness; self-will; lust.

Jacob. A human being embracing duplicity, repentance, sensualism. Inspiration; the revelation of Science, in which rigid mortal mindsets yield to the spiritual attitude of Life and Love.

Japhet (Noah's son). A kind of spiritual peace, flowing from the understanding that God is the divine Principle of all existence, and that people are God's idea, the child of Her care.

Jerusalem. Ever-changing human principles and knowledge gained from the physical senses; the arrogance of power and the power of arrogance; sensuality; envy; oppression; tyranny. Home, heaven.

Jesus. The best, physically tangible concept of the divine idea that the human mind can conceive, correcting error and bringing to light our immortality.

Joseph. A human being; a higher sense of Truth rebuking mortal certainties, or error, and showing the immortality and supremacy of Truth; pure affection blessing its enemies.

Judah. Human thinking progressing and disappearing; the spiritual understanding of God and spiritual beings appearing.

Kingdom of Heaven. The rule of harmony in divine Science; the domain of infallible, eternal, and omnipotent Mind; the atmosphere of Spirit, where Soul is supreme.

Knowledge. Evidence acquired from the physical senses; mortality; beliefs and opinions; human theories, doctrines, hypotheses; that which is not divine and is the origin of destruction, health problems, and death; not spiritual Truth and understanding.

Lamb of God. The spiritual idea of Love; unselfish alturism; innocence and purity; sacrifice.

Levi (Jacob's son). A corporeal and sensual belief; human person; denial of the fullness of God's creation; ecclesiastical despotism.

Life. See Review chapter, page 404.

Lord. In the Hebrew, this term is sometimes employed as a title, which has the inferior sense of master, a hierarchy, or privileged owner. In the Greek, the word *kyrios* almost always has this lower sense, unless specially coupled with the name God. Its higher signification is Supreme Ruler.

Lord God. Yahweh. Jehovah.

This juxtaposed term is not used in the first chapter of Genesis, the record of spiritual existence. It is introduced in the second and following chapters when the spiritual perception of God and of infinity is disappearing from the recorder's thought—when the true scientific statements of the Scriptures become clouded through a restricted perception of God as finite and with form. From this confusion follow idolatry and mythology—belief in many gods, or material intelligences, as something that can oppose the one Spirit, or intelligence, named Elohim, or God.

Matter. Mythology; mortality; another name for human mortal mind; illusion; intelligence, substance, and life in non-intelligence and mortality; life resulting in death, and death in life; sensation in the insensitive; mind originating in matter; the reverse of Truth; the contradiction of Spirit; the opposite of God; that of which immortal Mind takes no cognizance; that which human mind sees, feels, hears, tastes, and smells only in belief.

Matter/energy. Material energy; measurable, localized forces; a strata of mortal mind.

Mind. The only I, or Us; the only Spirit, Soul, divine Principle, substance, Life, Truth, Love; the one God; not that which is *in* man and woman, but the divine Principle of whom God's child is the full and perfect expression; Deity, which outlines but is not outlined. See Review chapter, page 404.

Miracle. That which is divinely natural, but must be learned humanly; a phenomenon of Science.

Morning. Light; symbol of Truth; revelation and progress.

Moses. A fleshly human being; moral courage; a type of moral law and the demonstration thereof; the proof that without the gospel— the union of justice and compassion—there is something spiritually lacking, since justice demands penalties under the law.

Mother. God: divine and eternal Principle; Life, Truth, and Love.

New Jerusalem. Divine Science; the spiritual facts and harmony of the universe; the kingdom of heaven, or domain of harmony.

Night. Darkness; doubt, fear.

Noah. A fleshly human being; knowledge of the nothingness of temporal things and of the immortality of all that is spiritual.

Oil. Dedication; altruism; gentleness; prayer; heavenly inspiration.

Person. The compound idea of infinite Spirit; the spiritual image and likeness of God; the full representation of Mind. Man and woman. See Review chapter, page 409.

Pharisee. Bodily and sensuous belief; self-righteousness; vanity; hypocrisy.

Pishon (river). The love of the good and beautiful, and their spirituality and immortality.

Principle. See Review chapter, page 401.

Prophet. A spiritual seer; disappearance of limited perceptions before the conscious facts of spiritual Truth.

Purse. Storing up treasures in material things; error.

Red Dragon. Error; fear; inflammation; sensuality; manipulation; hypnotism; jealousy; revenge.

Resurrection. Spiritualization of thought; a new and higher idea of immortality or spiritual existence; material belief yielding to spiritual understanding.

Reuben (Jacob's son). Corporeality; sensuality; delusion; mortality; error.

River. Channel of thought.
When smooth and unobstructed, it typifies the course of Truth; but muddy, foaming, and dashing, it is a type of error.

Rock. Spiritual foundation; Truth. Aloofness and stubbornness.

Salvation. Life, Truth, and Love understood and demonstrated as supreme over all; sin, sickness, and death destroyed.

Seal. The signet of error revealed by Truth.

Serpent (*nāhāš*, **in Hebrew**; *ophis*, **in Greek**). Subtle deceit; a lie; an error that conflicts with Truth; the first affirmation of mythology and idolatry; the belief in more than one God; hypnotism; the first lie of limitation; finiteness; the first claim that there is an opposite of Spirit, good, termed matter or evil; the first delusion that error exists as fact; the first claim that sin, sickness, and death are the realities of life. The first audible claim that God was not omnipotent and that there was another power named evil, which was as real and eternal as God, good.

Sheep. Innocence; inoffensiveness; those who follow their leader.

Shem (Noah's son). A structural, measurable human; kindly affection; love rebuking error; gratification of the flesh reproved.

Sin. Thoughts not based on and aimed toward the one Spirit. Disobedience to, and unawareness of, the one God and our spiritual selfhood.

Son. The Son of God, the Messiah or Christ. The son of human beings, the offspring of the flesh. "Son of a year."

Souls. See Review chapter, page 402.

Space/time. Empty area; interval; relative position and direction; a beginning and an end.

Spirit. Divine substance; Mind; divine Principle; all that is good; God; that only which is perfect, everlasting, omnipresent, omnipotent, infinite.

Spirits. Human beliefs; physicality; evil minds; supposed intelligences, or gods; the opposites of God; errors; fantasies. See Review chapter, page 402.

Substance. See Review chapter, page 404.

Sun. An example of Soul governing man and woman. The symbol of Truth, Life, and Love.

Sword. The idea of Truth; justice; Revenge; anger.

Temple. Body; the idea of Life, substance, and intelligence; the structure of Truth; the sanctuary of Love; a material structure where humanity congregates for worship.

Tenth. Contribution; tithe; showing reverence; gratitude; a sacrifice to the gods.

Thummim. Perfection; the eternal demand of divine Science.

The Urim and Thummim, which were to be on Aaron's breast when he went before Yahweh, were holiness and purification of thought and deed—the mindset which prepares us for the office of spiritual teaching.

Tigris (river). Divine Science understood and acknowledged.

Time. Mortal measurements; limits, in which are summed up all human acts, thoughts, beliefs, opinions, knowledge; matter; error; that which begins before, and continues after, what is termed death, until the mortal disappears and spiritual perfection appears.

Uncleanness. Impure thoughts; error; sin; dirt.

Ungodliness. Opposition to the divine Principle and its spiritual idea.

Unknown. That which spiritual sense comprehends. The unknown is unknown to the physical senses.

Some thinkers may believe God is unknowable, but Christian Science makes God known as the All-in-all, forever near.

Paul saw in Athens an "altar with the inscription, 'To an unknown god,'" and he said to the Athenians: "What therefore you worship as unknown, this I proclaim to you."[1]

---

[1]   Acts 17:23 (NRSV)

Urim. Light.

It was believed that the stones in the breastpiece of the high-priest had supernatural illumination, but divine Science reveals Spirit, not some device, as the illuminator of all. The illuminations of Science give us a sense of the nothingness of error, and they show the spiritual inspiration of Love and Truth to be the only fit preparation for admission to the presence and power of the Most High.

Valley. Depression; humility; darkness.

"Even though I walk through the valley of the shadow of death, I will fear no evil, for you are with me."[1]

Though the way is dark in mortal sense, divine Life and Love enlighten the way, destroy the restless human thinking, the fear of death, and the supposed reality of error. Christian Science, contradicting the feeling of depression, makes the valley to bud and blossom as the rose.

Veil. A cover; concealment; hiding; hypocrisy.

Veils are worn by women as a sign of reverence. Veils are also ritualistically worn as a mark of submission, in compliance with the notions of religious scholars.

Our motives and inclinations are paramount in religion. However, when rituals and ceremonies are the crux of religion, the motives and inclinations of a person are concealed by formal procedures and human routines. Jesus, as modest as he was mighty, rebuked this hypocrisy. Hypocrisy offers long petitions for blessings on physical rituals, but veils the crime, latent in thought, which is ready to spring into action and crucify God's anointed. The martyrdom of Jesus was the culminating sin of Pharisaism. Jesus' action rent the veil of the temple. It revealed the false foundations and structures of superficial religion, tore from bigotry and superstition their coverings, and opened the tomb with divine Science—immortality and Love.

Weeds. Mortality; error; sin; sickness; disease; death.

---

[1]   Ps. 23:4

Wilderness. Loneliness; doubt; darkness. Spontaneity of thought and idea; the entrance in which a mortal sense of things disappears, and spiritual sense unfolds the great facts of existence.

Will. The motive-power of error; human belief; animalistic power. The might and wisdom of God.
"It is God's will."[1]
Will, as a quality of so-called human mind, is a wrong-doer; therefore it should not be confused with the term as applied to Mind or to one of God's qualities.

Wind. That which indicates the might of omnipotence and the movements of God's spiritual government, encompassing all things. Destruction; anger; human passions.
The Greek word for wind, *pneuma,* is also used for spirit, as in John's Gospel where we read, "The wind [*pneuma*] blows wherever it pleases . . . So it is with everyone born of the Spirit [*pneuma*]."[2] Here the original word is the same in both cases, yet it has received different translations (as have other passages elsewhere in the New Testament). This shows how the Teacher had constantly to employ words that were significant to humanity in order to unfold spiritual thoughts. In the record of Jesus' supposed death, we read: "Jesus breathed his last."[3] Indeed, what Jesus gave up was air, an etherealized form of matter, for he never did give up Spirit, or Soul.

Wine. Inspiration; understanding. Error; fornication; temptation; emotionalism.

Winnowing Fork. Fan; separator of fable from fact; that which gives action to thought.

---

[1]   I Thes. 4:3

[2]   John 3:8

[3]   Luke 23:46; Mark 15:37

Year. A solar measurement of time; mortality; space for repentance. "With the Lord a day is like a thousand years."[1]

One moment of divine consciousness, or the spiritual understanding of Life and Love, is a foretaste of eternity. This exalted view, obtained and retained when the Science of being is understood, would bridge over with life discerned spiritually the interval of death, and humanity would be in the full consciousness of our spirituality and eternal harmony, where sin, sickness, and death are unknown. Time is a human thought, the divisor of which is the solar year. Eternity is God's measurement of Soul-filled years.

You. As applied to a physical body, a mortal human; finitude.

Zeal. The reflected animation of Life, Truth, and Love. Blind enthusiasm; human will.

Zion. Spiritual foundation and structure; inspiration; spiritual strength. Emptiness; unfaithfulness; desolation.

---

[1]   II Peter 3:8

INDEX

I

Illusion: 60, 64, 73, 80, 95, 104, 144, 189, 190, 209, 252, 255, 260, 266, 299, 301, 318, 341, 348, 464, 478, 499, 501, 507
Infatuation: 57, 160
Inflammation: 36, 150, 154, 323-324, 340, 347, 358, 363, 503, 509
Interpretation: 16, 20, 33, 37-38, 44-45, 60, 70, 100, 106, 199, 228, 252, 273-274, 298, 403, 412, 429, 438, 462, 469, 470, 482, 492, 496, 503, 505

J

Justice: 4, 15, 19, 29-30, 41, 45, 53, 89, 121, 191-192, 212, 241, 252, 276, 337, 338, 373-380, 401, 462, 466, 508, 511

K

Knowledge: 6, 22, 38, 40, 50, 70, 76, 80, 81, 88, 106, 109, 166-167, 169, 183, 215, 232, 236, 241, 280, 299, 340, 349, 384, 392, 401, 423, 452, 457, 467, 476, 499, 505, 506,511

L

Lack: 4, 34, 54, 56, 60, 65, 71, 106, 111, 139, 159, 208, 221,

246, 247, 298, 300, 316, 392, 508
Legitimate: 5, 103, 156-157, 194, 217, 450
Leukemia: 366
Life: 3, 9, 22, 53, 97, 163, 275, 328, 398, 402, 403, 417, 463
Lifestyle: 65, 297-280
Light: 29, 34, 60, 87, 104, 116, 130, 161, 175, 183, 254, 278, 290, 310, 317, 390, 413, 431, 437, 501, 506, 512
Lonely (loneliness): 36, 85, 513
Lord's Prayer: 13-14
Love: 2, 16, 80, 108, 111, 118, 145, 206- 207, 233, 236, 273, 315-316, 341, 349, 425, 470

M

Mahatma Gandhi: 411
Martin Luther: 33, 231
Martin Luther King, Jr.: 327
Martyr: 30, 114, 335, 512
Mathematics: 2, 92, 97, 166, 187, 273, 282, 298, 364, 470
Media: 121, 167,
Mind: 3, 37, 64, 82, 104-105, 133, 177, 213, 266, 287, 318-319, 382, 403, 404
Mineral: 133, 239, 436, 467, 479
Mother Teresa: 332
Motor system: 420, 422
Music: 22, 49, 68, 75, 124, 166, 182, 185, 219, 238, 261, 273, 326,